Intellectual Property and Information Rights for Librarians

INTELLECTUAL PROPERTY AND INFORMATION RIGHTS FOR LIBRARIANS

John Schlipp

LIBRARIES UNLIMITED®
An Imprint of ABC-CLIO, LLC
Santa Barbara, California • Denver, Colorado

Library of Congress Cataloging-in-Publication Data

Names: Schlipp, John, author.
Title: Intellectual property and information rights for librarians / John Schlipp.
Description: Santa Barbara, California : Libraries Unlimited, an imprint of ABC-CLIO, LLC, 2019. | Includes bibliographical references and index.
Identifiers: LCCN 2019014102 (print) | LCCN 2019016206 (ebook) | ISBN 9781440870712 (eBook) | ISBN 9781440870705 (print : alk. paper)
Subjects: LCSH: Intellectual property—United States. | Librarians—United States—Handbooks, manuals, etc.
Classification: LCC KF2980 (ebook) | LCC KF2980 .S35 2019 (print) | DDC 346.7304/802402—dc23
LC record available at https://lccn.loc.gov/2019014102

ISBN: 978-1-4408-7070-5 (paperback)
978-1-4408-7071-2 (ebook)

23 22 21 20 19 1 2 3 4 5

This book is also available as an eBook.

Libraries Unlimited
An Imprint of ABC-CLIO, LLC

ABC-CLIO, LLC
147 Castilian Drive
Santa Barbara, California 93117
www.abc-clio.com

This book is printed on acid-free paper ∞

Manufactured in the United States of America

CONTENTS

PREFACE

Teaching intellectual property (IP) and information rights is a proactive way to guide students and novice information users to be IP literate and to understand the vast range of IP issues. Comprehending IP is critical in today's world in order to negotiate the challenges associated with all kinds of IP. This book explores IP matters for today's information and communication students and professionals. The primary purpose of this book is to meet the growing need for librarians and specialists at libraries to learn more about IP as related to their work responsibilities, as well as to teach IP to their colleagues and customers. This book also provides ancillary support for professionals in information- or communication-based careers.

The ensuing chapters of this volume present copyrights, patents, trademarks, and other related rights, in relation to IP creators and consumers, including real-world scenarios and best practices. The first part of the book covers the legal and ethical aspects of IP and related rights, while the second part offers specific information associated with different types of libraries or information centers, as well as IP connected with information access and distribution. The content of this book contributes to three primary outcomes (goals) for its readers:

1. To develop an awareness of IP and information rights;
2. To apply IP to work in libraries, archives, and other professional information and communication environments; and
3. To encourage information professionals to pursue continuing education and to stay current with IP and information rights to support library workflow and customer outreach.

This book is one of the few comprehensive publications to address all types of IP for use by library professionals and customers. Information literacy (IL) is primarily a set of practical skills required for researchers to recognize the need for information and the ability to find, evaluate, interpret, and use such information effectively.[1] Content presented in this book addresses the growing need for informative and effective IL curricula for IP education. While many published resources on IL exist, surprisingly few examine IL tied to IP and integrating the two topics into a beneficial curriculum as well as a reference resource. The few published works are often inspired by sections of IL guidelines, which include IP topics such as ethical and legal use in "Information Literacy Competency Standards for Higher Education: Standard 5,"[2] as well as "Framework for Information Literacy for Higher Education: Information Has Value,"[3] both from the American Library Association. A noteworthy published editorial on this topic is Nicholas Joint's "Teaching Intellectual Property Rights as part of the Information Literacy Syllabus." In his article from *Library Review*, Joint promotes the logical connection between IP awareness and the IL curriculum. He believes that *reactive* IL is irrelevant, whereas *proactive* IL is everything.[4] This book promotes Joint's viewpoint that the best way to become IP literate is through *proactive* intellectual property information literacy (IPIL).

This book supports IPIL instructional objectives in higher education, facilitating students to be able to:

1. Identify the basic types of IP and related laws
2. Distinguish the conceptual difference between IP creators (authors, inventors, etc.) and consumers (users) in information-based situations
3. Recognize and apply practical applications of fair use and First Amendment rights of creators and consumers tied to information access
4. Comprehend and examine IP job-related applications for multiple types of library customers, media creators, and business branding specialists
5. Explore legal and ethical issues for libraries and other professional environments, such as intellectual freedom, internet regulations, privacy, cybercrime, and security

Although focused through the lens of libraries and information professionals, the content presented in this book also applies to subject disciplines dealing with IP, such as education, communication, business, computer and data science, and so forth. The subject matter is grounded in the reader's landscape of IPIL learning levels based upon the Dreyfus model of skill acquisition[5] (often applied in formal research about learning). The Dreyfus model classifies how students acquire competencies through formal instruction and practice in the field for their research and learning needs.[6]

Below are four stages, based upon the Dreyfus model, of how various levels of IPIL could be applied to readers of this book. Utilization of the four stages listed below will guide instructors and readers in learning the stated outcomes and objectives.

I. Beginner/Novice Level—Basic IP introduction and awareness as covered in Part I: General Section, Chapters 1 through 6.

II. Intermediate/Fluent Level—Subject familiarity, adeptness, and introductory competence for personal or work-related tasks associated with IP as covered in Part II: Specific Information (Access and Delivery), Chapters 7 through 10.

III. Proficient/Specialist Level—Practical work-related daily IP application, full competency, and/or certification, minimum academic degree (completed training), and some instruction to beginner and intermediate IPIL learners, as covered in all chapters.

IV. Expert (Mastery) Level—Related advanced degree (IP specialized study), such as a master's degree in library science, communication, information, technology, or law, tied to related subject research for authorship and/or instruction of IP. These experts in the field of specialized IP research and scholarship are referenced throughout the book.

Specific details and scenarios concerning historical milestones or contemporary topics involving IP are presented to engage instructors and students utilizing this book at various stages of the Dreyfus model. For example, Chapter 3 (on the fundamentals of patents) ties the historical account of the Wright brothers' efforts in patenting their invention of the first practical aircraft to the significance of strong patent claims. Additionally, Chapter 5 covers the contemporary world of fan culture and sports branding to teach trademark concepts. The author considers that such connections inspire further research and learning, which could prompt some students to pursue an IP focus in their chosen professions. In fact, the author of this book was bitten by the IP bug in graduate school, where IP was presented as a topic in advanced courses in library science.

NOTES

1. American Library Association, "IL Competency Standards for Higher Education," Presidential Committee on Information Literacy, Final Report (Chicago: American Library Association, 1989), http://www.ala.org/acrl/publications/whitepapers/presidential (accessed October 17, 2018); and Carol Collier Kuhlthau, "Information Skills for an Information Society: A Review of Research," Syracuse University (Syracuse, NY: ERIC Clearinghouse on Information Resources, December 1987), https://eric.ed.gov/?id=ED297740 (accessed February 15, 2019).
2. American Library Association, Institutional Repository, *Information Literacy Competency Standards for Higher Education*, https://alair.ala.org/handle/11213/7668#ildef (accessed October 18, 2018).
3. Association of College and Research Libraries, *Framework for Information Literacy for Higher Education* (Chicago: American Library Association, 2016), http://www.ala.org/acrl/standards/ilframework (accessed February 15, 2019).
4. Joint, Nicholas. "Teaching Intellectual Property Rights as Part of the Information Literacy Syllabus," *Library Review* 55, no. 6 (2006): 331.
5. Stuart E. Dreyfus and Hubert L. Dreyfus, "Five-Stage Model of the Mental Activities Involved in Directed Skill Acquisition," Operations Research Center, University of California, Berkeley, February 1980, Air Force Office of Scientific Research, U.S. Air Force, Washington, D.C., https://apps.dtic.mil/dtic/tr/fulltext/u2/a084551.pdf (accessed February 15, 2019).
6. Robert Farrell, "Reconsidering the Relationship between Generic and Situational IL Approaches: The Dreyfus Model of Skill Acquisition in Formal Information Literacy Learning Environments, Part I," *Library Philosophy and Practice* (November 2012): 1–16.

ACKNOWLEDGMENTS

The author of this book is sincerely thankful to all his professional colleagues, friends, and family, who have provided content, feedback, ideas, and support. Due to the limited space of an acknowledgment section, the following lists only significant highlights. At the top of the list, special thanks goes to two attorneys specializing in IP in higher education: Dwayne Buttler, JD, Endowed Chair for Scholarly Communication, University Libraries, University of Louisville, Louisville, Kentucky; and Jon M. Garon, JD, Dean and Professor of Law at Shepard Broad College of Law, Nova Southeastern University, Fort Lauderdale, Florida. Both Dwayne and Jon have served as mentors in my evolving role as an intellectual property librarian at the Intellectual Property Awareness Center (IPAC) of W. Frank Steely Library at Northern Kentucky University (NKU).

Additional acknowledgments go to the following professional colleagues for their support of research related to content in this book, as well as the instruction and outreach tied to this book: patent attorneys David Lafkas, JD, of the Eureka! Ranch®, and David Pressman, JD, author of *Patent It Yourself*; campus and community colleagues: John Alberti, Sharon and Arne Almquist, Andrea Brady, Andrea Brooks, Justine Burchell, Mary Carmen Cupito, Mary Chesnut, Allen Ellis, John Graham, Lois Hamill, Jane Hammons, Phyllis Hegner, Marcia Johnson, Linda Kocis, Danny Miller, Sheri Myers, Amanda Page, Ran Raider, Dave Schroeder, Sarah Schroeder, Lois Schultz, Dr. Jennifer Smith, Chris Strobel, Laura Sullivan, Mike Wells, Philip Yannarella, and Robert Zai III.

The author also wishes to thank other colleagues at NKU, including the Source Finder document delivery service at Steely Library, Cristen Ross, Erin Smith, Danny Lovell, and Deborah Stonehouse; the NKU Faculty Benefits Committee and Provost Sue Ott Rowlands for approving my sabbatical for further research and content for this book; former NKU graduate student assistants of the IPAC who proofed selected chapters, web pages, and lesson plans, including Lisa Schreihart, JD; Jill Liebisch; and Lauren Becker. The author is also grateful to his many students who utilized the work-in-progress version of this book as their textbook for LIN405 Intellectual Property & Information Rights for NKU's Bachelor's Degree in Library Informatics.

Many colleagues of the U.S. Patent & Trademark Office (USPTO) working within or supporting the Patent and Trademark Resource Centers Program (PTRCP) have been invaluable in providing instructional content referenced in this publication. PTRCP mentors include Amanda (Mande) Putnam, Martha Crockett Sneed, Christine Kitchens, Michael White, Tom Turner, Neil Massong, Robert Berry, Spruce Frasier, and many others. Suellen Hickey and Loretta Beck from the USPTO's Office of Trademark Quality Review & Training shared trademark searching examples from their many training sessions for PTRCs about the Trademark Electronic Search System (TESS) database. Alford Kindred and Robert Hodge, from the USPTO's Office of Innovation Development, shared diagrams and content about the patent application process from their Inventor Info Chat Series.

Thanks to all the members of the Patent and Trademark Resource Center Association for their shared information related to patent and trademark resources. Noteworthy examples include Donna Hopkins' instructional content for how to utilize patents to plot business trends for competitive intelligence; James Miller and Marian Armour-Gemmen's frequent support in answering questions related to advance patent searching on multiple patent databases; and Jan Comfort's patent and trademark college course instructional curriculum that provided a foundation for the author's initial design of portions of this book related to patents and trademarks.

Much appreciation goes to the financial support of a generous grant from the Cincinnati Bar Foundation that backed the Creative Thinking program in 2009. Content for Creative Thinking included copyright and plagiarism research and scholarship that inspired portions of this book.

Blanche Woolls and Emma Bailey, editors with ABC-CLIO/Libraries Unlimited, were instrumental in the advocacy and fine-tuning of the manuscript. In particular, Blanche brought many years of professional library experience to the organizing and staging of the author's IP knowledge to produce practical content in supporting this book. In conclusion, the author also thanks Paul Tenkotte, PhD, professor of history at NKU, for his review and editing of the original drafts of this book, utilized since 2011 as a textbook for LIN405 Intellectual Property & Information Rights. Without Paul's support, this book would not have been possible.

Chapter 1

INFORMATION LITERACY OF INTELLECTUAL PROPERTY (IP) AND INFORMATION RIGHTS

CHAPTER OBJECTIVES

- To identify librarians' and information professionals' intellectual property (IP) customers, namely, creators (authors or inventors) and consumers (users)
- To define IP and information rights
- To demonstrate the differences between all types of IP: copyrights, patents, trademarks, and alternative IPs
- To define IP information literacy and to understand how it is tied to the curriculum or outreach of our library colleagues and customers
- To instill a sense of responsibility as a professional to stay current with IP and information rights
- To recognize outreach opportunities for your library, such as IP awareness and information literacy for your customers
- To understand how technological advancements have led to the increased need for awareness of IP laws

INTRODUCTION

For most individuals, intellectual property (IP) is a mysterious legal topic that they believe only lawyers understand. As an overview and primer to IP, this chapter introduces IP creators and consumers and how the concept of IP relates to the creator's rights in relation to the consumer's use of IP. In your role as an information provider, you may be asked to help both IP creators and consumers understand their rights. This involves what IP creators need to do to protect their rights and what consumers need to do to make legal use of the creations and products protected by IP. The information in this chapter will provide a rudimentary explanation of IP as your basis for assisting both creators and consumers.

Copyrights, patents, and trademarks are the most common types of IP. Each type is vital to economic growth and employment within our local, state, and national economies, as revealed by a U.S. Department of Commerce report entitled "Intellectual Property and the U.S. Economy."[1] These IPs continue to drive the economy, supporting more than 45 million workers, or roughly 30 percent of all jobs in the United States, such as inventors and their inventions, artists and musicians and their creations, news media and software publishers, radio and television broadcasting outlets, sound recording and motion picture industries, computer and electronics products, and medical equipment and pharmaceuticals, among many others. IP contributes more than $6 trillion dollars, or 38 percent, of the U.S. gross domestic product (GDP).[2]

Aside from the economic data reported by the U.S. Department of Commerce, most educators, students, and the public at large are often unaware of IP. A study from 2013 in the United Kingdom, commissioned by the National Union of Students (NUS), revealed that students in higher education felt they did not know enough about IP for their future careers. Students often stated that their courses focused merely on plagiarism prevention, and "overwhelmingly, students believe a knowledge of IP is important, not only to their education, but to their future careers."[3] An informal survey[4] conducted by a UCLA engineering professor in

Figure 1.1

Intellectual Property Icon. (Courtesy U.S. Patent and Trademark Office, Intellectual Property Symbols Collection, Noun Project)

2012 revealed that some of his students were confused, while others were totally ignorant about various IPs. Among his survey of sixty engineering students, 21 percent could not answer the question "What is a patent?", 68 percent could not define "trade secret," 32 percent could not define "copyright," and 51 percent could not define "trademark." Clearly, librarians and educators are doing a poor job of informing students about IP. To address this challenge, one must first have a definition of IP.

WHAT ARE IP AND INFORMATION RIGHTS?

The World Health Organization defines IP as "the overall term for property in the creation of the mind, including inventions, literary and artistic works, but also images, and designs."[5] Kay Mathiesen, in the *Encyclopedia of Information Science and Technology,* defines information rights as "rights that specify claims and duties with regard to the communication, collection, access, use, and control of information. Information rights include the rights to privacy, intellectual property, free expression, and access to information."[6]

Throughout this book, information rights and policies associated with IP are presented. Fair use, free speech and freedom of expression, open access, freedom of information, and information management make up these diverse information rights facets.

IP is not just smart property, but when applied to creative works, it could be considered a return on investment to protect one's intellectual works; and it is associated with one's legal ownership and exclusive rights to authorize reproduction of one's intellectual works.[7] However, IP may also include original authorship or invention in relationship to the actual legal ownership. For example, an author or inventor could sell some or all of their IP rights to others. Or an author or inventor could be hired by an organization to create intellectual works, known as work-for-hire, where the rights belong to the hiring organization. In another scenario, the invention or intellectual work may be carried out by a researcher in a university, working either alone or with a team, and the rights belong to the university.

IP INFORMATION LITERACY

The Association of College and Research Libraries (ACRL) defines information literacy as a set of abilities requiring researchers "to recognize when information is needed and have the ability to locate, evaluate, and use effectively the needed information."[8] Facets of ethical and legal use of IP related to information literacy have often dealt with respecting authors by citing sources and also recognizing when to ask for copyright permission if portions of copyright works utilized were questionable fair use percentages, as covered in this book. Yet little research has been published that ties IP to information literacy. Recently phrases such as "intellectual property literacy" or "intellectual property information literacy" have been associated with educators across multiple subject disciplines as well as with commercial or nonprofit organizations' workshops or seminars for business or science and technology fields. In most cases, such information literacy outreach deals with the awareness of IP for both creators and consumers. In 2006, Nicholas Joint, who published one of the earliest scholarly references to IP information literacy,[9] emphasized that a proactive information literacy curriculum, including IP awareness, is the best way to enhance students' understanding of IP issues. In other words, the most effective way to avoid IP infringements, plagiarism offenses, or lack of IP awareness is proactive IP information literacy.[10] IP was the primary topic of a conference paper entitled "Exploring the Need for Intellectual Property Information Literacy for Business and STEM Disciplines," by Janis Tyhurst. The paper promotes the larger realm of IP awareness beyond copyright and fair use, such as including patents, among others. Tyhurst defines "intellectual property literacy" by using a former ACRL definition[11] for information literacy and substituting "intellectual property" in place of the word "information" from "information literacy": "Intellectual property literacy is a set of abilities requiring individuals to recognize when intellectual property is needed and to have the ability to locate, evaluate, and use effectively the needed intellectual property."[12]

Many of the instructional and outreach examples introduced throughout this book are examples of IP information literacy for library colleagues and customers requiring any type of IP awareness. The target audiences of such IP information literacy go beyond college students and IP specialists to other users such as schoolchildren, teenagers, and the general public.

PROTECTION OF IP AND INFORMATION RIGHTS

Almost from the beginning of U.S. history, IP was encouraged for the creation of new literary, artistic, and informational works for the ultimate benefit of society. In 1791, Article One, Section Eight of the U.S. Constitution gave Congress the power "to promote the progress of science and useful arts, by securing for limited times to authors and inventors the exclusive right to their respective writings and discoveries."[13] Without this right, authors and inventors might not be rewarded for creation of their intellectual works and most likely would not invest their time in such efforts. This book will discuss the rights of both the creators and consumers of IP, especially copyrighted works and what creative works may be protected. Likewise, multiple information rights associated with IP are covered, such as fair use, freedom of expression, open access, and others that are associated with library and information science and the culture of freedom of information.

Several kinds of works may be protected by IP. The first is copyright protection for the creative works of authors, musicians, or artists. The second covers a documented idea for an inventor's invention, a patent. The third discusses an entrepreneur's new business or service name which could be registered as a trademark. Although there are other types of IP, this chapter will concentrate more on the three basic, most prevalent types just mentioned because they are often associated with libraries and other information centers serving IP creators and customers.

KNOWLEDGE OF ALL IP TYPES

Librarians and information professionals need to be ready to explain IP. The term "intellectual property" itself has only come into common use in recent times. Until the World Intellectual Property Organization (WIPO) was founded by the United Nations in 1967, the term was associated with a few obscure legal documents and court cases. The IP name gained widespread usage after the passage of the Bayh-Dole Act, or Patent and Trademark Law Amendments Act[14] in 1980. The Act allowed universities, nonprofit research institutions, and small businesses to own, patent, and commercialize inventions created with federally funded research. The Act also led to the rise of technology transfer offices on campuses across the country, furthering the need for IP awareness in higher education. Many librarians and educators only associated IP with copyright, fair use, and plagiarism, when in fact patents, trademarks, and other intellectual works are included. Even the news media gets the terms "copyright," "trademark," and "patent" confused often. So it's no wonder when the public is puzzled about IP.

The word "catastrophe," with emphasis on "cat," is perhaps the best word to describe the 2018 headlines[15] behind a news story that further demonstrates the need for professionals connected with IP to understand and know the rights of IP users and the rights of IP owners. The copyright and trademark owner of the popular cultural icon Grumpy Cat® won over $700,000 from an infringing beverage maker selling an unlicensed coffee product, which exceeded the limits of its licensing agreement with Grumpy Cat's owner.

Grumpy Cat is a highly successful enterprise of an internet-famous feline's scowling image, first posted on social media in 2012. The owners of the sourpuss sensation built an effective and robust IP strategy, capitalizing on the likeness of Grumpy Cat on T-shirts, coffee mugs, books, and calendars. Grumpy Cat only licensed to sell a single product line of "Grumpy Cat Grumppucino," bottled iced coffees, to a beverage maker. The coffee producer later started selling other products, such as packaged Grumpy Cat Roasted Coffee and T-shirts, which went beyond the initial terms of the licensing agreement for Grumppucino bottled beverages. The sale of the packaged Roasted Coffee products and T-shirts by the beverage maker not only infringed on Grumpy Cat's copyrights and trademarks, but it also breached the terms of the license agreement.[16]

Grumpy Cat also sued the beverage maker Grenade Beverage for cybersquatting when it obtained the internet domain grumpycat.com using the trademark, again without permission. The lesson learned from this situation sustains the two sides of IP discussed throughout this book. The creator of an IP, should register his or her IP rights to the creation as soon as possible to be ready to guard those rights ferociously. The other side of the equation is the consumer or licensee respecting those rights.

It is important to explain to the person who wants to use an IP that it is essential to not only get permission, such as in the Grumpy Cat licensing setting, but also to read and clarify the fine print of any contract carefully to avoid such consequences. Just because a popular name such as Grumpy Cat is reposted on social media does not mean it is available to commercialize without permission. Some social media posts sharing images and headlines of this news story mistakenly refereed to Grumpy Cat's patents, which were not part of the story. The posts should have refereed to copyrights or trademarks.

Clearly, not only is knowledge about IP and information rights helpful for professionals in information-based careers who may be asked about this by their colleagues or library customers, but promoting awareness is also vital to support persons with questions from information outlets and media-creating customers, such as journalists, utilizing library research databases, which will be covered in Chapter 8. Such awareness helps IP creators and users overcome challenges associated with all types of IPs. Librarians promoting IP awareness are able to assist creative customers such as inventors, musicians, and authors with their own related IP needs. At the same time, there are some consumers of IP, such as journalists, teachers, scientists, artists, and nonprofit and small business specialists, who are allowed to use others' creative IP under fair use as permitted under copyright law. Copyright and fair use are introduced briefly here and covered extensively in Chapter 2.

Copyright is the concept most familiar to both the public and librarians in all types of libraries. Copyright covers authors and their literary, dramatic, musical, artistic, and certain other intellectual works, both published and unpublished. Turn the words around, and it authorizes the "right to copy." It protects the aesthetic or textual expression of ideas but not the ideas themselves. Copyright, compared to a patent or a trademark, is affordable and is registered with the U.S. Copyright Office at the Library of Congress. The "©" symbol, with the year and the owner of the copyright, is placed on the document. The website for further information is found at www.copyright.gov. The copyright owner is usually the original author or creator of the copyrighted work unless that ownership has been granted or sold to some other entity. Disputes over copyright frequently come with a consumer's copious use citing "fair use."

Librarians are commonly called upon to help define fair use and to explain whether fair use is a right or a privilege, especially when someone sees prohibitive copy warnings. In certain instances, publishers and producers of commercial intellectual works may post misleading prohibitive copy warnings that are not legally accurate and neglect to mention any fair use. This is evident in those forbidding FBI copyright warnings, which preface digital media or anticopy notices at the end of professional sports broadcasts. These are examples, despite the warnings, where fair use might permit some copying in limited portions for transformative reporting, criticism, or instruction. Transformative fair use is covered in Chapter 2. Compared to commercial copying scenarios, educational and personal use also have more tolerant copying rights with fair use. However, fair use does not mean unlimited use. More details about this are covered in Chapter 2 in the discussion of the First Amendment's tie to fair use and how the U.S. Supreme Court has promoted the public good of copyright ahead of an author's limited monopoly.

A patent protects unique processes, methods, and inventions. These are registered with the United States Patent and Trade Office (USPTO). Normally, the term of a patent is up to twenty years. U.S. patents are effective only within the

United States. Patent protection for other countries must be requested individually for each country. As exhibited on the USPTO website, there are three types of patents: utility, design, and plant. These will be discussed more fully in Chapters 3 and 4, as will the process of an application for a patent. These applications require lengthy research, and in the final stage, they may require the assistance of a patent attorney. This process can be quite onerous because of the requirements.

As technology changes, newer USPTO databases will replace those mentioned in this book. You may need to visit a Patent and Trademark Resource Center (PTRC) to learn the new technologies to locate patent and trademark information.

A trademark is a word, name, phrase, or symbol that identifies and distinguishes the business or provider of goods or services, and as with patents, their trademark applications, which are also granted by the USPTO, and the application requirements are very complex. Trademarks registered with the USPTO are national and are marked with an encircled letter "®," while those registered by a state government or common law are marked with "™."

To help understand the differences between the three major types of IP, it is helpful to think of something protected by all three IPs. The ever-popular board game Monopoly® had a utility patent, and it currently has trademarks, and copyrights associated with it.

The U.S. utility patent 2,026,082, displayed in figure 1.2, was issued in 1935 and has passed into the public domain. Hence, there are many regional and specialty "-opoly" games now available through various sources. The patent protected the functional invention of the game, and copyright still protects the expression of the published rules of the game and other creative expressions. Registered trademarks of the Monopoly game are still active along with other branding logos or game pieces.

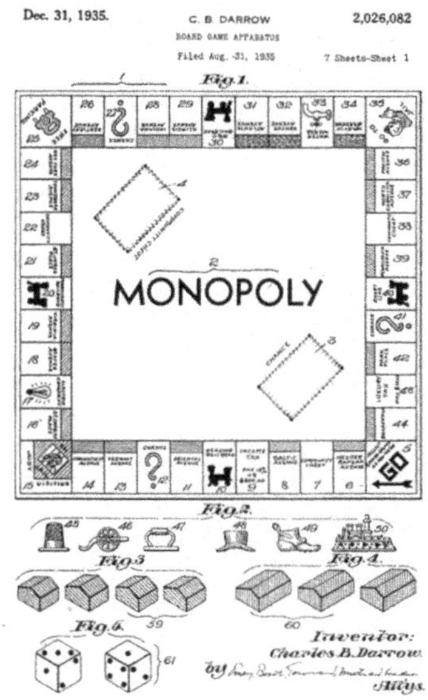

Figure 1.2
U.S. Utility Patent 2,026,082 for a Monopoly Game. (Courtesy of Hasbro. The MONOPOLY name and images are property of Hasbro, Inc. used with permission. © 2018 Hasbro, Inc.)

For more about the basics of copyrights, patents, and trademarks, see the websites of the Copyright Office at the Library of Congress and the U.S. Patent and Trademark Office. These are great starting points to direct most of your library customers to for their basic IP questions and registration or filing needs. Additional details on these IP resources will be covered in upcoming chapters.

IP AND YOU

You, other librarians, and information professionals can relate to IP when they consider their career ties. IP is integral to multiple library locations and roles. Here are just the most common examples: interlibrary loan and document delivery; electronic reserves and information delivery for educational instruction; scholarly communications; open educational resources; library database licensing; school library media centers; makerspaces; archives and special collections; science and technology libraries; art and music libraries; business and entrepreneur centers; technology transfer centers; and PTRCs, which are specially designated libraries representing the U.S. Patent and Trademark Office.

Your colleagues or family could create intellectual works in any number of ways. You may have a family member who has a good idea to make a better mousetrap. You may have teenagers who have decided to start a band and can't afford to use copyrighted music of others and so decide to write their own. If you do not have these in your family, you may have them among your library colleagues or users in almost all types of libraries.

Academic libraries have professors who write, create, and invent. Public librarians are as likely to have an author or journalist with copyright questions tied to their publishing, or a better mousetrap invention may be the product of the library's makerspace. School librarians have those same teenagers who have a band in someone's garage. Although special librarians are very likely to provide IP awareness to someone creating, it is probable that the company with which they are associated has legal counsel for patents and trademarks. Some of the following related scenarios are critical to understand:

- Respect of and legal adherence to computer software licensing agreements at work or home
- Assisting work colleagues, inventors, or businesspersons with review of IP registration or application information for their products or services
- Finding information for musicians about their creative works related to copyright registration
- Helping colleagues or customers become aware of fair use of others' intellectual works
- Explaining when and how to obtain permission of another's intellectual work when necessary
- Directing a journalist to a website for a FOIA form to access government information to write a news story

See figure 1.3 for a detailed chart that provides an overview of IPs by type and legal highlights. The chart should help your library colleagues or customers in understanding which right(s) apply to their specific IP need(s).

ALTERNATIVE IPS AND ADDITIONAL RESOURCES

Additional IP types include trade secrets, licensing, digital right management, public domain, open access/source, Creative Commons (CC), and orphan works. This summary begins with trade secrets.

Intellectual Property Overview (Highlights)

	Copyright	Trademark	Patent	Trade Secret
Law Source	U.S. Copyright Act (Federal) Title 17 U.S. Code	Lanham Act (Federal) Title 15 U.S. Code; state statutes; and common law	U.S. Patent Act (Federal) Title 35 U.S. Code	State statutes (Uniform Trade Secrets Act); common law
Subject Matter (Protected)	Art, writings and other forms of expression; not facts or ideas	Words, symbols, logos, designs or slogans that identify and distinguish products or services	Utility Patent: inventions Design Patent: ornamental (non-functional) designs	Formula, device, pattern, program, technique, or process
Protection Standard	Originality; authorship; fixation in tangible medium	Distinctiveness; secondary meaning; use in commerce	Novelty; non-obviousness; and utility (ornamentally for design patents; distinctiveness for plants)	Commercial value; unknown or unavailable information; effort to maintain secret
Protection Scope	17 U.S. Code §106: rights of reproduction, distribution, performance, public display, and derivative works	15 U.S. Code §1051: rights in U.S.; likelihood of confusion; and §1125(a) false designation of origin §43(a), false description, dilution	35 U.S. Code §154: right to exclude others from making, using, offering for sale, or selling the invention	Defense against misappropriation: acquisition by improper means or disclosure without consent
Protection Duration	Life of author plus 70 years	Perpetual until abandonment or loss of distinctness or secondary meaning	Utility/Plant: 20 years Design: 15 years	Potentially protected forever until publicly disclosed
Rights of Others	Fair use; compulsory licensing (music); independent creation	Truthful communication; fair use and collateral use (commentary)	Unless licensed, none.	Independent discovery; reverse engineering
Examples	Harry Potter books, movies and music soundtrack recordings	Coca-Cola name, distinctive logo and trade dress of bottle shape	iPhone mobile device, both utility and design aspects	Coca-Cola formula and KFC secret recipe

Figure 1.3
Intellectual Property Overview. (Highlights)

A trade secret is exactly what its name implies: valuable business information that is a secret and is not IP registered with a government agency. Trade secrets include formulas, patterns, compilations, programs, devices, methods, techniques, or processes. Trade secrets could last forever as long as they remain a secret. Famous trade secrets include the recipes for Coca Cola® and KFC®.[17]

Licensing has two sides for reflection within the IP focus. Just as there are two sides—creators and consumers—to our overarching IP constituents, the same applies to licensing. In simple terms, licensing is where one party grants another party the right to use its property, often with certain conditions and limited rights. According to Inc.com:

> A licensing agreement is a legal contract between two parties, known as the licensor and the licensee. In a typical licensing agreement, the licensor grants the licensee the right to produce and sell goods, apply a brand name or trademark, or use patented

> technology owned by the licensor. In exchange, the licensee usually submits to a series of conditions regarding the use of the licensor's property and agrees to make payments known as royalties.[18]

Licensing is significant for inventors or small businesses as licensors if they plan to license their patented invention or trademarked product with a company to manufacture or to market their IP as in our Grumpy Cat scenario. Music licensing or computer software licensing is the other side of the equation. Library customers may need to be alerted to the consequences of not heeding the licensing click-through agreements of such products.

Digital rights management is often a copy protection technique associated with licensed products. Specific examples about licensing are covered further in upcoming chapters related to copyrights, patents, and trademarks.

As covered earlier with the Monopoly® board game patent, public domain resources are often free to use without any need for permission. Public domain works should not be confused with public dissemination, such as most of the copyrighted content freely accessible on the web. Most content found on the web are copyrighted works unless otherwise noted. Upcoming chapters review how to determine when copyrights, trademarks, or patents have entered into the public domain.

In addition to public domain, there are alternative IP instances in which permission to copy and use the works of others is not questioned and sharing is encouraged. Open-access or open-source are open and free to use by others without permission. It is important to read the fine print of any open-access or open-source content, as making derivatives or interpolating with new copyrights or patents for commercial activity may be prohibited.

CC is an example of the growing open movement to publish and share with others to improve the public good of information access without placing works completely into the public domain.[19] Open access is vital to advancing the interests of library customers such as researchers, scholars, students, and the public. Open access is free, immediate, online access to scholarly research and publications and the right to reuse and redistribute these resources, often in the digital environment.[20] Scholarly communication librarians rely on the growing open-access culture to support their library customers who create and consume information.

Resources licensed with the CC are among popular examples of open access. The CC was founded by Stanford University Law Professor Lawrence Lessig and others who believed in sharing their intellectual content for free for noncommercial purposes such as personal, educational, and nonprofit environments. The CC offers "openly licensed creativity . . . freely available for legal use, sharing, repurposing, and reframing."[21] To promote universal access, the CC provides "a free, public, and standardized infrastructure that creates a balance between the reality of the Internet and the reality of copyright laws."[22] Not intended as a substitute for copyright, CC offers a free registration infrastructure for creators to file a license deed. This permits others to locate, recognize, and freely use their registered works in exchange for posting author attribution.

There are instances when a copyright owner of a work in question cannot be identified or found. These unique cases are known as orphan works. This condition has increased as a result of the Copyright Act of 1976, which eliminated the need to register copyrighted works with the Copyright Office. Orphan works of copyrighted works before 1978 could be traced in most cases, as historical copyright indexes exists of such Copyright Office registrations. Searching these indexes often provides names of copyright registrants and renewals.

KEEPING UP

The American Library Association (ALA) website affirms that "continuous learning is critical to renewing the expertise and skills needed to assist patrons in this information age. Library workers must continually expand their knowledge in order to keep up with the rate of change."[23] Such subject alertness training is even more vital for an IP librarian or specialist of a library supporting customers requiring IP awareness. Although associated library units or subject specialties vary from interlibrary loan and scholarly communication to patents and copyrights, there are multiple opportunities available for professional development related to IP.

Conferences and workshops range from national to regional programs sponsored by library associations; state libraries; library consortia; and individual libraries, colleges, and business and law schools. There are other like-minded organizations offering relevant training such as publishers, creative artists groups, local inventor's councils, and small business support groups.

The open access movement has further inspired regional copyright, fair use, and open access workshops and seminars. For example, Miami University Libraries in Oxford, Ohio, hosts an annual Copyright Conference,[24] (which draws national copyright experts from academia and law to educate librarians and educators about copyright, fair use, and open access. Furthermore, representatives of a group of libraries supporting inventors and entrepreneurs, known as PTRCs,[25] attend an annual PTRC training seminar at the U.S. Patent and Trademark Office in Washington, D.C. At this event, the library representatives sharpen their knowledge of patent and trademark searching and basic legal facts to provide IP awareness to their library customers.

Books, journal articles, online webinars, listservs, and websites offer vast continuing education and awareness resources related to IP for libraries and their customers. For example, scholcomm@lists.ala.org is a listserv on behalf of the Association of College and Research Libraries (ACRL) special interest group that shares information related to scholarly research and communication awareness and issues including copyright and open access topics. An example of an insightful website that covers all IPs is IP Watchdog®, located at https://www.ipwatchdog.com/. While the Watchdog site leans more toward the IP awareness topics tied to inventors and patents, it also offers useful articles related to copyrights and trademarks, which are written at the level needed for IP library experts.

Continuing education unit (CEU) programs and actual credit-bearing courses are offered for IP library professionals. Coursera's "Copyright for Educators and Librarians" continuing education course[26] is offered by copyright experts from the libraries at Duke University, Emory University, and the University of North Carolina at Chapel Hill. For a wider study of IP for library specialists, Northern Kentucky University offers a three-credit-hour course, entitled "Intellectual Property and Information Rights," for its online bachelor's degree in library informatics.[27] The library informatics course is targeted to library science students, yet students from electronic media and broadcasting, as well as students of sports business and entrepreneurship disciplines, also enroll in the class. This promotes changing the curriculum to broaden the IP scenarios covered. This, in turn, encourages a diverse subject-discipline student make-up, supporting interdisciplinary studies.

Such CEU and bachelor's degree courses, immersed in IP awareness and "training the trainer" concepts, provide an opportunity to tie IP awareness to information literacy. This information literacy opportunity is targeted to internal library colleagues and external library customers, including students and the general public. IP awareness tied to the information literacy curriculum is a proactive way of educating these target audiences. This proactive approach is covered below as it relates to outreach programming examples, and it also helps your library customers to avoid ethical plagiarism and legal infringement issues.

Later in this book, we discuss the U.S. Copyright Office, located at the Library of Congress. It is a helpful website for copyright awareness resources and offers many factual circular guides[28] on various matters related to copyright. In addition, the Library of Congress offers a blog[29] featuring timely topics posts including fair use. There is even a FAQ site[30] about copyright and a fair use index,[31] which offers a searchable database of court opinions, by category and type (e.g., digitization, music, parody, etc.).

OUTREACH

Teaching IP rights is a proactive way to coach and guide library customers and colleagues to be aware of and to understand the vast range of IP matters. Outreach affords IP librarians and specialists the opportunity to teach IP rights to such specialized library audiences. Comprehending IP is critical in today's world to negotiate challenges associated with all types of IP.

Outreach opportunities abound for IP awareness at libraries and information centers. There are two annual events to promote IP awareness at libraries. The first event is the World Intellectual Property Awareness Day,[32] celebrated since the year 2000, on April 26. The event is sponsored by WIPO. The international organization also provides many free resources on its website to conduct IP awareness training and events for library customers. Open Access Week[33] is celebrated during the last full week of October. Various libraries associated with the academic and research communities sponsor local workshops and events to inform their communities about open access and promote it as an alternative to the traditional copyright model of publishing scholarly research.

Throughout this book, other outreach best practices are presented related to each specific type of library. The most common target audiences are librarians, educators, students, inventors, authors, journalists, musicians, and artists. Academic and school libraries offer copyright and fair use awareness outreach for their instructors, students, and scholarly researchers. Academic and public libraries both provide outreach for inventors and entrepreneurs under the umbrella of the PTRCs. In certain instances, these PTRCs partner with one another. Hence, it is not unusual for an academic library to partner with a public library to present patent or trademark events to the wider, general public as public libraries tend to address IP for everybody from inventors and musicians to journalists and small businesses, as revealed in our chapter on public libraries.

LEARNING FROM PAST LEGAL CASES

The USPTO has stated, "Innovation and creativity are vital to this nation's prosperity and job growth."[34] IP laws are an integral part of protecting and promoting such innovation and creativity. Yet many innovators and creators are not aware of all of their IP rights. Given the importance of IP awareness, as covered in this book, the role of IP experts in libraries is vital in supporting productive citizens of the innovation culture and economy of today and tomorrow. This doesn't mean turning all of our library colleagues and customers into copyright, patent, and trademark experts. But it does mean ensuring that our related library constituents receive some instruction and training regarding their IP rights—and their civic duties respecting the IP rights of others. Significant legal cases associated with IP scenarios covered throughout this book will be examined from a very basic point of view. It is essential that readers of this book recognize the importance of learning from past legal cases as well as contemporary ones. The cases cited in this book will help teach colleagues and customers all about their IP and information rights.

This chapter has discussed information literacy of IP and information rights. It provided an introductory explanation of IP as a basis for assisting both creators and consumers of IP. In the next chapter, you will learn more about the unique types of IP creators and consumers and their awareness needs tied to copyright and fair use. In addition, alternatives to copyright and fair use will be covered.

NOTES

1. U.S. Department of Commerce, "Intellectual Property and the U.S. Economy: 2016 Update," https://www.commerce.gov/news/reports/2016/09/intellectual-property-and-us-economy-2016-update (accessed January 27, 2019). See full report at https://www.commerce.gov/sites/default/files/migrated/reports/ip-and-the-us-economy-september-2016.pdf.
2. Ibid.

3. Sarah McNicol, "Student Attitudes towards Intellectual Property—And What This Means for Libraries," *SCONUL Focus* 57 (2013), http://www.sconul.ac.uk/sites/default/files/documents/9_10.pdf (accessed September 30, 2015).

4. John Villasenor, "Intellectual Property Awareness at Universities: Why Ignorance Is Not Bliss," *Forbes* (Op-Ed), November 27, 2012, https://www.forbes.com/sites/johnvillasenor/2012/11/27/intellectual-property-awareness-at-universities-why-ignorance-is-not-bliss/#11be603d13ce (accessed October 17, 2018).

5. World Health Organization, "Intellectual Property," Health Topics, http://www.who.int/topics/intellectual_property/en/ (accessed October 17, 2018).

6. Kay Mathieson, "E-Human Rights," in *Encyclopedia of Information Science and Technology*, Third edition, Mehdi Khosrow-Pour, ed. (Hershey, PA: Information Science Reference, 2015), 2990.

7. John Schlipp, "What Is Intellectual Property?" Intellectual Property Awareness Center, https://inside.nku.edu/ipac/ipbasics.html (accessed December 15, 2018).

8. American Library Association, "Information Literacy Competency Standards for Higher Education," Presidential Committee on Information Literacy. Final Report (Chicago: American Library Association, 1989), http://www.ala.org/acrl/publications/whitepapers/presidential (accessed October 17, 2018).

9. Nicholas Joint, "Teaching Intellectual Property Rights as Part of the Information Literacy Syllabus," *Library Review* 55, no. 6 (2006): 330–336.

10. John Schlipp and Linda Kocis, "Using Popular Fiction to Spark Student Creativity and to Teach Intellectual Property Information Literacy (IPIL)," *Kentucky Libraries* 77, no. 1 (2013): 26–32.

11. American Library Association, Institutional Repository, Information Literacy Competency Standards for Higher Education, https://alair.ala.org/handle/11213/7668#ildef (accessed October 18, 2018).

12. Tyhurst Janis, "Exploring the Need for Intellectual Property Information Literacy for Business and STEM Disciples," in *Information Literacy in the Workplace*, 5th European Conference, ECIL 2017, Serap Kurbanoğlu et al., eds. (January 2018): 257–266.

13. U.S. Constitution Article I, §8, Clause 8 (1787).

14. 94. Statutes at Large, 3015, Patent and Trademark Law Amendments Act (1980).

15. Anca Draganescu-Pinawin, "Grumpy Cat: The Feline Who Grew a Business Empire with IP Rights," *WIPO Magazine* (February 2018): 47–48, http://www.wipo.int/wipo_magazine/en/2018/01/article_0008.html (accessed March 19, 2018); Steve Brachmann, "Grumpy Cat Wins $710,00 Verdict for Copyright, Trademark Infringement against Beverage Maker," IP Watchdog, January 27, 2018, http://www.ipwatchdog.com/2018/01/27/grumpy-cat-wins-copyright-trademark-infringement/id=92904/ (accessed March 19, 2018).

16. Brachmann, "Grumpy Cat Wins $710,00 Verdict for Copyright, Trademark Infringement against Beverage Maker."

17. Sue A. Purvis, "Fundamentals of Intellectual Property for the Entrepreneur," PowerPoint presentation, U.S. Patent and Trademark Office, https://www.uspto.gov/sites/default/files/about/offices/ous/121115.pdf (accessed October 10, 2018).

18. Inc.com,.Encyclopedia, Business Terms, "Licensing Agreements," https://www.inc.com/encyclopedia/licensing-agreements.html (accessed October 10, 2018).

19. Creative Commons, https://creativecommons.org/ (accessed December 26, 2018).

20. SPARK (Scholarly Publishing and Academic Resources Coalition), "Open Access to Scholarly and Scientific Research Articles," an open access fact sheet,

https://sparcopen.org/wp-content/uploads/2017/04/Open-Access-Factsheet_SPARC.11.10-3.pdf (accessed October 1, 2018).

21. Creative Commons, "Use & Remix," https://creativecommons.org/use-remix/ (accessed October 1, 2018).

22. Creative Commons, "About—Creative Commons," http://creativecommons.org/about (accessed March 31, 2011).

23. American Library Association: Tools, Publications & Resources, "Continuing Education (and Where to Find it)," September 23, 2013, http://www.ala.org/tools/atoz/continuing-education (accessed April 22, 2019).

24. Miami University Libraries, Copyright Conference, https://copyrightconference.lib.miamioh.edu/, (accessed April 22, 2019).

25. U.S. Patent and Trademark Office, Patent and Trademark Resource Center Program, Patent and Trademark Resource Centers, https://www.uspto.gov/learning-and-resources/support-centers/patent-and-trademark-resource-centers-ptrcs (accessed April 22, 2019).

26. Coursera, "Copyright for Educators and Librarians," https://www.coursera.org/learn/copyright-for-education (accessed December 26, 2018).

27. Northern Kentucky University, "College of Informatics, Bachelor of Science in Library Informatics," https://www.nku.edu/academics/informatics/programs/undergraduate/libraryscience.html (accessed December 26, 2018).

28. Library of Congress, "Circulars," https://www.copyright.gov/circs/ (accessed December 26, 2018).

29. Library of Congress, Blogs, "Copyright: Creativity at Work," https://blogs.loc.gov/copyright/ (accessed December 26, 2018).

30. Library of Congress, "Frequently Asked Questions about Copyright," https://www.copyright.gov/help/faq/ (accessed December 26, 2018).

31. Library of Congress, "Fair Use Index," https://www.copyright.gov/fair-use/index.html (accessed December 26, 2018).

32. World Intellectual Property Organization, "World IP Day," https://www.wipo.int/ip-outreach/en/ipday/ (accessed December 26, 2018).

33. Open Access Week, http://www.openaccessweek.org/ (accessed December 26, 2018).

34. Robert L. Stoll, Commissioner for Patents of the USPTO, "Protecting Intellectual Property Rights in a Global Economy: Current Trends and Future Challenges," statement before the Subcommittee on Government Management, Organization, and Procurement Committee on Oversight and Government Reform, United States House of Representatives, December 9, 2009, https://www.uspto.gov/about-us/news-updates/protecting-intellectual-property-rights-global-economy-current-trends-and (accessed October 17, 2018).

Part I

GENERAL INFORMATION

Chapter 2

COPYRIGHT AND FAIR USE

CHAPTER OBJECTIVES

- To identify the librarians' and information professionals' intellectual property (IP) customers: creators and users of copyrighted works
- To be familiar with the history of copyright
- To know that copyright registrations are administered by the Copyright Office, a division of the Library of Congress in Washington, D.C.
- To know copyright owners' exclusive rights and understand how these rights provide the owners control over the use of their copyrighted works, such as music
- To know what types of works may be copyrighted and how to register works with the U.S. Copyright Office
- To be familiar with copyright duration
- To understand copyright infringement
- To learn about various aspects of fair use
- To be able to show a library customer how to conduct a fair use analysis
- To be able to distinguish between different alternatives to traditional copyright and fair use

INTRODUCTION

Copyright is confusing. It has always been confusing for everyday persons, as Mark Twain expressed over one hundred years ago: "Only one thing is impossible for God: to find any sense in any copyright law on the planet."[1] The role of a librarian related to copyright information is often to help eliminate such confusion for copyright creators and copyright users visiting the library. For creators, librarians could help them understand their rights, how copyright protects them, and how to copyright their creations. For users of creative output, librarians, who are themselves users of creative output, especially in the print environment, could help users understand copyright and its restrictions, as well as fair use of copyrighted materials.

This chapter provides a broad introduction to help both library colleagues and customers understand multiple facets of U.S. copyright law, including copyright owners' exclusive rights, copyright registration and duration, copyright infringement, and fair use. Alternatives to copyright and fair use are also covered, including public domain, open access/source, Creative Commons (CC), digital collections, orphan works, interlibrary loan and document delivery, and licensing. Other types of licensing related to patents is covered in Chapter 3.

Besides inventors, aspiring musicians and songwriters are among the more frequent library customers needing assistance with copyright. Copyright law associated with music can be very intimidating compared to other types of copyrighted works. For example, an audio recording of a musical work consists of two separate copyrightable works: the actual published musical work content, such as sheet music, and the audio recording of the performance of the music. Meanwhile, the music business itself has complicated licensing methods. These address the various types of royalties, ranging from public performance rights to mechanical reproduction and distribution rights, as tied to the Section 106 exclusive rights of the copyright owners under copyright law, which is covered in this chapter.

Paul McCartney has been in the news for years regarding his quest to reclaim copyright ownership of lost publishing rights of his half of the Beatles® catalog composed between 1962 and 1970.[2] Yet, Paul McCartney and the other Beatles never lost their separate sound recording royalties connected to copyright. Again, different copyrights are associated with published musical works in sheet music as opposed to musical performances in sound recordings.

John Lennon once said, "Music is everybody's possession. It's only publishers who think that people own it."[3] And so it goes—Northern Songs was established in 1963 to take control of the music copyrights of Lennon and McCartney. The young music artists assigned all their copyrights to the publisher. Such licensing or assigning of copyrights is a standard practice, especially between new artists and music publishers. Executives of the fledgling publishing company and the trusted band manager held majority interest while John and Paul each owned a separate 20 percent. Soon the company went public to reduce a heavy tax liability for Lennon and McCartney's sudden fame and fortune. In time, such short-term income tax concerns were detrimental as Lennon and McCartney lost control of all their copyright publishing rights in 1969, when Northern Songs was sold to ATV Music.[4]

After multiple sales transactions, McCartney reflected, "The strange thing is that we never owned our own publishing, it was always getting bought and sold."[5] Ultimately, Sony was the last of many acquiring the former Northern Songs collection of Lennon and McCartney's music. Aware of a fifty-six-year copyright termination notice, covered in later in this chapter, McCartney successfully settled out of court with a confidential settlement agreement with Sony in 2017[6] to reclaim copyright of his comprehensive publishing catalog of Beatles tunes. U.S. copyright law (Section 304(c))[7] permits artists or authors to terminate the assignments of their initial copyright arrangements with a publisher, such as the Lennon and McCartney scenario, after a number of years—fifty-six years in this case.

The Beatles copyright scenario discussed above is the classic example of why any creative artist, author, or even a small business should be aware of both aspects of copyright as creators and users. Not only does one need to use caution to avoid potential copyright infringement, but one must also be aware of one's bundle of Section 106 exclusive rights under U.S. copyright law. Perhaps if Lennon and McCartney had spent some time with a helpful librarian at their neighborhood library, or with an attorney, they might have avoided their copyright conundrum. Academic and public libraries can often offer many books about copyright and the music business. Directing library customers to such books and offering workshops and programming related to specialized copyright topics, such as music, provide a worthy community service for such creative individuals.

Copyrighted works are more visible in our daily routine than other types of IP. Beginning in elementary school, students learn that using another's work without proper citation is called plagiarism. Plagiarism is usually not a legal issue; it is an ethical violation. However, if a work that is plagiarized is protected by copyright, the unauthorized use could be a copyright infringement. This moves to lessons about ownership of IP that is protected by the © symbol.

Copyright is a form of protection provided by the laws of the United States (Title 17, U.S. Code) to authors of "original works of authorship," including literary, dramatic, musical, artistic, and certain other intellectual works.[8] Copyrighted works are protected once created and fixed in a tangible format. Copyright owners have exclusive rights, while users of others' copyrighted works have limited fair use rights. Users often include students, teachers, authors, scholarly researchers, bloggers, journalists, musicians, documentary filmmakers, creative artists, and so forth. Therefore, it is equally good for both creators and consumers to know their rights as copyright owners (the creators) and copyright users (the consumers). Librarians specializing in IP are well suited to assist library colleagues and customers with their awareness needs of copyright and its related rights. Such copyright awareness advances the progress of knowledge for all consumers of information by giving the creator of copyrighted works an economic incentive to create new works. It enhances learning in educational environments while providing access to information to the public at large, and it also protects the authors and their works. Copyright law strives to balance the rights of public interest and the rights of authors while fair use ensures both freedom of speech and public access to information.

COPYRIGHT HISTORY

Legal copyright protection began early in U.S. history. Our legal history of copyright is derived from the British Statute of Anne from the early eighteenth century.[9] U.S. copyright was introduced in the late eighteenth century in the Constitution, Article I, Section 8, granting Congress the power in "securing for limited times to authors and inventors the exclusive right to their respective writings and discoveries." The *Copyright Act of 1976*[10] still applies to our copyright law today.

President George Washington signed the first federal copyright law, known as the Copyright Act of 1790.[11] The initial term of copyright was fourteen years, eventually followed by a renewal of another fourteen years. Over time, the legal duration of copyright in the United States lengthened. The Copyright Act of 1909[12] expanded the renewal period to twenty-eight years. The Copyright Act of 1976 expanded the term to life of the author plus fifty years. Ultimately, the term extended beyond the life of the author to seventy years in 1998 with the Sonny Bono Copyright Extension Act. For works prepared by multiple authors, copyright expires 70 years after the death of the last author, while works for hire last for 95 years from first publication, or 120 years from the date of creation, whichever expires first.[13]

When reviewing the history of copyright, it is essential to recognize that there is no such thing as an international copyright. Copyright law is territorial, and the laws of each country cover copyright protection in that country. However, there are treaties and conventions that protect such works in certain instances. The United States is a member of many treaties and conventions affecting copyright. The United States joined the Berne Convention in 1988. Each contracting state recognizes copyrighted works authored by nationals of other contracting states. Other significant treaties include the Universal Copyright Convention and the World Intellectual Property Copyright Treaty. Sections 104 and 104A of the U.S. Copyright Act cover the range of protection for foreign works. The copyright office website offers more details in *Circular 38A International Copyright Relations of the United States* at https://www.copyright.gov/circs/circ38a.pdf.

COPYRIGHT OWNERS' RIGHTS

Copyright law offers a bundle of exclusive rights to the author or creator of copyrighted works that are "fixed in any tangible medium of expression."[14] Under the Copyright Act of 1976, Section 106,[15] a copyright owner, such as a musician or an author, has six exclusive rights:

1. The right to reproduce the copyrighted work in copies or phonorecords;
2. The right to distribute copies or phonorecords of the copyrighted work to the public by sale or other transfer of ownership, or by rental, lease, or lending;
3. The right to display, in the case of literary, musical, dramatic, and choreographic works, pantomimes, and pictorial, graphic, or sculptural works, including the individual images of a motion picture or other audiovisual work, the copyrighted work publicly;
4. The right to perform, in the case of literary, musical, dramatic, and choreographic works, pantomimes, and motion pictures and other audiovisual works, the copyrighted work publicly;
5. The right to perform, in the case of sound recordings, the copyrighted work publicly by means of a digital audio transmission; and
6. The right to prepare derivative works based upon the copyrighted works.

These rights are the heart of the copyright law, as such rights give the owners control over the use of their copyrighted works. For example, a musician or an author could exercise any of these rights themselves or grant all or part of the rights to others. If another party makes unauthorized copies or performs publicly without permission of the copyright holder, it violates the rights of the musician or author, except for limitations of their exclusive rights allowed by fair use.[16] Limitations such as fair use on the rights of copyright holders will be covered soon in this chapter.

It is important to note that sometimes, an author or musician could relinquish part or all of their copyright to a publisher or to someone else, as covered above with the Beatles scenario. In made-for-hire works, the employer or the person or party for whom the work was prepared is considered the author. This is especially important to note with for-profit businesses, as covered in Chapter 10.

The first two exclusive rights of copyright holders deal with reproduction, that is, literally making copies, or distributing copies of a copyrighted work. Only the copyright holder has the right to make copies of his or her work. The right to distribute means that only the copyright holder has the right to sell, license, lease, or rent their work to whomever they please and for a fee if desired. These rights are the easiest for most people to understand. Perhaps this is due to that fact that the right to make copies (of anything—by authors, artists, map makers, musicians, etc.) was the only right of the original Copyright Act of 1790. Since then, other exclusive rights were added as works of authorship expanded and technology advanced.

The exclusive right to display publicly applies to objects such as works of art displayed in a public place, while the right to perform publicly deals with plays or musical works performed in a public place. A public place could also be a digital, virtual place, such as the internet. In 1995, a right was included that was more of a clarification for sound recordings to comply with changing digital technology: the right of public performance of sound recordings by means of digital audio transmission.[17] A digital audio transmission via an interactive system, such as a customizable song request website, implicates the performance rights of both the music composer and the recording artist performer.[18]

Finally, the right to prepare derivative works applies to the author, as only authors have the right to modify or revise their copyrighted work. One of the more common examples of this derivative right is when an author grants someone else the right to make a movie based upon his or her book. The copyright owner could even transfer part or all of his or her "exclusive rights" ownership by assignment.

COPYRIGHT AND MUSIC

Musicians, authors, and other creative artists often rely on related associations and organizations to administer legal matters such as contracts and IP. For example, the American Society of Composers, Authors, and Publishers (ASCAP); Broadcast Music, Inc. (BMI); and SESAC (formerly the Society of European Stage Authors and Composers) assist musicians in navigating the sea of granting permissions and gathering royalties in regard to public performances.

Although musicians could handle their own permissions and royalties, such performance rights organizations and related services are very accommodating. Once their works have been registered for copyright, covered in the next section of this chapter, musicians should turn to specific royalty rights agencies for licensing. In this instance, licensing is the process of granting permissions and gathering royalties. There are various royalty rights types of licensing, including:

- Mechanical Right Royalties for commercial recordings.
- Performing Right Royalties for public performances.
- Synchronization Right Royalties for television and movie music use.
- Print Right Royalties for scores and sheet music.
- Digital Right Royalties for online digital recordings.

When reviewing the list of royalty rights above by licensing type, think of the different needs of a music writer/composer (composition) versus an artist (sound recording). The typical garage band could simultaneously be original composers and recording artists. The composer would register his or her own music composition copyrights with the U.S. Copyright Office. If the composer is also the recording artist, copyright should be registered for both the compositions and the sound recordings. Although registration is not obligatory, it is required prior to filing an infringement lawsuit and affords the owner the right to seek attorneys' fees and statutory damages.

To review royalty rights in their simplest form, think of the royalties associated with the Beatles' *Sgt. Pepper's Lonely Hearts Club Band* album in 1967. The royalty rights listed above were divided three ways among the record label, the recording artists, and the musical works publisher. Today, digital rights would also be included for digital audio transmissions.

The following are scenarios that creative library customers could encounter related to copyright and the various royalties. If band members decided to record and sell their original music compositions, mechanical rights could be arranged by their publisher or an official representative to handle royalties. In such arrangements, artists would enter into a publishing agreement in which they would sign over all or part of their copyright exclusive rights in their compositions to a publisher in return for the administration of those compositions. However, the sound recording is often managed by a record company.

The exclusive rights of the copyright owner in Section 106[19] mentioned above provide a song composer the exclusive right to the first publication of the song under Section 115[20] of the Copyright Act. A song comprises a musical score and any lyrics. It does not include the sound recording, which is a separate right. Once the original recording has been made under the authority of the copyright holder, Section 115 (known as a compulsory license) allows any person to make his or her own recording of that song. To comply with the copyright law, the new recording artists must pay the U.S. Copyright Office a set royalty rate. This royalty is often referred to as the mechanical right royalty. Because of the challenges of working with the Copyright Office, most recording artists prefer to work with the rights organization known as the Harry Fox Agency, which serves as an intermediary for many commercial music publishers. Licensing the mechanical rights from the Harry Fox Agency provides a simplified method of obtaining the compulsory license needed to make a cover recording (new performer version) of previously released recordings.

The copyright owner of the composition retains the public performance rights in the song. A songwriter might retain these rights or might assign them to a music publisher. In exchange, the music publisher usually promotes the song, for example, in print, cover music, and commercial uses, as discussed in the Beatles scenario earlier with Northern Songs.

A band that plans to publicly perform music written by other artists requires a public performance license to do so. However, the common practice is for the venue of the performance to obtain the license. ASCAP, BMI, and SESAC each have a comprehensive catalog of music. Each band that appears in a dance club is covered by the same blanket license. The same is also true for the playing of prerecorded music, whether from a DJ or from the radio.

Now consider a different situation: a film producer wants to use a recording of a popular song for his or her new film. The producer would need to obtain three separate rights in this case: (1) to use the composition of the song; (2) to use the rights to reproduce the sound recording; and (3) for synchronization of the composition visually. For the composition copyright, the producer would need to obtain the right to publicly perform the song. This is necessary because public performance societies, such as ASCAP and BMI, are not permitted to license rights for motion picture theatrical distribution. The producer would also need to obtain the right to reproduce the composition and the right to "synchronize" the composition with the images from the visual track. These three rights are distinct, but fortunately, all come from the copyright holder of the composition. For the sound recording, there is no publication or synchronization right, but the producer must obtain the rights to reproduce the sound recording in association with the motion picture. Finally, if the producer wishes to create a soundtrack album, then he or she must obtain the reproduction rights from the composition copyright holder (or pay the compulsory license through the Harry Fox Agency) and the sound recording copyright holder.[21]

Print Right Royalties apply to a license for others to reproduce and distribute a copyrighted musical score in printed form such as sheet music. Examples include when additional copies are needed for a public performance or when another publisher wishes to print and sell a music score as part of an anthology or other special publications.

For digital sound recordings, Sound Exchange collects royalties from most digital radio or distribution services to pay recording labels and recording artists. On the other hand, performance rights organizations such as ASCAP and BMI handle royalties for songwriters.

Here are the corresponding Section 106 exclusive rights of the copyright owner, which are licensed for different types of royalty rights:

• To reproduce the copyrighted work in copies or phonorecords	• Mechanical right royalties for reproductions of recordings
• To distribute copies or phonorecords of the copyrighted work to the public	• Mechanical right royalties for reproductions of recordings
• To display copyrighted work publicly	• Print right royalties from the publisher
• To perform copyrighted nondramatic work publicly	• Performing right royalties for public nondramatic performances live or on recordings
• To perform sound recordings by means of a digital audio transmission	• Digital right royalties from Sound Exchange® or sound recording copyright owner directly
• To prepare derivative works based upon the copyrighted works	• Synchronization right royalties for reproduction of recordings in television and movies

There are two significant exemptions to the exclusive rights of copyright owners in Section 106 associated with school concerts and religious services, where permission to use is not required. Section 110(4), for school concert performances of musical works covered in Chapter 9, is often associated with K–12 schools. Without such an exemption, both classroom and school auditorium performances tied to pedagogy of learning about music could be at risk. Then Section 110(3) permits a choir and congregation to sing religious copyrighted music without permission from the copyright owners under certain conditions, covered in Chapter 10.

For additional reference on the complex topic of music business copyright and licensing, many research and law libraries hold a comprehensive book with more details, known as *Kohn on Music Licensing* by Bob Kohn and published by Wolters Kluwer. Nolo, the publishing company, also offers related music business reference such as *Music Law: How to Run Your Band's Business* by Attorney Rich Stim.

COPYRIGHT REGISTRATION AND PROTECTED WORKS

As Section 102[22] of the U.S. Copyright Act of 1976 establishes, copyright subsists automatically as soon as the work is created. One need not publish or register the work to be copyrighted. However, registration with the Copyright Office is advantageous for any future legal actions. See figure 2.1 for an image of the Copyright Office (https://copyright.gov/ homepage). The Copyright Office, a unit of the Library of Congress, administers the set of laws related to copyrights. The Copyright Office handles copyright registrations, the recordation of title and licenses, statutory licensing provisions, like compulsory license payments for recording reproduction and distribution, and other aspects of the 1976 Copyright Act.[23]

Registration establishes a public record of copyright claim. Before a copyright holder may file an infringement suit in court, registration is necessary. It allows the copyright owner to record the registration with the U.S. Customs Service for protection against importation of infringing copies, such as fake or counterfeit copies. It is easy to let others know you are the copyright owner. Just place your name or

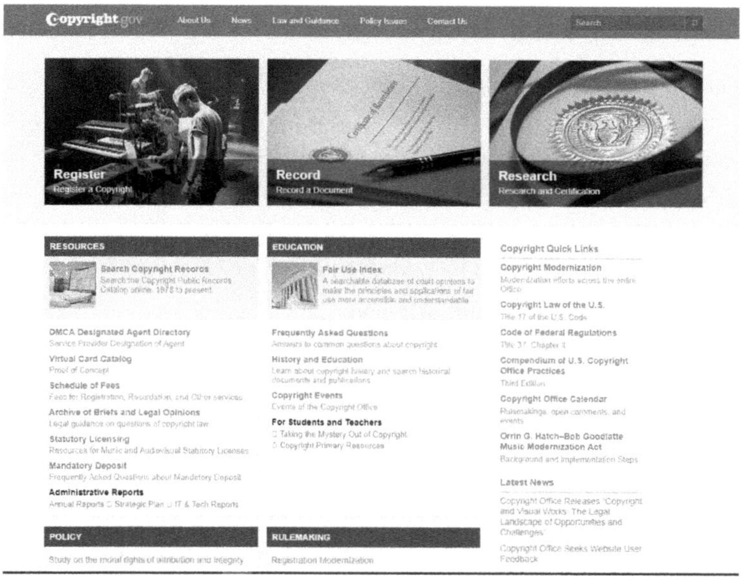

Figure 2.1
Home Page of U.S. Copyright Office Website

company name with the © symbol and year on the document or work: © 2019 John Schlipp.

To register a copyright, go to http://www.copyright.gov/eco/ for an online template. The current copyright cost is listed along with directions. Different types of works have different access points for registration. The following intellectual works may be protected by copyright:

- Literary works, including business brochures and product user manuals
- Musical works, including any accompanying words
- Dramatic works, including any accompanying music
- Pantomimes and choreographic works
- Pictorial, graphic, and sculptural works
- Motion pictures, sound recordings, computer software and games, and websites, among others
- Architectural works

Literary works are among the more commonly characterized examples of copyrighted works, expressed in tangible formatted fiction and nonfiction, manuscripts, poetry, contributions to collective works, compilations of date or other literacy subject matter, dissertations and theses, internet websites, computer programs, databases, student works, class notes, email, speeches, and so forth. Plays, dramas, and screenplays are categorized in the dramatic performing arts areas. The Copyright Office website provides more details on these categories of protected works at https://www.copyright.gov/.

Meanwhile, here is a list of works that may not be copyrighted:

- Works not in a fixed medium or that lack creative expression
- Works chosen to be available with no copyright restrictions by the author, such as open access or Creative Commons
- Most U.S. Government documents
- Facts, ideas, dates, names, and short phrases (ideas could be patented, and dates, names, and short phrases could be trademarked)
- Works that have entered the public domain

It is challenging to determine whether computer programs and software are copyrightable, patentable, or both. As covered in Chapter 3, software patents are associated with inventions that are functional and expressed in the form of a product or process, whereas software copyrights are associated with the expression of an idea and not an idea itself. Computer programs and software are considered copyright literary works, whereas the format or look of a database or website could be registered for copyright of its visual appearance. Copyright registration is especially useful to shield unauthorized copying of software source code and to pursue infringement lawsuits.

However, free and open source software collaboration is customary with operating systems such as Linux. The underlying source codes are distributed under an open-source General Public License (GPL) that promotes sharing, while commercial amenities such as Red Hat® offer service support.[24]

COPYRIGHT DURATION

The year 2019 brought two significant changes to public domain of copyrighted works. Since the twenty-year freeze enacted by the Copyright Extension Act of 1998 ended, plenty of popular culture of the 1920s resumed entering into the public domain. From this point forward, each year will now free up access to timeless music, movies, and books. In addition, the enactment of the Music Modernization Act (MMA) of 2018 reduced the public domain period for sound recordings published prior to 1972.[25]

Copyrighted works enter into the public domain according to when each work was copyrighted. For most U.S. works published before 1978 that are ninety-six years old or older, there is usually no question that they are in the public domain. Copyrighted works published and registered up to 1963 that were not renewed may have expired and have also entered into the public domain. However, copyrights of works up to 1963 that were renewed last up to ninety-five after the publication date. Works published and registered between 1964 and 1977 retain the copyright up to ninety-five years after the publication date, and works created since 1978 are copyrighted for at least seventy years past the copyright author's death.[26] See figure 2.2's highlighted portion of Cornell University's *Copyright Term and the Public Domain in the United States* chart to determine if a work has entered into the public domain. Directions on how to trace copyright registrations and renewals before 1978 to determine copyright status are covered later in this chapter.

Copyright Term and the Public Domain in the United States chart by Peter B. Hirtle*

Works Registered or First Published in the U.S.
(except sound recordings and architecture)

Date of Publication	Conditions**	Copyright Term***
96 years or older	None	None. In the public domain due to copyright expiration
Up through 1977	Published without a copyright notice	None. In the public domain due to failure to comply with required formalities
1978 to 1 March 1989	Published without notice, and without subsequent registration within 5 years	None. In the public domain due to failure to comply with required formalities
1978 to 1 March 1989	Published without notice, but with subsequent registration within 5 years	70 years after the death of author. If a work of corporate authorship, 95 years from publication or 120 years from creation, whichever expires first
Up through 1963	Published with notice but copyright was not renewed	None. In the public domain due to copyright expiration
Up through 1963	Published with notice and the copyright was renewed	95 years after publication date
1964 through 1977	Published with notice	95 years after publication date
After 1977	Published with or without notice**	70 years after the death of author. If a work of corporate authorship, 95 years from publication or 120 years from creation, whichever expires first
Anytime	Works prepared by officer or employee of US Government as part of official duties	None. In the public domain in the United States (17 U.S.C. § 105)

Never Published, Never Registered Works

Type of Work	Copyright Term***
Unpublished works	Life of the author + 70 years
Unpublished anonymous and pseudonymous works, and works made for hire (corporate authorship)	120 years from date of creation
Unpublished works when the death date of the author is not known	120 years from date of creation

*Used under a Creative Commons BY 3.0 license from the Cornell University Library and Peter B. Hirtle.
** See Peter B. Hirtle's most current Cornell University Library chart at https://copyright.cornell.edu/publicdomain for additional conditions, especially works created and published after 1977.
*** All copyright terms run through the end of the calendar year in which they would otherwise expire. A work enters the public domain on the first of the year following the expiration of its copyright term. For example, a book published on March 15, 1924 would enter the public domain on January 1, 2020, not March 16, 2019.

Figure 2.2
Cornell University's Copyright Term and the Public Domain in the United States Chart. (Used by permission of the Copyright Information Center and under a Creative Commons BY Attribution Only License)

The MMA changed the public status of some classic pre-1972 recorded music. The MMA brings a substantial number of sound recordings into the public domain sooner than the state copyright laws that it preempts. Federal protection for pre-1972 recordings will expire ninety-five years—subject to certain additional periods—after the date of their first publication, depending on the date range.

The earliest music recordings made before 1923 will enter the public domain on January 1, 2022.[27] Disposition of subsequent years are noted on published public domain time frame charts such as the complete version of the Cornell University website *Copyright Term and the Public Domain in the United States*,[28] located at https://copyright.cornell.edu/publicdomain.

Unpublished works are often a challenge when it comes to determining their copyright status. Museums, special collections, and archives deal with this conundrum often, as covered in Chapter 10. The Cornell University *Copyright Term and the Public Domain*, figure 2.2, includes a section specifically addressing never-published, never-registered works.

The U.S. Copyright Act of 1976 offers copyright owners a subsequent opportunity to terminate copyright assignment transfers and reclaim copyright, as in the Lennon and McCartney scenario mentioned earlier in this chapter. Section 203[29] covers termination of assignment transfers made since 1978, while Section 304(c)[30] covers termination of transfers made before 1978. Works made for hire are not eligible. Such termination rights are especially helpful for authors and songwriters.

SWEEPING NEW LEGISLATION TRANSFORMS MUSIC LICENSING IN U.S.

The Music Modernization Act (MMA), signed into law[31] on October 11, 2018, reforms music licensing in the United States. The MMA updates Section 115 of the U.S. Copyright Act. Karyn A. Temple, Acting Register of Copyright and Director of the U.S. Copyright Office emphasized that, "The MMA changes the law for licensing musical works and pre-1972 sound recordings, as well as the distribution of sound recording royalties to producers, mixers and sound engineers."[32] The MMA comprised three separate titles, which included overhauling music licensing, clarifying copyright on pre-1972 recordings, and codifying the royalty-payment system. The U.S. Copyright Office published a pamphlet with full details of the enacted legislation entitled *Amendments to the Copyright Act as a result of the Orrin G. Hatch-Bob Goodlatte Music Modernization Act* located at https://www.copyright.gov/legislation/2018_mma_amendments.pdf.

COPYRIGHT INFRINGEMENT

Headlines in the news remind us that library customers such as young students and even adults are not immune to copyright infringement. Perhaps their confusion is due to lack of IP information literacy about copyright and file sharing of media and music. In July 2009, a federal jury ordered a twenty-five-year-old Boston University graduate student to pay music companies $675,000 for file-sharing two dozen songs. A year later, a U.S. District Court Judge reduced the student's fine by 90 percent, claiming the initial penalty was excessive.[33] Such examples in the news attests to why authors, musicians, artists, students, and others can benefit from IP information literacy. Students in high school and college often download commercial music or media without permission. Even adults in commercial

Figure 2.3
Jump Start © 2007 Robb Armstrong. Reprinted with permission of ANDREWS MCMEEL SYNDICATION. All rights reserved.

businesses take content freely from the Web and repost it with no thought of asking for permission. At times, librarians specializing in IP are called upon to educate such groups at their schools and in the community.

One reason for the lack of awareness could have something to do the fact that the word "infringement" is not something often used in our daily vocabulary as displayed in cartoonist Robb Armstrong's humorous *Jump Start* comic in figure 2.3. BusinessDictionary.com defines infringement as a "violation of the terms of an agreement, encroachment, trespass, or disregard of others' rights, such as invasion of an exclusive right of intellectual property."[34] Copyright infringement is the unauthorized use of a copyrighted work. Section 501 of the U.S. Copyright Act states that an infringer is "anyone who violates any of the exclusive rights of the copyright owner."[35] Those exclusive rights are the rights emphasized in Section 106 as defined as copyright infringement by the U.S. Copyright Office as occurring "when a copyrighted work is reproduced, distributed, performed, publicly displayed, or made into a derivative work without the permission of the copyright owner."[36]

Evaluating an alleged copyright infringement is not always easy to determine. Returning to our music scenarios related to the Beatles, George Harrison was the first Beatle to garner a solo number one hit with his own musical composition, "My Sweet Lord," in 1970. He was accused of plagiarizing a 1962 pop tune entitled "He's So Fine" by the Chiffons. The court ruled[37] that Harrison was guilty of subconscious plagiarism. Although copyright infringement and plagiarism are separate offenses, here is an unusual instance where each overlapped. To hear a comparison of the two songs, listen on YouTube at https://youtu.be/sYiEesMbe2I or go to a search engine and enter keywords: George Harrison "My Sweet Lord" copyright Lydia Hutchinson, or http://performingsongwriter.com/george-harrison-my-sweet-lord/.

A copyright owner must demonstrate three elements to prove infringement: first, ownership of a valid copyright; second, that the work was copied without authorization; and three, elements copied were an improper appropriation of the copyright protected expression, or in other words, substantially similar.[38] A copyright owner who successfully proves an infringement claim is entitled to statutory damages up to $30,000[39] per each work infringed, plus attorney fees and other costs[40] incurred by the plaintiff. In the case of willful infringement, the statutory damages could run up to $150,000[41] per work infringed. A willful infringement is when the alleged infringer knew that the act was an infringement.

Library customers should be aware of the Digital Millennium Copyright Act (DMCA)[42] enacted in 1998, which increased the penalties for criminal copyright infringement to as high as $1,000,000 and up to ten years' imprisonment.[43] The DMCA regulates the legality of digital copyrighted works such as circumventing copyright protection technology. Section 1201 of the DMCA asserts, "No person shall circumvent a technological measure that effectively controls access to" a copyrighted work.[44] Such copyright protection technology is often known as Digital Rights Management (DRM) covered below in the ILL and Licensing section of this chapter.

Besides revising sections of the U.S. Copyright Act of 1976, Sections 1201 and 1202 of this complex law affect library information polices related to their online services, library employees, and library customers. The DMCA "affords to copyright owners rights against those who circumvent copy protection technologies and insulates online service provides from liability for infringing acts of their subscribers subject to various limitations."[45] Such limitations on copyright infringement liability for service providers is covered in Chapter 6. In addition, circumvention of technological protection measures is permitted for specified exemptions,[46] such as classroom instruction covered under the TEACH Act covered in Chapters 7 and 9.

As many librarians tend to be upstanding copyright advocates for both respecting copyright owners and exercising the fair use rights of library customers, legal challenges associated with libraries and librarians are uncommon. At the time of publishing this book, the author was only aware of two instances: one case with a school library discussed in Chapter 9 and another case with customers of an academic library discussed in Chapter 7. No doubt, there are other occasions where libraries get cease-and-desists letters or settle out of court, but these are generally not matters of public record.

Another reason library related infringement cases are uncommon is that in certain instances, infringement penalties are reduced (or eliminated) for what copyright owners could fiscally collect from nonprofit librarians and educators if an alleged infringement were job related or an intended fair use, per Section 504(c)(2)[47] of the Copyright Act. Even if huge statutory damages are excluded, a nonprofit infringer could still be liable for some damages and injunctions. In addition, lawsuits are inconvenient and consume time, energy, and incur possible out-of-pocket expenses. Such proceedings are also a serious drain on one's emotions and community support. Later chapters cover specific conditions tied to potential copyright infringement for different library scenarios by library type.

Promoting copyright awareness to library colleagues and customers, including potential infringement liability, is crucial to avoid the scenarios just mentioned. However, there is one major exception to copyright infringement, which follows in the next section on fair use.

FAIR USE AND OTHER EXCEPTIONS

IP basics include knowing about copyright and fair use. The Fair Use Doctrine[48] of the U.S. copyright law strives to balance public interest rights and individual author rights. Fair use ensures freedom of speech and public access to information, yet it supports the spirit of the U.S. Constitution, Article One, Section Eight, which promotes "... the progress of science and useful arts, by securing for limited times to authors and inventors the exclusive right to their respective writings and discoveries."[49] Fair use is a legal doctrine of U.S. copyright law. It promotes free expression and free speech by permitting the unlicensed use of copyright-protected works within certain conditions.[50] To further support freedom of expression, Section 102 affirms that copyright only protects expression and not ideas or facts.[51]

> The Fair Use Doctrine protects First Amendment rights, as it allows "later authors to use a previous author's copyright to introduce new ideas or concepts to the public." SunTrust Bank v. Houghton Mifflin Co., 268 F.3d 1257, 1265 (11th Cir. 2001).

Fair use is tied to copyright with Section 107 of the Copyright Act of 1976,[52] which provides the media, educators, researchers, and others with limited fair use rights to copy and use portions of copyrighted works without violating copyright. Fair use is one of the primary exceptions listed in the U.S. Copyright Act, which relates to the rights of copyright owners discussed earlier in this chapter.

Throughout this book, the following sections of the Copyright Act are most common: 107, 108, 109(a), 110(1), and 110(2), as these deal with the daily needs of most libraries. Other sections may apply to your unique circumstances, and when they do, you should consult with legal counsel specializing in your specific scenario. Exceptions listed within the Copyright Act that could apply to libraries and their constituents include:

- Section 108: Reproduction by libraries and archives. In other words, photocopying and preservation exceptions for research, study, and interlibrary loans.[53]
- Section 109(a): The First Sale Doctrine. Allows consumers to resell their legally acquired copyrighted works. It also makes it legal for libraries to lend resources.[54]
- Section 109(c): Exception for public displays. Makes it legal for anyone to display a single legally acquired copy of a work publicly where the work is located.[55] For example, artwork in a museum or even book cover images on your libraries online catalog.
- Section 110(1): Display and performance in face-to-face teaching.[56] Applies to the classroom of most educational environments from preschool through higher education.
- Section 110(2): Display and performance in distance learning.[57] Also known as the TEACH Act covered in Chapters 7 and 9.

- Section 117: Computer software. Allows owners of a copy of a computer program to modify to work on or make an archival copy for their computer.[58] Otherwise, any license agreement would provide details for that copy.
- Section 120: Architectural works. Permits anyone to capture a picture of the architectural work of a publicly displayed building.[59] Keep in mind this applies to a copyright exception only. Some buildings have federally registered trademarks, such as the Chrysler Building in New York and the Wrigley Building in Chicago. Trademark fair use is covered in Chapter 5.
- Section 121: Special formats for persons who are visually impaired or have other disabilities. Allows some libraries and other organizations that serve the needs of those with disabilities to reproduce or to distribute copies of previously published, nondramatic literary works in special formats for use by those with such disabilities.[60]

The primary exemption covered for this chapter is fair use. Fair use (Section 107) promotes social benefit and is vital to the growth of knowledge. As Supreme Court Justice Sandra Day O'Connor observed in 1991, the primary purpose of copyright is to "build freely upon the ideas and information conveyed by a work. . . . It is the means by which copyright advances the progress of science and art."[61] O'Connor is saying that fair use of copyrighted works favors progress. A study of the Computer and Communications Industry Association found that fair use adds to U.S. economic growth, accounting for 16 percent of the economy, employing one in eight workers and contributing $2.8 trillion to the GDP.[62]

While fair use does not mean unlimited use, the following types of limited uses are regularly deemed fair use per Section 107[63] of the U.S. Copyright Act:

- Criticism, commentary, and news reporting such as quoting or excerpting
- Scholarship and research quoting for illustration or clarification of researcher's reflection
- Nonprofit teaching and classroom use such as photocopies of limited portions for classroom instruction

Fair use allows flexibility favoring the public's limited use of copyrighted works without permission from the author in such scenarios.

Laura Gasaway authored an insightful article entitled "Fair Use: A Right or a Privilege?"[64] In this article she states, "Fair use excuses conduct that ordinarily would be infringement, but because of the existence of certain factors, the conduct is exempted." Some even go so far to call fair use an affirmative defense to copyright infringement.[65]

There are four fair use factors one must review in assessing whether the limited use is fair use.[66] You should become familiar with these fair use factors from the Fair Use Doctrine, as librarians specializing in IP are often called upon to demonstrate how to apply these four factors to various customer scenarios (see figure 2.4 for helpful visual diagram and figure 2.6 for a checklist to share for such demonstrations). Each scenario must be evaluated on a case-by-case basis by your customers, balancing these four factors:

1. the **purpose** and character of the use, including whether such use is of a commercial nature or is for nonprofit educational purposes. NOTE: if the copyrighted work is being used for a different purpose than that of the original, it may be a transformative use. Examples include quotations incorporated in a report or multimedia mash-ups included in commentary or criticism. More on transformative use later.
2. the **nature** of the copyrighted work, factual versus creative.
3. the **amount** and substantiality of the portion used in relation to the copyrighted work as a whole; for example, the small quantity of content and portion used is not central or significant to entire work.
4. the **effect** to the market of the use of, or value of, the copyrighted work.

When at least three of the four factors favor fair use, then more than likely the scenario is a fair use. When the factors are evenly split, you must decide whether or not it is worth the risk.[67] Your customers might contact their organization's legal counsel. If still in doubt, ask for permission. When less than half of the factors favor fair use, then authorization should definitely be obtained. Fair use applied to you or your IP customer's specific situation may vary depending on the type of use as well as the type of user, for example, education versus commercial use. Fair use is discussed in various chapters by library types and unique scenarios.

One way to help you or your customers remember the four-part factors of a fair use analysis is to refer to a windowpane mnemonic illustrated in figure 2.5: PANE—Purpose, Amount, Nature, and Effect.

Although the order of the four factors listing is not exactly the same as listed earlier from the actual law, it does trigger one's memory when giving a presentation

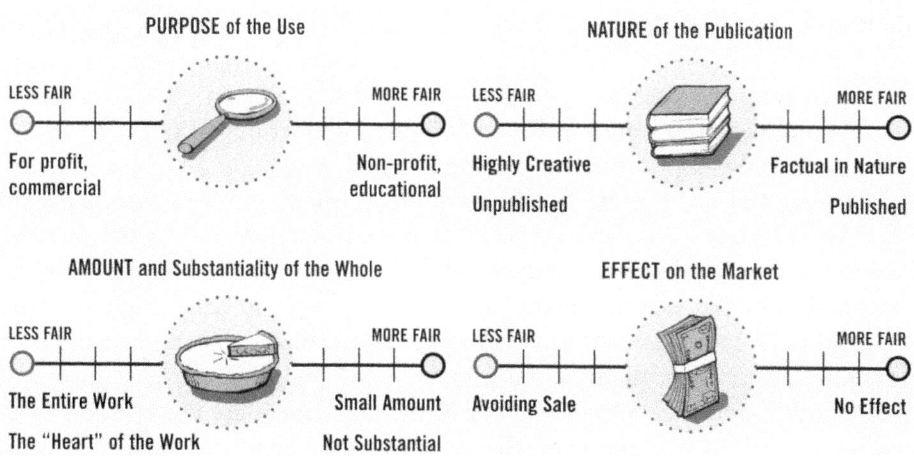

Figure 2.4

Fair Use Continua by Carrie Russell from *Complete Copyright: An Everyday Guide for Librarians,* 2004, American Library Association. (Used by permission by Carrie Russell and under a Creative Commons BY Attribution Only License)

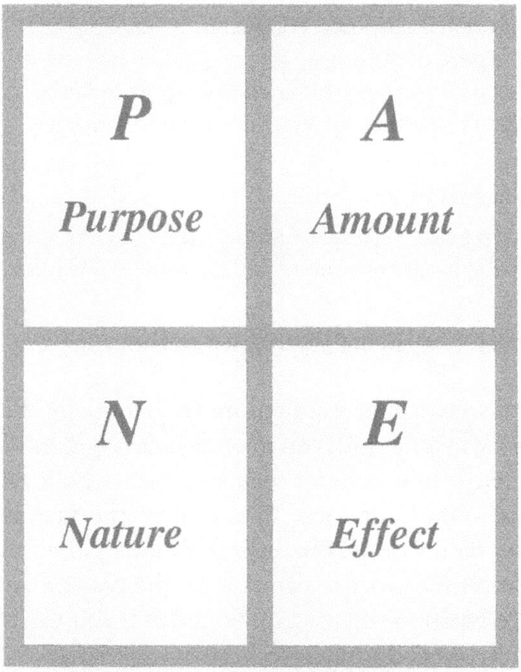

Figure 2.5
Fair Use Window PANE by author John Schlipp

or reviewing the four factors on the fly while assisting library customers. Figure 2.6 from Kenneth Crews and Dwayne Buttler shown here has become the de facto checklist for a fair use analysis.

All of the fair use graphics provided above are tools to assist librarians when reviewing fair use with library customers. Although one should review all four factors together when determining whether one's use is indeed fair use, each of the four factors is discussed in greater detail below.

When congress constructed the Fair Use Doctrine of the Copyright Act of 1976, the "purpose" factor aimed to favor nonprofit education such as libraries, while it was less favorable toward for profit and commercial applications. However, for-profit, commercial use could be fair use in certain instance. For example, for-profit journalists employ commentary, and commercial rap musicians could exploit parody as covered below as a transformative fair use, which often weighs in favor of fair use. Meanwhile, nonprofit educators and librarians should realize there are limitations to their more favorable "purpose" factor. This is why one should consider all four fair use factors together for each instance of a fair use analysis with the graphic tools shown here.

The "nature" factor, as noted in Russell's figure 2.4, features a continuum where copying and using highly creative or unpublished works are less likely fair use, while copying and using more factual content, especially published, is favored by the Fair Use Doctrine. Nonfiction historical or scientific published works are more conducive to copying fair use portions, while imaginative or creative expressions such as fiction books, entertainment movies and music, and other highly creative works tend to be more resilient to unauthorized uses, thus requiring permission or smaller amounts used to qualify as fair use.

The "amount" and substantiality factor of the percentage used in relation to the copyrighted work as a whole generally favors smaller-quantity portions. Yet one must be careful not to use portions of a work that are considered the heart of the work, or in which the importance of a few qualitative paragraphs is tied to the central message of the work. For example, the Supreme Court ruled in *Harper & Row Publishers, Inc. v. Nation Enterprises* (1985) that the *Nation* magazine exceeded fair

FAIR USE CHECKLIST ______________________________
(instructional project name)

Instructor ______________________ Date ________ Prepared by ______________________

Please complete and retain a copy of this form in connection with each possible "fair use" of a copyrighted work for your project.

Favoring fair use	Opposing fair use
PURPOSE	
☐ Teaching (includes multiple copies for classroom use)	☐ Commercial activity
☐ Research	☐ Profiting from the use
☐ Scholarship	☐ Entertainment
☐ Nonprofit educational institution	☐ Bad-faith behavior
☐ Criticism	☐ Denying credit to original author
☐ Comment	
☐ News reporting	
☐ Transformative or productive use (changes the work for new utility)	
☐ Restricted access (to students or other appropriate group)	
☐ Parody	
NATURE	
☐ Published work	☐ Unpublished work
☐ Factual or nonfiction based	☐ Highly creative work (art, music, novels, films, plays)
☐ Important to favored educational objectives	☐ Fiction
AMOUNT	
☐ Small quantity	☐ Large portion or whole work used
☐ Portion used is not central or significant	☐ Portion used is central to or "heart of the work"
☐ Amount is appropriate for favored educational purpose	
EFFECT	
☐ User owns lawfully purchased or acquired copy of original work	☐ Could replace sale of copyrighted work
☐ One or few copies made	☐ Significantly impairs market or potential market for copyrighted work or derivative
☐ No significant effect on the market or potential market for copyrighted work	☐ Reasonably available licensing mechanism for use of the copyrighted work
☐ No similar product marketed by the copyright holder	☐ Affordable permission available for using work
☐ Lack of licensing mechanism	☐ Numerous copies made
	☐ You made it accessible on the web or in other public forum
	☐ Repeated or long-term use

The original Fair Use Checklist, developed by Dr. Kenneth D. Crews, Director of Columbia University Libraries/Information Services Copyright Advisory Office, is available as a PDF from: http://copyright.columbia.edu/copyright/fair-use/fair-use-checklist/

revised 10 JAN 2012

Figure 2.6

Fair Use Checklist by Kenneth Crews, formerly of Columbia University, and Dwayne K. Buttler of University of Louisville. (Used under a Creative Commons BY Attribution License from the Copyright Advisory Office of Columbia University)

use when it quoted approximately 300 words from President Ford's forthcoming memoir before the sale of the 200,000-word book by authorized publisher Harper & Row. The court held that the "amount" factor weighed against fair use because the 300 words quoted were the heart of the work related to Ford's pardon of President Nixon.[68] In this scenario, the heart of the work aspect was also triggered the next "effect" factor of fair use.

The "effect" of the use on the market or value of the copyrighted work is often considered the most important factor with the courts,[69] such as the *Harper & Row* case cited above. If it can be established that such use reduced sales of the copyrighted work, it might be an infringement. This is why familiarity of fair use and copyright law is vital for IP librarians and specialists who support work colleagues or customers who need to conduct a fair use analysis. Legitimate fair use is a defense to a potential copyright infringement as it permits limited use of a copyrighted work without asking for permission. But which scenarios are legitimate, and which are not? The following sections in this chapter and upcoming chapters by library types review specific examples to clarify fair use in most library situations.

When making or distributing reproductions of copyrighted works for public use which are fair use (or lawful under other exemptions covered in later chapters), always try to retain and indicate the unaltered copyright notice from the original work. This provides other users notice that the work is copyrighted and whom to contact for permission for further distribution. If such copyright details are not available, one should post a notice stating something like, "This material may be protected by copyright law (Title 17 U.S. Code)."[70] Failure to include copyright notice of others could make your unlicensed use vulnerable to a claim of willful infringement.[71]

Fair use and distance learning, also known as distributed learning relies on the TEACH Act (Section 110(2)) or fair use (Section 107). Although the TEACH Act primarily applies to higher education, some K–12 and other educational environments are taught online. IP librarians or specialists are often called upon to assist online instructors with supplementary readings in electronic reserves, information about the TEACH Act and fair use, licensing requirements of subscription database content posted online, and so on. For more about how copyright applies to online instruction see Chapters 7 and 9.

Since the introduction of the U.S. Copyright Act of 1976, there have been multiple best practices and guidelines to assist libraries, schools, higher education, cultural heritage organizations, public media, and other nonprofit groups navigate fair use with specific benchmarks endorsed by fair use experts in each field. Such guidelines are not the actual Section 107 Fair Use Doctrine. These guidelines are safe harbor tools. Applying the actual Fair Use Doctrine is often more generous for nonprofit and educational applications. Most fair use guidelines are for educators. Librarians are often called upon for assistance. The following highlighted list of fair use guidelines are covered in detail throughout this book:

Agreement on Guidelines for Classroom Copying in Not-for-Profit Educational Institutions with Respect to Books and Periodicals, H.R. Rep. No. 94-1476, at 68–70 (1976).

Codes of Best Practices in Fair Use, Center for Media & Social Impact at American University (multiple *Codes* published since around 2004).

Fair Use Guidelines for Educational Multimedia, Consortium of College & University Media Centers (1996).
Guidelines for Educational Uses of Music, H.R. Rep. No. 94-1476, at 70–71 (1976).
Guidelines for Off-Air Recordings of Broadcast Programming for Educational Purposes, H.R. Rep. No. 97-495, at 8–9 (1982).
Guidelines on Photocopying and Interlibrary Arrangements, National Commission on New Technological Uses of Copyrighted Works (CONTU) Public Law 93-573 (1974).
Model Policy Concerning College and University Photocopying for Classroom, Research and Library Reserve Use, American Library Association (1982).
Statement on the Digital Transmission of Electronic Reserves, Music Library Association (2010).
Using Electronic Reserves: Guidelines and Best Practices for Copyright Compliance, Copyright Clearance Center (2005).

IS FILE SHARING FAIR USE?

Today's world of the internet has provided new opportunities for both creators and consumers of media such as music and movies. However, with this digital technology comes legal and ethical responsibility. The digital aspect of the Web allows for wonderful innovations such as portable media/MP3 players, but fair use should be practiced to avoid possible copyright infringement. When you download music without paying for it, or share it with others without their paying for it, the copyright creators, the musicians, film talent and technicians, and recording and film studios, among others, are not fully compensated for their labor. Recording companies and their professional associations consider this stealing.

The Recording Industry Association of American (RIAA), accessed at http://www.riaa.com/physicalpiracy.php, is the professional organization that represents the recording companies. RIAA has reacted with legal actions against some file sharers. School use or personal use copying should be limited to respectful, legal, fair use portions of media content and always obtained from legal sources.

A common scenario related to file sharing and fair use would be when your library patron purchases the latest hits songs from iTunes or another legitimate subscription service, which he or she burns to a personal media player. This patron, or any patron, can download audio files from one of your library's subscription music databases. This library patron frequently shares these music files with friends. Two separate legal matters should be considered here: first, the personal use of copying to one's own music player device, and second, sharing with others. Depending on the licensing agreement of the subscription music services, he or she may or may not be able to share legally with others.

TRANSFORMATIVENESS AND FAIR USE

Transformer-type toys change into different things that are not copies of their original form—new things such as cars, animals, and planes, which are far removed

Figure 2.7
Stegowagenvolkssaurus sculpture by Patrica A. Renick, 1974, titled to and owned by Northern Kentucky University, 2011. (Photo used with permission by Michael Providenti and W. Frank Steely Library, Northern Kentucky University)

from their original form (see figure 2.7). When library customers choose brief bits of information from books, limited music, or movie clips, and add something original, their own ideas—music beats, or art images—this is transformative use, also known as a "mash-up." The courts favor most transformative uses, especially for instructional or personal, noncommercial use.

Transformative principles are outlined and specifically applied for the classroom in *The Code of Best Practices in Fair Use for Media Literacy Education* developed by the Center for Media and Social Impact. This *Code* is found at http://cmsimpact.org/code/code-best-practices-fair-use-media-literacy-education/. Based on the fair use doctrine, particularly the *Code's* fourth and fifth points, the students' transformative use is specifically applied.

In the classroom, instructors and students may under some circumstances use copyrighted work excerpts in creating their own new material; and distribute their works digitally if their work incorporates, modifies, and re-presents a portion of existing media content in a transformative way. As Joyce Valenza has stated on her *School Library Journal* blog:

> When a user of copyrighted materials adds value to, or repurposes materials for a use different from that for which is was originally intended, it will likely be considered transformative use; it will also likely be considered fair use. Fair use embraces the modifying or existing media content, placing it in a new context.[72]

The Center for Media and Social Impact provides other similar *Codes of Best Practices in Fair Use* that apply transformativeness for other specific disciplines, ranging from academic and research libraries to documentary filmmakers. See http://cmsimpact.org/program/fair-use/ for a complete listing.

Temple Media Education Lab also provides a great film to use when introducing the concept of fair use and transformative use to library customers. It is a short, fun music video entitled "User Rights, Section 107." This three-minute film is a great introduction about user rights and fair use related to copyright. Other related educational films, lesson plans, and activities are also included. See it at: https://mediaeducationlab.com/news/music-videos-help-educators-and-students-conquer-copyright-confusion.

FAIR USE: PARODY, SATIRE, OR INFRINGEMENT?

"Satire is a lesson; parody is a game."
—Vladimir Nabokov, *Strong Opinions*[73]

Is there a difference between parody and satire? Parody usually spoofs or pokes affectionate fun at a work, such as humorous sketches on late-night television variety programs, while satire is usually more of a jibe using humor to attack or ridicule. The First Amendment often protects parody as a form of free speech, where satire is protected less frequently. Parody is another form of free speech. Reviewing parody is an engaging way to learn more about the first of the four fair use factors, "purpose and character" of the use.

Parody is one of the more heavily litigated types of uses that fall under the "purpose" factor, and the "comment and criticism" category. Parody can be an extremely effective mode of comment and criticism and is greatly favored by the First Amendment because it clothes its message in humorous form.[74] To visually illustrate parody at its best, go to www.youtube.com on the web and keyword search: went with the wind. You should get a list of links to view the classic *Carol Burnett Show* movie parody entitled *Went with The Wind.*[75] The comedic artistry of Carol Burnett and the fashion ingenuity of Bob Mackie figuratively and literally dressed a "comedic tour de force" parody of *Gone with The Wind.*[76] Notice how Carol Burnett and her cast fondly poke fun at the characters and the story. It represents "parody" because there is no malicious intent, and their performance does not detract from the original or harm the commercial viability of Margret Mitchell's book or the classic MGM motion picture. Even Carol Burnett believed that this was one of the finest examples of parody.[77] Fashion Designer Bob Mackie's sketch of Carol Burnett in costume for this parody is displayed here in figure 2.8.

Figure 2.8
Carol Burnett as Miss Starlett by Bob Mackie. (Courtesy of Bob Mackie. Used with permission © Bob Mackie Design Group, Ltd.)

However, another parody of *Gone with the Wind* was a cause of litigation in another case. In 2001, the estate of Margaret Mitchell's copyrighted *Gone with The Wind* legally challenged the published book *The*

Wind Done Gone. The new book's publisher asserted it was a critical parody protected by fair use. In turn, the U.S. Circuit Court of Appeals in Atlanta suggested that the parody constituted fair use and that it was tied to the First Amendment principles of protecting critical parodies. The Circuit Court held that the new work was specific criticism of the depiction of slavery and the relationships between blacks and whites in *Gone with The Wind*. The case was ultimately settled out of court.[78]

Dr. Seuss Enterprises, L.P. v. Penguin Books USA, Inc. is a somewhat similar 1997 court case where the spoof writer claimed parody. An author creatively imitated the definitive style of Dr. Seuss books to express the story of the O. J. Simpson murder court trial in his book entitled *The Cat NOT in the Hat! A Parody by Dr. Juice*. The court determined that this book was indeed a satire, as it did not poke fun at Dr. Seuss. It conveyed a story about O. J. Simpson that had nothing to do with the Dr. Seuss style or the well-known *Cat in the Hat* character. The court declared that the author's commercial book was not transformative fair use and not a parody.[79]

The courts appear to see a difference between satire and parody, as the American Bar Association (ABA) points out in a published Roundtable Discussion entitled "The Satire/Parody Distinction in Copyright and Trademark Law—Can Satire Ever Be a Fair Use?"[80] While a parody imitates the original work to create a new expression, a satire uses the work to criticize something else, which requires justification for the very act of borrowing from the original. As a result, the court appears to favor parody under fair use, while disfavoring satire.[81]

An example of a definitive fair use parody case went all the way to the Supreme Court. It is generally known as the "Pretty Woman" case. The ABA Roundtable Discussion affirms that this case qualified as fair use as it used some elements of a prior author's work to create a new work with commentary. It offered social benefit and, in the process, created a new work. Parodies are transformative, as opposed to superseding, works.[82] Other books, articles, and websites refer to this case to illustrate the transformative aspect of fair use that applies to librarians, educators, and their colleagues, as they add value to or repurpose copyrighted works for a use different than that for which the work was originally intended.

The "Pretty Woman" case is officially known as *Campbell v. Acuff Rose*.[83] It goes back to the 1990s when rap group 2 Live Crew borrowed not the melody but a few lines from the first part of "Pretty Woman." The other lyrics and all of the music performed were an original composition of the rap group. The group had attempted to get permission and to pay for the use, but they were denied. The music publisher felt the rap performance was risqué and ultimately sued 2 Live Crew for copyright infringement. To view the actual use of the few lyrics, go to YouTube or a search engine on the Web and use the search terms: pretty woman 2 live crew.

The Supreme Court determined their use was indeed a transformative fair use as it only borrowed a small portion of the lyrics from the original song. In addition, the transformed parody was intended for a very different audience than the original song. As the Supreme Court recognized in this case, the important question when dealing with transformative use is:

> whether the new work merely supersedes the objects of the original creation, or whether and to what extent it is "transformative," altering the original with new expression, meaning, or message. The more transformative the new work, the less will be the significance of other factors, like commercialism, that may weigh against a finding of fair use.

Once again, the transformative use concept introduced by the Supreme Court in this instance of parody had a major impact on fair use for librarians and educators. This transformative concept applies to students and teachers in library research and writing as well as customers of public libraries.

Many copyright scholars, such as Edward Lee Lamoureux,[84] have also discussed how the first fair use factor "purpose and character of the use" was predominant in the Supreme Court's final decision of the "Pretty Woman" case in favor of transformative fair use. The Court then viewed the remaining three fair use factors, nature of work, amount, and market effect through the analysis of the first "purpose and character of the use" factor. In reviewing this case, one might wonder if all four fair use factors are *not* equal. Could some be more important than others? This validates why every fair use analysis must be evaluated on a case-by-case basis. Many librarians and educators fall into the trap of using an amount of 10 percent as fair use quantity and believing that if it is educational, then it is fair use no matter what. However, by reviewing the four fair use factors on a case-by-case basis, one's analysis may result in a more generous or meager amount to apply as fair use than what guidelines suggest. Yet often, the case-by-case analyses for librarians and educators tend to be more favorable than applying guidelines mentioned earlier.

Another topic closely related to parody is when musicians sample music. If you view brief film clips from the 2010 Independent Lens (Indiepix Films) documentary, *Copyright Criminals*, at www.pbs.org/independentlens/copyright-criminals/classroom.html, the documentary examines both sides of the debate about whether musicians sampling the music of others is copyright infringement or not. It has four short film modules to view that will provide background on this topic. Comparing to the "Pretty Woman" parody case and viewing these short films here about musicians and sampling the music of others, one might wonder whether the copyright owners of the original music sampled are eligible for compensation, or is it fair use? Parody and transformative use could be argued as fair use; yet, if the use of another musician's music is not transformed and not parody, then it could be an infringement. This is when a fair use analysis is highly advised.

The next section covers free-to-share type services using other IP labels related to copyright. They are alternatives to fair use, which may offer some attributes of public domain.

ALTERNATIVES TO TRADITIONAL COPYRIGHT AND FAIR USE

This section includes information about public domain, open access, open source, the CC, and digital library repositories among others. These are all alternatives to relying on fair use that help creators protect their works in an open culture as well as to help others locate works in a free and open IP setting.

Authored works in the public domain are not protected by copyright. For example, older works published before the early twentieth Century, such as the traditional story *Snow White and the Seven Dwarfs*, are usually in the public domain. Public domain legally belongs to the public and may be used by anyone for free.[85] The popular animated television series, *The Simpsons*, featured a spoof of Disney's animated film classic *Snow White*. Disney has legitimately exploited numerous stories from the public domain,[86] creating new copyrighted expressions of such works, and then fiercely protected their new expressions. The *Simpsons* animators transformed the Disney iconic characters with their own *Simpsons* characters in place of the Disney dwarfs; they sang a parody of Disney's "Heigh Ho," as "Ho Hi." The final line of the "Ho Hi," lyrics went, "If Disney sues, we'll claim fair use Ho Hi, Ho Hi."[87] This does not mean that the Disney film, *Snow White*, introduced in 1937, is in the public domain at the time of writing this book. It does, however, illustrate again how transformativeness is often fair use.

Other exceptions to copyright that are in the public domain include U.S. government documents. Common facts may not be copyrighted, such as "George Washington was the first president of the United States," and neither can the names listed in a telephone book or the ingredients of a recipe found in a cookbook.

Continuing with the fair use with facts aspect of copyrighted works, there is a significant copyright case that went to the Supreme Court that is referenced often among related copyright awareness and information literacy. *Feist Publications, Inc. v. Rural Telephone Service Co.*, 499 U.S. 340 (1991) addressed how facts are not copyrightable, but the compilation of facts might be protected if there is some creativity. Feist Publications collected listings of names, addresses, and telephone numbers from Rural Telephone's directory to print its own private directory. Rural Telephone objected, claiming that its phone directory listings were its creative property. The Supreme Court held that no one may claim originality of the facts, because facts do not owe their origin to an act of authorship. The distinction is between creation and discovery: the first person to find and report a particular fact has not created the fact; he or she has only discovered its existence. This is the case with all facts—scientific, historical, and contemporary news reports, among others. Facts are not copyrightable and are public domain. However, the compilation of facts could be copyrightable if there is some modicum of creativity. In this case, a basic arrangement of names and phone numbers did not qualify as original. Neither was the content sufficient creativity to garner copyright protection.[88]

The Library of Congress offers a fee-based research service for customers at https://www.copyright.gov/rrc/, where Copyright Office specialistscan search onsite copyright records to verify copyright registrations. Besides reviewing the *Copyright Term and the Public Domain* chart (figure 2.2) from Cornell University Library, it is also possible for anyone to trace copyright registrations, and renewals on their own to determine copyright status of most works registered works. Besides the LOC's onsite registrations, a few Federal Depository Library Program libraries hold the *Catalog of Copyright Entries* published by the Copyright Office. In addition, most *Catalogs* are searchable online via the internet archive at https://archive.org/details/copyrightrecords. Because copyright registration in the United States was mandatory before 1978, these volumes are insightful for locating such registrations and renewals, especially through 1963, when renewals were not automatically completed. Circular 22 from the U.S. Copyright Office, entitled *How to Investigate the Copyright Status of a Work* (https://www.copyright.gov/circs/circ22.pdf), offers additional details. Also, see the author's IPAC website, for a guide entitled "Researching & Tracing Copyright Renewal Records." It offers instructions on tracing copyright registrations to determine if a work is in the public domain at https://inside.nku.edu/ipac/worksofothers/copyright-renewals.html.

OPEN ACCESS AND CREATIVE COMMONS

Besides public domain resources, which are open and free to use by others without permission, there are alternative IP instances where permission to use the works of others is not questioned. Open access and CC are examples of the growing open movement to publish and share with others to improve the public good of information access. Open access is vital to advancing the interests of library customers such as researchers, scholars, students, and the public. Open access is free, immediate, online access to scholarly research and publications and the right to reuse and redistribute these resources, often in the digital environment.[89] The other form of access for researchers and scholars is the CC.

Resources licensed with the CC[90] are among popular examples of open access. The CC was founded by Stanford University Law Professor Lawrence Lessig and others who believed in sharing their intellectual content for free for noncommercial purposes such as personal, educational, and nonprofit environments. Professor Lessig's research is focused on law and technology, especially as it affects copyright. Lessig supports fair use in the digital world, where these rights appear to be in decline. To address this challenge, the CC offers "openly licensed creativity . . . freely available for legal use, sharing, repurposing, and reframing."[91] To promote universal access, the CC provides "a free, public, and standardized infrastructure that creates a balance between the reality of the Internet and the reality of copyright laws."[92] Not intended as a substitute for copyright, CC offers a free registration infrastructure for creators to file a license deed. This permits others to locate, recognize, and freely use their registered works in exchange for posting author attribution.

The CC license options are combinations of the following four conditions:

- BY (attribution) allows others to use your work but only if they attribute the way you request. BY is required for all CC licenses.
- NC (noncommercial) allows others to use your work—but for noncommercial purposes only. This does not mean that works cannot be used for commercial purposes, but separate licenses must be obtained by a user who wishes to make commercial use of the work.

- ND (no derivatives) allows others to copy, distribute, display, and perform only verbatim copies of your work, not derivative works. The right to make adaptations can be licensed with a separate agreement.
- SA (share alike) allows others to make derivatives from your original, work but they are allowed to distribute derivative works only under the same terms as the license of your work or a license that is compatible with your terms. SA is used to prevent others from taking something from the CC and then blocking it with a more restrictive license.[93]

All four CC licenses are based on copyright law and thus are applicable only to copyrightable works. CC also offers CC0 (Creative Commons Zero), a way to release works into the public domain. See https://creativecommons.org/ for the most current information. Other public domain uses discussed here are those transferred into digital collections.

OPEN DIGITAL COLLECTIONS

The open access movement has spawned multiple free alternatives for publishing and sharing open resource. A major use of public domain or open access materials is found in Project Gutenberg, Wikimedia Commons, and similar sites. Project Gutenberg, at https://www.gutenberg.org/, has provided free full-text books since 1971. It was founded by writer Michael S. Hart while attending the University of Illinois. Hart received a grant to help digitize books on the ARPANET computer network that eventually was part of ARPANET, the early internet. This site offers a treasure trove of some of the world's finest literature from the public domain with no restrictions on viewing or redistributing. No fees are required. New resources are once again being added to the collection as the public domain is now growing each year, as the moratorium of the Sonny Bono Copyright Extension Act ended on December 31, 2018.[94]

Wikimedia (https://commons.wikimedia.org/wiki/Main_Page) is a media file repository offering over forty-nine million media files from the public domain and freely-licensed educational media content such as images, sound and video clips available to use for free.[95] Attribution is often the primary concern of media content contributors. Licensing terms of each media file is located on each description page. Although Wikimedia hosts Wikipedia and other free knowledge projects, not all media files posted on Wikipedia are from Wikimedia Commons. Awareness of Wikimedia Commons or CC licensing notices are helpful to determine open access usability of image posted on Wikipedia. Another site similar to Wikimedia is Picryl https://picryl.com/. Picryl claims to be the largest search engine for public domain content, including images, documents, music, and videos. Both sites encourage users to verify the public domain status of each work, as other rights besides copyright may apply.

While Project Gutenberg was among the first digital libraries, it was followed later by the Library of Congress. Initially, digital libraries were more often nonprofit and offered their public domain content for free. Later, commercial players such as Google and nonprofit academic consortiums under the HathiTrust group, a coalition of research libraries, began providing free access to scanned public domain books and limited previews of books with active copyright, ranging from a few lines to limited pages depending on copyright circumstances. Google and HathiTrust felt these previews were lawful and fair use. Both Google and HathiTrust were sued by commercial publishing interests.

The settlement of Google's book scanning project ultimately helped to cultivate another aspect of transformative fair use: creating a "new utility" from an existing work such as its "search and find" snippets feature.[96] HathiTrust's partnership with Google dealing with the same type of scanning work resulted in a similar legal decision. In the end, such transformative character permits libraries to engage in other beneficial uses of resources in their collection, such as digital repositories or online special collections.

In 2004, Google began to scan and digitize millions of books, predominantly nonfiction and some in the public domain. However, in response to the copyrighted works scanned and displayed, the Author's Guild and other parties sued Google in 2005[97] claiming Google's digital library prompted book sales declines and threatened their "exclusive rights"[98] protected by copyright. In 2008, the Author's Guild agreed on a $125 million settlement. The settlement terms, including a Book Rights Registry to compensate authors, were rejected in 2011 by New York's federal Second Circuit Court judge, Denny Chin.[99] In the end, Google was not required to pay royalties to any authors for scanning their books.

Meanwhile, HathiTrust and other libraries collaborated with Google to provide books for its scanning project. HathiTrust was separately sued[100] for use of the digital works, which Google scanned from its collections. Judge Baer of the United States District Court affirmed that HathiTrust's use of digitized works was fair use.[101] The circuit court also affirmed the case as fair use.[102]

After much litigation over alleged copyright infringements versus fair use defenses, the Google Books' case was appealed to the U.S. Supreme Court in 2014, which in turn denied "certiorari." This means the Supreme Court refused to review the circuit court's decision. Hence, the 2013 decision of the lower Second Circuit remained as final; Google's book-scanning project was indeed fair use.[103] The transformative fair use conclusiveness of this case now offers readers a universal library, as well as a clearer legal track for librarians to become "more confident about pursuing forms of broader digital access" for the public good.[104]

The open movement has encouraged the growth of quality open access journals. The Directory of Open Access Journals (DOAJ) https://doaj.org/ is an online directory that indexes and provides access to open access, quality peer-reviewed journals for multiple subject disciplines.

ORPHANED WORKS

Orphaned works are another condition librarians should be aware of. This condition affects how libraries digitize their collections and how their customers use such works in question. The U.S. Copyright Office defines orphan works as a "situation where the owner of a copyrighted work cannot be identified and located by someone who wishes to make use of the work in a manner that requires permission of the copyright owner."[105]

While not a law yet, the Orphan Works Act of 2008[106] addressed a universal challenge in finding copyright owners for permission to use after a realistic good faith search. The Act has promoted prospective future legislation that may limit the copyright owners in demanding only reasonable reimbursement, so long as the author of the work has provided attribution. Moreover, such future legislation would try to assure that a user's "good faith" and "reasonable effort" to locate a copyright owner should be sufficient to protect them from later potential copyright infringement liability.[107]

In 2014, the Copyright Office reviewed the challenge of orphan works.[108] The Office produced a document in 2015 entitled *Orphan Works and Mass Digitization: A Report of the Register of Copyright*. In it, the Copyright Office expressed concern that mass digitization can sometimes be impeded by a user's inability to locate copyright owners of various works despite one's best searching efforts. Further, the Office stressed that mass digitization projects for public access could be hindered by trying to obtain authorization for "the sheer number of individual permissions required."[109]

The *Orphan Works and Mass Digitization* report concluded that "legislation addressing both orphan works and mass digitization could do much to further the objectives of the copyright system by providing legal certainty to users, establishing reliable mechanisms for the compensation of authors, and making vast numbers of long forgotten works available for the public good."[110]

Although Congress has not passed any specific legislation related to orphan works as of 2018, the MMA does include provisions for nonprofit streaming of out-of-print, pre-1972 recordings when the rights holder cannot be located and if such recordings are not available commercially. It is then the responsibility of the user to file a notice with the Copyright Office, for which any copyright holder has ninety days to object to its use. The potential user could also establish a noncommercial fair use in certain conditions.[111]

INTERLIBRARY LOAN (ILL) AND DOCUMENT DELIVERY

This section covers ILL and Document Delivery in relation to U.S. Copyright Act, Sections 107 and 108, plus an integral guideline known as the CONTU Rule of Five, as well as database licensing agreements and the permissions process. These are all vital in assuring copyright compliance of an ILL and document delivery workflow. Understanding and applying copyright compliancy and fair use also supports our library customers in obtaining resources to fulfill their information needs.[112]

Limited funding for acquiring new resources and serials inflation are unavoidable in any type of library. It has become a challenge to collect every book or periodical which we believe our users will need. Consequently, libraries rely on ILL and related delivery alternatives. According to the Interlibrary Loan Code for the United States, "Interlibrary loan is the process by which a library requests material from, or supplies material to, another library. The purpose of interlibrary loan as defined by this code is to obtain, upon request of a library user, material not available in the user's local library."[113]

ILL activity helps libraries expand their *access* to resources unavailable to their local users beyond their locally *owned* holdings by borrowing from other libraries. This became a common practice in the mid-1950s when standardized ILL request forms were developed. During the 1960s, union catalogs and union lists of serial holdings emerged listing holdings of a group of several libraries or collections. However, the delivery process of items lent was as not as quick as it is today. It could take over a month to obtain one book from an interlibrary lending source, as postal mail was the typical library request communication method. Journal article lending became more accessible as the cost and quality of photocopies improved in the 1970s. When OCLC introduced its ILL subsystem in 1979 using electronic requesting communication, the turnaround time improved for lending.[114] Consortia agreements were also introduced to enhance ILL services. Today, ILL electronic delivery of resources directly to patrons has transformed the role of libraries in delivering information. A library may easily purchase a copyright compliant copy of an article from a publisher or document delivery website or acquire a book or media items from a bookseller within a few business days.

The First Sale Doctrine from Section 109 of the Copyright Act not only provides libraries the legal opportunity to lend books, it also supports interlibrary lending. The First Sale Doctrine allows for a legally acquired copy of a copyrighted work to be sold, leased, lent, displayed, or disposed of without permission of the copyright owner. Section 109(a) states that "the owner of a particular copy or phonorecord lawfully made under this title, or any person authorized by such owner, is entitled, without the authority of the copyright owner, to sell or otherwise dispose of the possession of that copy or phonorecord."[115] However, the purchaser or borrower of a book or other copyrighted work cannot make copies without permission of the copyright owner, or with certain fair use exceptions. As covered in other chapters of this book, ILL relies on Section 108 of copyright law, while Section 107 provides fair use for customers when they make limited copies of library resources for their research needs.

The First Sale Doctrine also supports libraries in selling used resources for fundraising, such as book sales. In theory, it would even permit a library to lease parts of its collection to another library or museum if it so wished. However, when a library leases electronic resources (such as journal article databases) from a publisher, the contractual agreement may not permit lending to other libraries. Yet there is an exception in Section 109 of the Copyright Act for library lending of licensed works to other libraries, as discussed later in this chapter.

Given the commonplace use of photocopiers and the recent ease of electronic delivery, it has become exceptional for libraries to lend entire journal issues or bound volumes. Journal or magazine articles are now copied and delivered to a requesting library. As this method evolved, publishers expressed their concern for copyright infringement. Today, the internet has made this process even more convenient and cost effective, as librarians may easily scan articles and send via facsimile, using Adobe® PDF files or other electronic methods. However, the publishers' concerns over copyright infringement remain.

Librarians copy and distribute journal or magazine articles legally under Section 108 of the U.S. Copyright Act.[116] This law offers limitations on a copyright holder's exclusive rights, such as reproduction by libraries and archives, and allows librarians to make copies and to receive copies of articles, chapters, and other short works for purposes of private study and research. Fair use plays a smaller role within ILL, as it comes from Section 107 of the Copyright Act.

Section 108(a) of the Copyright Act states that libraries may "reproduce no more than one copy . . . of a work . . . or . . . distribute such copy," if the following conditions apply: (1) the copies are made without any commercial advantage; (2) the library's collections are open to the public or available persons doing research in a specialized field other than those associated with the library; and (3) the copy or distribution of the work includes a copyright notice on the copy that this work may be protected by copyright.

Section 108(d) and Section 108(e) provide further limits:

- The copy becomes the property of the user.
- The library may copy no more than one article, one "other contribution" to a copyrighted collection, or a small part of any other copyrighted work (an exception may be allowed for when an entire work is extremely short, e.g., a pamphlet).
- The library or archive must prominently exhibit a warning of copyright where copy requests are placed (online or face-to-face order forms) in accordance with requirements issued by the Copyright Office:
    - The copyright law of the United States (title 17, United States Code) governs the making of photocopies or other reproductions of copyrighted material. Under certain conditions specified in Section 108, libraries and archives are authorized to furnish a photocopy or other reproduction. One of these specific conditions is that the photocopy or reproduction is not to be "used for any purpose other than private study, scholarship, or research." If a user makes a request for, or later uses, a photocopy or reproduction for purposes in excess of fair use, that user may be liable for copyright infringement. This institution reserves the right to refuse to accept a copying order if, in its judgment, fulfillment of the order would involve violation of copyright law.[117]

Section 108(g) specifies that the allowances only apply to the "isolated and unrelated reproduction or distribution of a single copy . . . of the same material on separate occasions."[118] The allowances do not pertain when the library, or its employees, is aware that copying is carried out for use of "related or concerted reproduction or distribution of multiple copies . . . of the same material,"[119] whether made on one occasion or over a period of time, and whether intended for aggregate use by one or more individuals. Neither does it apply where the library or its employees engage in the systematic reproduction or distribution of single or multiple copies of materials as a substitution for a subscription or purchase.

Based on the need to clarify Section 108(g) related to ILL, the CONTU Rule of Five guidelines[120] were developed by publishers, teachers, and librarians. If a library is open to the public or others researching in a specialized field outside its primary patron group,[121] the CONTU Rule of Five guidelines[122] supports a library in acquiring limited photocopies or electronic copies of journal articles published within the last five years. Under Section 108(a)2, for-profit academic institutions or profit-oriented company information centers could also use the CONTU Rule of Five, but they would need to be open to the public or provide virtual access by offering document finding services and ILL.[123]

The CONTU Rule of Five guidelines are such that for the current calendar year, borrowing libraries may not take delivery of more than five copies of articles from a single title published within the last five years. For example, let's say the ILL staff receives a sixth article request for *Marmalade Magazine* during the current calendar year in October. The CONTU Rule of Five calendar does not start over until the first day of January each year. What are the options for interlibrary when the sixth request for *Marmalade Magazine* arrives?

Borrowing the magazine from another library or canceling the request is the most prudent option, but it is not necessarily in the best interest of the customer. As an alternative, the Copyright Clearance Center or commercial document delivery services are available when permission and royalties are necessary for the sixth copy. Purchasing pay-per-use, single articles online from the publisher is another option. Document delivery service or publisher purchases usually cover the copyright royalties for individual customer use.

As noted above, the CONTU guidelines do not include requests for articles over five years old at the date of request. Generally, it is considered that Section 107 of the Copyright Act related to fair use should cover requests for articles that were published five years ago or earlier, as the "effect on the market" factor is no longer significant. Exemption from following the CONTU guidelines is permitted when the library owns a copy of the journal, but it is not available due to being not yet received from the publisher, is missing or stolen, or is long overdue from a borrowing patron. However, licensing contract agreements may supersede these exemptions for embargo periods of database journal issues.

The borrowing library must also specify whether its article request is copyright compliant with the CONTU guidelines on the request form (paper or electronic). The borrowing library must clearly indicate on each request for photocopies whether it "Conforms to the CONTU Copyright Guidelines" (CCG) or "Conforms to the Copyright Law" (CCL). CCG is indicated when the borrowing library does not currently subscribe to a magazine or journal title, it is of the first five copies from a title request for the current calendar year, and the material requested was published within five years of the date of request. CCL is indicated on requested articles published at least five years before the date of the request or when the article copied is considered fair use under Section 107 of the Copyright Law. The borrowing library is responsible in maintaining the copyright compliance records. The lending library is not responsible for maintain copyright records.

Commercial document delivery services are available for both nonprofit and for-profit libraries to supplement ILL. Usually these services will assure that their delivery of documents are copyright compliant for a specific library's needs.[124] Document delivery means different things to different people. Is it the document-on demand commercial service that provides an academic library a hard-to-locate document or one that requires copyright compliance? Is it the library's in-house photocopy service or scanning service to its users of its own in-house journal articles or intra-library loan within its library system, that is, another branch or campus library? Or is it conventional ILL?

Ronald Dekker and Leo Waaijers define document delivery as bridging the gap between where the customer is and where the document is. Dekker and Waaijers expand the explanation from two perspectives: those of the user and the library. A user sees a document delivery service as a transparent, reliable way of obtaining his or her document, whereas a librarian sees document delivery as a known quality service and efficient process that fills the gap between the customer and the requested document. User-friendly, seamless access, as much digital delivery as possible, to hybrid collections of both paper and electronic resources is also fundamental in meeting the needs of the document delivery customer.[125]

From a library customer's viewpoint, ILL and document delivery are the same thing. They see this as a way to borrow books and other media or obtain copies of articles not available from their library at the time of their request. Hence, document delivery may continue to move toward purchasing and acquiring books, non-print media, and journal articles in lieu of ILL borrowing. This is a growing popular trend and an effective collection development method, especially where research patrons need a specific resource. Also known as "purchase instead of borrow" or "just-in-time," this has been researched and reported in library literature often; see endnote for further information.[126]

ILL AND LICENSED RESOURCES

Just as copyright serves two parties, consumers and creators, licensing follows the same structure. Librarians specializing in collection acquisitions, IP, or ILL should be cognizant of licensing implications on fair use.

Licensing is an issue with lending some audiovisual and media resources. Similar to computer software, some media resources are no longer sold but rather licensed to libraries. Licensing potentially allows the copyright holder to take away some statutory rights, including the First Sale Doctrine of the U.S. Copyright Act. In this scenario, the library is not only restricted in interlibrary lending, it may also prohibit lending to its own customers. When purchasing audiovisual resources, watch for any licensing restrictions associated with the materials. Some signs to look for include shrink-wrapped packing with fine print license, a "splash page" in addition to the customary FBI copyright notice, or other special sales terms posted on the publisher's catalog or website.[127]

However, David Ensign proposes that there may be exceptions to lending licensed works in Section 109(b)(1)(A) of the Copyright Law. "Under some circumstances, individuals and institutions may not be permitted to lend or lease computer programs or sound recordings, but specific provisions included in the Copyright Act permit nonprofit libraries and educational institutions to lend these items to one another."[128]

ILL and subscription databases of serials and e-book deal with the customer or user aspects licensing. Library acquisitions should negotiate for the permission to use such database content for ILL lending as well as instructional needs for academic, school, and special libraries. Licensing almost always overrules fair use because a legal contract is involved. If fair use applications are not mentioned, such uses could apply to a more restricted degree. The publisher may stipulate any requirements. Libraries should carefully examine any contractual details to be aware of what is defined for ILL, electronic sharing, authorized users, and any other research use of the licensed content. Whether for large-scale annual subscriptions or unique, single document delivery purchases, it is best to get all licensing agreements in print. One should never rely on any verbal agreements.[129]

It cannot be emphasized how important contract negotiations are for libraries related to "right to use" conditions for ILL lending. A library has the right to ask for reasonable revisions in a contract in order to help its customers. Recently, interlibrary lending of some electronic content has been permitted with negotiated licensing agreements by some vendors. As licensing agreement contracts may be overloaded with many legal terms and unclear conditions for librarians, it is helpful to have your institution's legal counsel review the fine print in the negotiation process. For libraries dealing with database acquisitions, there are three basic licensing agreement categories:

1. Statutory or Compulsory License: Third parties, such as libraries legally make use of copyrighted works without copyright owner's authorization as long as it complies with legal requirements and royalties are paid when applicable. This is more the exception than the rule. The Digital Performance Rights in Sound Recordings is one of six compulsory licenses accepted by U.S. copyright law. It likely would not apply to licensing of databases for library acquisition.
2. Shrink-Wrap License: Also known as Click-On, these are licensing agreements that are non-negotiable. Everyone is familiar with this type of licensing associated with computer software and some online resources. A buyer or user of the resource agrees to the terms by virtue of opening the package or clicking on an "I Accept" agreement of online software or resource. It is usually associated with a single user of the resource, and it is not intended to be reviewed for negotiation. However, as a conservative measure, libraries should review agreements that are unclear with their legal counsel to avoid any legal risks for the library and its parent institution.
3. Negotiable License: These are mainly associated with library acquisition of leased databases. As most library databases are intended for use by a larger scale community than most Shrink-Wrap single users, negotiation is important to define terms and conditions for their specific users and obtain a competitive price.[130]

Digital Rights Management (DRM) is utilized for some content delivered via ILL or document delivery. The ALA defines DRM technology as a way "to control access to, track and limit uses of digital works."[131] DRM consists of practices such as encryption, watermarks, and password restriction incorporated in the technology that delivers information. Some digital media content publishers maintain that DRM technologies are essential to prevent revenue loss due to unauthorized copying of their copyrighted works. Conversely, others argue that conveying control of the use of media from consumers to the media will lead to the loss of existing fair use rights and suppress innovation in the flow of information and ideas.

DRM could negate fair use, especially for ILL or document delivery. As with licensed databases, there may be agreements associated with single purchased digital copies of articles or database digital copies permitted for ILL lending. Since this technology, as it relates to copyright law and licensing agreements is developing, librarians should keep an eye on the latest DRM developments and its impact for ILL and document delivery customers. One such development is middleware software, which has been developed to authenticate and authorize individuals through an online negotiator process that works on behalf of DRM vendors and DRM users. Hypothetically, a researcher using DRM content might request to make fair use copies of a document through middleware online prompts without requesting permission directly from a copyright holder.[132]

ILL codes, consortia networks, and reciprocal agreements offer collaboration between libraries to work together to garner sharper pricing or licensing terms of resources such as databases. Codified polices assist the ILL daily workflow including following licensing agreement as well as copyright compliance. The primary code, which virtually all ILL departments follow, is known as the *National Interlibrary Loan Code*,[133] also available as the *Interlibrary Code for the United States*,[134] with supplementary guidelines to clarify the original *National Code* document. The *Code* promotes open-minded interlibrary policies for state, regional, and local applications. These groups often create their own code based on the *National Code*. State and regional policies are usually tied to consortia, network, or reciprocal agreements that assist with tight budgets.

Networks may be created at the local level to provide express courier services and reciprocal agreements. *A Model Interlibrary Loan Code for Regional, State, Local or Other Special Groups of Libraries* was made available by the ALA in 1984. It was "intended to provide guidelines for any group of libraries interested in developing an interlibrary loan code to meet special needs."[135]

ILL codes are also helpful for clarifying who is responsible for what, such as the fact that borrowing libraries are responsible for any damaged or lost items borrowed. Many libraries post the *National ILL Code* for their customers to view on their websites. The *National ILL Code* is helpful when consortia create and implement their own codes for lending and borrowing agreements.

Copyright and fair use knowledge are vital to working within the law for ILL. Gretchen McCord Hoffmann firmly believes that we should know the rules and when they apply—and follow them. She also emphasizes the importance of knowing your institution's policy about copyright and ILL. When in doubt, always consult your institution's legal counsel for any questions. And most importantly, maintain documentation related to the workflow of all ILL activity.[136]

CONCLUSION

Copyright advances the progress of knowledge for all consumers by giving an economic incentive to authors and artists to create new works. The copyright owner has exclusive rights to prohibit others from trespassing of their copyrighted work. Fair use is an exception to those exclusive rights. It provides users of copyrighted works with limited fair use rights to copy and use portions of such works without violating copyright. Fair use also ensures freedom of speech and public access to information. Alternatives to traditional copyright and fair use include public domain, open access, open source, the CC, and digital library repositories, among others.

Librarians and information providers have a responsibility to be aware of copyright issues if they are going to impart IP information literacy to both creators and users of copyrighted works. With this awareness, one can identify alternatives that the law allows and make decisions about copyright that best advance their objectives.[137] Obviously, there is even a civic responsibility for your clientele regarding the ethical and legal use of copyrighted resources. The next chapter will review patents, another IP for which librarians and their constituents need awareness to support their research, creativity, and innovation.

NOTES

1. Mark Twain, *Mark Twain's Notebook*, May 23, 1903, cited in *Mark Twain at Your Fingertips: A Book of Quotations*; compiled and edited by Caroline Thomas Harnsberger (New York: Cloud, Inc., Beechhurst Press, 1948), 69.
2. Robert Hilburn, "The Long and Winding Road," *Los Angeles Times*, September 22, 1985, https://www.latimes.com/la-et-hilburn-michael-jackson-sep22-story.html (accessed December 31, 2018); Sean Michaels, "Paul McCartney to Regain Beatles Back Catalogue?" *Guardian*, August 11, 2009, https://www.theguardian.com/music/2009/aug/11/paul-mccartney-beatles-back-catalogue (accessed December 31, 2018).
3. John Lennon quote in Beth Dreher, "10 Quotes That Will Change the Way You Think about John Lennon," *Reader's Digest*, https://www.rd.com/culture/john-lennon-quotes/ (accessed December 31, 2018); Johnny Rogan, *Complete Guide to Music of John Lennon* (London: Omnibus Press, 1997), 90.
4. Russell Sanjek, *American Popular Music and Its Business: The First Four Hundred Years: Volume III From 1900 to 1984* (New York: Oxford University Press, 1988), 473–474; Paul Rutter, *Music Industry Handbook* (London: Routledge Taylor & Francis Group, 2016), 104–105; Dan Rys, "Brief History of the Ownership of the Beatles Catalog," Billboard, https://www.billboard.com/articles/columns/rock/7662519/beatles-catalog-paul-mccartney-brief-history-ownership (accessed December 31, 2018); and Hilburn, "The Long and Winding Road." For additional details see Brain Southall and Ruppert Perry's *Northern Songs: The True Story of the Beatles Song Publishing Empire* (London: Omnibus Press, 2016) and Paul Robertson's *How the Beatles Lost Control of their Song Publishing Rights*, http://www.ptrob.com/Music/Beatles/Song_Rights/song_rights.html (accessed December 31, 2018).
5. Paul McCartney quote in introductory section of book by Rupert Perry, *Northern Songs: The True Story of the Beatles Song Publishing Empire* (London: Omnibus Press, 2006).

6. McCartney v. Sony/ATV Music Publishing LLC et al., U.S. District Court, Southern District of New York, No. 17-00363; Agence France-Presse, "Beatles Song Rights Dispute: Paul McCartney and Sony ATV Work It Out," *Guardian*, July 3, 2017, https://www.theguardian.com/music/2017/jul/04/beatles-song-rights-dispute-paul-mccartney-and-sony-atv-work-it-out (accessed December 31, 2018); and Reuters, "Paul McCartney Settles with Sony/ATV to Reclaim Beatles' Song Copyright," June 30, 2017, http://fortune.com/2017/06/30/sony-beatles-copyright/ (accessed December 31, 2018).

7. 17 U.S. Code § 304—Duration of Copyright: Termination of Transfers and Licenses Covering Extended Renewal Term.

8. U.S. Copyright Office, "Copyright in General," https://www.copyright.gov/help/faq/faq-general.html (accessed October 15, 2018).

9. An Act for the Encouragement of Learning, by vesting the Copies of Printed Books in the Authors or purchasers of such Copies, during the Times therein mentioned. 8 Anne c.19 (1710 Statute of Anne).

10. *Copyright Act of 1976*, Public Law 94-553, *U.S. Statutes at Large* 90 (1976): 2541.

11. 1 Statutes at Large, 124.

12. 35 Statutes at Large, 1075.

13. 90 Statutes at Large, 2541.

14. 17 U.S. Code §102(a)—Subject Matter on Copyright.

15. 17 U.S. Code §106—Exclusive Rights in Copyrighted Works.

16. 17 U.S. Code § 107—Limitations on Exclusive Rights: Fair use.

17. *Digital Performance Rights in Sound Recordings Act of 1995*, Public Law 104-39, U.S. Statutes at Large 109 (1995): 336.

18. 17 U.S. Code § 114(d)—Limitations on Exclusive Rights: Sound recordings.

19. 17 U.S. Code § 106—Exclusive Rights in Copyrighted Works.

20. 17 U.S. Code § 115—Scope of Exclusive Rights in Nondramatic Musical Works: Compulsory License for Making and Distributing Phonorecords.

21. For more details about copyright clearances for filmmakers, see Jon Garon's "Chapter 14: Music," in *Independent Filmmaker's Law and Business Guide: Financing, Shooting, and Distributing Independent and Digital Films* (Chicago: Chicago Review Press, 2009).

22. 17 U.S. Code §102—Subject Matter on Copyright.

23. U.S. Copyright Office, "Overview of the Copyright Office," https://www.copyright.gov/about/ (accessed October 15, 2018).

24. Linux, "What Is Linux?" https://www.linux.com/what-is-linux (accessed December 31, 2018).

25. Kevin J. Hickey, "Music Modernization Act: Extending Copyright Protection to Pre-1972 Sound Recordings," *Congressional Research Service—Legal Sidebar*, October 15, 2018, https://fas.org/sgp/crs/misc/LSB10181.pdf (accessed December 1, 2018); and U.S. Copyright Office, Music Modernization Act, https://www.copyright.gov/music-modernization/ (accessed December 1, 2018).

26. Peter B. Hirtle, Cornell University Library, "Copyright Term and Public Domain in the United States," January 1, 2019, https://copyright.cornell.edu/publicdomain (accessed January 2, 2019).

27. Ibid.

28. Ibid.

29. 17 U.S. Code § 203—Termination of Transfers and Licenses Granted by the Author.

30. 17 U.S. Code § 304—Termination of Transfers and Licenses Covering Extended Renewal Term.

31. Public Law No: 115-264 (October 11, 2018), H.R.1551—Orrin G. Hatch-Bob Goodlatte Music Modernization Act, 115th Congress (2017–2018).

32. Karyn A. Temple, "United States Modernizes Its Music Licensing System," *WIPO Magazine* 6 (December 2018): 14, https://www.wipo.int/wipo_magazine/en/2018/06/article_0002.html (accessed January 29, 2019).

33. Jonathan Saltzman, "Judge Slashes Downloading Penalty," *Boston Globe*, July 10, 2010, http://archive.boston.com/news/local/massachusetts/articles/2010/07/10/file_sharing_damages_reduced_tenfold/ (accessed December 29, 2018).

34. Business Dictionary, http://www.businessdictionary.com/definition/infringement.html (accessed September 15, 2018).

35. 17 U.S. Code § 501—Infringement of Copyright.

36. U.S. Copyright Office – Frequently Asked Questions About Copyright: Definitions, https://www.copyright.gov/help/faq/faq-definitions.html (accessed December 29, 2018).

37. Bright Tunes Music v. Harrisongs Music 420 F. Supp. 177 (S.D.N.Y. 1976).

38. Jason Sloan, "An Overview of the Elements of a Copyright Infringement Cause of Action—Part I: Introduction and Copying," American Bar Association, January 27, 2012, https://www.americanbar.org/groups/young_lawyers/publications/the_101_201_practice_series/elements_of_a_copyright/ (accessed December 29, 2018); Jason Sloan, "An Overview of the Elements of a Copyright Infringement Cause of Action—Part II: Improper Appropriation," American Bar Association, August 27, 2013, https://www.americanbar.org/groups/young_lawyers/publications/the_101_201_practice_series/part_2_elements_of_a_copyright/ (accessed December 29, 2018); Kurt Saunders, *Intellectual Property Law: Legal Aspects of Innovation and Competition* (St. Paul, MN: West Academic Publishing, 2016), 376, 926; Carrie Russell, *Complete Copyright: An Everyday Guide for Librarians* (Chicago: American Library Association, 2004), 116.

39. 17 U.S. Code § 504—Remedies for Infringement: Damages and Profits.

40. 17 U.S. Code § 505—Remedies for Infringement: Costs and Attorney's Fees.

41. 17 U.S. Code § 504(c)(2)—Remedies for Infringement: Damages and Profits.

42. Public Law 105–304 (1998); 112 Stat. 2860 (1998).

43. 17 U.S. Code § 1204—Criminal Offenses and Penalties.

44. 17 U.S. Code. § 1201(a)(1)(A)—Violations Regarding Circumvention of Technological Measures: Copyright Protection Systems.

45. Peter S. Menell, Mark A. Lemley, and Robert P. Merges, *Intellectual Property in the New Technology Age: 2017, Volume II: Copyrights, Trademarks & State IP Protections*, Copyright Law (Berkeley, CA: Clause 8 Publishing, 2017), 496.

46. 17 U.S. Code § 1201(a)(1)(C)-(D)—Violations Regarding Circumvention of Technological Measures: Copyright Protection Systems.

47. Kenneth Crews, "Chapter 14: Responsibilities, Liabilities, and Doing the Right Thing," in *Copyright Law for Librarians and Educators: Creative Strategies and Practical Solutions* (Chicago: American Library Association, 2012), 101–107, cites 17 U.S.C. § 504(c)(2) and U.S. Constitution, Eleventh Amendment; Russell, *Complete Copyright*, 4, cites Copyright Act of 1976, 17 U.S.C. § 504(c)(2), regarding remission of statutory damages and limit on the remedies which rights holders could expect to collect if they sued schools or libraries; also cites U.S. Constitution, Eleventh Amendment, protecting state entities from federal prosecution without consent.

48. 17 U.S. Code §107—Limitations on Exclusive Rights: Fair Use.

49. U.S. Constitution Article I, §8, clause 8 (1787).

50. U.S. Copyright Office, "More Information on Fair Use," https://www.copyright.gov/fair-use/more-info.html (accessed October 16, 2018).

51. 17 U.S. Code § 102—Subject Matter of Copyright.

52. *Copyright Act of 1976*, U.S. Code 17 (2005), §107 (Historical Revisions and Notes).

53. 17 U.S. Code § 108—Limitations on Exclusive Rights: Reproduction by Libraries and Archives.

54. 17 U.S. Code § 109(a) – Limitations on Exclusive Rights: Effect of Transfer of Particular Copy or Phonorecord: First Sale Doctrine.

55. 17 U.S. Code § 109(c)—Limitations on Exclusive Rights: Effect of Transfer of Particular Copy or Phonorecord: Public Display.

56. 17 U.S. Code § 110(1)—Limitations on Exclusive Rights: Exemption of Certain Performances and Displays: Face-to-Face Teaching.

57. 17 U.S. Code § 110(2)—Limitations on Exclusive Rights: Exemption of Certain Performances and Displays: TEACH Act of 2002.

58. 17 U.S. Code § 117—Limitations on Exclusive Rights: Computer Programs.

59. 17 U.S. Code § 120—Scope of Exclusive Rights in Architectural Works.

60. 17 U.S. Code § 121—Limitations on Exclusive Rights: Reproduction for Blind or Other People with Disabilities.

61. Feist Pubs., Inc. v. Rural Tel. Svc. Co., Inc., 499 U.S. 340 (1991).

62. Heather Greenfield, "Study Shows Fair Use Industries Make Up One Sixth of the Economy," Computer and Communications Industry Association, http://www.ccianet.org/2017/06/study-shows-fair-use-industries-make-up-one-sixth-of-the-economy/ (accessed December 31, 2018).

63. 17 U.S. Code § 107—Limitations on Exclusive Rights: Fair use.

64. Laura Gasaway, "Fair Use: A Right or a Privilege?" in *Get Copyright Right* (Alexandria, VA: Special Libraries Association, 2006), 75.

65. David Muradyan, "'Fair Use': An Affirmative Defense to 'Copyright Infringement,'" The IP Law Blog, May 6, 2011, https://www.theiplawblog.com/2011/05/articles/copyright-law/fair-use-an-affirmative-defense-to-copyright-infringement/ (accessed October 15, 2018); Kevin Smith, "Free Speech, Fair Use, and Affirmative Defenses," Duke University Libraries, Scholarly Communications @ Duke, November 3, 2014, https://blogs.library.duke.edu/scholcomm/2014/11/03/fair-use-affirmative-defense/ (accessed October 15, 2018).

66. U.S. Code 17 §107—Limitations on Exclusive Rights: Fair use.

67. See Checklist for Conducting a Fair Use Analysis before Using Copyrighted Materials @ http://www.copyright.cornell.edu/policy/Fair_Use_Checklist.pdf on how to handle factor analysis when evenly split.

68. Harper & Row Publishers, Inc. v. Nation Enterprises, 471 U.S. 539, 564-566 (1985).

69. Ibid., 566.

70. Richard Stim, Library Photocopying, Stanford University Libraries, https://fairuse.stanford.edu/overview/academic-and-educational-permissions/library-photocopying/ (accessed December 31, 2018); and Russell, *Complete Copyright*, 93.

71. Wai Choy, "Infringing Copyright? Think Twice Before Removing the Copyright Notice—It Could Be Deemed 'Copyright Management Information' Under the DMCA," Proskauer New Media and Technology Law Blog, August 5, 2013, https://newmedialaw.proskauer.com/2013/08/05/infringing-copyright-think-twice-before-removing-the-copyright-notice-it-could-be-deemed-copyright-management-information-under-the-dmca/ (accessed December 15, 2018).

72. Joyce Valenza, "Fair Use and Transformativeness: It May Shake Your World," School Library Journal, April 1, 2008, http://blog.schoollibraryjournal.com/neverendingsearch/2008/04/01/fair-use-and-transformativeness-it-may-shake-your-world/ (accessed April 1, 2018).

73. Alfred Appel, Jr., "Nabokov's Interview," *Wisconsin Studies in Contemporary Literature* VIII, no. 2 (Spring 1967), http://lib.ru/NABOKOW/Inter06.txt_with-big-pictures.html (accessed December 31, 2018).

74. Kathleen Olson, "First Amendment Values in Fair Use Analysis," *Journalism & Communication Monographs* 5, no. 4 (Winter 2004): 185.

75. CBS Television, *Carol Burnett Show*, Season Ten, Episode Eight, segment entitled "Went with The Wind," November 13, 1976.

76. Jesse Rhodes, "Carol Burnett—We Just Can't Resist Her!" *Smithsonian*, https://www.smithsonianmag.com/smithsonian-institution/carol-burnettwe-just-cant-resist-her-50924199/ (accessed December 31, 2018).

77. Frank DeCaro, *Unmistakably Mackie: The Fashion and Fantasy of Bob Mackie* (New York: Universe Publishing, 1999), 83.

78. Associated Press, "Settlement Reached Over 'Wind Done Gone,'" May 10, 2002, www.freedomforum.org/templates/document.asp?documentID=16230; and SunTrust Bank v. Houghton Mifflin Co., 268 F.3d 1257, 1264-65 (11th Cir. 2001).

79. Dr. Seuss Enterprises, L. P. v. Penguin Books USA, Inc., 109 F.3d 1394 (9th Cir. 1997); Richard Stim, Summaries of Fair Use Cases, Stanford University Libraries, https://fairuse.stanford.edu/overview/fair-use/cases/ (accessed December 30, 2018).

80. IP Roundtables—ABA Section of Litigation, Satire/Parody Distinction in Copyright and Trademark Law, http://apps.americanbar.org/litigation/committees/intellectual/roundtables/0506_outline.pdf (accessed March 29, 2011).

81. Ibid.

82. Ibid.

83. Campbell v. Acuff-Rose Music, 510 U.S. 569. (1994).

84. Edward Lee Lamoureux et al., "Chapter 2: Three Copyright Issues," in *Intellectual Property Law and Interactive Media: Free for a Fee* (New York: Peter Lang, 2009), 70–75.

85. John Schlipp, Public Domain, Intellectual Property Awareness Center, https://inside.nku.edu/ipac/ipbasics/publicdomain.html (accessed December 31, 2018).

86. Derek Khanna, "50 Disney Movies Based On The Public Domain," *Forbes*, February 3, 2014, https://www.forbes.com/sites/derekkhanna/2014/02/03/50-disney-movies-based-on-the-public-domain/#4bc339a2329c (accessed December 31, 2018).

87. Simpsons Wiki, "Time to Say Goodbye," http://simpsons.wikia.com/wiki/Time_to_Say_Goodbye (accessed September 30, 2018).

88. Feist Publications, Inc. v. Rural Telephone Service Co., 499 U.S. 340 (1991).

89. SPARK (the Scholarly Publishing and Academic Resources Coalition), "Open Access to Scholarly and Scientific Research Articles," an open access fact sheet, https://sparcopen.org/wp-content/uploads/2017/04/Open-Access-Factsheet_SPARC.11.10-3.pdf (accessed October 1, 2018).

90. Creative Commons home page https://creativecommons.org/ (accessed October 16, 2018).

91. Use & Remix—Creative Commons, https://creativecommons.org/use-remix/ (accessed October 1, 2018).

92. About—Creative Commons, http://creativecommons.org/about (accessed March 31, 2011).

93. Licensing Types—Creative Commons, https://creativecommons.org/share-your-work/licensing-types-examples/ (accessed October 1, 2018).

94. Project Gutenberg, "Free Books – Project Gutenberg," https://www.gutenberg.org/ (accessed October 1, 2018).

95. Wikimedia Commons, "Commons Welcome," https://commons.wikimedia.org/wiki/Commons:Welcome (accessed October 1, 2018).

96. Kenneth Crews, guest interview, "Fair Use in Authors Guild v. Google, Inc.," *Legal Talk Network*, comments on legal talk network podcast from November 13, 2015, https://legaltalknetwork.com/podcasts/lawyer-2-lawyer/2015/11/fair-use-authors-guild-v-google-inc/ (accessed October 6, 2018).

97. Edward Wyatt, "Writers Sue Google, Accusing It of Copyright Violation," *New York Times*, September 21, 2005, https://www.nytimes.com/2005/09/21/technology/writers-sue-google-accusing-it-of-copyright-violation.html (accessed October 7, 2018).

98. 17 U.S. Code § 106—Exclusive Rights in Copyrighted Works.

99. *Authors Guild v. Google, Inc.*, 770 F. Supp. 2d 666 (SDNY 2011).

100. Julie Bosman, "Lawsuit Seeks the Removal of a Digital Book Collection," *New York Times*, September 12, 2011, https://www.nytimes.com/2011/09/13/business/media/authors-sue-to-remove-books-from-digital-archive.html (accessed October 7, 2018).

101. Authors Guild, Inc. v. HathiTrust, 902 F. Supp. 2d 445, (SDNY 2012).

102. Authors Guild v. HathiTrust, 755 F.3d 87 (2d Cir. 2014).

103. Authors Guild v. Google, Inc., 804 F.3d 202 (2d Cir. 2015), *cert denied*, 136 S. Ct. 1658 (2016; lawsuit filed in 2005, ruled in favor of Google in 2013 and again on appeal in 2015).

104. Dan Cohen, "What the Google Books Victory Means for Readers: Is a Universal Library Finally Within Reach?" *Atlantic*, October 22, 2015, https://www.theatlantic.com/technology/archive/2015/10/what-the-google-books-victory-means-for-readers-and-libraries/411910/ (accessed October 6, 2018).

105. U.S. Copyright Office, *Report on Orphan Works: Report of the Register of Copyrights*, January 2006, p. 1, https://www.copyright.gov/orphan/orphan-report.pdf (accessed August 15, 2018).

106. Shawn Bentley Orphan Works Act of 2008, S. 2913, 110th Cong. (2008); and the Orphan Works Act of 2008, H.R. 5889, 110th Cong. (2008).

107. U.S. Copyright Office, "A Report of the Register of Copyrights: Report on Orphan Works," January 2006; also see http://www.copyright.gov/docs/regstat030806.html (accessed December 31, 2018).

108. U.S. Copyright Office, Orphan Works, https://www.copyright.gov/orphan/ (accessed December 1, 2018).

109. U.S. Copyright Office, *Orphan Works and Mass Digitization: Report of the Register of Copyrights*, June 2015, p. 1, https://copyright.gov/orphan/reports/orphan-works2015.pdf (accessed December 31, 2018).

110. Ibid., 106.

111. Mitch Stoltz, "New Music Modernization Act Has a Major Fix: Older Recordings Will Belong to the Public, Orphan Recordings Will Be Heard Again," *Electronic Frontier Foundation*, September 19, 2018, https://www.eff.org/deeplinks/2018/09/new-music-modernization-act-has-major-fix-older-recordings-will-belong-public (accessed December 29, 2018); and Tim Brooks, "Music Modernization Act, With Changes Advocated by ARSC, Represents a Major Advance for Preservation and Access to Historical Recordings," October 17, 2018, https://arsc-audio.org/blog/2018/10/17/mma_success/ (accessed December 29, 2018).

112. This section of this chapter on interlibrary loan and document delivery is from an earlier chapter published by the author and the publisher of this book. John Schlipp, "Chapter Six: Electronic Reserves and Information Delivery," in *Distributed Learning and Virtual Librarianship*, Sharon Almquist, ed. (Santa Barbara, CA: Libraries Unlimited, 2011).

113. American Library Association, Interlibrary Loan Committee, *National Interlibrary Loan Code for the United States, (1993)*, http://www.nmrls.org/ill/illcode.shtml (accessed April 18, 2009).

114. Kate Nevins, "An Ongoing Revolution: Resource Sharing and OCLC," *Journal of Library Administration* 25, no. 2–3 (1998): 65–71, co-published simultaneously in *OCLC, 1967–1997: Thirty Years of Furthering Access to the World's Information*, edited by K. Wayne Smith (New York: Hayworth Press, 1998), 65–71.

115. 17 U.S. Code § 109(a)—First Sale Doctrine.

116. 17 U.S. Code § 108—Limitations on Exclusive Rights: Reproductions by Libraries and Archives.

117. *Code of Federal Regulations*, title 37, vol. 1, sec. 201.14 (2008), pp. 485–486. See http://www.gpo.gov/fdsys/pkg/CFR-2008-title37-vol1/pdf/CFR-2008-title37-vol1-chapII-subchapA.pdf (accessed April 16, 2019).

118. 17 U.S. Code § 108(g)—Limitations on Exclusive Rights: Reproductions by Libraries and Archives.

119. Ibid.

120. For more on the CONTU Rule of Five, see http://www.copyright.gov/circs/circ21.pdf (accessed April 16, 2019).

121. 17 U.S. Code § 108(a)(2)—Limitations on Exclusive Rights: Reproductions by Libraries and Archives.

122. *1975 Senate Report on the New Copyright Law*, Senate Judiciary Committee, 94th Cong., 1st Sess. (1975): S. Rep. No. 94-473, 70–71.

123. Carol Helgerson, "Copyright Issues in For-Profit Libraries: A Handbook for Non-Lawyers," *Special Libraries Management Handbook: The Basics (2004)*, http://www.libsci.sc.edu/bob/class/clis724/SpecialLibrariesHandbook (accessed August 11, 2009).

124. James S. Heller, "Impact of Recent Litigation on Interlibrary Loan and Document Delivery," *Law Library Journal* 88, no. 2 (1996): 158–177, for libraries wishing to implement their own document delivery.

125. Ronald Dekker and Leo Waaijers, "Beyond the Photocopy Machine: Document Delivery in a Hybrid Library Environment," *Interlending & Document Supply* 29, no. 2 (2001): 69–75.

126. Access (just-in-time) versus ownership (just-in-case) collection development research affirms more effective fulfillment results for researcher document or book requests. This collection method may require shifting funds from the traditional ownership (just-in-case) acquisition for journal subscriptions and books to accessing (just-in-time) to fill requested journal articles and books on demand. See the following articles for more: Kristine J. Anderson et al., "Buy, Don't Borrow: Bibliographers' Analysis of Academic Library Collection Development through Interlibrary Loan Requests," *Collection Management* 27, no. 3–4 (2002): 1–11; Sharon A. Campbell, "To Buy or to Borrow, That Is the Question," *Journal of Interlibrary Loan, Document Delivery & Electronic Reserves* 16, no. 3 (2006): 35–39; Gayle Rosemary Y. C. Chan, "Purchase Instead of Borrow: An International Perspective," *Journal of Interlibrary Loan, Document Delivery & Electronic Reserves* 14, no. 4 (2005): 23–34; Suzanne Ward, "Books on Demand: Just-in-Time Acquisitions," *Acquisitions Librarian* 14, no. 27 (2002): 95–107; Suzanne Ward, Tanner Wray, and Karl

E. Debus-López, "Collection Development Based on Patron Requests: Collaboration between Interlibrary Loan and Acquisitions," *Library Collections, Acquisitions, and Technical Services* 27, no. 2 (2003): 203–213.

127. Carol Simpson, "Interlibrary Loan of Audiovisuals May Bring a Lawsuit," *Library Media Connection* 25, no. 5 (February 2008): 26–28.

128. David Ensign, "Resource Sharing and Copyright Among Library Consortia Members," in *Growing Pains: Adapting Copyright for Libraries, Education, and Society*, Laura Gasaway, ed. (Littleton, CO: Rothman & Co., 1997), 151–171.

129. Leslie Ellen Harris, *Licensing Digital Content: A Practical Guide for Librarians* (Chicago: American Library Association, 2009), 112; Stephen Bosch et al., *Guide to Licensing and Acquiring Electronic Information* (Lanham, MD: Scarecrow Press, 2005), 53.

130. Audrey Fenner, "Introduction: Managing Digital Resources," *Managing Digital Resources in Libraries* (New York: Haworth Press, 2005), 1–2. Co-published simultaneously in *The Acquisitions Librarians* no. 33–34, 1–2, pp. 11–12; Bosch, *Guide to Licensing and Acquiring Electronic Information*, 53–57.

131. American Library Association, *Digital Rights Management (DRM) & Libraries, 2007*, http://www.ala.org/ala/aboutala/offices/wo/woissues/copyrightb/digitalrights/digitalrightsmanagement.cfm (accessed April 18, 2009).

132. Russell, *Complete Copyright*, 104; Pramod Jamkhedkar et al., "Middleware Services for DRM," Communication Systems Software and Middleware, COMSWARE 2007, Second International Conference on COMmunication System softWAre and MiddlewaRE (January 7–12, 2007), 1–8, http://www.ece.unm.edu/~drake/products/COMSWARE_07.pdf (accessed August 15, 2009); also archived at https://web.archive.org/web/20100614091101/http://www.ece.unm.edu/~drake/products/COMSWARE_07.pdf (accessed May 2, 2019.)

133. American Library Association, Interlibrary Loan Committee, *National Interlibrary Loan Code for the United States, 2003*, http://www.nmrls.org/ill/illcode.shtml (accessed April 18, 2009).

134. American Library Association, RUSA Reference Guidelines, *Interlibrary Loan Code for the United States, 2001.* http://www.ala.org/ala/mgrps/divs/rusa/archive/protools/referenceguide/interlibrary.cfm (accessed April 18, 2009).

135. American Library Association, Coalition for Networked Information, Information Policies, *Model Interlibrary Loan Code for Regional, State, Local, or Other Special Groups of Libraries* (1984), http://www.cni.org/docs/infopols/ALA.html (accessed May 7, 2009).

136. Gretchen McCord Hoffmann, *Copyright in Cyberspace 2: Questions and Answers for Librarians* (New York: Neal-Schuman Publishers, Inc., 2005), 42.

137. Kenneth D. Crews, *Copyright Law for Librarians & Educators: Creative Strategies and Practical Solutions* (Chicago: American Library Association, 2006), viii.

Chapter 3

PATENT FUNDAMENTALS

CHAPTER OBJECTIVES

- To be able to explain what a patent is and to distinguish between utility, design, and plant patents
- To be aware of patent claims and understand their importance for protecting a patented invention
- To recognize the difference between a provisional and a nonprovisional application
- To understand how the application and examination process works
- To know about patent owners' rights, such as maintenance, protection, assignments and licensing, trade secrets, nondisclosures, and open source, among others
- To become aware of infringement challenges, including mobile technologies and software patents, patent trolls, patent pools, and standards.
- To understand the significance of the American Invents Act regarding "first to invent" versus "first to file."

INTRODUCTION

While librarians may have some knowledge of the importance of patents, they may find themselves asked by a member of their campus or community about how to patent an invention. This may even apply to school librarians dealing with those technically inclined students who wish to follow in Bill Gates's footsteps. Understanding patent law basics is vital for inventors, entrepreneurs, and new business start-ups. Such knowledge helps to avoid costly mistakes. When inventors come to the library, librarians also need to be able to help them understand the financial and competitive significance of their intellectual property (IP). The following chapter focuses on the legal facets of patents, including patent types, patent claims, provisional and nonprovisional applications, the examination process, maintenance and protection, assignments and licensing, infringements, and other related topics. Patent searching resources and techniques are covered in the next chapter. Aspects of patent legal topics are presented in this chapter through the retrospective lens of the Wright brothers and their patented inventions, which changed history and revolutionized the way we travel. Yet, history repeats itself, as similar patent infringement challenges faced by the Wright brothers loom with the latest technologies such as smart phones.

WRIGHT BROTHERS' PATENTS

"No bird soars in a calm."
—Wilbur Wright

On the frigid morning of December 17, 1903, wind gusts of up to twenty-seven miles per hour swept across Kitty Hawk, North Carolina. The Dayton, Ohio, natives Orville (1871–1948) and Wilbur (1867–1912) Wright were about to make history. At 10:35 a.m., a photograph (see figure 3.1) captured the momentous occasion as their "Wright Flyer" took flight from the sandy beach dunes of Kill Devil Hills. It was the first sustained, powered, and controlled flight in human history. Five local

Figure 3.1
First Flight, December 17, 1903, 120 Feet in 12 Seconds, 10:35 a.m.; Kitty Hawk, North Carolina. (Courtesy of Library of Congress)

people witnessed the brothers' invention as it flew overhead, with Orville at the controls and Wilbur standing nearby to keep the machine in balance.[1]

It would take a few years to perfect the Wright Flyer as a fully practical airplane. The brothers meticulously researched "prior art" discoveries, such as the hang-gliding flights of German inventor Otto Lilienthal. These earlier discoveries inspired their mastery of powered flight, which they achieved by controlling the three primary axes of yaw, pitch, and roll. Many identify the Wrights as the first aeronautical engineers and test pilots.[2] As a matter of fact, Orville Wright would serve as one of the original members of the National Advisory Council on Aeronautics (NACA), which eventually became the National Aeronautics and Space Administration (NASA).

The story of the Wright brothers' early airplane patents offers practical IP lessons for librarians to share with their clientele, and these experiences are discussed throughout this chapter. Such lessons include the importance of filing patent applications early and often for one's invention. Their experience also demonstrates how new technologies and patent claims often become tangled in unanticipated "patent thickets" and "patent trolls." "Patent pools" or cross licensing established by standards-setting organizations may be needed to sort out infringement issues and to streamline licensing opportunities.

In the early twenty-first century, patents appear to be in transition. News reports and articles are replete with headlines about litigation and "patent trolls." Economists and business experts, however, recognize that patents fuel innovation, which, in turn, feeds the economy.

To learn more about the way patents work, access https://www.fjc.gov/publications/patent-process-overview-jurors or enter the following search terms in a web search engine: patent process overview jurors federal judicial center. This seventeen-minute online tutorial from the Federal Judicial Center describes patents and why they are needed, how inventors get a patent, the United States Patent Trade Office (USPTO) role, and why disputes over patents occur. Although this film was designed for juries of patent-related court cases, librarians and independent inventors may find it very helpful when they are learning how to do a patent search. It is also a great IP refresher for patent specialists at Patent Trade Resource Centers (PTRCs).

PATENT OVERVIEW

You should now begin to recognize the difference between patents and copyrights. Copyrights are often confused with patents. Perhaps this is because historically, copyrights and patents were introduced simultaneously in the late eighteenth century in the U.S. Constitution, Article I, Section 8,[3] which grants Congress power in "securing for limited times to authors and inventors the exclusive right to their respective writings and discoveries." Notice the phrase "limited times" tied to the "exclusive right" of authors and inventors in the Constitution. This affirms that the founding fathers intended to promote progress by limiting the duration of protection, such as patents, so that ultimately such works would enter the public domain and allow others to build freely upon them.[4]

President George Washington signed the Patent Act of 1790 to officially initiate U.S. patent law. Thomas Jefferson, secretary of state, served as the first administrator and patent examiner of granted U.S. patents. In the year 1952, U.S. patent laws were codified in Title 35 of the U.S. Code.[5]

Obtaining a patent is much more difficult than copyright registration, which is automatically protected when the copyright expression is recorded in a tangible form. An inventor's work is only protected after the application for an invention undergoes strict appraisal by patent examiners before a patent might be granted.[6] This is also why a professional patent attorney or agent is highly advisable to improve the likelihood of a successfully granted patent. Except for computer software codes and certain ornamental designs, patents and copyrights usually do not overlap on the same creation. Generally, patents are associated with inventions that are functional and expressed in the form of a product or process, while copyrights are associated with an expression of an idea and not an idea itself.

Patents are issued by inventors for patentable subject matter, which means it has to be a "process, machine, manufacture, or composition of matter."[7] In addition to being protectable subject matter, a prospective patent application must meet the following additional requirements: First, the invention must be useful and serve some utility function (or ornamental function in the case of special patents for designs).[8] Second, it must be novel and unknown to others.[9] Third, the invention must not be obvious to someone who has ordinary skill in the specific state of the art for the invention.[10] It must also include specifications to enable any person familiar with the associated technology to be able to build the invention.[11] A patent cannot be obtained for laws of nature, natural phenomena, mathematical formulas, and abstract ideas.[12]

The best way to determine if one's invention is indeed unique, new, and original is to perform a preliminary prior-art patent search, which is covered in the next chapter. A preliminary patent search attempts to find all patents issued and literature in the related field of the invention to make certain it is the first of its kind.

> The easiest method to locate a patent is if you have the patent number or the inventor name. Then you could use one of the patent databases to quickly find it. However, if one wish to see if their idea for a product or a new service is indeed original, a comprehensive search process is rather complex. The next chapter offers details about PTRCs. These libraries teach inventors, entrepreneurs, and others how to conduct their own free preliminary patent searches of prior-art.

In the United States, a patent is a property right granted by the federal government that gives an inventor "the right to exclude others from making, using, offering for sale, or selling" during the term of his or her patent. An inventor's exclusive rights term is up to twenty years from the date on which the patent application was filed in the United States.[13]

A patent is often referred to as a contract between society and an inventor. To promote innovation, society agrees to protect an inventor's control over an invention, and in return, the inventor must publicly disclose the details of the invention. The information made available thus potentially spurs further innovation.[14]

Figure 3.2
U.S. Patent and Trademark Office Seal

A patent application is a disclosure document describing an invention that is suitable for filing at a patent office in order to apply for a patent on the invention.[15] The USPTO (see figure 3.2) is a branch of the U.S. Department of Commerce and the agency for filing patent applications in the United States. While librarians may teach clientele how to search to make sure the invention is the first of its kind, their instructional reference responsibility for the application should end there.

Although there is no such thing as a single international patent, the Office of International Patent Cooperation (OIPC) supports inventors and businesses in protecting their patent rights worldwide via the Patent Cooperation Treaty (PCT). The PCT is an international agreement where one may apply for patent protection simultaneously from foreign patent offices by filing a single international patent application (or PCT application) instead of filing several separate foreign patent applications.[16] Subsequently, such sets of patents for different countries covering the same invention are commonly known as patent families.

Once an invention has been developed into a working embodiment, a functional prototype, or enabling description, the inventor or a qualified attorney or agent hired by the inventor completes an application. Due to the potential high costs associated with a patent application, the role of the librarian is teaching the inventor how to perform a prior-art search of other similar patents and published disclosures before filing an application, and then encouraging the inventor to meet with a patent attorney or agent. Ultimately, the Wright brothers had to hire a qualified attorney to execute their patent applications (see sidebar about Wrights' patent application)—something you can help your clients understand rather than make Orville and Wilbur's error.

The Wrights attempted to prepare their own patent application, but it was rejected by the U.S. Patent Office, which claimed that their description was "vague and indefinite" and "incapable of performing its intended function." So the Wrights hired patent attorney Henry Toulmin of Springfield, Ohio. Toulmin advised the brothers to avoid patenting the mechanisms which controlled the wings, but more strategically to patent the idea of wing-warping. Such a broad aviation patent claim of a new and useful method of controlling a flying machine (powered or not) defeated virtually all future infringement cases in court. Their attorney also advised the brothers to avoid public disclosure until their patent was granted. After three years of patience, the Wright brothers' patent was granted for a "new and useful improvement in Flying Machines."

THREE TYPES OF PATENTS

An inventor may apply for one of three types of patents: a utility patent, a design patent, or a plant patent. A utility patent is the most common type of patent and offers protection for new and useful inventions, such as a process including business methods, machine, article of manufacture, or composition of matter.[17] These examples are categorized into three types of utility patents: chemical, mechanical, and electrical. Pharmaceuticals would be an example of the chemical kind. A machine or manufactured article would be of the mechanical variety, whereas software for a computer device would be placed in an electrical group. A utility patent is the most common type of patent for typical gadget inventions and lasts for up to twenty years.

The Wright brothers' first patent (No. 821,393) for their 1902 Flying Machine[18] was not for its motorized flight feature. The new and useful utility claims were for its three-axis glider controls for yaw, pitch, and roll. These patented claims were truly unique, and planes use them today. These controlling functions are essential to motorized flight as much as movable wheels are to controlling automobiles. See figure 3.3 for Wright brothers' patent drawing illustrating its three-axis glider control motion.

A design patent offers protection of a design, appearance, or ornamentation of an invention, not how it works.[19] The letter "D" appears before a design patent number to distinguish it between utility and design patent numbers. Design patents in certain instances could overlap with copyrights or trademarks. According to the USPTO website, "an ornamental design may be copyrighted as a work of art and may also be subject matter of a design patent . . . [while] a design patent and a trademark may be obtained on the same subject matter."[20] Design patent protection lasts for up to fourteen years.

Perhaps one of the most famous design patents is D48,160 for the original iconic Coca-Cola bottle. In addition to beverage containers, the ornamental appearance

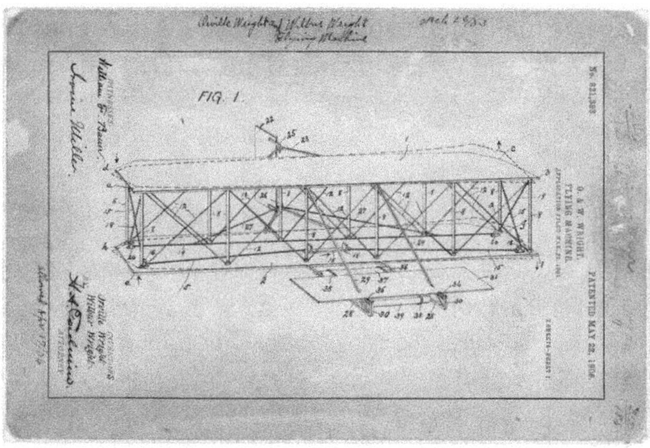

Figure 3.3
Wright Brothers' Flying Machine U.S. Patent 821,393 Drawing, May 22, 1906. (Courtesy of National Archives and Records Administration)

of jewelry, furniture, computer icons, automobiles, and even superhero costumes and gadgets have been patented in the United States for design.

A plant patent protects new varieties of asexually reproduced plants such as roses and fruit.[21] Asexual reproduction means growing a genetically identical plant without the use of seeds. Eligible applications for plant patents include those reproduced by grafting, budding, or cutting. These may include cultivating different types of plants to produce mutants or hybrids and also newly found seedlings. Plant patents may not be granted for naturally occurring plants. The letters "PP" appear before a plant patent number. In addition, some plants may be protected with utility patents[22] or the Plant Variety Protection Act (PVPA).[23] Both a utility patent and a plant patent could support the same invention, provided each patent deals with different subject matter.[24] The Linda Porter Rose (PP 1,507) is a distinguished example of a famous plant patent. It was assigned to Linda's famous husband, Great American Songbook composer Cole Porter, in memory of her passing. Plant patent protection lasts for up to twenty years.

Once inventors or their attorneys determine which kind of patent applies to their invention, they should begin to think about how the invention is unique, new, and original. Then they should reflect on the scope and boundaries making up the inventive concepts to help craft claims for the patent application.

PATENT CLAIMS

According to the World Intellectual Property Organization (WIPO): "Claims mark the boundaries of the protection provided by a patent, just as a physical boundary such as a fence, marks the limits of a parcel of real property."[25] Each claim is a single numbered sentence defining a patent owner's exclusive rights. IP librarians could make inventors aware of the importance of developing strong claims for their patent applications. Besides defining the scope and boundaries of the invention, claims state the legal rights of the patent property owner. Just like real property, patents may be bought, sold, or licensed. It is the means by which the invention is separated from the public domain.[26]

Claims are the most significant inclusive section to read when comparing one's invention to prior art in published patents and related disclosures of others during a preliminary patent search (covered in Chapter 4). Claims are the heart of a patent. Without strong claims, a patent is useless.

Returning to the Wright brothers' first patent, their patent attorney constructed eighteen impervious claims to establish their IP boundaries around their three-axis glider controls for yaw, pitch, and roll. In particular, claim number seven demonstrates how their attorney crafted this claim for their exclusive combined wing warping and adjustable rudder for controlling their airplane:

> In a flying machine, the combination, with an aeroplane, and means for simultaneously moving the lateral portions thereof into different angular relations to the normal plane of the body of the airplane and to each other, so as to present to the atmosphere different angles of incidence, of a vertical rudder, and means whereby said rudder is caused to present to the wind that side thereof nearest the side of the aeroplane having

the smaller angle of incidence and offering the least resistance to the atmosphere, substantially as described.[27]

This claim also demonstrates the effective broad scope of its patent boundary to exclude others from making, using, or selling an airplane using such an aerodynamic control. Modern airplanes today still employ this same basic concept. Until the Wrights' various patents expired, there were numerous patent infringement battles that will be discussed later. Ideally, claims should be narrow enough to identify uniqueness from previous developments but broad enough to protect against similar inventions. Knowledge and review of prior art references assist an attorney or agent in finding the right balance in constructing effective claims. Claims are also reviewed as part of the patent searching discussion in the next chapter.

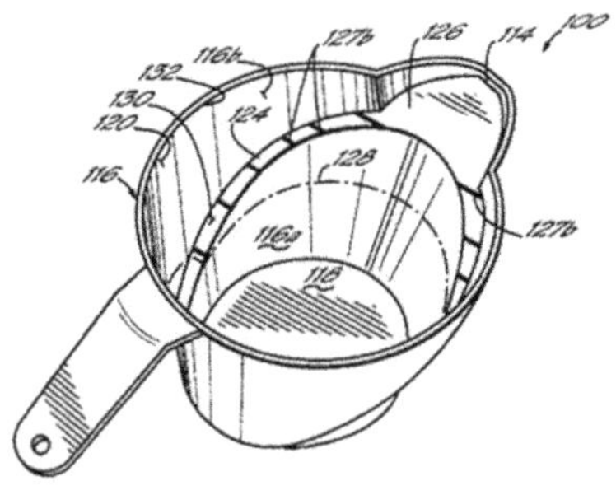

Figure 3.4
Measuring Cup U.S. Patent 6,263,732 Drawing, July 24, 2001, Hoeting et al. (Courtesy U.S. Patent and Trademark Office)

Another example of an effective angular relations claim dealt with a diagonal dimension plane for a common houseware measuring cup. U.S. Patent 6,263,732 was granted to an independent inventor for an innovative, new way to view measurements of cup contents by looking down into the cup (see figure 3.4) rather than holding it up to match contents to line on the cup. Merely titled "Measuring Cup," this cup features a unique diagonal indicia ramp on the cup's inner sidewall. This distinctive measuring cup was effectively licensed by the inventor to Oxo® to manufacture and successfully sell as part of their Good Grips® brand. The single claim of the patent was so strong, that imitations came nowhere near the long-term sales success by Oxo.

Here is the single, solid claim published for Hoeting's U.S. Patent 6,263,732 Measuring Cup—A measuring device, comprising:

a bottom wall and a generally vertical and encircling side wall having a lower edge and an upper edge, said sidewall defining an upwardly opening cup with an upper end;

a spout attached integrally to said sidewall; and

a pair of continuously sloping ramps formed integrally with and radially inward in relief from said sidewall, said ramps extending from about said bottom wall generally opposite said spout toward said open upper end generally adjacent said spout, wherein said ramp is coextensive with said spout, said ramp having an upwardly directed surface and indicia located on said upwardly directed surface being at least one of standard and metric units of measurement providing a readily observable indication of the volume of the contents contained within said cup.[28]

At the time of preparing the manuscript for this book, there appeared to be only two newer patents that attempted to provide similar utility function and outcome without employing the same claimed method from Hoeting's US Patent 6,263,732. Below are these two U.S. Patents granted since Hoeting's Agular Measuring Cup, which use similar angular measurement methods without infringing. Notice that these subsequent patents required more than one single claim to fend off future competitors.

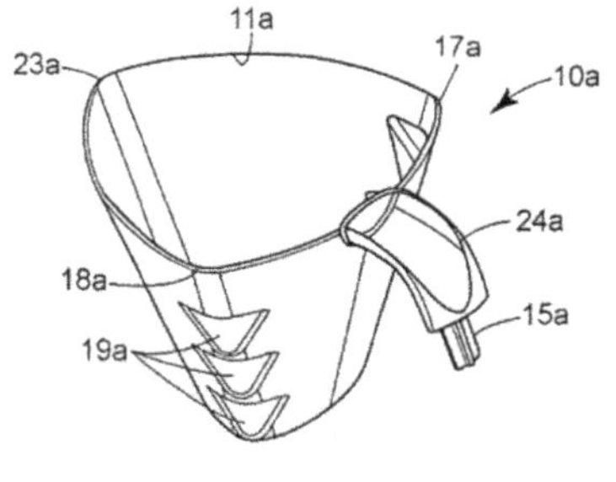

Figure 3.5
Measuring Cup U.S. Patent 7,306,120 Drawing, December 11, 2007, Hughes. (Courtesy U.S. Patent and Trademark Office)

Here is the primary claim highlight out of 18 claims for the second measuring cup (see figure 3.5) by Hughes U.S. Patent 7,306,120: ". . . a plurality of vertically spaced apart steps disposed inside the cup with each step having a top horizontal surface marked with volumetric indicia. . . ."[29]

Here is the primary claim highlight out of 17 claims for the third measuring cup (see figure 3.6) by Breit U.S. Patent 9,354,098:

> [A] reference member disposed substantially in a central portion of the space formed by the sidewall, the reference member having volumetric indicia that are at least partially upwards-facing; and a receptacle capable of receiving a substance, the receptacle formed by a portion of the space between the reference member and the sidewall, wherein the volumetric indicia of the reference member indicate a volume of the substance deposited in the receptacle.[30]

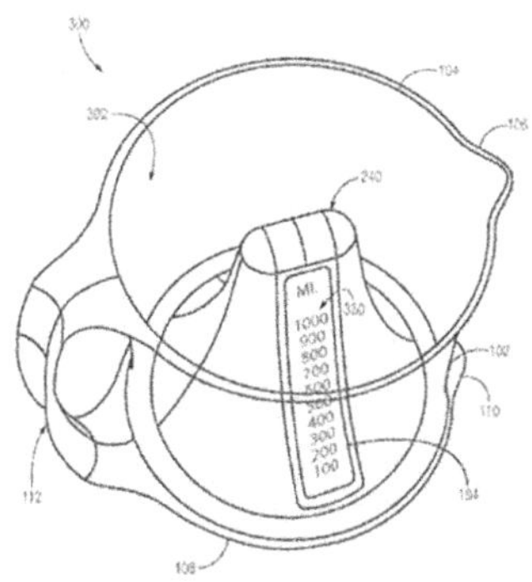

Figure 3.6
Measuring Cup U.S. Patent 9,354,098 Drawing, May 31, 2016, Breit. (Courtesy U.S. Patent and Trademark Office)

Patent drawings further support the claims of a patent application. The old saying that a picture is worth a thousand words is obvious when seeing the drawings of measuring cups displayed above. Notice how each drawing further supports the cited claims. Inventor drawings developed before meeting with a patent attorney or agent are also a helpful guide to visualizing what an invention does. The three patent drawing examples included in this chapter display numbers and letters, which are used as reference characters in the actual claims.[31] Such reference characters in drawings often help strengthen claims. Furthermore, patent drawings could be created by anyone with artistic talent so long as he or she follows the requirements of the USPTO included within its document, entitled *Guide for the Preparation of Patent Drawings* available at most PTRCs or online at HathiTrust. Further, consult the *General Information Concerning Patents* document on the USPTO site at https://www.uspto.gov/patents-getting-started/general-information-concerning-patents.

Drawings are necessary for most patent applications (except chemical-related patents). Drawings often help a patent examiner to better understand the subject matter of a patent application. Patent drawings must follow standards established by the USPTO or the Patent Cooperation Treaty (PCT) for international applications for foreign patents. Drawings should be black and white line drawings unless otherwise specified by the USPTO.

Besides claims and drawing, awareness of the structure of a patent document assists one in efficiently reviewing and researching prior art before submitting one's new patent application. Librarians should point out to their customers that the summary cover page offers researchers essential information, such as patent number, inventor names(s), serial number, application and granted publication dates, abstract summary, classification numbers, prior art references, best representative drawing, and so forth. Additional pages of a patent include supplementary drawings, specifications, and its indispensable claims listed last. A granted patent could range from a few pages to one hundred pages, depending on the invention and technology. See figure 3.7 for highlighted parts of a patent document.

PROVISIONAL AND NONPROVISIONAL APPLICATIONS

Patent applications are either provisional or nonprovisional. Provisional patent applications are often touted as a quick and easy way to obtain a patent. On its own, this is not really an application for a patent. Rather, it's a conditional document establishing an inventor's priority to invention, as long as a regular nonprovisional patent application is filed within one year.[32] A provisional patent application is an option for utility or plant patents only, and not for design patents. According to the USPTO website, provisional patent applications were introduced in 1995 to provide a lower-cost first patent filing option. A provisional application for a patent has a pendency lasting twelve months from the date that the provisional application is filed.[33]

Consequently, an applicant who files a provisional application must file a corresponding nonprovisional application for a patent that is reviewed by a patent examiner at the USPTO during the twelve-month pendency period of the provisional application (figure 3.8) in order to benefit from the earlier filing of the provisional application. Provisional applications not only permit one to claim patent pending, it also allows the licensing applicant to publicly disclose the invention to determine if there is a viable market. A provisional application is a lower cost method in establishing an early effective filing date placeholder. This is critical for an inventor to consider as the United States uses a first-to-file patent system and no longer a first-to-invent system. This could save an inventor added expenses if it is determined to forego a nonprovisional examiner reviewed patent application. For more information on provisional applications, see http://www.uspto.gov/patents/resources/types/provapp.jsp.

The twenty-year patent protection duration for a nonprovisional patent is subject to the payment of maintenance fees. The term of a patent begins on the date the patent issues and ends twenty years from the date the earliest filed application. Thus, if a provisional application is linked to the nonprovisional, the provisional would be considered the earliest date.

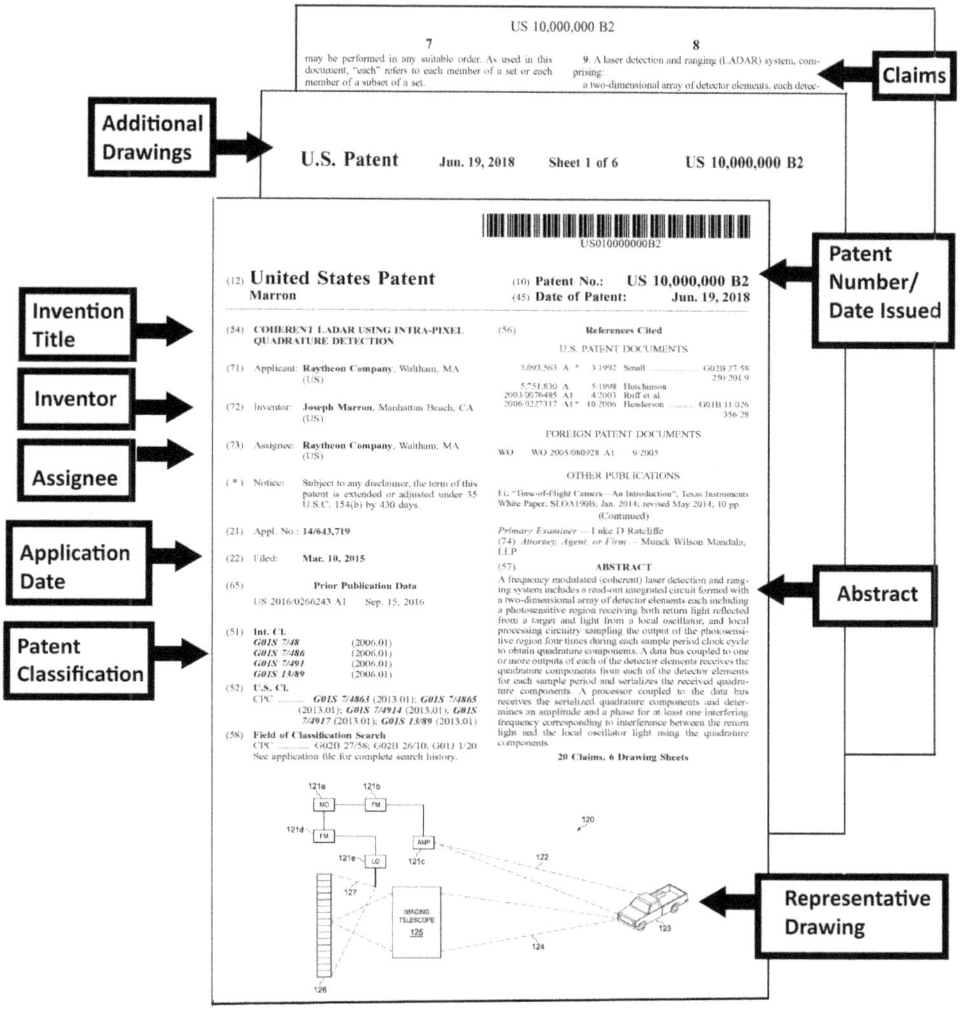

Figure 3.7
Parts of a Patent Document. (Patent Images Courtesy of U.S. Patent and Trademark Office)

The patent application process flow chart shown in figure 3.9 offers a simplified overview of the application steps with the USPTO. Inventors have two paths for their initial patent application disclosures: provisional or nonprovisional. A patent examiner at the USPTO only reviews nonprovisional patent applications, not provisional applications. Yet, both application types are a valid entry point for patent pendency. Ultimately if an inventor chooses to start with a provisional application, they must apply with a corresponding nonprovisional patent application within twelve months.

When and if a nonprovisional patent application is filed, it is assigned to a patent examiner at the USPTO who is an expert in the field of the invention. The examiner determines if the invention is potentially patentable and verifies

Provisional	Non-provisional
• Not examined or published • One-year time limit • Only for utility patents • A low-cost way to establish an early effective filing date (priority date) in a non-provisional patent application with few formalities	• Examined • Published 18 months from earliest filing date (unless a request for a non-publication at filing) • Can become a patent • In general, 20-year patent protection from filing date

Figure 3.8

Provisional or Nonprovisional Applications. (Diagram and Content Source: USPTO Inventor Info Chat Series: Types of Patent Applications. Office of Innovation Development. Used by Permission of Alford Kindred and Robert Hodge. February 16, 2017)

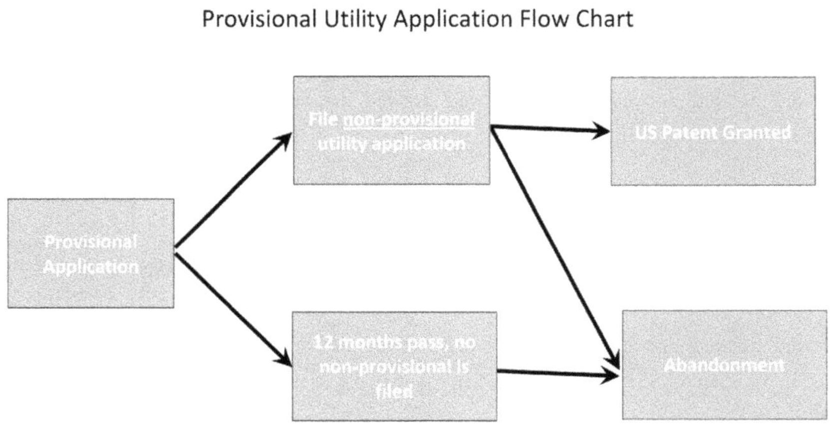

Figure 3.9

Application Flowchart. (Diagram and Content Source: USPTO Inventor Info Chat Series: Types of Patent Applications. Office of Innovation Development. Used by Permission of Alford Kindred and Robert Hodge. February 16, 2017)

whether or not the application meets the filing requirements. Next, the examiner conducts a thorough prior-art search, utilizing multiple patent databases. The patent examiner will establish communication with the party who submits the application.

Hypothetically, inventors could submit their own applications. Books such as David Pressman's *Patent It Yourself* offer thorough step-by-step details. However, librarians should encourage these clients to seek a patent attorney or agent specializing in invention technology and licensed to practice before the USPTO. This path is more likely to result in a granted patent with strictly enforceable, resilient claims. A database listing of attorneys and agents registered with the USPTO may be searched at https://www.uspto.gov/ (keyword search: attorney roster) for easy access.

> The term "patent pending" implies that a patent application has been submitted to the USPTO. It offers no legal protection until a patent is granted. However, it is a useful marketing technique to alert potential copycats. It is unlawful to post "patent pending" on an item if an application is not on file and current.

EXAMINATION PROCESS

After an inventor, a patent attorney, or an agent has submitted the patent application, it goes through what is commonly known as patent prosecution process. An examiner is assigned the application for inspection. After an examiner verifies that that the application meets the requirements for filing, he or she conducts a very thorough search of prior art from the field of the claimed invention. Ultimately, the examiner either grants or rejects the patent. Below is a short summary of their prosecution process.

A Non-Final Office Action is usually the initial feedback to an applicant or his or her representing attorney or agent. If an examiner finds two or more inventions claimed in a single patent application, the applicant is restricted to limit the application to just one of the inventions. The other invention is eligible for a separate application with a filing date of the first application. Other initial Office actions include patent rejection or objection. A rejection is often issued due to insufficient claim(s) directly corresponding to patentable subject matter. A rejection may also relate to a claimed invention lacking novelty or non-obviousness. Very few applications are granted without some Office action related to rejection of claim(s). An objection to an application is often easiest to remedy. It usually means there is a format issue.[34]

An applicant or his or her attorney or agent will reply to an examiner's Office action rejection and/or objection with an amended application. According the USPTO, "the applicant must clearly point out why he or she thinks the amended claims are patentable in view of the state of the art disclosed by the prior references cited or the objections made. He or she must also show how the claims as amended avoid such references or objections."[35] The examiner of the application will reconsider, based upon the reply, and a second Office action typically follows.

A final rejection or allowance is the eventual phase of examination process. An allowance ultimately becomes a granted patent. Otherwise, an appeal process is required if the applicant does not agree with a rejection as the final decision. An appeal should be directed to the Patent Trial and Appeal Board (PTAB) at the USPTO.[36]

Once a patent has been granted, it is up to the inventor to maintain the patent. If the patent is not maintained and ultimately expires, the protection it offers ceases to exist.

MAINTENANCE AND PROTECTION OF PATENTS

An inventor, once granted a patent, is responsible for protecting the patent rights to exclude others from making or distributing the patented invention. The USPTO does not offer a patent police force to monitor and to alert inventors of looming infringements. Although an inventor customer of your library may not discover aeronautics, his or her idea is worthy of protection, a lesson learned over time by the Wright brothers.

The Wright brothers not only discovered the correct combination of precise prior arts to perfect the first sustained, powered, and controlled flight, but they also discovered that it was just as challenging to maintain and protect their patents. Ultimately, they sued nine competitors for infringement, while three suits were brought against them. An ugly patent war commenced. The brothers fiercely protected their IP and won virtually all cases. Initially it tarnished their business reputation until their company later merged with a major competitor. Ultimately, the United States government was forced to step in to create "patent pools," as the United States entered World War I. Further discussion of patent wars and "patent pools" are covered below.

Similar to real estate property taxes, there are USPTO maintenance fees over the life of the patent, or up to twenty years in the United States. Patent insurance businesses offer services to protect inventions from any unexpected enforcement or defense litigation expenses. Patent owners have other associated options to consider such as assignments and licensing, trade secrets, nondisclosures, standards, and open access.

During the life of an active issued patent, an owner's rights could be lost, invalidated, or terminated in any one of three ways:

1. failure to pay USPTO maintenance fees,
2. inequitable conduct during the application process or the active life of patent; or
3. finding prior art that shows the patent is not novel or is obvious.

The first is failure to pay fees. Patent maintenance fees for the USPTO are due at 3.5, 7.5, and 11.5 years from the date the patent is granted. Failure to pay current fees in a timely manner may result in the expiration of the patent. The USPTO does not remind patent owners when maintenance fees are due. The USPTO attempts to send reminders only after fees are not paid when due. Such reminders offer a six-month grace period, including a surcharge. If a patent fee is not paid, the patent expires on the date the grace period ends.[37] Plant patents and design patents are not subject to maintenance fees. See USPTO website for current fees and details.

According to the USPTO's *Manual of Patent Examining Procedures*: "A finding of 'fraud,' 'inequitable conduct,' or violation of duty of disclosure with respect to any claim in an application or patent, renders all the claims thereof unpatentable or invalid."[38] Inequitable conduct could occur when a patent applicant falsifies or leaves out information to purposing deceive the patent examiner. Such inequitable conduct could be questioned at the time of the patent application or during the active period of the granted patent. If a competitor or another party finds prior art that shows that a granted patent was not new, novel, or obvious at the time of application, this could jeopardize the livelihood of the patent either before or after it is granted.

Since the introduction of the America Invents Act (AIA), discussed in more depth later in this chapter, additional patent opposition procedures were implemented. Most significant of these are a procedure for supplemental examination to provide a patent applicant the opportunity to request a reexamination to correct their errors or omissions to avoid any inequitable conduct accusations from others.[39] Some patent experts refer to the supplemental examination as a patent "amnesty program" for applicants.

To correct minor mistakes such as typographical errors, misspelled names, word choices used to describe a claim, missing drawing, or most honest minor omissions, reissued patents with new numbers are issued. Reissued patent numbers are prefaced with the letters RE.

PATENT ASSIGNMENTS AND LICENSING

A patent, like real property ownership, can be sold, licensed, or transferred outright to another person. A patent owner could be the patent inventor or an assigned party, and this may be more than one inventor on a patent application. It is important to recognize inventorship versus ownership of a patent. Only the named person(s) may be listed as the inventor(s). Businesses may not be named as inventors.

Patent assignment occurs when an inventor has transferred patent ownership to another party. For example, hired-to-invent or an employee agreement in a professional work environment automatically assigns an employee's inventions made within the scope of their related work for a company. It is customary for scientists at companies such as Procter & Gamble to sign employee agreements whereby all of their work-related IP, including patents, is automatically assigned to their employer. Therefore, a patentee has two primary ownership options on how to assign his or her patent rights:

1. A patent can be transferred or sold outright, by assigning all of its rights.
2. A patent could be licensed exclusively to one party only or nonexclusively to a variety of parties.

The patent law in the United States permits the transfer or sale of a patent, or of an application for patent, by a documented means known as an assignment. The assignee becomes the owner of the patent and acquires the same rights that the original patentee possessed.[40]

Where assignment of a patent transfers inclusive owner rights to the assignee, the licensing of a patent is a formal agreement often made between an inventor as licensor and a company as licensee. It is a contract that conveys a bundle of selected rights to produce, market, sell, and/or use the product or service in exchange for either royalties from product sales or a fixed payment. In terms of real property, think of licensing as renting or leasing property. Such conveyed rights are less than the entire ownership interest. A license is not an assignment of the patent. Such rights may be limited to time, geographical area, or field of use.[41]

Inventors have four types of licenses and two approaches to licensing. The four types of licenses for patents could include the following:

1. The license to use is actually as worded; the licensee may only use the patent (or other IP). For example, a click through licensing agreements for software on your computer or mobile device.
2. The manufacturing-only license is often the licensed party to whom the inventor goes to for manufacturing their invention as a product.
3. The sales-only license is often the licensed party to whom the inventor makes an agreement as the authorized sales agent of his or her invention as a product. This could be wholesale distributor(s) and/or retailer(s).
4. The license to manufacture, sell, and use, or a combination of two or all three.

The two approaches to licensing are exclusive and nonexclusive licenses. An exclusive license is granted by the patent owner to a licensee. It prevents the patent owner or another licensee from competing with that exclusive licensee for the contracted geographic region, length of time, and/or field of use, set forth in the license agreement.[42] A nonexclusive license could allow multiple licensees for the same geographic region, length of time, and/or field of use.

Submitting a provisional patent application allows an inventor to claim patent pending for his or her invention. When potential licensees are considering an invention, patent pending suggests perception of ownership, which could increase one's royalties from a licensing transaction. Patent pending entices prospective licensees or assignees of your prospective nonprovisional patent.[43]

Licensing can also be established through standards. Standards are published specifications and procedures intended to assure reliability of products, materials, and services.[44] According to the Licensing Executives Society (LES), fair and reasonable licensing arrangements are often developed with standards, as there are often disagreements between negotiation parties.[45]

TRADE SECRETS AND NONDISCLOSURES

Trade secrets are confidential IPs protected by their secrecy rather than by a publicly disclosed document with a government agency. Such trade secrets may be disclosed by authorization with confidentiality agreements. Often those who know the secret are required to sign nondisclosure or noncompeting agreements. Trade secrets remain valuable and effective as long as the IP remains confidential. Trade secrets may last forever. Trade secrets provide the owner a competitive advantage. Ideally, only a few people should know a trade secret. In addition, the trade secret should be difficult to reverse-engineer.

Trade secrets are frequently an alternative to patents. Trade secrets do not require novelty to be patentable subject matter or require expression of an idea for copyrightable requirements.[46] Thus, multiple types of IPs could be protected as trade secrets. Specific situations include confidential formulas, business practices and processes, proprietary in-house customer activity lists, and so one. Among the more famous trade secrets are the formula for Coca-Cola® and the search engine algorithms of Google®.[47]

Maintaining and protecting trade secrets has become a challenge with the growth of global commerce and rapid communication via the internet, mobile devices, and cloud data storage. Competitive spying or trade secret theft costs companies millions of dollars in confidential proprietary information losses. Once a trade secret has been illicitly disclosed, its owner loses all protection.[48]

Nondisclosure agreements or confidentiality agreements are frequently used to protect trade secrets within business settings, with parties ranging from internal employees to external licensees manufacturing a product or service protected by a trade secret. A nondisclosure agreement is a legally enforced contract prohibiting an individual from divulging or making use of the invention without permission. If such a contract is violated, that individual may be liable for monetary damages and also legally prevented from using or patenting such an invention.[49]

Laws related to trade secrets differ from patent and copyright laws. Rather than liability for unauthorized use, violators improperly use, acquire, or disclose a trade secret by way of wrongful or unethical conduct, such as theft, fraud, or breach of a confidential agreement.[50] Two legal principles in the United States that help address such infringements are the Uniform Trade Secrets Act and the Economic Espionage Act.

Originally, trade secrets were disparate common laws based upon court precedence in each state. To simplify and unify this inconsistency, nearly all states have adopted the Uniform Trade Secrets Act.[51] The Act codifies the common law of trade secrets with clarification of legal rights and remedies. This is especially helpful for businesses operating in multiple states by attempting to standardize the uneven challenges between different states' common laws related to trade secrets.

Congress passed the Economic Espionage Act of 1996, which makes theft or misappropriation of trade secrets a federal crime. This Act provides individual fines of up to $500,000 and imprisonment for up to fifteen years. It provides organizational fines of up to $10,000,000 for violations.[52]

Trade secrets are also protected by case laws or court-made doctrines related to rulings. These rulings have been established over time.

STANDARDS AND OPEN SOURCE

Standards and open source are topics not often associated with patents. Both practices are becoming more relevant for certain types of patented inventions. Both standards and open source promote a shared or more collaborative attribute generally not connected with patents. Therefore, a patent applicant needs to be aware of standards and open source when searching prior-art and/or preparing a patent application.

The open access concept has different names in potential relationships to patents, such as open source license and open patent, among others. It is still the same premise as open access; another party has disclosed his or her invention and wishes to share his or her IP openly with others, so long as inventor attribution is provided and there is no restriction to modifying the IP or commercial exploitation directly from the IP. However, commercial gain by selling customer service for such is often freely allowed, as with the Linux operating system.

The Linux operating system utilizes an open source GNU Public License (GPL). Open source is the most common open licensing associated with software patents. Patent rights could be jeopardized for a newly patented invention based upon a Gnu Public License per the closing of the GPL preamble:

> [A]ny free program is threatened constantly by software patents. We wish to avoid the danger that redistributors of a free program will individually obtain patent licenses, in effect making the program proprietary. To prevent this, we have made it clear that any patent must be licensed for everyone's free use or not licensed at all.[53]

Such an open source license conflicts with the customary goal of economic gain tied to a patent. Hence, any patentee who uses IP from an open source license must read the fine print before interpolating such open source IP into his or her new patent.

Just like open licensing, industrial standards may affect new patent applications. Government and/or nonprofit operated departments, agencies, or associations produce standards. Such groups may be designated geographically, such as a state, national, or international group, as well as by technology or industry designation. The International Organization for Standardization (ISO) defines a standard as a "document, established by consensus and approved by a recognized body, that provides, for common and repeated use, rules, guidelines or characteristics for activities or their results. . . ."[54] The specification and criteria of standards often provide a quality benchmark. Ideally, standards enable products or services to flow smoothly through various industry commercialization stages. They are especially vital for comprehensive adoption of newly developing technologies, including products, processes, services, interfaces, or materials.

For companies to comply with standards, authorization for use of a competitor's patent may be required. It is the primary purpose of a standard-setting body, in collaboration with concurring companies, to establish standardized technology for the benefit of product and service compatibility, as well as consumer safety. If a patent owner member of a standards group blocks the development of a standard by refusing to license or by demanding unreasonably high royalties, this defeats the purpose of an industry standard.[55] Consequently, good-faith rules of standards groups frequently include the following requirements for companies participating in a standards-setting process related to patents:

- Members must disclose patents or patent applications that cover a proposed standard.

- Members must offer commercially reasonable and fair licenses when their patents are included in a standard.[56]

Antitrust enforcement may occur if a standards group fails to disclose and/or block patent rights related to a standard. Some groups have covenants for members for such conditions. So, if a patent is part of a standard, the patent owner member will not sue the association or assert an infringement claim against another member.[57] Ideally, reasonable and fair licensing is applied.

Working with open licenses and/or standards has several advantages. Both methods prohibit offensive patent infringement claims against other members of an agreement, such as competitors or patent trolls. In addition, both methods eliminate or simplify any fair and reasonable licensing needs.

Returning to the story of the Wright brothers and their patent conflicts with initial competitive airplane products, one can see how standards are essential for new technologies. Patent pools are often a resolution reached to maintain such patent standards to avoid "patent thickets" which is "a dense web of overlapping intellectual property rights that a company must hack its way through in order to actually commercialize new technology."[58] Such patent thickets could stifle, rather than encourage, innovation. Patent pools have pros and cons. Most standards organizations promote these pools as offering a positive effect on competition and innovation, yet in some situations, possible countercompetitive scenarios may arise stifling innovation, such as price fixing or development of an industry cartel.

> "History has shown that an invention typically is not made from a single 'flash of genius,' but from an assembly of incremental innovative developments. Patent thickets should not be viewed as a block on innovation but rather a milestone of progress and a natural part of the evolution of a complex, marketable and successful product."[59]—Jeffrey I. D. Lewis and Ryan M. Mott

After the Wright brothers won their patent infringement suits, the federal government intervened by organizing a consortium of aviation companies known as the Manufacturer's Aircraft Association and eventually known as the Aerospace Industries Association. Each member of the Association was required to pay a fair and reasonable fee for use of the patents of the Wright brothers and their key aviation competitor, Glenn Curtiss, for every airplane produced. Ultimately, Wilbur Wright died in 1912, and Orville Wright sold his company in 1915 and retired. Curtiss became the leading aircraft manufacturer, as World War I commenced. Nearly a decade after the war, the Wright's company merged with Curtiss Aeroplane and Motor Company becoming a major aeronautical manufacturer known as Curtiss-Wright.[60] Such patent conflicts are common when new technologies are introduced, such as recent patent wars between manufacturers of mobile smartphones and charges of patent infringement resulting in litigation.

PATENT INFRINGEMENT

Creators of new things, whether they are music, another measuring cup, or a smartphone, will need effective research guidance from their librarian to find related factual information resources to save them from potential infringement. Patents filed and granted, as well as patent litigation, have dramatically expanded in the twenty-first century.[61] According to a 2016 federal Government Accountability Office (GOA) report, 60 percent of the growth in infringement cases was related to software patents.[62] The advancements in mobile information technology demonstrate how patented inventions help to drive the U.S. economy and improve our lives. Although multiple types of IP are associated with mobile phones and other technology, it is the patents themselves that are highly coveted and guarded. As of 2012, there were over 250,000 active U.S. patents that affected smartphones.[63] That is, one in six active patents are associated with smartphone inventions. This does not include patents for other mobile electronic devices or for the wireless technology itself. It is likely that the number of patents in this field will continue to grow, adding fuel to our economy while further enhancing our lives, especially virtual connectivity and access to knowledge.

Many patents are associated with mobile devices that everyone owns. Check a copy of your mobile device's instructional manual or user guide. Skim through the contents and see if you can locate patent number references. How many patents are listed? Most likely, more than you'd ever need to know!

Instances of such essential patents in your mobile device guide demonstrates the need for cross-licensing or a patent pool to construct and market a smartphone or computer. As an example, the curved design exterior of smartphones is an Apple® U.S. Design Patent No. D618,677, and the swiping finger across a screen to unlock the display of your Kindle® or your smartphone is also an Apple® U.S. Utility Patent No. 8,046,721. The feature of accessing an email message pushed to the phone without accessing the server is a Motorola® U.S. Utility Patent No. 6,272,333. All of these patent enhancements are carefully monitored, and litigation is begun if infringement is seen.

No doubt the patent litigation process is often complex, mysterious, and costly, especially with regard to patent infringement cases. Yet major innovative technology businesses are using their patents and in some cases trademarks "as competitive weapons to capture and defend markets, outflank rivals, and increase revenue. These firms regard patent strategy as a new core competency of the modern enterprise and an important factor in their success."[64] Instead of litigation, some parties may opt for an alternative dispute resolution to an alleged infringement such as mediation, arbitration, or private trials to settle the patent battle.

Librarians can help their clientele avoid infringement by helping them conduct associated patent searches for similar inventions. Dedicated research libraries for patents, known as Patent and Trademark Resource Centers (PTRCs), offer such help. A listing of PTRC locations nationwide is located at the USPTO website https://www.uspto.gov/learning-and-resources/support-centers/patent-and

-trademark-resource-centers-ptrcs. These are covered further in the next chapter on patent searching.

Earlier in this chapter, the differences between utility, design, and plant were discussed. An infringement of a utility patent takes place when one makes, uses, or sells an item covered by the claims of a valid, in-force patent without the patent owner's permission. After such infringement, a patent owner may sue for infringement in a federal court.[65] Federal courts have exclusive jurisdiction over patent infringement lawsuits. In the *Apple v. Samsung* smartphone case, both design patents and utility patents were involved.[66] Design patent claims are associated with patent drawings and novelty of the patented design. Design patents do not protect functionality as do utility patents. When combined, as in the case with Apple, they may strengthen a larger IP portfolio of a single product such as a smartphone.[67] If patent holders have genuine reason to protect an alleged infringement of their patent, then they must file a patent infringement action in a U.S. District Court. Since the *Apple v. Samsung* case, some business experts believe that companies may reconsider dealing with competitors during product development and execute more risk assessments.[68]

As a preventive measure during product development, a librarian may show an inventor how to perform a patent infringement search. This helps to determine whether the invention infringes any valid in-force patents. Librarians might also recommend that the inventor use a professional advanced patent searcher to execute the patent infringement search to discover whether an invention is infringing any of those valid, in-force patents. An infringement search is much narrower in scope than a fundamental patent search, which covers all prior art.[69]

A patent validity search is another type of patent search to help a defendant in a patent infringement lawsuit. The librarian could provide instruction on how to locate information that would potentially invalidate the patent for which the inventor was alleged of an infringement. As described in the next chapter on patent searching, to avoid an accusation of practicing law, the librarian should not perform the actual patent search. Librarians should merely demonstrate how to perform such a patent search. A validity search involves re-reviewing the prior art and patents cited for the granted patent by a patent office. The goal is to show that the patent office would not have approved the application if the examiner had known about any newly discovered prior art. Conversely, if a plaintiff patentee needs to validate a patent by confirming that others could not locate invalidating prior art,[70] a librarian may possibly demonstrate similar patent searching techniques for such a customer. Once again, the librarian should use caution by not performing the actual search to avoid giving legal advice. Experienced IP librarians should only offer hypothetical searching examples.

All of these searches discussed above are much more advanced than the preliminary patent searching covered in the next chapter. As stated often in this book, it is highly advisable for a layperson, such as an independent inventor or general business associate, to obtain the services of an experienced patent attorney or agent for these highly complicated types of specialty searches. To demonstrate just how involved these infringement battles can be, the Mobile Phone Patent War is described below.

MOBILE TECHNOLOGY PATENT INFRINGEMENTS

The following mobile phone patent war scenarios demonstrate the need for a patent strategy, considering the risk surrounding the introduction of a new invention into the marketplace. It is vital for inventors, entrepreneurs, or businesses to be knowledgeable about all potential prior arts in the IP minefield of their new innovation.

Multiple headlines in newspapers, weblogs, trade magazines, and legal journals have cited patent wars between smart phone manufacturers. The first example has helped others protect their IP, an earlier lesson learned from BlackBerry's manufacturer, Research in Motion, and its patent battle with a small patent holding company named NTP Incorporated. The plaintiff firm, NTP, was categorized by many as a patent troll, as it assertively enforced it patent portfolio against larger, well-known companies.[71] The infringement charged in this case was for a necessary feature of the BlackBerry phone and the way it received email messages. This case was settled in 2006, whereby BlackBerry's manufacturer paid NTP a substantial $612.5 million. As Apple and Samsung smart phones have grown in popularity, this infringement case, merely speculating a potential shutdown of the BlackBerry's service, certainly has not helped BlackBerry's mobile phone business.[72]

The Apple patent war with Samsung lingered in the news headlines for seven years. Apple brought charges against Samsung smartphones in the summer of 2012. Shortly thereafter, on August 24, a jury for the *Apple v. Samsung* case in San Jose, California, found that Samsung violated six out of seven Apple patents on trial. Samsung was ordered to pay over $1 billion in damages for patent violations. During the summer of 2014, Apple stopped its injunction against certain Samsung mobile models in its smart phone patents war. During this same period, Apple's mobile phone iOS market share had declined to just under 12 percent while Android held 85 percent and Microsoft's Windows and BlackBerry share was less than the remaining 3 percent.[73] In 2015, a federal appeals court blocked the sale of some Samsung smartphones, while a federal circuit ordered Samsung to pay Apple $548 million dollars. Samsung appealed again as the USPTO reexamined some Apple patents in question and found one utility patent invalid.[74] However, this "David versus Goliath" battle continued as Apple fiercely guarded its IPs. This case continued all the way to the Supreme Court.[75] After a second appearance at the Supreme Court, the Court announced in November 2017 that it would not hear the appeal from Samsung, leaving the District Court's ruling in Apple's favor.[76] Apple and Samsung reached a final settlement in mid-2018, after Apple was awarded $539 million dollars by a U.S. jury.[77]

SOFTWARE PATENTS

The discussion of patent infringement battles between the mobile phone giants are also related to IP protection of computer software. Both patent law and copyright law may apply to the IP defense of certain facets of computer software. A computer software patent is often referred to as a Computer-Implemented Invention (CII) when dealing with a patent attorney or agent registered with the USPTO. See https://www.uspto.gov/web/offices/com/sol/og/con/files/cons092.htm for more.

The question of which IP to apply to one's new software comes up frequently at PTRCs. The answer is not so obvious and often requires the assistance of an IP attorney specializing in software. In its simplest terms, both patents and copyrights could apply to most computer software including mobile apps. However, as apps are more akin to the latest fashions in that they may change or morph with the seasons, trademark is a supportive IP utilized to protect the branding of such transformative apps. In simple terms, patents protect the idea, while copyright protects the written code. Trade secrets and licensing are other IPs that could apply to computer software protections. See list below for determining which type of IP could apply to a computer.

- Utility patent could protect the underlying algorithm function of computer software.
- Copyright can protect against unauthorized copying of software script/code and even database formats.
- Copyright term of protection is 70+ years versus 20 years for a utility patent.
- Copyright is used for most computer software copyright registrations, as well as for format/appearance of a database or website.
- Trademark may apply to the software product branding name.
- Trade secret is another option for protection of computer software.

The first publicly acknowledged U.S. Patent No. 3,380,029 for software processing to sort data on a computer was granted to Martin Goetz in 1968.[78] Additional software copyrights and patents surfaced in the early 1980s in the United States, but were slower to develop in the other countries. By the mid-1990s, software patents in the United States became more common. Nevertheless, this continues to be a hotly debated issue, as more open source proponents believe that software patents discourage the public good aspect whereby software should be open and free to use and improve.

The term free does not necessarily imply free of cost, as open software such as Linux is free to obtain and use, but there is often a service cost associated with such open-source software. Even Linux is not immune to alleged IP infringement, as an IP insurance firm claimed that Linux potentially infringes 283 patents.[79] Those who oppose such proprietary conditions or believe that software IP should be open promote legislative review of the issue. Conversely, many in the commercial business of software development promote patents and copyright protection measures incentives for future innovations. In addition, trademarks could be applied to the branded names of software.

U.S. courts have differentiated between the purposes of copyright and patent laws related to software. Copyright protects the expression of the computer software code and appearance of its formatted view. Copyright also permits independently created authorship that is identical to another copyrighted work by coincidence, while patents must be totally novel and of a single authorship party. The main shortcoming of copyright is that it does not protect the algorithm or the underlying sequence of computer commands, only the computer code itself. Broader protection could be granted by a patent that demonstrates novelty and non-obviousness. Since 1981, a hotly debated issue associated with software patents involves software embedded algorithms patented that include combinations of prior art and basic mathematics which some believe are in the public domain.

In June 2014, the Supreme Court made it more challenging to obtain patents for software in the *Alice Corp. v. CLS Bank International* case,[80] as it ruled that patent claims regarding abstract ideas of Computer-Implemented Inventions (CII) were not eligible subject matter for a patent. According to the Martin Goetz, pioneer commercial software inventor and the first acknowledged patentee of a software patent, the Supreme Court decision:

> was a great victory for those that believe that inventors that [sic] use a digital computer to innovate can get a patent on their invention. . . . The Supreme Court unanimously agreed that the critical issue is whether there is an inventive concept (and not on how an invention is implemented) . . . [it] finally ended the debate on whether computer-implemented inventions are patentable.[81]

Thus, the *Alice Corp. v. CLS Bank International* case still had some vague eligible subject matter analysis aspects, which required further clarification for patent examiners to follow. Therefore, the USPTO revised its guidance in 2019 for subject matter eligibility under Title 35 of the US Code Sections 101 and 112 related to the questionability of abstract ideas related to software patents. The new framework for evaluating eligibility should help some prospective software patent applicants avoid rejection by identifying certain subject matter groups that are or are not abstract ideas, by integrating abstract ideas into a practical application that is indeed truly innovative, and by focusing on aspects of their inventions that relate to practical implementations of an improvement in technology.[82] However, one should watch for future reviews by the Supreme Court of the 2019 revised guidance for subject matter eligibility of computer software, as it may not be final.

PATENT TROLLS

Librarians could help their clientele understand the challenge of patent trolls. Larger consumer electronics companies and some legal and business analysts believe that the current patent system permits patent trolls to unexpectedly pounce on larger companies that allege them of infringing. Consequently, larger technology companies believe that the current patent system allows too many broadly established claims, while many patent trolls may profit from this allowance.

Patent trolls are parties who obtain patents with no intention of marketing or producing the patented invention. Instead, the patent becomes an opportunistic tool to merely sue for infringement to establish licensing agreements or collect royalties.[83] The name "patent troll" is derived from the fabled model of trolls that lurked beneath countryside bridges and unexpectedly surprised passing travelers demanding ransom-like tolls to allow passage. Some defensive patenting and patent trolls are prevalent among controversial software patents noted above. Patent-holding trolls aggressively pursue big tech businesses such as Apple, Motorola, and Google with patent infringement suits, or they demand licensing fees for the most basic components of smartphone functions. For example, NTP has resurfaced, targeting companies with wireless email patent infringements like those it placed on Blackberry in 2006 mentioned earlier. The *Wall Street Journal* reported that patent licensing trolls often "use patents for offensive purposes, licensing them as broadly as possible and asserting them in infringement suits against companies that refuse to take a license."[84]

AMERICA INVENTS ACT (AIA)

Many small businesses and independent inventors favor the Leahy-Smith America Invents Act (AIA) introduced in 2011, which claimed to "spur innovation and economic growth by streamlining the patent application process and introducing new procedures to ensure patent quality."[85] The most significant change shifts the U.S. patent system from a "first to invent" claim to a "first to file" submission system.[86] Some believe that the AIA will reduce the patent approval turnaround time and "will reduce incremental, duplicative, and strategic patents, eroding the armaments available to wage a patent war,"[87] like infringement lawsuits in the smartphone industry.

The "first to file" concept is not new. Other technologically advanced countries have utilized it for years. Previously, the United States valued and legally enforced "first to invent" for patent applications, which, when a dispute occurred, was often documented with a simple inventor's notebook.

Many critics believe that new "first to file" policy for the United States will create a fierce rivalry between patent competitors. Some factions feel this fosters a winner-takes-all condition for larger corporations, rather than supporting smaller, independent inventors. This is more common in highly competitive, lucrative markets. Defensive patenting is often deemed necessary to gain competitive market share or to gain licensing income from permissions for competitors' use of one's patent. Provisional applications for patents, covered earlier in this chapter, are helpful for independent inventors and small businesses to capitalize on the advantages of the new "first to file" patent application process.

CONCLUSION

It is likely that, in the twenty-first century, the nature of patents in the United States may encounter new, unforeseen challenges paralleling contemporary technological and political changes. Just as the Wright brothers confronted obstacles in maintaining and protecting their patents, so too must today's innovators. Librarians and their knowledge of the facts and where to locate accurate information related to patents are vital for all information professionals if they are going to help their customers avoid legal challenges related to patents as well as others. In the next chapter, you will apply all that you now know about patents to learning how to teach library customers patent searching.

NOTES

1. David McCullough, *The Wright Brothers* (New York: Simon & Schuster, 2015).
2. G. D. Padfield and B. Lawrence, "The Birth of Flight Control: An Engineering Analysis of the Wright Brothers' 1902 Glider," *Aeronautical Journal* 107, no. 1078 (December 2003): 697–718.
3. U.S. Constitution Article I, Subsection 8, clause 8 (1787).
4. Rich Goldstein, *ABA Consumer Guide to Obtaining a Patent: A Practical Resource for Helping Entrepreneurs & Inventors Protect Their Ideas* (Chicago: American Bar Association, 2016), 40.
5. United States Patent and Trademark Office, *General Information Concerning Patents* (2015), 2.
6. Edward Lamoureux, *Intellectual Property Law & Interactive Media* (New York: Peter Lang, 2009), 94.
7. 35 U.S. Code § 101—Inventions Patentable.
8. Ibid.
9. 35 U.S. Code § 102—Conditions for Patentability; Novelty.
10. 35 U.S. Code § 103—Conditions for Patentability; Nonobvious Subject Matter.
11. 35 U.S. Code § 112—Specification.
12. U.S. Patent & Trademark Office, *Manual of Patent Examining Procedure*, 2106 Patent Subject Matter Eligibility [R-08.2017], https://www.uspto.gov/web/offices/pac/mpep/s2106.html (accessed January 12, 2019).
13. 35 U.S. Code § 154—Contents and term of patent; and David Pressman, *Patent It Yourself*, 14th edition (Berkeley, CA: Nolo, 2009), 9.
14. Timothy Wherry, *Intellectual Property: Everything the Digital-Age Librarian Needs to Know* (Chicago: American Library Association, 2008), 10.
15. David Pressman, *Patent It Yourself*, 14th edition (Berkeley, CA: Nolo, 2009), 9.
16. U.S. Patent and Trademark Office, International Patent Cooperation, https://www.uspto.gov/patents-getting-started/international-patent-cooperation (accessed January 14, 2019).
17. 35 U.S. Code § 101—Inventions Patentable.
18. U.S. Patent no. 821, 393, Orville and Wilbur Wright, Flying-Machine, May 22, 1906.
19. 35 U.S. Code § 171—Patents for Designs.
20. U.S. Patent & Trademark Office, *Manual of Patent Examining Procedure*, 1512 Relationship between Design Patent, Copyright, and Trademark [R-07.2015], https://www.uspto.gov/web/offices/pac/mpep/s1512.html (accessed February 21, 2017).
21. 35 U.S. Code §§ 161–164 (1994).
22. 35 U.S. Code §§ 111 (101, 102, 103, 112).
23. 7 U.S. Code §§ 2321 et seq.—Plant Variety Protection Act; also see USDA site for details at https://www.ams.usda.gov/rules-regulations/pvpa (accessed January 20, 2019).

24. Shubo (Joe) Zhou, *Intellectual Property Protection for Plants in the United States*, Power Point presentation at PTRC Program Training Seminar, USPTO, Alexandria, Virginia, March 24, 2016.
25. World Intellectual Property Organization, WIPO Patent Drafting Manual, 67, http://www.wipo.int/edocs/pubdocs/en/patents/867/wipo_pub_867.pdf (accessed February 25, 2017).
26. Joseph P. Kennedy and Wayne H. Watkins with Elyse N. Ball, *How to Invent and Protect Your Invention: A Guide to Patents for Scientists and Engineers* (Hoboken, NJ: Wiley, 2012), 52.
27. U.S. Patent no. 821,393, claim 7.
28. U.S. Patent no. 6,263,732, single claim.
29. U.S. Patent no. 7,306,120, primary claim.
30. U.S. Patent no. 9,354,098, primary claim.
31. U.S. Patent & Trademark Office, *Guide for the Preparation of Patent Drawings* (2002), 9, 31, 36.
32. Kennedy and Watkins, *How to Invent and Protect Your Invention*, 57.
33. U.S. Patent & Trademark Office, "Provisional Application for Patent," https://www.uspto.gov/patents-getting-started/patent-basics/types-patent-applications/provisional-application-patent (accessed February 17, 2017).
34. United States Patent and Trademark Office, *General Information Concerning Patents* (2015), 24.
35. Ibid., 25.
36. Ibid., 25–26.
37. Ibid., 29.
38. U.S. Patent & Trademark Office, *Manual of Patent Examining Procedure*, 2016, Chapter 2000, Section 2016, Fraud, Inequitable Conduct, or Violation of Duty of Disclosure Affects All Claims [R-08.2012], https://www.uspto.gov/web/offices/pac/mpep/s2016.html (accessed October 15, 2018).
39. Deborah E. Bouchoux, *Intellectual Property: The Law of Trademarks, Copyrights, Patents, and Trade Secrets* (Boston: Cengage Learning, 2018), 392–393.
40. United States Patent and Trademark Office, *General Information Concerning Patents* (2015), 30.
41. U.S. Patent & Trademark Office, *Manual of Patent Examining Procedure*, 301 Ownership/Assignability of Patents and Applications [R-07.2015], https://www.uspto.gov/web/offices/pac/mpep/s301.html (accessed March 8, 2017).
42. Ibid.
43. Gene Quinn, "Patent Pending: The Road to Obtaining a U.S. Patent," *IP Watchdog*, December 15, 2018, https://www.ipwatchdog.com/2018/12/15/patent-pending-u-s-patent/id=102130/ (accessed December 17, 2018).
44. Dr. Konstantinos Karachalios, Managing Director of the Institute of Electrical and Electronics Engineers' Standards Association (IEEE-SA), "Expert Interview: The Importance of Industry Standards," *European Patent Office* website, 2017, https://www.epo.org/news-issues/issues/standards.html (accessed October 21, 2018).
45. Richard Lloyd, LES completes crucial step in drive to introduce standards to the IP market, Intellectual Asset Management (IAM) blog, February 16, 2017, http://www.iam-media.com/Blog/Detail.aspx?g=df904e6d-86df-48de-978f-f53a4db3779c (accessed February 17, 2017).
46. Shubha Ghosh, Richard Gruner, Jay P. Kesan, and Robert I. Reis, *Intellectual Property: Private Rights, the Public Interest, and the Regulation of Creative Activity* (St. Paul, MN: West Academic Publishing, 2007), 7–8.

47. Kennedy et al., *How to Invent and Protect Your Invention*, 106–107.

48. Kurt M. Saunders, *Intellectual Property Law: Legal Aspects of Innovation and Competition* (St. Paul, MN: West Academic Publishing, 2016), 23.

49. Kennedy et al., *How to Invent and Protect Your Invention*, 108–109.

50. Kurt M. Saunders, "Law and Ethics of Trade Secrets: A Case Study," *California Western Law Review* 42, no. 2 (2006, Article 3): 210.

51. National Conference of Commissions on Uniform State Laws, *Uniform Trade Secrets Act* 14 U.L.A. 433 (1985), http://www.uniformlaws.org/Act.aspx?title=trade%20Secrets%20Act (accessed March 7, 2017).

52. Economic Espionage Act of 1996, 18 U.S.C. §§ 1831–1839.

53. Free Software Foundation, *GNU General Public License, Version 2*, Preamble, https://www.gnu.org/licenses/old-licenses/gpl-2.0.en.html (accessed March 11, 2017).

54. International Organization for Standardization, *ISO/IEC Guide 2, Standardization and Related Activities, General Vocabulary*, 2004, Section 3.2, https://www.iso.org/standard/39976.html (accessed March 11, 2017).

55. Jefferson C. Glassie, Eileen Morgan Johnson, and Dana O. Lynch, *Intellectual Property for Nonprofit Organizations and Associations* (Washington, D.C.: Association Management Press, 2012), 90–93; World Intellectual Property Organization, *Standards, Intellectual Property Rights (IPRs) and Standards-Setting Process*, http://www.wipo.int/sme/en/documents/ip_standards_fulltext.html (accessed January 23, 2017).

56. Ibid.

57. Ibid.

58. Ian Hargreaves, "Digital Opportunity: A Review of Intellectual Property and Growth," May 2011, https://www.gov.uk/government/uploads/system/uploads/attachment_data/file/32563/ipreview-finalreport.pdf, 18 (retrieved March 16, 2017); and Carl Shapiro, Navigating the Patent Thicket: Cross Licenses, Patent Pools, and Standard-Setting (March 2001), 1–2. Available at SSRN: https://ssrn.com/abstract=273550 or http://dx.doi.org/10.2139/ssrn.273550.

59. Quote from Lewis and Mott's article entitled, "The Sky Is Not Falling: Navigating the Smartphone Patent Thicket," *WIPO Magazine*, February 2013, p. 10. Also, see HTML version of article at http://www.wipo.int/wipo_magazine/en/2013/01/article_0002.html.

60. Smithsonian National Air and Space Museum, The Wright Brothers: The Invention of the Aerial Age, The Aerial Age Begins: Many Law Suits, https://airandspace.si.edu/exhibitions/wright-brothers/online/age/1910/lawsuits.cfm (accessed March 12, 2017); Phaedra Hise, "How the Wright Brothers Blew It," November 19, 2003, https://www.forbes.com/2003/11/19/1119aviation.html (accessed March 12, 2017).

61. Mark A. Lemley, "Surprising Resilience of the Patent System," *Texas Law Review* 95, no. 1 (November 2016): 1–2.

62. United States Government Accountability Report, Intellectual Property: Patent Office Should Define Quality, Reassess Incentives, and Improve Clarity, GAO-16-490, June 2016.

63. Daniel O'Conner, "One in Six Active U.S. Patents Pertain to the Smartphone," Disruptive Competition Project (DisCo), October 17, 2012, http://www.project-disco.org/intellectual-property/one-in-six-active-u-s-patents-pertain-to-the-smartphone/#.WJ3QpSgdXao (accessed February 10, 2017).

64. Kevin Rivette and David Kline, *Rembrandts in the Attic* (Boston: Harvard Business School Press, 2000), 3.

65. United States Patent and Trademark Office, *General Information Concerning Patents* (2015), 31.
66. *The Economist*, "Apple v. Samsung: Swipe, Pinch and Zoom to the Courtroom," September 1, 2012, p. 61, https://www.economist.com/business/2012/09/01/swipe-pinch-and-zoom-to-the-courtroom (accessed December 10, 2019).
67. Gene Quinn, "Design Patents: The Under Utilized and Overlooked Patent," IP Watchdog, December 20, 2011, http://www.ipwatchdog.com/2011/12/20/design-patents-the-under-utilized-and-overlooked-patent/id=21337/ (accessed September 24, 2012).
68. Rodd Zolkos, "Apple's Patent Victory Puts Focus on Tech Risks," *Business Insurance* 46, no. 34 (September 3, 2012): 1.
69. Richard Stim, *Patent, Copyright & Trademark: An Intellectual Property Desk Reference*, 12th edition (Berkeley, CA: Nolo, 2012), 96–97.
70. Thomas Wolff, "What's So Special about Patent Invalidity Searching?," *Online* (July/August 2012): 28–33.
71. Stephen Wellman, "Will NTP Sue Every Wireless Company?" *Information Week* blog, September 12, 2007, http://www.informationweek.com/mobility/business/will-ntp-sue-every-wireless-company/229214957 (accessed September 24, 2012).
72. David Weston, "Blackberry: A Teaching Case for WIPO," Intellectual Property Research Institute of Australia, October 2008, http://www.wipo.int/export/sites/www/academy/en/about/global_network/educational_materials/cs2_blackberry.pdf (accessed October 20, 2018).
73. Barry Levine, "Android Hits 85 Percent Smartphone Market Share," Top Tech News, August 1, 2014, http://www.toptechnews.com/article/index.php?story_id=0030003DMG66 (accessed August 3, 2014).
74. Howard Mintz, "Apple v. Samsung: Samsung slapped with injunction," *Silicon Valley*, September 17, 2015, http://www.siliconvalley.com/apple-vs-samsung (accessed October 22, 2015); Bret Swanson, "Will the Apple-Samsung Battle Help Modernize Patent Law?" *Computer World*, October 12, 2015, http://www.computerworld.com/article/2991912/technology-law-regulation/will-the-apple-samsung-battle-help-modernize-patent-law.html (accessed October 13, 2015); Matthew Bultman, "Samsung Can't Put Off Paying $548M in Apple Smartphone War," Law 360, October 13, 2015, http://www.law360.com/articles/713655/samsung-can-t-put-off-paying-548m-in-apple-smartphone-war (accessed October 14, 2015).
75. Derek Dahlgren, "Saga Continues: Apple v. Samsung, Next Stop Supreme Court," IP Watchdog, September 29, 2015, http://www.ipwatchdog.com/2015/09/29/apple-v-samsung-next-stop-supreme-court/id=62065/ (accessed September 30, 2015); Robert Mann, "Opinion Analysis: Justices Tread Narrow Path in Rejecting $400 Million Award for Samsung's Infringement of Apple's Cellphone Design Patents," SCOTUS Blog, December 6, 2016, http://www.scotusblog.com/2016/12/opinion-analysis-justices-tread-narrow-path-in-rejecting-400-million-award-for-samsungs-infringement-of-apples-cellphone-design-patents/#more-249662 (accessed October 21, 2018).
76. Joe Mullin, "Supreme Court Won't Hear Apple v. Samsung Round Two," ARS Technica, November 6, 2017, https://arstechnica.com/tech-policy/2017/11/supreme-court-wont-hear-apple-v-samsung-round-two/ (accessed October 9, 2018).
77. Jan Wolfe and Stephen Nellis, "U.S. Jury Awards Apple $539 Million in Samsung Apple Retrial," *Reuters*, May 24, 2018, https://www.reuters.com/article/us-apple-samsung-elec/u-s-jury-awards-apple-539-million-in-samsung-patent-retrial-idUSKCN1IP3Q1 (accessed January 10, 2019); Shawn Knight, "Apple Awarded $539 Million in Samsung

Patent Infringement Retrial," *Techspot*, https://www.techspot.com/news/74809-apple-awarded-539-million-samsung-patent-infringement-retrial.html (accessed January 10, 2019); and Jacob Kastrenakes, "Apple and Samsung Settle Seven-Year-Long Patent Fight over Copying the iPhone," *The Verge*, June 27, 2018, https://www.techspot.com/news/74809-apple-awarded-539-million-samsung-patent-infringement-retrial.html (accessed January 10, 2019).

78. U.S. Utility Patent no. 3,380,029, April 23, 1968.

79. Stephen Shankland, "Group: Linux Potentially Infringes 283 Patents," CNET News.com, August 1, 2004, http://news.cnet.com/Group-Linux-potentially-infringes-283-patents/2100-7344_3-5291403.html (accessed October 4, 2012).

80. *Alice Corp. v. CLS Bank International*, 573 U.S. 208, 134 S. Ct. 2347 (2014).

81. Martin Goetz, "Why Alice v. CLS Bank is a Victory for Software Patents," IP Watchdog, February 6, 2015, http://www.ipwatchdog.com/2015/02/06/alice-v-cls-bank-is-a-victory-for-software-patents/id=54489/ (accessed February 10, 2015).

82. U.S. Patent and Trademark Office, "U.S. Patent and Trademark Office Announces Revised Guidance for Determining Subject Matter Eligibility," Press Release 19-01, January 4, 2019, https://www.uspto.gov/about-us/news-updates/us-patent-and-trademark-office-announces-revised-guidance-determining-subject (accessed January 10, 2019); Gene Quinn, "Revised Patent Eligibility Guidance Effectively Defines What is an Abstract Idea," IP Watchdog, January 4, 2019, https://www.ipwatchdog.com/2019/01/04/patent-eligibility-guidance-abstract-idea/id=104754/ (accessed January 10, 2019); Gene Quinn, "Software Patent Drafting Lessons from the Key Lighthouse Cases," IP Watchdog, January 9, 2019, https://www.ipwatchdog.com/2019/01/09/software-patent-drafting-lessons-key-lighthouse-cases/id=104874/ (accessed January 14, 2019); and Paul S. Hunter and Daniel Rose, "New USPTO Guidance on Patent Subject Matter Eligibility Seeks to Standardize Abstract Idea Analysis," *National Law Review*, January 7, 2019, https://www.natlawreview.com/article/new-uspto-guidance-patent-subject-matter-eligibility-seeks-to-standardize-abstract (accessed January 10, 2019).

83. Richard Posner, "Why There Are Too Many Patents in America, *Atlantic*, July 2012, http://www.theatlantic.com/business/print/2012/07/why-there-are-too-many-patents-in-america/259725/ (accessed September 20, 2012); and Kennedy et al., *How to Invent and Protect Your Invention*, 81.

84. Stuart Weinberg and Anupretta Das, "Multiple Bidders Are Emerging for Nortel's Wireless Patents," *Wall Street Journal*, February 3, 2011, http://online.wsj.com/article/SB40001424052748703960804576120463615113454.html (accessed September 24, 2012).

85. USPTO, "Historic Patent Reform Implemented by U.S. Patent and Trademark Office," Press Release, 1259, September 17, 2012, http://www.uspto.gov/news/pr/2012/12-59.jsp (accessed September 20, 2012).

86. Ibid.

87. Mary Anne Gobble, "Arming for a Patent War," *Research Technology Management* 54, no. 6 (Nov/Dec 2011): 2–3.

Chapter 4

PATENT SEARCHING

CHAPTER OBJECTIVES

- To recognize library customers that need the patent searching support of a Patent & Trademark Resource Center (PTRC) such as inventors and entrepreneurs
- To understand what a PTRC is and what resources and services it provides the public
- To be able to instruct library customers of the importance and benefits of a preliminary prior art patent search via free United States Patent and Trademark Office (USPTO) and other free online databases
- To describe how to provide effective intellectual property (IP) information literacy through reference and library instruction, which may be promoted through library outreach programming as discussed in Chapter 1.

INTRODUCTION

The previous chapter covered the fundamentals of patents, including basic legal information associated with the application process and maintenances of patents. In this chapter, you will learn about the patent basics background to teach library customers how to conduct their own patent searches. Patent searching is one of the primary aspects of patent information that IP librarians will encounter most often. Much of this interest is rooted in the growing emphasis on STEM (science, technology, engineering, and mathematics) in education and business entrepreneurship. A patent search is highly advisable before submitting one's potential application for a patent. Although the patent application process is one that few inventors or entrepreneurs should implement on their own, prior art patent searching and reviewing other literature in the field of one's invention is something most people can do after a librarian teaches them how. Thus, once an inventor feels confident that his or her invention is indeed unique, new, and novel, and it is not found within an exhaustive search, then meeting with a patent attorney or patent agent to review his or her options, such as an application, is ideal.

PATENT SEARCHING CUSTOMERS

Business incubators and accelerators are all around. Some are in the community, while similar business and STEM programs are part of secondary and higher education. One challenge for many of the inventors or entrepreneurs associated with these start-up support networks is the lack of patent searching awareness. Patent information provided by IP librarians offers start-ups an edge to know their potential patent and other IP rights and thus safeguard their new products or services. IP librarians who collaborate with such start-up networks are also able to extend their library customer base. Generally, the patent searching instruction covered in this chapter is highly sought out by inventors and entrepreneurs utilizing startup support services.

To help IP librarians prepare for patent searching customers and other IP customer queries, it is helpful to view the highly popular reality television series known as *Shark Tank*. Watching *Shark Tank* is great training for IP librarians to start thinking about what types of patents or other IP may apply to any library customers' newly invented products or services.

Most recognize the stereotypical image of a male inventor tinkering in his garage and coming up with trite, corny ideas such as a heated toilet seat or an electric hammer. Yet, there are more women inventors and entrepreneurs today, which helps dispel the passé "male inventor" perception. For example, a study conducted at the School of Informatics and Computing at Indiana University, Bloomington, found that patent filings by women have risen significantly within higher education.[1]

However, it is still those iconic images of Thomas Edison, or more contemporary comparisons of inventors like Steve Jobs of Apple, that linger in our social psyche. Even pop culture lampoons this image often, as was the case with the timeless animated Fox Network series, *The Simpsons*, when Homer Simpson's midlife crisis prompts him to quit his job and become the next Edison in an episode entitled the "Wizard of Evergreen Terrace."[2] The "Wizard" episode title is a play on the popular nickname for Edison as the "Wizard of Menlo Park." Ultimately, Homer does come up with a useful, novel invention: an un-tippable chair, after which he coincidentally finds one displayed in the Edison Museum. In his hijinks to destroy the Edison model chair in the museum, he sees a poster that reveals Edison had fewer inventions than Leonardo da Vinci. So Edison had a role model, just as Edison inspired Homer. This makes Homer feel better as he abandons his idea to destroy Edison's chair while he leaves behind his own unique invention, an electric hammer. The following day a newscast reports the discovery of the model chair and an electric hammer just found in the museum, which are likely to make millions for Edison's family. Perhaps if Homer had visited a PTRC library (figure 4.1) nearby to conduct a prior art patent search, he would have learned that his electric hammer invention was indeed novel and new. At that point, Homer could have patented his original invention before the Edison heirs' discovery of his new hammer. This reflection of the de facto inventor stereotype should help us prepare for what types of imaginative personalities come to libraries for assistance with patent searching.

Figure 4.1
Logo of the Patent and Trademark Resource Center Program. (Courtesy of the Patent and Trademark Resource Center Program at the USPTO)

PATENT AND TRADEMARK RESOURCE CENTERS (PTRCS)

When a library offers patent resources of the U.S. Patent and Trademark Office, usually inventors and entrepreneurs will visit, phone, or email with the following types of questions:

- How do I get a patent for my idea for an invention?
- How do I find out if my idea has been patented before?
- How do I bring my invented product to the marketplace?

Most public and academic libraries in the United States featuring patent and trademark resources are PTRCs, but there are a few special libraries in the PTRC family, such as state or law libraries. PTRCs were originally known as Patent and Trademark Depository Libraries (PTDLs), but they were officially renamed as PTRCs on October 1, 2011, per an official federal government press release entitled "USPTO Rebrands National Library Network as Patent and Trademark Resource Centers."[3] The document reported that the new "Centers" designation indicates the transformation to modern electronic resources and assistance, rather than the former paper depository format. As part of their membership in the PTRC program, these libraries can help inventors and entrepreneurs answer the frequently asked questions above. According to the USPTO website, PTRCs are a nationwide network of public, state, and academic libraries that are designated by the USPTO to disseminate patent and trademark information and to support the diverse IP needs of the public. By accessing the patent and trademark information at a PTRC with the help of a trained specialist, one is able to determine if someone else has already patented an invention or obtained a federal registration for a trademark on goods or services. PTRCs also have access to PubEAST and PubWEST, examiner-based advanced patent searching systems. These trained specialists may also help library customers with specific questions regarding the patent and trademark processes, but they will not provide legal advice. Of the over eighty PTRCs in the United States, most are also FDLP libraries and house Government Printing Office

(GPO) documents. For a list of all the PTRCs and to determine the closest one to you, see https://www.uspto.gov/learning-and-resources/support-centers/patent-and-trademark-resource-centers-ptrc/ptrc-locations.

PTRCs offer free public access to large, up-to-date collections of patent and trademark databases; pertinent search and reference resources; helpful, knowledgeable staff; and confidentiality. It is very important to convey this confidentiality policy so inventors feel comfortable in sharing some limited information. Confidentiality is critical as public disclosure by an inventor to another party could prevent allowance of a granted patent. Public disclosure is discussing or disclosing your invention to the public such as a trade show display, a newspaper article, a website announcement, and so on.

You have most likely seen commercials on television that advertise businesses ready to assist inventors in making millions of dollars for their new widget ideas. The majority of these inventor business services are questionable and usually misleading. It is not uncommon for some of these businesses to charge independent inventors thousands of dollars for what they could have accomplished on their own at their regional PTRC library. Such an investment with a professional patent attorney or agent would be a healthier financial risk. Many questionable inventor promotion firms have been challenged by the Federal Trade Commission (FTC) for misrepresenting independent inventors and often by swindling them. The FTC and the USPTO offer informative websites and brochures to support PTRCs in promoting an awareness on this topic (see, for instance, https://www.uspto.gov/sites/default/files/documents/ScamPrevent.pdf.

In addition, many inventors believe that sending their ideas to themselves in a sealed envelope via the postal service is as good as a patent. This is an old wives' tale and legally has no merit. Submitting a provisional application for a patent, as discussed in the previous chapter, is the answer and more affordable for most people.

Many PTRCs offer free classes and outreach programs to raise awareness among potential IP user groups. Target audiences range from school and college entrepreneur and science classes to independent inventors and business start-ups in the community. For all of these outreach efforts, educational information is presented for children, teens, and adults related to IP and inventing. These outreach efforts not only raise awareness of library services and resources but also contribute to a community's innovation and economic development.[4]

Ethical and legal use of information based upon the American Library Association's Information Literacy Standards are often associated with IP awareness for school and college instruction. Such examples include the *Code of Ethics of the American Library Association*,[5] the *Standards for the 21st-Century Learner*[6] of the American Association of School Librarians (AASL), and the more recently published *Framework for Information Literacy for Higher Education*[7] from the Association of College & Research Libraries (ACRL) and *AASL Standards Framework for Learners*[8] of the AASL. Later chapters in this book cover these special types of instruction and outreach for these varying audiences.

The associated patent resources available at PTRCs serve multiple purposes ranging from typical inventors' needs to the research of genealogists. Besides historical data, genealogists are able to study and document family ancestry and accomplishments from patent literature. Historic patents include signatures of decedent inventors as well as residential records and business associate names. Businesses are able to map out product development cycles, economic trends, or competitor advances via patent landscape searching. From fusion to fashion, U.S. patents offer us a rich technological and cultural history documented in over ten million documents. Patents are often cited as the first source of information on new technologies.[9]

PATENT SEARCHING PROCESS OVERVIEW

Searching existing patents helps inventors determine whether or not a patent has already been issued for their invention. Patent searching and obtaining a patent are challenging. However, the initial preliminary prior-art patent searching process is achievable by most people who are adept at using online information databases. This type of search is defined as a prior art or novelty search. It has nothing to do with artwork paintings or graphic designs. It is searching the state of the art connected with the subject matter of the invention. PTRC specialists routinely teach inventors how to search existing patents. Such instruction offers inventors background on keyword searching and classification searching. After completing a comprehensive search, an inventor can determine whether to invest the money to hire an attorney to pursue submitting an application to the USPTO.

Before teaching library customers how to search, please be aware of the *Code of Ethics* published by the ALA, which advises librarians to clarify their role as information providers and not as interpreters of information when assisting customers with specialized information, such as health, patents, or other legal issues. Librarians should only provide instruction to library customers on how to find needed specialized information independently and effectively.[10] Patent searching specialists and support staff at a PTRC should not perform patent searches for inventors. Just as stated above, librarians do not offer medical or legal advice but rather help customers do their own searches. Utilizing a planned, hypothetical example for a patent search demonstration reduces the chance of a malpractice suit for "unauthorized practice of law."

A few exceptions when a librarian might search for a noninventor customer include citing isolated historical patents or those patents related to business or technical information research.[11] A common example of a noninventor search would include historic patents for genealogy research. It is always important to remember that the role of an IP librarian is to provide information assistance rather than legal advice. Only a patent attorney or agent registered with the USPTO should perform searches or provide legal advice for inventors with new patent prospects. However, librarians do provide IP information literacy that infuses needed concepts and skills for patent searchers such as accessing and managing patent documents via established classifications. In addition to IP library instruction, librarians answer inventors' basic questions to topics such as those covered in the previous chapter, Patent Fundamentals.

As library customers perform their own search, they should document proof that their processes, methods, or inventions have *not* been patented before. This means maintaining a list or spreadsheet of patents found that are similar. Such patents, if found, should be referenced on an inventor's actual patent application for his or her new invention. There are intricate patent classification systems that one should use to search patent databases effectively. Keyword searching alone may not reveal previous patents issued which are similar. Librarians or specialists at PTRCs are trained by the USPTO to instruct inventors, entrepreneurs, and others how to search the patent databases, including unique onsite databases, PubEAST and PubWEST, at each Resource Center library.

It is important to remember that as technology changes, newer USPTO databases will replace those mentioned in this book. Visiting a regional PTRC is the best way to learn how to make use of the most current technology for locating patents and trademarks.

When an IP librarian starts the instruction of patent searching, he or she must provide an introduction about patents, including basic legal facts, as mentioned in the previous chapter. It is vital that librarians make it clear that for an invention to potentially qualify to become a granted patent, one must search all patents issued, including literature, in the related field of the invention to make certain it is the first of its kind. This satisfies the novelty requirement of 35 U.S.C. §102 for patentability, which requires that a patent application demonstrates that the invention is indeed new. Second, a patent must also be useful and serve a function. Third, the invention must be nonobvious to those in its field. Fourth, the invention must be able to be built by someone familiar with the associated technology.

Reviewing the format of a patent document is helpful to present during a patent searching instruction session with library customers. Merely looking at the front page of a contemporary U.S. patent document says much about a patent. It tells the tale of the patent quickly and succinctly. A patent searcher can review specific sections of the front page to get what he or she needs to quickly progress through a prior art patent search. Figure 4.12, U.S. Patent "Umbrella Having and Anti-Inversion Mechanism," listed later in this chapter, displays key bibliographic points to know for a patent searching evaluation. These significant parts of a patent or patent application include elements such as:

- patent number and issue date to determine the age of the patent;
- title and abstract to define the subject matter;
- filing dates to determine the enforceability period of the patent; and
- inventor name(s); assignee (owner); classification codes; principal drawing; cited references; patent examiner and attorney names; and note regarding number of claims and drawing sheets.

The subsequent pages of a patent document (displayed in Figure 3.7 in Chapter 3) include the specifications, claims, and drawings. As discussed in Chapter 3, the claims are the most significant points to read as these determine the scope or boundary of patent protection. The claims are comparable to the metes and bounds description in a real property deed.

The USPTO website offers two versions of patents published since 1976: a PDF version, which is a copy of the official patent document issued, and an HTML version, which is revised as classifications are updated. It is important to note that the classification numbers found on PDF versions of patents are the classes at the time of the patent issue date. Patent classifications change over time. The HTML webpage view of patents offer the current classifications, which are useful in a prior art search. However, the PDF versions include drawings, which are not included on the HTML versions.

The easiest way to locate a patent is to have the patent number or the inventor's name. Then you can search one of the patent databases to quickly find the patent. This is often the case when a historian or genealogist is looking for historic patents. However, if you or your customer, the inventor, wish to see if the idea for a product or new service is original, the search process is not so simple. So, why should one perform a patent search?

- To prepare for the application process
- To improve awareness of their invention field
- To locate prior art required in an application
- To determine whether an application is feasible
- To prepare for consultation with a patent attorney or agent

PATENT SEARCHING VIA USPTO OR ESPACENET WEBSITE

Two search methods are available for finding lists of patents from online databases, namely, keyword or classification searching. In addition, when one only needs to find a single patent by its patent number, there is a separate patent number search page on the USPTO site.

Keyword searching is quick. It requires few specialized search skills. It is more appropriate for very recently developed technologies where patent office classifications have not yet been developed. Keyword searching matches words, phrases, and terms on the patent documents contained within each database. At minimum, most patent databases offer Boolean connectors such as "and," "or," and "and not" to form search queries. Google Patents offers an easy to use site for keyword searching. Although it is not ideal for an all-inclusive invention search as with the USPTO or Espacenet, keyword searching in Google Patents is helpful for when one is unable to locate a classification code for searching in the USPTO or Espacenet sites, as covered below.

However, keyword searching is not comprehensive. Pre-1976 patents from the USPTO's online PatFT (Patent Full-Text) database must be searched by classification or patent number. Only Espacenet of the European Patent Office (EPO) on the web or the PubEAST or PubWEST patent databases (available at PTRCs) provide optical character recognition (OCR) keyword searching before 1976 (often

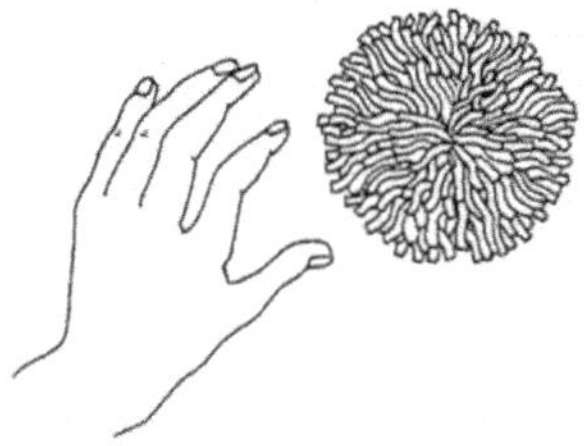

Figure 4.2
U.S. Utility Patent 4,756,529 Generally Spherical Object with Floppy Filaments to Promote Sure Capture. (Courtesy U.S. Patent and Trademark Office)

back to the 1920s). Google Patents is not as comprehensive, but it also offers OCR keyword searching back to the early 1800s. This is useful for historians and genealogists. As patent databases offered by the USPTO and Espacenet change in the future, it will be important to continue to contact nearby PTRCs for updates and instructional assistance.

As an example of some of the challenges of keyword searching, take a look at the patent drawing shown in figure 4.2. It's for a Koosh® ball. How would you or your inventor begin to describe the Koosh ball for a patent search? Spongelike? Floppy? Strands? The U.S. Utility Patent 4,756,529 cover page titles it "Generally Spherical Object with Floppy Filaments to Promote Sure Capture." This demonstrates why keyword searching most likely would not have located it, whereas the classification controlled-vocabulary would have found it.

The second method of searching is classification searching. Library patent specialists should be aware of the two classification types for U.S. patents. One is the USPTO classification system, or U.S. Patent Classification System (USPC). The second is the Cooperative Patent Classification (CPC) introduced in 2012, which replaced the USPTO classification system. Both classification methods are comprehensive. These classification systems are organized by the invention features as described in a patent. This chapter discusses the preferred CPC method for searching U.S. Utility patents. The USPTO classification system will continue to be available for U.S. Design and Plant patents, but since 2015, the CPC structure is used for searching all utility patents, including foreign patents.

Patent classification systems are thesaurus or controlled-vocabulary structures similar to library subject headings. The classified structures are categories of technology in which such inventions fit.[12] Both the USPTO and CPC structures are hierarchal systems to organize patents. Each is concept based.

For Design or Plant Patents, the U.S. Patent Classification scheme (located at https://www.uspto.gov/sites/default/files/patents/resources/classification/overview.pdf) may be used. If this link is no longer current, keyword search USPC or U.S. Patent Classification from the USPTO's home page search box. However, for this book, the demonstrated example will be to find a utility patent with the newer CPC scheme.

To perform a CPC patent search, it may be helpful to consult *Seven Step Strategy*, published by the USPTO. The seven-step search process has been changed and enhanced over time. For the most current version of the seven-step patent search, see https://www.uspto.gov/learning-and-resources/support-centers/patent-and-trademark-resource-centers-ptrc/resources/seven. There should be an HTML web and PDF handout version of the *Seven Step Strategy*.

A very helpful 40-minute tutorial https://www.uspto.gov/video/cbt/ptrcsearching/ on the USPTO website reviews patent searching utilizing the *Seven Step Strategy.* It may take up to an hour to complete this tutorial carefully. The basic search methodology is most important to learn. Whenever assisting a library customer searching for patents, always refer them to the most current *Seven Step Strategy* and latest database posted on the USPTO website.

A current version of the *Seven Step Strategy*[13] (at the time of writing this book) from the PTRC program office follows, with a hypothetical example of a new umbrella, to help you see how to conduct a utility patent search. The USPTO's recommended search process is listed here twice: first for using the free USPTO online version as of early 2019, and a second alternate free database, the EPO Espacenet site. Each begins with finding keywords to locate proper classification codes.

Some patent searchers prefer the CPC classification search template of the EPO as it searches additional patent content to locate classifications compared to the USPTO site. To be thorough, one should perform the classification search with both online databases. Otherwise, the PubEAST or PubWEST databases found onsite at most PTRCs is another free option.

USPTO's Online Patent Searching PatFT and AppFT Databases (as of January 2019)

There are three primary web pages of the USPTO that are utilized as gateways for our primary searching scenario:

USPTO homepage https://www.uspto.gov

PatFT (PatentFull-Text) page http://patft.uspto.gov/netahtml/PTO/search-bool.html

AppFT (Application Full-Text and Image) page http://appft.uspto.gov/netahtml/PTO/search-bool.html

Conducting a patent search requires brainstorming keywords, using your terms to find initial relevant CPC, reviewing the classification definition linked to the CPC classification. These steps are expanded below.

Step 1. Brainstorm Keywords

The USPTO recommends thinking of terms that describe the invention. A patent searcher should answer a few basic questions in the first step to help brainstorm and come up with words that describe the invention:

- What is the purpose of my invention?
- Is it a process or a product?

- What is it made of? Physical composition?
- How is it used? Method?
- What are common and technical terms used to describe the nature of the invention?

For this search example from the USPTO, the invention is an umbrella.

Purpose: *Umbrella has a new rib design to eliminate an umbrella collapsing or inverting due to high winds.*
Invention: *An improvement in umbrellas to eliminate need for frequent replacement of umbrellas.*
Invention Components: *Framework with ribs, stretchers and a main frame, securing rings, mounting brackets, joint connectors, fabric connectors, fabric, linkage bar.*
How used: *As needed in protection from the elements.*
Other terms (in addition to above): *Parasol, sunshade, support assembly or apparatus, windproof, wind-resistant.*

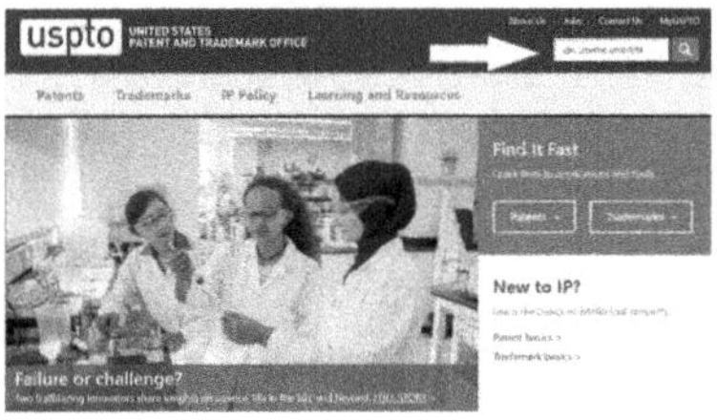

Figure 4.3
USPTO Website Screenshot Heading. (Courtesy U.S. Patent and Trademark Office)

Step 2. Access and Review CPC Scheme

Use your terms to find initial relevant CPC using the USPTO website's search box (https://www.uspto.gov/). In the search box, found in the top right-hand corner of the home page, (see figure 4.3), enter the terms "CPC scheme" plus any keywords(s) describing invention. For example, to find CPC classifications for patents related to umbrellas, you would enter "CPC scheme umbrella" without quotation marks. Scan the resulting classification's scheme that are class schedules to determine the most relevant classification to the invention.

When an inventor gets zero results in this search, suggest substituting the word(s) used to describe the invention with synonyms or alternative terms from those chosen in Step 1. For example, if searching for "CPC scheme car mirror" is not getting satisfactory results, try substituting the word "car" with "vehicle," like this: "CPC scheme vehicle mirror." When the CPC classification search results continue to be disappointing, an inventor could look for search words in the International Patent Classification (IPC) *Official Catchword Index* located at https://www.wipo.int/portal/en

CPC is based on IPC, so classifications found in the *Official Catchword Index* often provide better results. Librarians or specialists should not suggest synonyms for their customers. Instead, reference a thesaurus or catchword index as suggested.

As this book went to press, the USPTO introduced a new CPC searching tool which no longer requires one searching the patent website to include "CPC scheme" with keywords entered for a classification search. The new classification resources gateway is located at https://www.uspto.gov/web/patents/classification/index.htm or found as a CPC classification link under main patent sections displayed at the USPTO home page.

Based upon our umbrella invention, your search should reveal the potential CPC scheme sections show in the snippet view in figure 4.4.

The first listed section "A45B Walking Sticks; Umbrellas; Ladies' or Like Fans" appears to be the best match. Click on that section to get the A45B section in detail shown in figure 4.5 below. Scan the classification titles in the class scheme for A45B looking for the most relevant classification. Dot indents are used to show hierarchical relationships in the scheme. The more dots the more specific the concept is. Some titles may have references in parenthesis following the title that aid in the classification selection.

It seems that A45B 25/22 is a possible good match based on the title "Devices for increasing the resistance of umbrellas to wind." Nothing under A45B 25/22 with two dots is more specific, so this should be a good choice.

Figure 4.4
CPC Scheme Selections Screenshot. (Courtesy U.S. Patent and Trademark Office)

Figure 4.5
Details of Umbrellas Screenshot. (Courtesy U.S. Patent and Trademark Office)

The hierarchy structure of the CPC scheme is similar to an outline for a typical presentation or research paper. It consists of a main topic, major point, sub point, minor point. The *Guide to CPC (Cooperative Classification Classification)*[14] publication by EPO/USPTO demonstrates the structure of the CPC system with each classification consisting of a section, class, subclass, and group. In our umbrella example above, labeled "Devices for increasing the resistance of umbrellas to wind," the letter "A" represents the section; "A45" is the class; "A45B" signifies the subclass level; and "A45B 25/22" is the subgroup within the group level. See figure 4.6 below for details.

The hierarchical level of CPC subgroups is determined by the number of dots as shown below in figure 4.7. The subgroup hierarchy is not determined by the numbering in the symbol of the subgroups. There is an additional dot for each indented subgroup. Indention is a notation for illustrating dependency. The main group has no dots, as it is the highest level for the group. The indent level of a subgroup is displayed as a series of dots immediately preceding the title of the subgroup in the main group schedule.

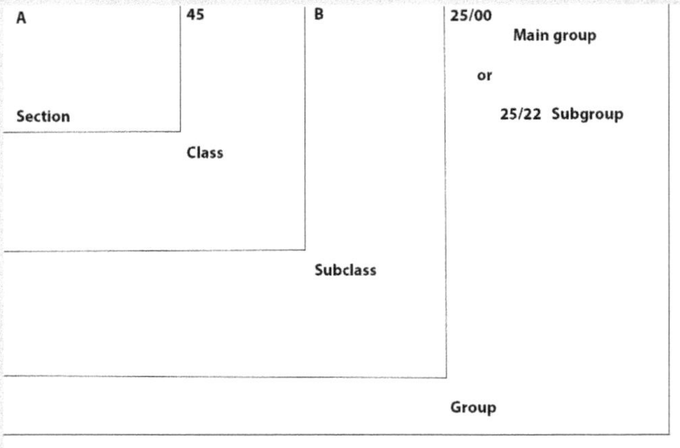

Figure 4.6

CPC Scheme, Main Trunk: Section, Class, Subclass, Group Diagram of Devices for Increasing the Resistance of Umbrellas to Wind. Derivative Based upon Content from Guide to CPC Publication by EPO/USPTO, Version 1.0, Revision 4.00. (Courtesy EPO and USPTO)

Explanation	Symbol	Hierarchical Level	Title
CPC main group	A45B 25/00		Details of umbrellas
CPC subgroup	A45B 25/22	•	Devices for increasing the resistance of umbrellas to winds
CPC subgroup	A45B 25/24	•	Protective coverings for umbrellas when closed
CPC subgroup	A45B 25/26	• •	Ventilated coverings

Figure 4.7

Example of Hierarchical Level of CPC Subgroups. CPC Scheme, Main Trunk: Hierarchical-Level Dots Chart of Devices for Increasing the Resistance of Umbrellas to Wind. Derivative Based upon Content from Guide to CPC Publication by EPO/USPTO, Version 1.0, Revision 4.00. (Courtesy EPO and USPTO)

Step 3. Verify CPC Relevancy

Review classification definition linked to the CPC classification selected. Verify the relevancy of CPC classification found by reviewing the CPC classification definition linked to it, if there is one. The example (figure 4.8) relies solely on images, but some CPC definitions use text.

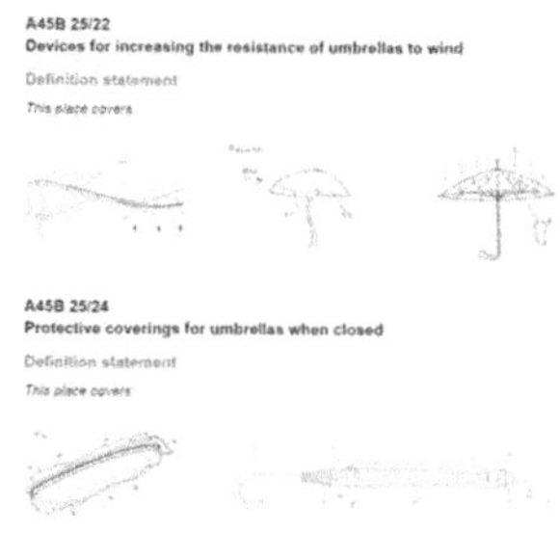

Figure 4.8
CPC Definition Statement Illustration at USPTO website. (Courtesy U.S. Patent and Trademark Office)

Step 4. Retrieve Full-text Patent Documents from PatFT Database

Access and review issued U.S. patents using the selected CPC Classification from the Patents Full-Text and Image (PatFT) database. Return to the USPTO homepage (https://www.uspto.gov/). Click on PatFT under Patents button/tab in Find It Fast section shown in figure 4.9.

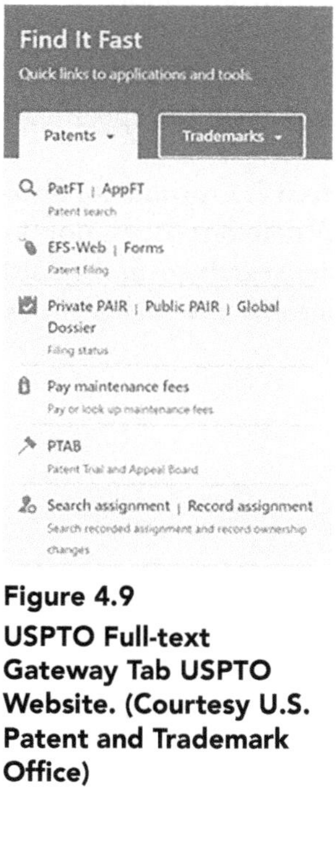

Figure 4.9
USPTO Full-text Gateway Tab USPTO Website. (Courtesy U.S. Patent and Trademark Office)

Once you arrive at the PatFT database site, enter the identified class code in Term 1 Box. It is very important to close the gap in the middle of any CPC class code when doing a PatFT search, so enter our example as "A45B25/22." In the Field 1 drop-down box, select "Current CPC Classification." Leave the Term 2 Box blank. For Select Years, use the drop-down box example below (figure 4.10) to select "1790 to present [entire database]." Click on the Search button.

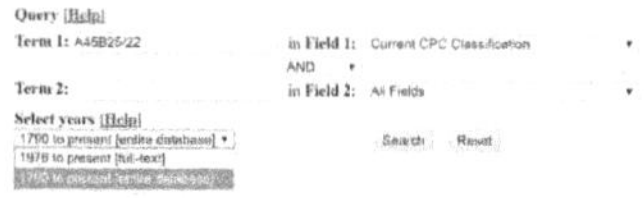

Figure 4.10
USPTO Full-text Search Template USPTO Website. (Courtesy U.S. Patent and Trademark Office)

From the results listing shown in figure 4.11 example below, review the most relevant patent publications listed. Click links to access HTML webpage version of each patent.

Step 5. Conduct Thorough Review of Patents

Using this selected set of most relevant patent publications, review each document (figure 4.12) in-depth for similarity to this example invention, paying close attention to the additional drawing pages, the specification, and *especially the claims*. Every unique feature of an invention should be found in the claims. Claims are the heart of what is protected in a patent. References cited in a patent viewed may lead you to additional relevant patents. Print or download the most relevant U.S. patents found. A PDF version of each patent (figure 4.13) is available. Click on the Images button near the top of the page to access PDF documents.

Results of Search in US Patent Collection db for:
CPC/A45B25/22: 201 patents.
Hits 1 through 50 out of 201

Next 50 Hits

Jump To

Refine Search CPC/A45B25/22

	PAT. NO.		Title
1	10,092,069	T	Umbrella having an anti-inversion mechanism
2	10,064,462	T	Rope guiding device and walking stick chair having the same
3	10,039,352	T	Beach umbrella anchor with an integral shovel
4	9,986,799	T	Wind-proof dual canopy system
5	9,943,148	T	Protector for rib tip of umbrella
6	9,844,250	T	Anti-turning umbrella frame
7	9,839,268	T	Wind-resistant umbrella frame structure
8	9,826,807	T	Umbrella support apparatus
9	9,788,617	T	Pull rib of wind-resistant umbrella
10	9,756,912	T	Wind resistant umbrella
11	9,756,911	T	Wheelchair having an umbrella assembly
12	9,668,554	T	Umbrella having an anti-inversion mechanism

Figure 4.11

USPTO Full-Text Database Results List Top of 200 Patents from CPC Search for A45B25/22. (Courtesy U.S. Patent and Trademark Office)

Otherwise, create a list or spreadsheet to note the patent numbers, titles, and dates to assess patents for final disposition to submit an application.

Step 6. Access and Review Published Patent Applications

Retrieve pending U.S. published patent applications from the AppFT database (http://appft.uspto.gov/netahtml/PTO/search-bool.html). Utilize the same CPC classifications selected in Step 3. Follow the same search approach used in Step 4 of first narrowing down your results to the most relevant patent applications by studying the abstract and representative drawings of each on its front page. Then examine the selected published patent applications closely, paying close attention to the pages of additional drawings, the specifications and especially the claims.

Step 7. Options for Broadening a Patent Search

When one does not locate many inventions like their own, try broadening the search to find additional U.S. patent publications. There are many ways to accomplish this, such as performing a separate keyword search to supplement

USPTO PATENT FULL-TEXT AND IMAGE DATABASE

Home | Quick | Advanced | Pat Num | Help

Hit List | Next List | Next | Bottom

View Cart | Add to Cart

Images

(1 of 201)

United States Patent **10,092,069**
Haythornthwaite , et al. **October 9, 2018**

Umbrella having an anti-inversion mechanism

Abstract

An umbrella has a plurality of ribs attached to a runner by main struts. The umbrella has an anti-inversion mechanism formed of a plurality of anti-inversion struts. Each anti-inversion strut is pivotally coupled to one respective main strut and is pivotally connected to a floating joint member that is freely movable along a length of one respective rib. The anti-inversion mechanism also includes a stop that is fixedly attached to the rib and restricts the degree of travel of the floating joint member along the rib and is positioned to prevent the respective rib from inverting in response to an applied force.

Inventors: **Haythornthwaite; David** (Fujian Province, CN), **Haythornthwaite; Andrew** (Fujian Province, CN)
Applicant: **Name** **City** **State Country Type**

Shedrain Corporation Portland OR US
Assignee: **SHEDRAIN CORPORATION** (Portland, OR)
Family ID: **59275264**
Appl. No.: **15/409,088**
Filed: **January 18, 2017**

Figure 4.12

USPTO Full-Text Database Relevant Patent Publication. (Courtesy U.S. Patent and Trademark Office)

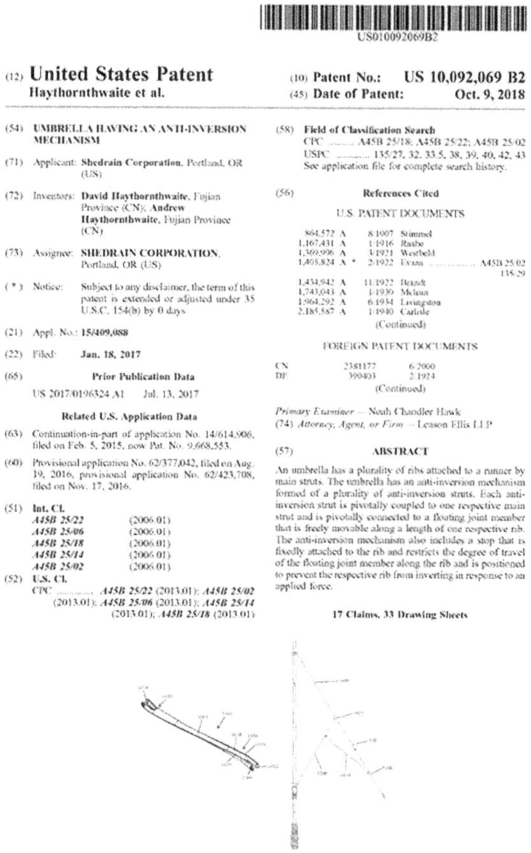

US010092069B2

(12) **United States Patent**
Haythornthwaite et al.

(10) **Patent No.: US 10,092,069 B2**
(45) **Date of Patent: Oct. 9, 2018**

(54) **UMBRELLA HAVING AN ANTI-INVERSION MECHANISM**

(71) Applicant: **Shedrain Corporation**, Portland, OR (US)

(72) Inventors: **David Haythornthwaite**, Fujian Province (CN); **Andrew Haythornthwaite**, Fujian Province (CN)

(73) Assignee: **SHEDRAIN CORPORATION**, Portland, OR (US)

(*) Notice: Subject to any disclaimer, the term of this patent is extended or adjusted under 35 U.S.C. 154(b) by 0 days.

(21) Appl. No.: **15/409,088**

(22) Filed: **Jan. 18, 2017**

(65) **Prior Publication Data**

US 2017/0196324 A1 Jul. 13, 2017

Related U.S. Application Data

(63) Continuation-in-part of application No. 14/614,906, filed on Feb. 5, 2015, now Pat. No. 9,668,553.

(60) Provisional application No. 62/377,042, filed on Aug. 19, 2016, provisional application No. 62/423,708, filed on Nov. 17, 2016.

(51) **Int. Cl.**
A45B 25/22 (2006.01)
A45B 25/06 (2006.01)
A45B 25/18 (2006.01)
A45B 25/14 (2006.01)
A45B 25/02 (2006.01)

(52) **U.S. Cl.**
CPC ***A45B 25/22*** (2013.01); ***A45B 25/02*** (2013.01); ***A45B 25/06*** (2013.01); ***A45B 25/14*** (2013.01); ***A45B 25/18*** (2013.01)

(58) **Field of Classification Search**
CPC A45B 25/18; A45B 25/22; A45B 25/02
USPC 135/27, 32, 33.5, 38, 39, 40, 42, 43
See application file for complete search history.

(56) **References Cited**

U.S. PATENT DOCUMENTS

864,572 A		8/1907	Stimmel	
1,167,431 A		1/1916	Raabe	
1,369,996 A		3/1921	Westbeld	
1,405,824 A	*	2/1922	Evans	A45B 25/02 135/29
1,434,942 A		11/1922	Brandt	
1,743,043 A		1/1930	Mclean	
1,964,292 A		6/1934	Livingston	
2,185,587 A		1/1940	Carlisle	

(Continued)

FOREIGN PATENT DOCUMENTS

CN	2381177	6/2000
DE	390403	2/1924

(Continued)

Primary Examiner — Noah Chandler Hawk
(74) *Attorney, Agent, or Firm* — Leason Ellis LLP

(57) **ABSTRACT**

An umbrella has a plurality of ribs attached to a runner by main struts. The umbrella has an anti-inversion mechanism formed of a plurality of anti-inversion struts. Each anti-inversion strut is pivotally coupled to one respective main strut and is pivotally connected to a floating joint member that is freely movable along a length of one respective rib. The anti-inversion mechanism also includes a stop that is fixedly attached to the rib and restricts the degree of travel of the floating joint member along the rib and is positioned to prevent the respective rib from inverting in response to an applied force.

17 Claims, 33 Drawing Sheets

Figure 4.13

U.S. Patent 10,092,069 "Umbrella Having and Anti-Inversion Mechanism" PDF Front-Page Image. (Courtesy U.S. Patent and Trademark Office)

your CPC listing of patents found. Keyword searching could be more effective for new technologies for which classifications have not yet been established. In addition, keyword searching might retrieve a few patents missed from a CPC search.

Perhaps utilizing other databases or classifications are worthwhile, too. For example, conducting a supplementary search utilizing the EPO's Espacenet database is covered next in this chapter. In addition, one could apply the former USPC to search pre-2015 U.S. utility patents. See a patent librarian at a PTRC for information about the USPC classifications. Also, details about the USPC are found at the USPTO website (https://www.uspto.gov/patents-application-process/patent-search/classification-standards-and-development). As inventions could also be found in nonpatent resources, try searching items such as books, journals, websites, and other technical literature disclosures of inventions at your nearest PTRC (https://www.uspto.gov/learning-and-resources/support-centers/patent-and-trademark-resource-centers-ptrc/ptrc-locations).

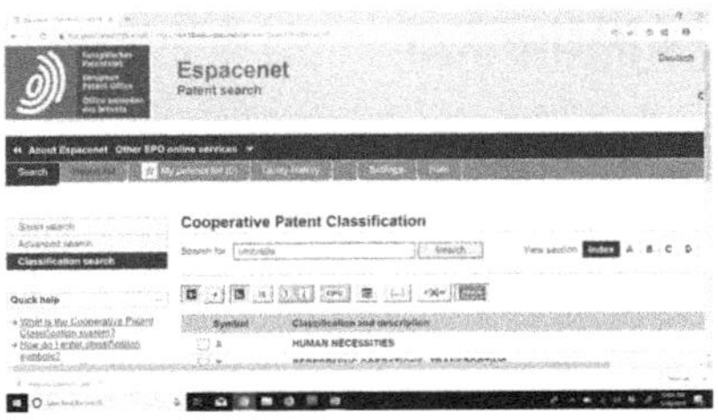

Figure 4.14
Espacenet Cooperative Patent Classification Search Gateway. (Courtesy Espacenet at the European Patent Office)

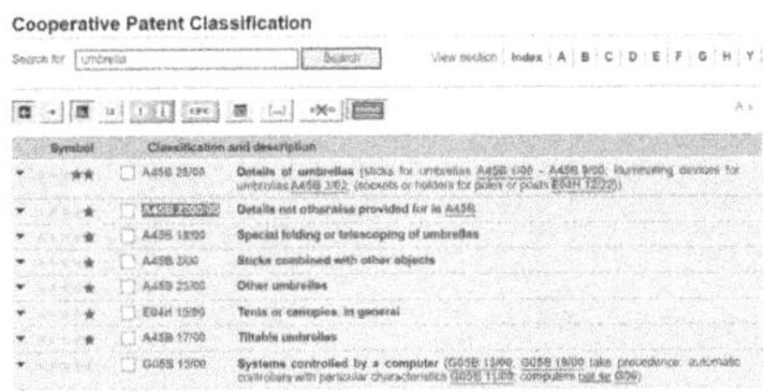

Figure 4.15
CPC Scheme Sections for Umbrella Inventions. (Courtesy of Espacenet at the European Patent Office)

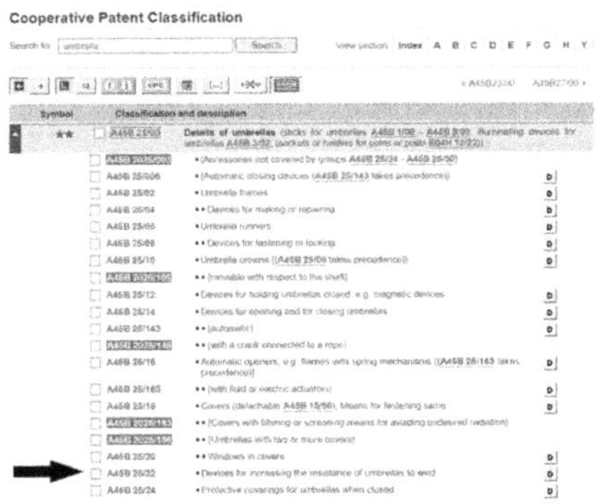

Figure 4.16
Cooperative Patent Classification Search Results for "Umbrella." (Courtesy of Espacenet at the European Patent Office)

If inventors have still not found inventions similar to theirs, then they probably have not done a thorough enough search and must try again. Remember, although an idea may be truly new and original, inventors should find similar inventions to include in their patent application.

Espacenet Database Alternative Searching Method

As discussed earlier, one should consider a supplementary search of CPC classes in the EPO's Espacenet database for an exhaustive classification search. Some patent searchers perform the USPTO's *Seven Step Strategy* in both the USPTO and EPO databases to be thorough. The following are the same seven steps—but applied for use with the EPO's Espacenet free patent searching database.

1. Brainstorm keywords and subject terms that describe an invention based upon its purpose, composition, and use. See hypothetical umbrella search scenario above for keyword examples.
2. Access and review CPC scheme using the Espacenet CPC webpage (figure 4.14) at https://worldwide.espacenet.com/classification?locale=en_EP. Or keyword search: CPC and Espacenet from a search engine such as Google® or Bing® to locate the CPC gateway at Espacenet. Enter the search term "umbrella."

   There is no need to include the search term "CPC scheme" as with the USPTO site, as this is the CPC classification home. Merely entering keyword(s) such as "umbrella" is enough to locate CPC classes. Based upon our umbrella invention, your search should reveal the potential CPC scheme sections shown in figure 4.15.

Results are shown in order of relevance. Star symbols indicate the most relevant. The first listed section A45B 25/00 appears to be the best match. Click the highest relevance classification to reveal the entire classification scheme under A45B 25/00. You may need to return to this step to search other higher star relevancies for a comprehensive review. On the new page displayed above (figure 4.16), scan the classification titles in the class scheme for A45B 25/00 looking for the most relevant classification.

As we discovered in our USPTO site search earlier, A45B 25/22 is a possible good match based on the title "Devices for increasing the resistance of umbrellas to wind."

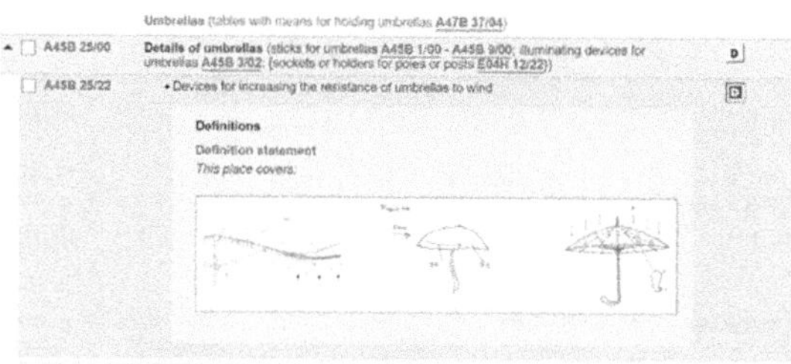

Figure 4.17

Definition Statement Illustration at Espacenet Site. (Courtesy of Espacenet at the European Patent Office)

3. Review classification definition linked to the CPC classification you selected. Verify the relevancy of CPC classification found by reviewing the CPC Classification Definition linked. The example above (figure 4.17) relies solely on images, while some CPC definitions display text.

Figure 4.18

Patents Retrieved. (Courtesy of Espacenet at the European Patent Office)

4. Retrieve and review issued U.S. patents using the selected CPC classification A45B 25/22 from the PatFT database (https://www.uspto.gov/). Or remain at the Espacenet site and check mark the box next to the CPC classification A45B 25/22. The CPC class will automatically appear in a gray box on the left, as shown in figure 4.18.

   If the Find Patents button is clicked in figure 4.18, a full list of U.S. and foreign patents will appear. However, to limit your list to a smaller and more manageable group of U.S. patents, you should click on the Copy to Search Form button. On the following template displayed in figure 4.19, simply add the letters "US" on the Publication Number box. Then press the Search button at the bottom of the template page.

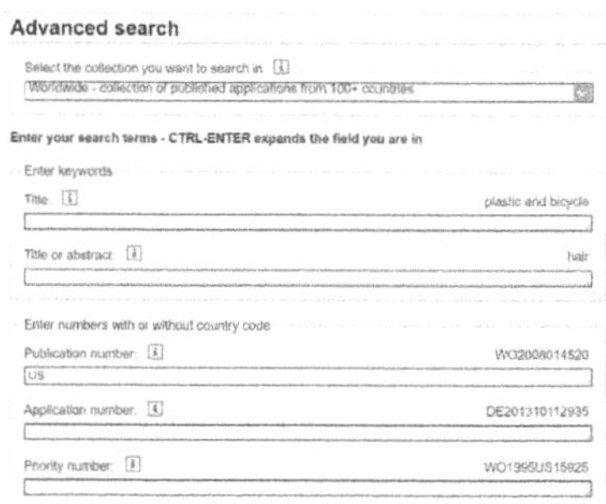

Figure 4.19

Copy to Search Form. (Courtesy of Espacenet at the European Patent Office)

   A listing of U.S. umbrella patents is shown in figure 4.20.

5. Using this selected set of most relevant patent publications displayed in figure 4.20, review each document in-depth (figure 4.21) for similarity to this example invention, paying close attention to the drawings pages, the specifications, and especially the claims. Remember, claims are the heart of the patent.
6. Retrieve pending U.S. published patent applications with the CPC classification selected in Step 3 in the AppFT database (http://appft.uspto.gov/netahtml/PTO/search-bool.html). Otherwise, if you use the Espacenet site, you have already viewed applications, as these are displayed simultaneously in Step 5 above.

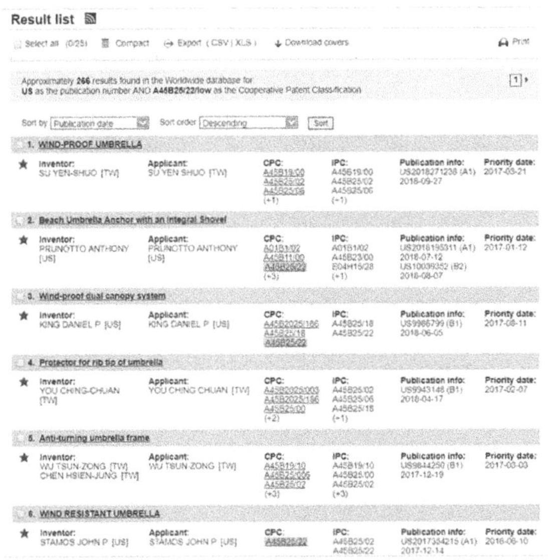

Figure 4.20
Search Results. (Courtesy of Espacenet at the European Patent Office)

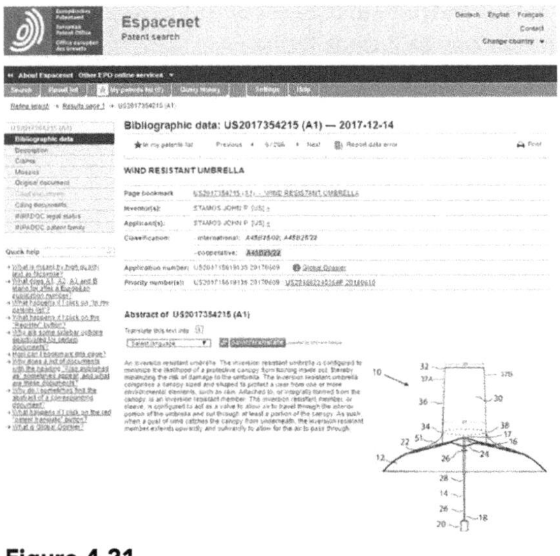

Figure 4.21
Review Each Relevant Patent. (Courtesy of Espacenet at the European Patent Office)

7. Broaden your search to find additional U.S. patent publications using keyword searching in either the USPTO or Espacenet databases. However, you will need to use the Espacenet database to locate foreign patents. Once again, try searching for other disclosures of inventions using the free electronic and print resources of your nearest PTRC.

HELP BEYOND THE IP LIBRARIAN

When the search moves beyond an IP librarian's or an inventor's capabilities, a patent attorney or agent may be an inventor's best friend. The legal language of patent application preparation is a challenge, as covered in the previous chapter. It is highly advisable for inventors and entrepreneurs to see a local patent attorney or agent. As an inventor wants a successful patent application, a patent attorney is more experienced in preparing patent applications. A librarian will then need to show the inventor how to find a local patent attorney.

There is a USPTO attorney and agent listing database at https://oedci.uspto.gov/OEDCI/practitionerSearchEntry. From this site, enter your city and state. Then locate an attorney or agent registered with the USPTO from your city. If there is no listing from your city, try to find another city nearby. This list is helpful to refer inventors to when they ask for references to find an attorney or agent, because it doesn't tie the librarian to the recommendation. You will not be making a reference, merely providing directions on how to use the USPTO attorney and agent listing database.

Other types of patent searches besides a prior art search for prospective patents of new inventions include infringement/validity or right-to-use searches and patent landscape analysis for competitive intelligence. A patent infringement/validity search is another type of search utilized for a defendant in a patent infringement lawsuit to locate information that would invalidate the patent for which they were alleged of an infringement. A validity search involves re-reviewing the prior art and patents cited for the granted patent by a patent office. The goal is to show that the patent office would not have approved the application if the examiner had known about any newly discovered prior art. Conversely, the plaintiff patentee may want to validate the patent by confirming that others could not locate invalidating prior art.[15]

As a preventive measure during product development, an advanced patent searcher may want to execute a patent infringement or right-to-use clearance search to discover whether an invention infringes any valid, in-force patents. An inventor might even perform this type of search as an initial step in deciding whether to develop a particular invention. An infringement search is much narrower in scope than a preliminary patent search which covers all prior art.[16]

Another common type of patent searching is a patent landscape analysis for competitive intelligence. Such an investigation of patents provides an overview or snapshot of patents in a specific subject area or technology. It helps to identify and understand product development of competitors and new market opportunities. Chapter 10 on special libraries covers this type of business patent searching.

All these searches discussed above are much more advanced than the preliminary prior art patent searching discussed in this chapter. As stated often in this book, it is highly advisable for a layperson, such as an independent inventor or general business associate, to obtain the services of an experienced patent attorney or agent for these highly complicated types of specialty searches. However, it's vital for an inventor, entrepreneur, or business to be knowledgeable of all potential prior arts in the IP mine field of his or her new innovation.

ADVANCED PATENT SEARCHING POSSIBILITIES

When one utilizes general information databases from a library, one often encounters simplified interfaces that resemble Google® and Bing® search engines. At the very least, Boolean operators are included such as "and," "or," and "not." When demonstrating classification searching for patents on USPTO or Espacenet databases, the "and" Boolean operator is utilized more often to narrow down overwhelming results listing of patents. Espacenet offers its Smart search interface, which is a Google-like method of searching with no need to think about Boolean operators. These databases all provide searching fields for patent numbers, titles and abstracts, inventor names, specifications and claims, classification schemes, publication dates, and so on.

Consequently, when one needs to narrow the vast list of patents found from his or her initial keyword or classification search, the utilization of advanced searching interfaces and techniques are helpful. At the time of this book preparation, the

USPTO offers a Quick Search interface as well as an Advanced Search option for both its PatFT and AppFT databases. In addition, there is a separate Patent Number Search page for looking up a single patent document. The EPO's Espacenet database offers a default Smart Search, an Advanced Search template, and a Classification Search option. In addition, most PTRCs offer two advanced patent searching databases onsite, PubEAST and PubWEST, which are the same databases that the USPTO patent examiners utilize to complete patent examinations of applications. We will apply advanced patent searching guidelines for assisting patent searchers with the USPTO website and Espacenet. The Espacenet database is, most likely, what future versions of the USPTO database will ultimately resemble. That is why we include both database examples here.

To illustrate the advanced searching options on these sites, let's start with the basics. If our library customer has invented a better mousetrap with electronic features, he or she might use the following search terms, mouse and trap, to find how many mousetrap patents exists. Unfortunately, there are over twenty thousand associated U.S. patents. To begin to narrow this search, one might add related synonyms such as "electric," "battery," and "power," to narrow the number of patents. For example, mouse and trap and (electric or battery or power). Notice how parentheses are utilized to nest synonyms together to supplement the primary terms. If one enters this on the USPTO Advance Search interface, it only narrows the search to over eight thousand patents. The USPTO site structure allows one to narrow one's search to individual fields found within the patents with Field Codes listed at the Advanced Search page, as shown in figure 4.22.

Field Code	Field Name	Field Code	Field Name	Field Code	Field Name
PN	Patent Number	PRAD	Priority Filing Date	AN	Assignee Name
ISD	Issue Date	PCT	PCT Information	AC	Assignee City
TTL	Title	PTAD	PCT Filing Date	AS	Assignee State
ABST	Abstract	PT3D	PCT 371c124 Date	ACN	Assignee Country
ACLM	Claim(s)	PPPD	Prior Published Document Date	EXP	Primary Examiner
SPEC	Description/Specification	REIS	Reissue Data	EXA	Assistant Examiner
CCL	Current US Classification	RPAF	Reissued Patent Application Filing Date	REF	Referenced By
CPC	Current CPC Classification	AFFF	130(b) Affirmation Flag	FREF	Foreign References
CPCL	Current CPC Classification Class	AFFT	130(b) Affirmation Statement	OREF	Other References
ICL	International Classification	IN	Inventor Name	COFC	Certificate of Correction
APN	Application Serial Number	IC	Inventor City	REEX	Re-Examination Certificate
APD	Application Date	IS	Inventor State	PTAB	PTAB Trial Certificate
APT	Application Type	ICN	Inventor Country	SEC	Supplemental Exam Certificate
GOVT	Government Interest	AANM	Applicant Name	ILRN	International Registration Number
FMID	Patent Family ID	AACI	Applicant City	ILRD	International Registration Date
PARN	Parent Case Information	AAST	Applicant State	ILPD	International Registration Publication Date
RLAP	Related US App. Data	AACO	Applicant Country	ILFD	Hague International Filing Date
RLFD	Related Application Filing Date	AAAT	Applicant Type		
PRIR	Foreign Priority	LREP	Attorney or Agent		

Figure 4.22

USPTO Full-text Database Advanced Search Field Codes. (Courtesy U.S. Patent and Trademark Office)

To apply a field code, one merely prefaces one's search terms with a field code followed by a forward slash. As demonstrated in our example above, if one does not select a specific field, the text of the entire patent is searched. So if we enter the following search utilizing the Specification (spec/) field: spec/(mouse and trap and (electric or battery or power)), over six thousand patents are found. Conversely, if we apply the same search to the narrower Abstract (abst/) field: abst/(mouse and trap and (electric or battery or power)), only three patents are found.

However, one must use caution when applying field codes to a search, as your choice could broaden or narrow your search results found as shown in figure 4.23. In most instances utilizing the Title (ttl/) and/or Abstract (abst/) fields are effective for narrowing most overwhelming patent search lists. Yet searching only title or abstract fields could overlook important documents. If one must narrow one's search, then Abstract is often the preferred choice over Title.

Just as right truncations or wildcards are helpful to retrieve variant word endings in other information databases, this is also very helpful with advanced patent searching. Currently the USPTO site offers the dollar sign "$" symbol for such needs. Applied to our electronic mousetrap, this could add missing patents that utilize plural or other suffixed variations to the accompanying synonyms keywords: abst/(mouse and trap and (elec$ or batter$ or power$)), eight patents were found, which is five additional patents beyond the originally located three above. Keep in mind our hypothetical search scenarios above are by no means comprehensive prior art searching. It is only for demonstration purposes of advanced patent searching techniques. For instance, the plural word for mouse is mice, so the wildcard approach might not apply. An "or" Boolean combination with mouse or mice would be recommended. Other synonyms for mouse could include rodent and rat.

The USPTO site offers date range limiters and phrase searching with quotation marks. It is important to note that phrases with quotation marks cannot be truncated. Currently the USPTO site does not offer proximity operators, so one should

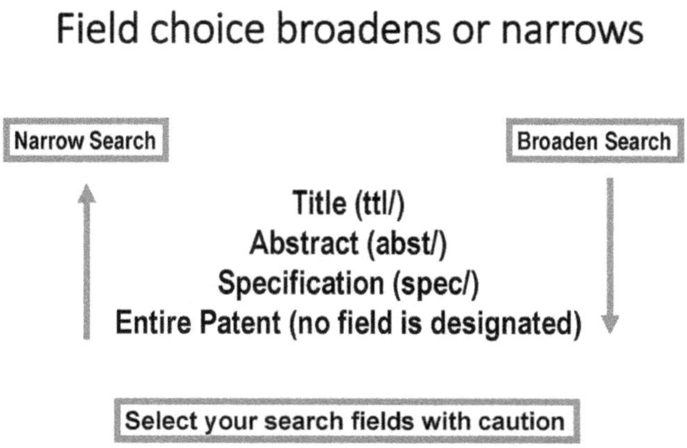

Figure 4.23
Field Codes to Search. (Original Artwork of Author)

use caution when using phrases. Searching for specific phrases may lead to missing patents with words inverted or separated within a sentence.

The advanced patent databases PubEAST and PubWEST, available at most PTRCs, offer proximity operators and other advanced searching capabilities. Espacenet also offers limited proximity operators for narrowing one's search. For more about using the Advance Search interface at the USPTO site, see http://patft.uspto.gov/netahtml/PTO/help/help.htm.

Ideally, a library patent searching customer should be able to combine his or her CPC classification searches with the advanced search techniques covered here to complete a comprehensive prior art search of his or her invention. This should help the customer decide on pursuing a patent application with a patent attorney or agent registered with the USPTO.

Espacenet is the European equivalent of the USPTO website. It was developed by the EPO with member states of the European Patent Organisation. Espacenet offers advanced patent searching features similar to those of the USPTO site. Espacenet provides free access to over one hundred million patent documents from around the world. There is even a way to separate U.S. patents and applications from other countries in your searching implementations. Besides an easier to navigate CPC classification interface, it also offers a single line Smart Search template, as well as Advanced Search.

The Espacenet Advanced Search template does not offer the same search query precision as the Advanced Search interface on the USPTO. Nevertheless, when supplemented with the USPTO PatFT and AppFT databases, it makes a good database team to search prior art patents. It is primarily a tool to help narrow your CPC scheme searches, which are more flexible to find on Espacenet. Once one locates one's appropriate CPC code for the classification of the invention, a Selected Classification prompt directly integrates with a Copy to Search Form on the actual Advanced Search page. When one presses the Copy to Search Form button, it automatically enters the CPC classification code onto the Advanced Search template. At that point, one is able to narrow one's patents to a specific country or enter other terms. Fields such as keyword in title, abstract, or full text are supportive for such refinement of patent listings. In addition, other fields include dates, inventor name, applicant name, and publication numbers.

Espacenet offer a free form Smart search template, which provides keyword searching in the title and/or abstract of a patent. One can also built a Contextual Query Language (CQL) command-line statement using field identifiers, Boolean, proximity, and comparison operators. Right, or suffix, truncation includes three options for varying number ranges of characters. One can search full text in an abstract, specification (description), or claims with appropriate field identifiers.

The Espacenet result listings offer cutting-edge features normally only found on commercial databases. For example, there is direct integration of a CPC popup when viewing a listing of patents. This allows a quick glance at classification details without leaving the patent results listing. A preferred "My Patents List" feature is useful to save favorite patents on one's computer. Plus, a selected list of patents may be exported to an Excel spreadsheet for compilation of relevant patents found. For more details, see Espacenet's help tab at https://worldwide.espacenet.com/ or a list of user guides at https://www.epo.org/searching-for-patents/technical/espacenet.html#tab-1.

Additional free-access patent searching databases exist, such as Google Patents, Patentscope, Free Patents Online, and so forth. Each have their pros and cons, but are worth reviewing to see if they offer features that meet your unique needs. When utilized together, the free USPTO site and EPO's Espacenet offer U.S. inventors and entrepreneurs an ideal platform to perform a preliminary prior art search to determine the patent feasibility of their inventions.

CONCLUSION

This chapter has covered patent searching for inventors and entrepreneurs. It introduced PTRC libraries and their relationships with the PTRC Program. Most importantly, you should feel comfortable in instructing library customers in how to do a preliminary, prior-art patent search via free online databases such as the USPTO site and Espacenet. All of this IP information background allows you to provide effective IP information literacy through reference and library instruction. This supports inventors and entrepreneurs in their patent searching and related IP information needs. It is suggested that you conduct IP reference and library instruction for both IP creators and customers through outreach programming, as advised throughout this book. The next chapter covers trademarks.

NOTES

1. Indiana University Bloomington, "Patent Filings by Women Have Risen the Fastest in Academia, IU Study Finds," IU Bloomington Newsroom, July 8, 2015, http://archive.news.indiana.edu/releases/iu/2015/07/women-patents.shtml (accessed October 22, 2015).
2. Fox Television, *The Simpsons*, Season Ten, Episode 205, "Wizard of Evergreen Terrace," September 20, 1998.
3. U.S. Patent & Trademark Office (USPTO), "USPTO Rebrands National Library Network as Patent and Trademark Resource Centers," New and Updates, September 28, 2011, https://www.uspto.gov/about-us/news-updates/uspto-rebrands-national-library-network-patent-and-trademark-resource-centers (accessed April 1, 2018).
4. John Schlipp, "Best Practices and *InventorFest*: Community Partners and Patent and Trademark Depository Libraries (PTDLs)," *Intellectual Property (IP) Journal of the PTDLA* 4.2 (November 2007); Jeffrey L. Furman, Markus Nagler, and Martin Watzinger, "Disclosure and Subsequent Innovation: Evidence from the Patent Depository Library Program," NBER Working Paper no. 24660, May 2018, https://www.nber.org/papers/w24660 (accessed June 6, 2018).
5. American Library Association, Code of Ethics of the American Library Association, Principle 4, "We Respect Intellectual Property Rights and Advocate Balance between the Interest of Information Users and Rights Holders," 2008, http://www.ala.org/tools/ethics (accessed September 23, 2018).
6. American Association of School Librarians, *Standards for the 21st-Century Learner*, section regarding respecting copyright and intellectual property of other, and sections

on ethical use and legal use of information (Chicago: American Association of School Librarians, 2007), 4, 6, 7.

7. Association of College & Research Libraries, *Framework for Information Literacy for Higher Education*, Frame: Information Has Value, "As Creators and Users of Information, Experts Understand Their Rights and Responsibilities when Participating in a Community of Scholarship" (Chicago: Association of College and Research Libraries, 2016), http://www.ala.org/acrl/standards/ilframework (accessed September 23, 2018), 16.

8. American Association of School Librarians, AASL Standards Framework for Learners, "Frame 6, 'Engage: Demonstrate Safe, Legal, and Ethical Creating and Sharing of Knowledge Products Independently while Engaging in a Community of Practice and an Interconnected World," 2018, https://standards.aasl.org/wp-content/uploads/2017/11/AASL-Standards-Framework-for-Learners-pamphlet.pdf (accessed September 23, 2018).

9. Patent & Trademark Resource Center Program, "Patents: The Collection for All Reasons," 2011, information flyer.

10. For more about the ALA Code of Ethics and providing information service, see *RQ* 31 (Summer Issue 1992): 554–555, prepared by the Standards and Guidelines Committee, Reference and Adult Services Division, American Library Association, 1992.

11. Kevin Harwell, "Legal Issues Relating to Patent Searching in Publicly Accessible Libraries," *Journal of Government Information* 25, no. 2 (1998): 34.

12. Rich Goldstein, *ABA Consumer Guide to Obtaining a Patent: A Practical Resource for Helping Entrepreneurs & Innovators Protect Their Ideas* (Chicago: American Bar Association, 2016), 28.

13. USPTO, "Seven Step Strategy" (for conducting preliminary searches of U.S. patents and published applications), https://www.uspto.gov/learning-and-resources/support-centers/patent-and-trademark-resource-centers-ptrc/resources/seven (accessed October 27, 2018).

14. European Patent Office and USPTO, "Guide to CPC (Cooperative Patent Classification)," publication by EPO/USPTO, Version 1.0, Revision 4.00, https://www.cooperativepatentclassification.org/publications/GuideToTheCPC.pdf (accessed October 27, 2018).

15. Thomas Wolff, "What's So Special about Patent Invalidity Searching?," *Online* (July/August 2012): 28–33.

16. Richard Stim, *Patent, Copyright & Trademark: An Intellectual Property Desk Reference*, 12th edition (Berkeley, CA: Nolo, 2012), 96–97.

Chapter 5

TRADEMARKS

CHAPTER OBJECTIVES

- To be able to describe what a trademark is and explain its purpose and function
- To become familiar with the history of marks including the Lanham Act
- To explore trademark law in relation to the needs of libraries and library customers
- To recognize unique nontraditional trademarks
- To recognize library customers that need the trademark searching support of Patent & Trademark Resource Center (PTRC)
- To be able to instruct library customers of the importance and benefits of trademark searching via free United States Patent and Trademark Office (USPTO) and other free online state databases
- To understand how the registration and maintenance process works
- To understand trademark fair use as it is related to freedom of expression from the first amendment
- To be familiar with additional related topics including licensing, right of publicity, domain names, and so forth

INTRODUCTION

Paul Goldstein states, "If copyright is the law of authorship and patent is the law of invention, trademark is the law of consumer marketing."[1] It was not until the beginning of the twenty-first century that trademarks became so significantly tied to smaller businesses and entrepreneur start-ups. The trademark of a small business is perhaps one of its most important assets in today's global and online economy. No longer do all local businesses rely on local market activities. Many rely on infinite online customers outside of their local turf. So even a local, small business must be aware of its name or trademarks in relation to the vast online competition nationally, or even globally, to avoid potential infringement issues.

A perfect example of small businesses needing to protect their trademarks is revealed in news headlines discussing how some smaller chocolate confectionary businesses have been daunted with "cease and desist" letters by a larger, well-known chocolate bar manufacturer regarding alleged trademark issues. As many smaller mom-and-pop candy companies lack the resources of a chocolate giant like the one from Pennsylvania, they often settle out of court.

However, a fledgling gourmet chocolatier from New York City would not back down after getting a stern "cease and desist" letter from the chocolate giant alleging trademark infringement. The artisanal chocolatier felt the trademark "customer confusion" infringement accusation was unfounded. The giant chocolate company believed that the chocolatier's luscious Champagne Kiss chocolate truffle squares, with faux red lipstick smooch marks, diluted the trademark of its well-known brand of inexpensive foil-wrapped, flat-bottomed teardrop chocolates. The New York gourmet chocolate shop continued to sell the Champagne Kisses for Valentine's Day. It appeared that the larger chocolate manufacturer backed down.[2]

What does this David and Goliath story teach us? Lack of IP awareness, including trademarks, is detrimental for both new and established smaller businesses. Even when established small to midsized companies have regionally marketed their brands for decades, an examination of its IP, such as trademarks in this case, could avoid such legal hassles. This chapter covers such protective measures like understanding basic trademark law and trademark searching. This information helps a business to determine whether another entity is already utilizing a similar trademark. Such facts are vital for small to midsized businesses that call on PTRCs or libraries offering assistance with these types of IP resources.

A trademark is a word, name, slogan, design, symbol—or even a color, smell, product configuration, or combination of any of these—that identifies and distinguishes the business or provider of goods or services. Trademarks registered with the USPTO are marked with an encircled letter "®," while those registered by a state government or common-law use are marked with a "TM" after the trademarked name or symbol.

The USPTO describes common-law rights existing from actual use of a mark.[3] Common law allows posting a TM symbol without registration, but it is not as secure as registration with the federal government or a state government agency. You may also hear the expression "service mark" or see the tag "SM," which is basically the same. Where trademarks apply to product or brand identifiers, service marks apply to services by indicating the source of the service rather than a product. For example, Target® is a service mark of a retail service, while Tide® is a trademark identifier of a laundry detergent product. A name or logo associated with a plumbing service is another example of a service mark, such as Roto-Rooter®, while the Nike® product name and swoosh logo illustrates a typical trademark. To simplify this further, a trademark identifies a product created by a business, while a service mark identifies a service offered by the business.

From an economic standpoint, according to ipwatchdog.com, "a trademark is just a symbol that allows a purchaser to identify goods or services that have been acceptable in the past and reject goods or services that have failed to live up to the desired standards, which will vary from consumer to consumer."[4] Innovative trademarks have always been vital to successfully identify the goods or services of a business. In fact, nearly one-quarter of all new businesses reported trademarks as the most commonly maintained form of intellectual property (IP), according to Kaufmann Firm Studies.[5] Such data implies that trademarks offer the best chance of making a good first impression with new business start-ups.

This chapter prepares those IP library specialists interacting with entrepreneurs and small businesses who are more likely to need support with the trademark resources of the USPTO and state agencies, such as secretary of state offices. Federal and state trademarks have different database records, guidelines, agencies, and fees. To qualify for registration, a mark must be unique and actively used. This applies to trademarks of both nonprofit and for-profit organizations. If an organization or individual holder continues to use the mark in commerce and pay its maintenance fees, the mark could be owned and used forever. Other related topics in this chapter include U.S. trademark law basics, searching trademarks, registration and maintenance of marks, freedom of expression issues, licensing and right of publicity matters, internet domain names, and protecting one's mark against fakes and counterfeit goods.

BRIEF HISTORICAL TIMELINE OF TRADEMARKS (INCLUDING LANHAM ACT)

Marks of varying types have been around for as long as man has needed to identify things. For instance, Western movies show how cattle were branded for ownership designation. Ownership of animals has even been documented on cave drawings of early man as far back as 5,000 BCE. Pottery from First Dynasty Egypt has marks believed to be ownership marks. Among the earliest widely recognized trademarks were those stamped on swords and weaponry created by blacksmiths, as well as building bricks, pottery, lamps, and even loaves of bread made during the Roman Empire.

Separate states in the United States have offered trademarks since the early 1800s. However, trademarked brands as we know today became more common by 1870. In that year, the first federal legislation for trademarks was introduced. In addition, the *Official Gazette* was first published to report trademarks granted by the USPTO. The foundation of the current trademark law in the United States is the Lanham Act of 1946.[6] According to the McKinney Engineering Library, a PTRC at the University of Texas at Austin, the purpose of the Lanham Act was "to eliminate unfair competition in marketing goods and services and to provide the owners of marks protection against confusion of similar marks."[7]

To visualize the progression of the historical development of branded marks, look at our Trademark History Timeline, based on an online timeline from the

Figure 5.1
Trademark History Timeline. (Courtesy McKinney Engineering Library at University of Texas at Austin)

McKinney Engineering Library website (http://legacy.lib.utexas.edu/engin/trademark/timeline/tmindex.html).

Reviewing this trademark timeline (figure 5.1), one can see that marks have existed since the cave painting of prehistoric humans around 5,000 BCE. This is the estimated year the earliest marks were found to designate presumed ownership of bison. The range of years where the economic use of trademarks documented on bricks in the Roman Empire was 500 BCE to 500 CE. The year of the earliest English law on trademarks was known as Bakers Marking Law in 1266 for baker merchants.

Trademark legislation was passed in 1870 in the United States based on the commerce clause of the Constitution. The Lanham Act became a law in 1946. It is the contemporary statutory framework for federal examination and registration of trademarks. A mark must demonstrate actual use in commerce (or intent to use within a reasonable time) to receive a federal registration. This is officially known as "use in commerce." Section 1127 of the Act currently defines "use in commerce" as: "the bona fide use of a mark in the ordinary course of trade, and not made merely to reserve a right in a mark."[8] In particular,

> a mark shall be deemed to be in use in commerce—
>
> 1. on goods when—
>   a) it is placed in any manner on the goods or their containers or the displays associated therewith or on the tags or labels affixed thereto, or if the nature of the goods makes such placement impracticable, then on documents associated with the goods or their sale, and
>   b) the goods are sold or transported in commerce, and
> 2. on services when it is used or displayed in the sale or advertising of services and the services are rendered in commerce, or the services are rendered in more than one State or in the United States and a foreign country and the person rendering the services is engaged in commerce in connection with the services."[9]

The "use in commerce" requirement is the threshold to the trademark rights of the trademark owner. It stems from the fact that the federal government has no constitutional authority to regulate marks that are utilized within a single state border. The federal government may only regulate goods or services that travel across state or international borders or that involve commerce across these boundaries. This is rooted in the Trade-Mark Supreme Court Cases 100 U.S. 82 (1879) that were a set of three cases consolidated into a single appeal that ruled that the Copyright Clause[10] of the U.S. Constitution gave Congress no power to regulate trademark. This resulted in the Trade Mark Act of 1881,[11] based on the Commerce Clause,[12] that was determined to be constitutional. The *Trademark Manual of Examining Procedure (TMEP)* also affirms that offering services via the internet is considered interstate use in commerce.[13] Use in commerce is important to relate to the trademark search and registration with the USPTO covered later in this chapter.

According to the Constitution statement covered in Chapter 1: "The Congress shall have power. . . . To promote the progress of science and useful arts, by securing for limited times to authors and inventors the exclusive right to their respective writings and discoveries . . ."[14] from *Article One, Section 8(8) of the U.S. Constitution*, Federal Convention of 1787. Notice that the Constitution does not include anything about branding or trade markings. However, patents and federal trademarks are granted by the USPTO under the U.S. Department of Commerce, which is an executive branch of the federal government. As mentioned in Chapters 1 and 2, copyrights are registered by the Copyright Office at the Library of Congress, which is a part of the legislative branch of the federal government.

LEGAL ESSENTIALS FOR SELECTING A STRONG MARK AND AVOIDING INFRINGEMENT

It is helpful for IP specialists and their customers to have a basic understanding of the legal facts of trademarks for those selecting a mark or trying to avoid a potential infringement. The following is a very brief legal overview. When library customers have detailed questions related to these legal matters, refer them to factual online resources, such as the USPTO's Trademark Basics guide at https://www.uspto.gov/trademarks-getting-started/trademark-basics. In addition, you might encourage them to find a local, licensed attorney specializing in trademarks for further support. Moreover, most libraries and booksellers offer legal self-help books, which are perfect to address such advanced questions.

For a legal introduction to trademarks, try to study our topic in the context of the IP owners and users. Just as copyrights and patents have two sides, the same applies with trademarks.

Principally, library customers may need to know how to avoid infringing on other trademarks when staring a new business. Yet such customers potentially are creators of their own new unique marks, which need to be strong, distinctive marks to be eligible for federal registration. Trademark infringement is defined by the USPTO as "the unauthorized use of a trademark or service mark on or in connection with goods and/or services in a manner that is likely to cause confusion, deception, or mistake about the source of the goods and/or services."[15] Typical infringement scenarios include finding out that a competitor has an identical or similar branded mark for a comparable product or service. Or a business gets a firm cease-and-desist letter from another company's legal counsel alleging infringement. On the other hand, fair use could apply with certain library customers when using trademarks to describe their expression in copyrighted works such as books and media. In addition, some marks could be ethically controversial as covered later in this chapter.

Besides state trademark registrations and common law trademarks by use, as covered earlier, the federal Lanham Act,[16] a statute also known as the Trademark Act of 1946, is what this chapter follows for federal registration and trademark searching information. Following the Lanham Act and other registration requirements found at the USPTO site are helpful in obtaining a federal trademark registration as well as avoiding potential infringement.

It is also important to remind library customers that a trade name registration within the state where the business operates is not the same thing as a trademark. Trade names are registered with a state agency to avoid duplication of business names. However, a trade name could be the same word(s) as a trademark if the conditions for federal or state registration are met and approved by the federal or state agency.

Similar to patents, federal trademark applications go through an exacting examination process at the USPTO. Before thinking about federal registration for a trademark, the USPTO suggested that one should consider, first, whether the mark you want to register is registrable and, second, how difficult it will be to protect your mark based on the strength of the mark selected.[17]

Foremost when selecting a mark, one should make certain there is no likelihood of confusion with other marks. Such potential likelihood of confusion is the most common reason for refusal of applications. The USPTO determines that a likelihood of confusion occurs when "(1) the marks are similar, and (2) the goods and/or services of the parties are related such that consumers would mistakenly believe they come from the same source."[18] Similarity of marks rejected by the USPTO include sound, appearance, meaning, among others. Sound-alike rejections include different spellings with same pronunciation or close spellings or sounds. Conflicting similar appearance often comprise where logos are the same content but stylized differently. Meaning could include synonyms or foreign equivalent words, such as water, aqua, and agua.

In addition to challenges with likelihood of confusion, one's mark should be distinctive or unique to obtain registration. A distinctive mark is fanciful, arbitrary, or suggestive. A fanciful mark is a coined word often with no meaning such as Kodak® or Xerox®. An arbitrary mark has meaning but is not associated with it type of goods or services, such as Apple® computers. A suggestive mark suggests but does not describe, like Coppertone® suntan lotion, which suggests the result of using the product.

While distinctive marks are strong trademarks, generic and descriptive words for marks are weak and less likely to qualify as federal trademarks. Surnames or generic words or phrases are common examples of such weak marks. For example, McDonald's® restaurants most likely had to prove secondary meaning of the surname associated with its restaurant service or food goods sold.

Often, distinctiveness is acquired by secondary meaning or acquired distinctiveness of the mark, where customers are familiar with the mark as a source indicator. In other words, the customer "associates that mark with a particular producer, rather than the underlying product."[19] Often, secondary meaning is acquired through long-term use and/or publicity and advertising.

Marks that are merely descriptive cannot be registered with the USPTO until secondary meaning is proven. Customarily, the USPTO admits secondary meaning of a descriptive mark after five years of its continuous use in commerce supported by significant advertising, sales, and customer feedback, which affirms their association of the mark to it goods or service.

In addition to the challenges of weak trademarks or service marks getting federal registration, nontraditional marks such as a trade dress has similar challenges. In addition to secondary meaning, a trade dress must demonstrate that such trade dress is not associated with the functionality of the product. Just as a generic term cannot be registered as a wordmark because it cannot serve as source indicator, so it goes with functionality of design marks such as trade dress. When such a product feature serves as a function, it is ineligible for federal trademark registration. An attempt to clarify the functionality, product feature, challenge with trade dress was codified as an official Functionality Doctrine in 1998.[20]

Trade dress protects the characteristics and distinctive visual presentation of a product packaging such as graphics, color, or shape and, after sufficient use in commerce, of actual product configuration. Trade dress goes beyond the branded name or logo. Design patents, covered in our patent chapters, are similar to trade dress. Design patents that are for ornamental inventions may also apply to the look and feel of an object. Although U.S. design patents only last for fifteen years, Coca Cola® extended its ornamental design patent protection of its classic beverage bottles with a trade dress in U.S. trademark registration 1,057,884 in 1977, as shown below in figure 5.2.

Unlike design patents, trade dress in the United States refers to one aspect of a nontraditional subset of trademark law whereby the visual characteristics of a product or its package are protected by trademark. Such nontraditional trademarks are granted by the USPTO only when serving as a source identifier, when having an acquired distinctiveness and not currently registered for the same goods and services classification by another party, used in commerce, and primarily nonfunctional.[21]

Trade dress includes distinctive packaging, coloring, or other design facets of a brand beyond an insignia or logo. Just as traditional trademarks or service marks serve as source identifiers to consumers, so does the function of trade dress. The origin of trademark and trade dress both stem from the federal Lanham Act designed to protect consumers of such goods and services. Trade dress infringement cases are often brought to federal courts as unfair competition under section 43(a) of the Lanham Act.[22] Unfair competition denotes the legal decisions

Int. Cl.: 32

Prior U.S. Cl.: 45

United States Patent Office — Reg. No. 1,057,884
Registered Feb. 1, 1977

TRADEMARK
Principal Register

The Coca-Cola Company (Delaware corporation)
310 North Ave. NW.
Atlanta, Ga. 30313

For: SOFT DRINKS, in CLASS 32 (U.S. CL. 45).
First use July 8, 1916; in commerce at least as early as Sept. 1, 1916.
The mark consists of the three dimensional configuration of the distinctive bottle as shown.
Owner of Reg. No. 696,147.

Ser. No. 88,384, filed May 25, 1976.

JOHN C. DEMOS, Examiner

Figure 5.2
Trademark for Coca Cola® Bottle Trade Dress. (Courtesy U.S. Patent and Trademark Office)

and statutes that protect against such unethical business practices associated with trademarks.[23]

Trade dress is often associated with the "look and feel" of a brand. It is a growing area of IP protection for the fashion industry. With fashion, items can include everything from shoes to jewelry. For instance, what do most fine jewelry aficionados think of when they see a small robin's egg blue–colored gift box with a white satin ribbon? The color and design of the container usually invokes an explicit connotation and expectation of a charming fine jewelry product of Tiffany & Co. The robin's egg blue–colored package took years for Tiffany to establish. Once such ornamental trade dress is firmly established as source-identifying in the minds of one's customers, distinctiveness is acquired. Protecting a color with trade dress is complex, as functionality should not be associated with its use. A competitive business may fiercely guard its iconic branding with a federally registered trade dress in specific goods and services classifications.

Sound marks are another type of nontraditional trademark that is commonly heard and not seen. Perhaps the most famous are the roar of the MGM® lion and the bell tones of the NBC® chimes. According to the USPTO, a sound mark identifies and distinguishes a good, service, or collective membership organization and indicates its source.[24] For audio samples of such sound marks, listen at the following site: https://www.uspto.gov/trademark/soundmarks/trademark-sound-mark-examples.

TRADEMARK SEARCHING

Some popular music artists have registered their professional names as trademarks with the USPTO website. For example, both Paul McCartney and Lady Gaga have their names registered. Taylor Swift's trademark filings have raised some eyebrows as revealed in the following *Mondaq* news headlines, "Is Taylor Swift Trying to Use Trademark Protection to Monopolize Common Phrases?" and "Can Taylor Swift Shake off Accusations of Trademark Greed?" One *Mondaq* article by John Scruton reported on the extraordinary number of trademarks that Ms. Swift filed with the USPTO. In particular, there are many catchphrases from some of her lyrics featured in her successful album entitled *1989*. Phrases such as "This Sick Beat" and "Party Like It's 1989" are examples. Many observers were concerned that such actions were controlling common expressions. However, Ms. Swift may only dictate use of such term(s) if the USPTO approves the application(s), and then only for specific goods and services in commerce. For example, applications submitted included goods and services such as entertainment services, electronic newsletters, contests, fan club services, clothing, jewelry, ring tones, and so on.[25]

Before beginning your basic training on utilizing the Trademark Electronic Search System (TESS) database to search for trademarks, try the following test-drive exercise to get an idea of what the TESS database does and how it works. Locate the TESS database from the USPTO home page https://www.uspto.gov/ or go directly to http://tmsearch.uspto.gov/. In the Basic Word Mark Search (New User) template, enter the name of one of the music personalities listed above. Notice the listing that appears. The name of the celebrity is the actual trademark registered in the TESS database. The primary pieces of the trademark are indexed, such as the serial and registration numbers, the word mark, check status, and if the mark is LIVE or DEAD. Click on the name of the celebrity to see a full record of the trademark registration. Notice the International Goods and Services numbers listed, the owner of the word mark, and an actual visual example near the top of the document for logos, images, and signatures, among others.

As one begins a formal trademark search, one should keep in mind that the federal TESS database is not the only place to search for trademarks; there are state trademark databases to search, too. In addition, it is smart to review trade magazines, phone directories, competitive business catalogs, and the internet for similar marks. However, the federal searching and registration process is the first place to start.

FEDERAL TRADEMARK SEARCHING

Library customers who use a trademark database are usually searching to see if a trademark has been registered or applied for that is similar to their mark and that falls under the same goods and services classification. To search for federal trademarks, go to the USPTO Trademark site (located at https://www.uspto.gov/trademark) for a virtual tour. This URL offers all types of backgrounds and introductions to basic trademark information for entrepreneurs and small businesses. Just as patent searching is important before an inventor applies for a patent, the USPTO provides TESS to search federally registered trademarks. Usually searching trademarks is not as complicated as a patent search.

The USPTO provides a *Conducting a Trademark Search* guide, similar to its seven-step patent searching guide, at https://www.uspto.gov/learning-and-resources

/support-centers/patent-and-trademark-resource-centers-ptrc/resources. Below are the seven steps suggested by the USPTO as published in 2018.[26] After reviewing the seven steps, this chapter elaborates further on the actual trademark searching within the TESS database below. It is important that those searching the TESS database find the class(es) related to the goods or services associated with their prospective trademark. An abbreviated listing of the International Schedule of Classes of Goods and Services is listed before the TESS database searching section.

CONDUCTING A TRADEMARK SEARCH

1. Describe the Products or Services being sold with the mark.
2. Identify specific terms for your product or service using the online Acceptable Identification of Goods & Services Manual. Begin with this alphabetical listing of acceptable terms for the identification of goods and services. The Goods and Services Manual is searchable on the USPTO Web site at: https://tmidm.uspto.gov/. Locate terms that describe your good or service. For example, "flying discs" is the acceptable identification term for a flying saucer–type toy.
3. Determine international class. The entry for your product or service in the online Acceptable Identification of Goods and Services Manual (http://www.uspto.gov/trademark/trademark-updates-and-announcements/nice-agreement-current-edition-version-general-remarks) will also list the appropriate international class for that product or service. While providing the class for your goods or services is not a requirement for an application, knowing your international class can aid in focusing your search.
4. Determine related goods or services, and their classes. Identify terms for related goods and/or services that are used, advertised or sold with your product. For instance, peanut butter is sold and used with jellies and jams in the Acceptable Identification of Goods & Services Manual. Also scan the International Classification of Goods and Services for classes that are related to your product or service (http://www.uspto.gov/trademarks/notices/international.jsp)
5. Develop a basic search strategy. Brainstorm several alternatives to your mark in case your first choice is taken. Are there reasons why the USPTO might reject your mark? (See common refusals at http://tess2.uspto.gov/webaka/html/Likelihood/Likelihood_of_Confusion.html). If your mark includes a phrase, what are the most important keywords? Don't forget to use truncation devices (*) or wildcards (?) to look for marks with word stems similar to yours.
6. Broaden your search strategy. Consider searching with alternative spellings and homonyms to your mark. Use words that have the same or similar meanings to your mark. Also try words that have similar sounds or appearances or even phonetic equivalents. If necessary, the strategy can be narrowed later by limiting your search results with the goods/services you found in Step 2 or the International Class you found in Step 3.
7. Conduct the search. Search on TESS--the USPTO's web-based Trademark Electronic Search System-at your local PTRC (www.uspto.gov/ptrc) or at home if you have internet access.

NOTE: Search Logos and Designs if needed. Use the Design Search Code Manual (http://tess2.uspto.gov/tmdb/dscm/index.htm) to determine the correct design search code(s) for your mark's graphic design components (if it has any). Use these design codes in a search on TESS to see if there are other marks with a similar design element for similar products/services as yours.

As you may see from the USPTO's *Conducting a Trademark Search* guide, some may prefer the assistance of an IP attorney for the application process if there are any special needs.

Similar to patents, U.S. trademarks are classified with codes. However, as noted below, there are only forty-five goods and services categories. These can be found at the International Schedule of Classes of Goods and Services on the USPTO website, https://www.uspto.gov/trademark/trademark-updates-and-announcements/nice-agreement-tenth-edition-general-remarks-class. The trademark classification groups are much easier for the average person to digest than patent classifications. Two different trademark holders could use the same name if they are used for different goods or services. For example, the federal trademark for the Delta® airline service with International Classification 039 for Transporting and Travel Services may be subsequently used in commerce by the noncompeting Delta® faucet manufacturer with International Classification 011 Appliances. Another noncompeting example would include Dove® chocolates and Dove® soap.

The following listing of international trademark classifications are established by the Committee of Experts of the Nice Union and set forth in the International Classification of Goods and Services for the Purposes of the Registration of Marks (Nice Classification), published by the World Intellectual Property Organization (WIPO).[27]

International Trademark Classes	
001—Chemicals	**024—Textiles**
002—Paints	**025—Clothing**
003—Cleaning Substances	**026—Lace and Embroidery**
004—Industrial Oils	**027—Carpets and Floor Coverings**
005—Pharmaceuticals	**028—Games and Sporting Goods**
006—Common Metals	**029—Meat, Fish, and Poultry**
007—Machines	**030—Coffee, Tea, and Baking Goods**
008—Hand Tools	**031—Grains and Agriculture**
009—Computers and Scientific Appliances	**032—Beers and Beverages**
010—Medical Materials	**033—Alcoholic Beverages (excluding Beers)**
011—Appliances	**034—Tobacco Goods**
012—Vehicles	**035—Advertising and Business Services**
013—Firearms	**036—Insurance and Finance Services**
014—Precious Metals	**037—Construction and Repair Services**
015—Musical Instruments	**038—Telecommunications Services**
016—Paper Goods	**039—Transporting and Travel Services**
017—Rubber Goods	**040—Materials Treatment Services**
018—Leather Goods	**041—Education and Entertainment Services**
019—Building Materials	**042—Science and Technology Services**
020—Furniture	**043—Food and Drink Services**

021—Household Utensils	044—Medical and Vet Services
022—Ropes and Textile Goods	045—Legal and Security Services
023—Yarns and Threads	

A library customer wishing to conduct his or her own trademark search in the federal TESS database should consider the following points:

- There are two aspects of marks for which one could search via the TESS database: a graphic symbol versus a word or a phrase. Searching for a word is much simpler than locating a graphic symbol. However, searching for graphic symbols is easy once one understands the differences and where to locate these on the USPTO site.
- One must be familiar with the International Schedule of Classes of Goods and Services listed above before starting any searching of marks. This is a comprehensive listing by 45 categories for the related goods and services.
- One should have some prerequisite background of, or guidance from a librarian or specialist familiar with, the unique searching techniques associated with TESS as well as some advanced database searching experience. If not, it is the job of an IP librarian to educate such customers on how to use these types of IP databases, as demonstrated below.

The TESS database offers searching of a U.S. Trademark that has been registered, or for which an application has been submitted. These include trademark applications that are pending, registered, abandoned, canceled, or expired. TESS offers three search options for finding trademarks.

The first option is known as *Basics Word Mark Search* (New User). This basic search template is suitable for merely entering simple words or phrases for a few fields such as owner name, and serial or registration number. Not recommended for a comprehensive search because most of TESS's core function and feature are not available. For example, it cannot be used to search design marks.

Word and/or Deign Mark Search (Structured) is the second option. This structured form search template is ideal for novice users as it has all of the options of the advanced Free Form search by way of helping one to build a search with drop down field choices.

Expert searchers will appreciate the third advanced option, which is the *Word and/or Design Mark Search* (Free Form) template. It is most effectual when utilizing its field codes and search query operators.

TESS offers additional search interfaces for a Design Search Code Manual, a Browse Dictionary word listing catalog, and an Official Gazette gateway search template. See the TESS home page (figure 5.3).

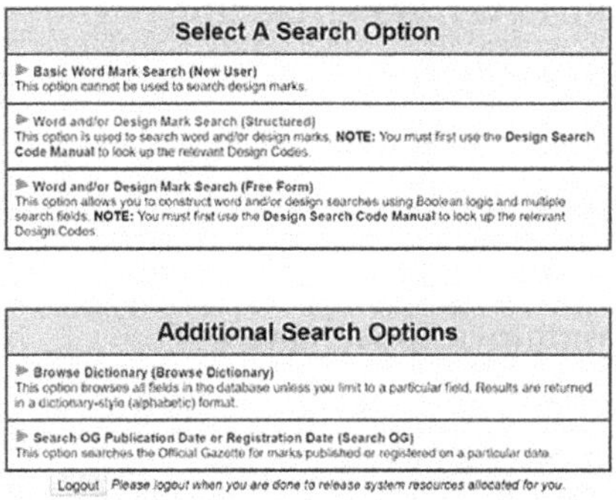

Figure 5.3
TESS Home Page Graphic (Courtesy U.S. Patent and Trademark Office)

The Basic Word Mark Search (New User) interface shown, is simple to use but limited. For example, if you search for Delta, over two thousand results would be displayed (figure 5.4).

Figure 5.4

TESS Search for "Delta." (Courtesy U.S. Patent and Trademark Office)

The Word and/or Design Mark Search (Structured) interface, shown below in figure 5.5, is ideal for intermediate level searchers with little knowledge of search term strategy building. It offers the capability of combining two search terms with drop down fields to narrow one's search. It is very important to note that the Structured interface offers a Boolean operator drop drown at the right, which defaults with the "or" operator. Generally, library customers need the "and" operator for their typical trademark searching needs. It is important to remind trademark searchers often of the Boolean "and" operator option shown below. Otherwise, searchers may get false hits unrelated to their specific trademark search.

Figure 5.6 reveals over ninety records in which the term Delta is located combined with the International Schedule of Classes for Goods and Services code 039 for Transporting and Travel Services. To help one determine which records to click on to reveal the full display, there are several fields worth noting. The serial number and the registration numbers are important when a searcher already knows these numbers. However, most of your trademark library customers usually have no references except their own word(s) or image for their prospective trademark. The LIVE or DEAD indicator is shown, indicating if the mark is still active or no longer in use. When a mark is DEAD, it is most likely possible to use in the same goods or services class. If one scrolls down on the list shown below, there are two examples discussed further.

Below in figure 5.7 is an iconic classic example of a Delta jet from our demonstrated search of a design mark plus words, letters, and/or numbers. It is significant to note that the design mark is still active as its Live/Dead Indicator field states LIVE near the bottom of the displayed record.

Figure 5.5

TESS Structured Search for Delta and IC 039. (Courtesy U.S. Patent and Trademark Office)

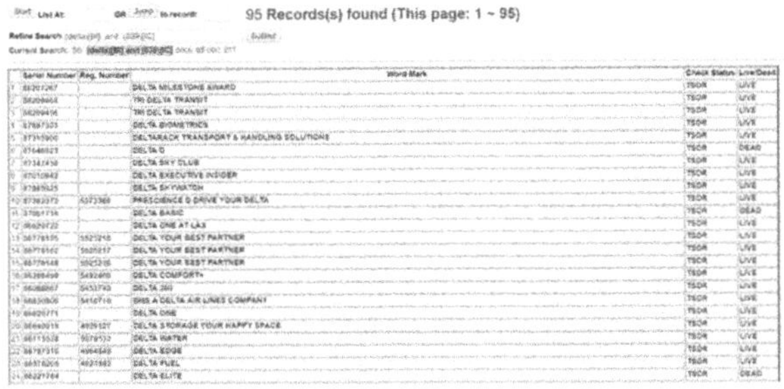

Figure 5.6
TESS Results Listing for Delta. (Courtesy U.S. Patent and Trademark Office)

However, when you open another record from the same results listing, you will find a retrospective record shown in figure 5.8 below of a famous 1970s advertising slogan that is no longer active as its Live/Dead Indicator field states DEAD.

Reviewing the details from each trademark record provides owner and location information as well as filing and registration dates. The three blue buttons at the top of each record offer links out to other databases which additional information. The first link is for the TSDR (Trademark Status and Document Retrieval) system. It provides complete electronic records, including details about the registration process and maintenance information. The second link is for the ASSIGN Status,

Figure 5.7
TESS Live Record for Delta®. (Courtesy U.S. Patent and Trademark Office)

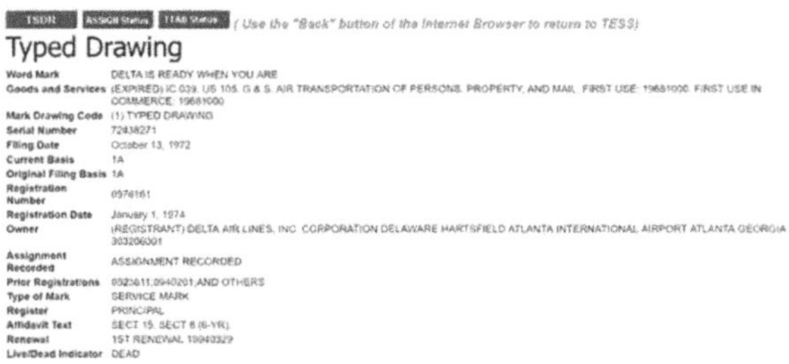

Figure 5.8
TESS Dead Record for Phrase "Delta is ready when you are." (Courtesy U.S. Patent and Trademark Office)

US Trademark Field Codes

Code & Name	Code & Name	Code & Name
[AD] Abandonment Date [AF] Affidavits [AR] Assignment Recorded [AT] Attorney of Record [BI] Basic Index [CB] Current Basis [CC] Coordinated Class [CD] Cancellation Date [CR] Change in Registration [DC] Design Search Code [DD] Design Description [DE] Description of Mark [DM] Decimal Mark [DS] Disclaimer [FD] Filing Date [FM] Full Mark [GS] Goods and Services	[IC] International Class [IR] International Registration Number [LD] Live/Dead [MD] Mark Drawing Code [MI] Mark Index [MN] Mark Non-Punctuated [MP] Mark Punctuated/Word Mark [OB] Original Filing Basis [OD] Other Data [ON] Owner Name [OW] Owner Name and Address [PD] Priority Date [PF] Physical Filing Date [PO] Published for Opposition [PM] Pseudo Mark [PI] Pseudo Mark Index [PR] Prior Registrations	[RD] Registration Date [RE] Renewals [RG] Register [RN] Registration Number [SF] Section 44 Indicator [SD] Single Design Code [SN] Serial Number [SO] Serial - Other Formats [ST] Standard Characters Claimed [SR] Date Amended to Current Register [TC] Trademark Search Facility Classification Code(limited to 8-28-07 through 1-31-11) [TD] Total Designs [TF] Distinctiveness Limitation Statement [TI] Translation Index [TL] Translation [TM] Type of Mark [UD] Update/Load Date [US] US Class

Figure 5.9
TESS Free Form Advanced Field Codes. (Courtesy U.S. Patent and Trademark Office)

which provides assignment information such as a change of owner. It is also useful for information about any mark name changes. The third link is for the TTAB Status database to see if any mark is involved in proceedings at the Trademark Trial and Appeal Board. If found, the site links to documents pertaining to such legal records, including final decisions.

The Word and/or Design Mark Search (Free Form) interface offers a template for trademark searchers with advanced database searching skills. It allows a searcher to combine terms and data, classification or design, and codes from specific fields found in a trademark record. Unlike the other TESS search options, it facilitates more than two fields to be combined with search terms or codes. Most IP librarians and specialists should be adept at using such free form settings, and they should be capable of training trademark-searching customers of their library on how to use it. See figure 5.9 above for display of complete field codes and names.

Besides trademarked words and phrases, some trademarks include logo designs. Among the field codes shown above, there are trademark design codes [DC] and design descriptions [DD], which enable searching content within the USPTO's Design Code Manual. Some trademarks consist of logos or designs, often combined with names or words. Just as searching with the [IC] code for International Classifications helps to narrow one's search for those trademarks in the same goods or services area, searching with a [DC] code within the Design Search Code Manual allows one to locate specific types of images. These images are classified into specific categories with a numerical arrangement which resembles the Dewey Decimal classifications of three hierarchical sections by tens, hundreds, and thousands. The USPTO Design Code Manual codifies design figurative elements to assigned six-digit numbers separated by decimals into three hierarchical levels by categories, divisions and sections. Specific categories include twenty-nine design topics, such as 01 Celestial Bodies, 02 Human Beings, and 03 Animals, as shown from highlights of the Table of Categories:

01	**Celestial bodies, natural phenomena, geographical maps** This category includes objects that appear in the sky, including clouds, stars, moons, sun, planets, and constellations. Additionally, designs associated with weather conditions such as rainbows, lightning, and snowflakes are found here. Maps of countries and continents are also in 01.

02	**Human beings** This category includes representations of men, women and children regardless of the activity they are engaged in or how they are dressed. Stylized humans, those in caricature form, stick figures, and parts of the human body are also in this category.
03	**Animals** This category includes most animals, except mythological animals. Animals found here include mammals, birds, kiwi, kiwi birds, fish, reptiles, and insects. Prehistoric animals, stylized animals and animals with human attributes are also coded in category 03.

Such design categories are then expanded under narrower divisions, such as 01 Celestial Bodies: 01.01 Stars; 01.03 Constellations; 01.05 Sun; 01.06 Globes; and so on. Then each division is narrowed further into sections. For example, a five-pointed star would be coded in category 01 (celestial bodies, natural phenomena and geographical maps), division 01 (stars, comets), and section 03 (stars with five points). The complete design code for a five-pointed star is 01.01.03, as displayed in figure 5.10.

Figure 5.10
Design Code Manual, Table of Divisions in Category 01, Celestial Bodies, 01.01.03, Single Star with Five Points. (Courtesy U.S. Patent and Trademark Office)

The [DD] field is used to search corresponding entries from the Alphabetical Index of the Design Search Code Manual for a design code. Links to access the Design Search Code Manual are found at various sections of the TESS home page. One can keyword search or scan an index or contents list to locate codes in the Design Search Code Manual. A hypothetical example of searching for a design code of a branding logo tied to a phrase for a prospective trademark registration is demonstrated further below.

Familiarity of all these trademark-searching components come together for demonstrating how to use the Word and/or Design Mark Search (Free Form) interface. Here is a hypothetical scenario where a library customer, Pete, is marketing a new series of tennis rackets for his sporting goods business. Pete has already secured patents for his new line of rackets. Now he needs to make certain nobody else has trademarked the name Blue King for tennis rackets. Returning to the *Conducting a Trademark Search* guide above, this effort addresses the first two steps of the USPTO's *Conducting a Trademark Search* guide. To verify that "tennis rackets" are the acceptable terms for the identification of goods and services, locate the Goods and Services Manual at https://tmidm.uspto.gov and enter the words: tennis rackets.

Then the following results list is displayed as figure 5.11. Notice that International Class 028 is associated with basic tennis racket products, such as the types in our scenario. This confirms for the steps three and four of the *Conducting a*

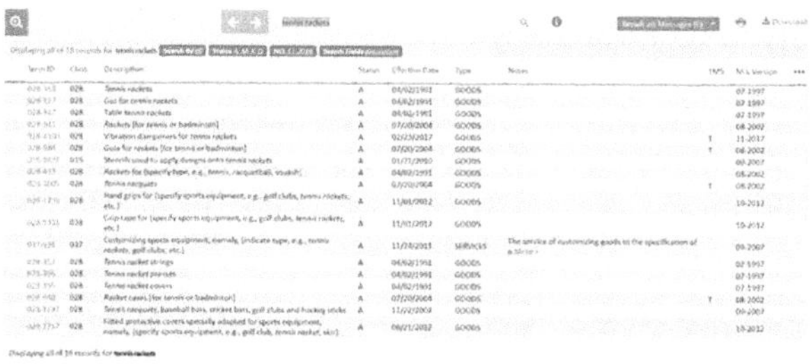

Figure 5.11
ID Manual Results Listing for Tennis Rackets. (Courtesy U.S. Patent and Trademark Office)

Trademark Search guide that the terms tennis rackets are the appropriate goods or services and their matching class(es) associated with the term(s).

Steps five and six of the *Conducting a Trademark Search* guide involves developing a basic search strategy utilizing the TESS database to verify that our customer's branded mark is not registered with the same goods and services class. TESS offers operators for truncations, phonetics, Boolean, and proximity searching methods. Combined with the field codes discussed earlier, this offers precision searching capabilities for trademark searchers. Hypothetical searcher Pete might need to broaden his search with alternative spellings and homonyms, as demonstrated below.

Pete's initial search strategies could be entered in either the Structured or Free Form interfaces in TESS. For example, he might do a simple search of the words in his mark: blue and king. Next applying truncation, Pete could broaden his search allowing for alternate spellings of the words:

blu and *king*
bloo and *king*

Pete could also search for possible variations of the distinctive word "king" alone:

k$ng

The $ symbol permits phonetic searching as it only retrieves different characters, such as extra "n" letters or a "i" or "y" substitution, such as KYNG or KINNG. The asterisks placed on either side will retrieve marks where the term entered will appear at the beginning, middle, or end of a mark found.

Step six of the *Conducting a Trademark Search* guide could be applied to either the Structured or Free Form interfaces in TESS. Initially, our trademark searcher Pete uses the Structured Search interface (figure 5.12 below) entering blue and king with the Basic Index field. It is very important to note that the "and" Boolean operator is selected at the right of the Structured Search template.

If Pete enters his same search on the Free Form interface, he would combine the terms blue[BI] and king[BI]. From either interface, 40 total records were retrieved.

Figure 5.12
TESS Search Template for Blue and King. (Courtesy U.S. Patent and Trademark Office)

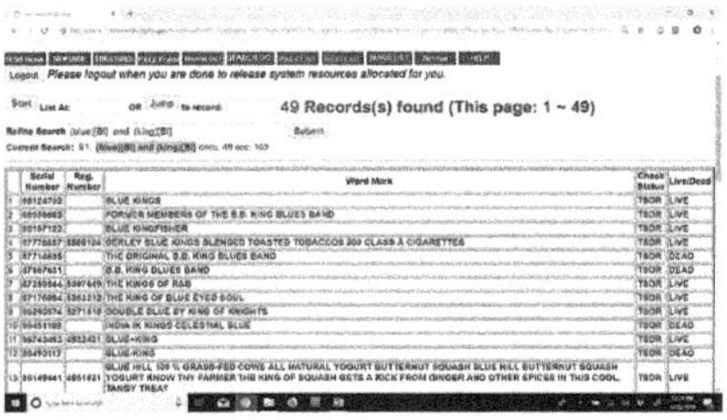

Figure 5.13
TESS Search Results Listing for Blue and King. (Courtesy U.S. Patent and Trademark Office)

The top ten hits are shown below in figure 5.13 to demonstrate the visual format of the results listing.

As Pete did not combine the unique International Class for his goods code IC 028 Games and Sporting Goods, non-competing marks of other goods and services appear. He could either combine this with his next search or merely review all forty-nine records to read the Goods and Services classifications.

Next, Pete might conduct a phonetic search utilizing the truncation and wildcard operators. From either Structured or Free Form interfaces, he would enter two different search queries as separate searches:

bloo[BI] and *k$ng*[BI]
blu[BI] and *k$ng*[BI]

Detailed result listings are displayed for both searches conducted. This permits Pete to determine if his Blue King brand is potentially a viable federal trademark. However, if he wants to make certain he has not overlooked overlapping or similar Goods and Services classes for tennis rackets, he should click on the [CC] field listed among the field codes near the bottom of the Free Form interface in TESS. Coordinated Classes are groups of related classes that might include goods or services similar to your selected class. For example, the identified class IC 028 for Games and Sporting Goods reveals possible similarities with the following International Classes: 028, 009, 016, 020, 025, 035, 041, and 042. One should read these classes just in case their identified good or service could also be classified in one of these classes. For example, class IC 041 Education and Entertainment might include an educational tennis instruction service known as Blue King.

Finally, Pete has a created a branding logo, which consists of a man wearing a blue crown for his trademark Blue King. Pete should review the Design Search Code Manual for crowns and possible the color blue. He might combine a Design Search Code for Men Wearing Crowns 02.01.03 [DC] with his word mark terms: blue and king.

It is very important to remind trademark searchers that even if no similar trademark is found from their own search in TESS, they should not assume that their trademark application will be automatically registered at the USPTO. This is not the same as a copyright registration, where the expression is protected immediately based upon original authorship. After trademark application is registered, a trademark examiner reviews the application by performing a comprehensive search, which may result in their refusing to register the trademark. The primary reason why the USPTO might reject an application is most often related to a statutory basis[28] due to the likelihood of confusion of the applicant's mark to another established mark already used in commerce or pending before the USPTO. For more details on likelihood of confusion, see the USPTO website: http://tess2.uspto.gov/webaka/html/Likelihood/Likelihood_of_Confusion.html.

State and Common Law Trademark Searching

In certain instances, state trademark registration could be better suited to small businesses such as neighborhood restaurants or new traditional business start-ups that rely mainly on local or regional customers. The cost for a single state trademark is usually easier to obtain and much more affordable than a federal trademark. However, if a product or service is marketed nationally through internet commerce, then federal registration makes more sense. In that instance, it is not only more cost effective, but federal registration also offers national protection of your trademark.

Business trade names such as Amazon.com may function as a trademark, but only because such names are also associated with a mark of its product or service. As mentioned earlier, businesses register their actual trade names at the state level separately. However, federal registration or state registration for trademark purposes is a separate process.

Web links to a few national state-by-state trademark databases and directories are listed below. Each database is set up differently and may have dissimilar search commands and techniques. The common search points often include mark keywords, mark description, owner/registrant name, goods and services classification, registrant number/ID, and mark disposition or status.

Here are the links to the state trademark databases:

USPTO's State Trademark Information Links

https://www.uspto.gov/trademarks-getting-started/process-overview/state-trademark-information-links

Find Law's State Trademark Information

https://smallbusiness.findlaw.com/intellectual-property/state-trademark-information.html

Coordinated Legal Tech's Secretaries of State

http://www.coordinatedlegal.com/SecretaryOfState.html

Common law trademarks exist as soon as a mark is put to use and notated with a TM symbol. When searching to make certain your customer's mark is unique, they should also check the web, regional yellow pages, national trade magazines, and company directories in the marketplace for a mark, as well as other local or regional publications for possible common law trademarks. This is especially important for regional trademarks.

REGISTRATION PROCESS AND MAINTENANCE

As covered in our searching section, trademarks are classified by goods and services, such as Class 25 for clothing, footwear, and headgear. Depending on the size and scope of product or service offerings of a company, one may need to file for more than one classification. Plus, the mark must prove "actual use in commerce" (or "intent to use" within a reasonable time) before a federal registration is even considered. "Actual use" means packaged, marketed, and sold or transported in commerce.

Registration of a trademark is not legally mandatory. Many small mom-and-pop businesses have a common law trademark associated with their business without registering. The major advantage to state or federal registration is the documentation, which becomes public record along with validity, ownership, and, in the case of federal registration, distinctiveness.[29]

Federal registration establishes a legal presumption and national notice of your customer's ownership and exclusive rights to use the mark in connection with its goods/services listed except where the mark is currently in use by preceding users who have not registered the mark such as common law. It makes it easy for other to find the registration of the mark. It is a notice to others that the mark is unavailable. This discourages others from using a similar mark.[30]

Federal registration also shifts the burden of any disputes from the documented owner onto the opposing party. It also offers the registrant the ability to bring an action concerning the mark in federal court, such as to prosecute an infringement claim. Federal registration supports the feasibility of foreign registration as well as registration with U.S. Customers and Border Protection to prevent importation of fake and counterfeit goods. Lastly, and most importantly, federal registration gives the owner the right to use the ® symbol.[31]

Registration Process—How to File a Federal Trademark Application

The four parts of the registration process are listed below. It is not difficult for one to prepare and submit one's own trademark application. The USPTO website offers helpful trademark application guides, including engaging video tutorials on what to do before, during, and after one files an application. The steps are described below.

1. Compile required information needed for your application such as good and service class(es) identified and concluding your mark is distinctive and one-of-a-kind based upon a completing a thorough "due diligence" search for similar trademarks. A comprehensive search should go beyond merely searching the TESS database at the USPTO website. When one is uncertain if one's prospective mark is in fact distinctive in its class(es), consulting with a licensed attorney specializing in trademark applications is a wise investment. Other information needed includes first-use date of the mark, as the mark should actually be used in commerce (or "Intent to Use" within a reasonable time) to even be considered, as well as demonstrating an image of how the mark is actually being used, known as a specimen.

NOTE: If you are not currently using the mark in commerce at the time of your application, you must submit an intent to use application instead.

2. Prepare your Trademark Electronic Application System (TEAS) online application found at the USPTO site https://www.uspto.gov/trademarks-application-process/filing-online. At the time of preparing this book, the USPTO required the following on an application to get a filing date:
    - Owner of the mark or applicant's name
    - Name and address for correspondence
    - Depiction of the mark as a clear drawing for design marks
    - Description of goods/services for which mark is used
    - Application filing fee for each class submitted
    - Basis for filing or current use in commerce or intent to use
    - Specimen for use-based applications means the applicant should attach and describe tag or label used for goods; business sign or advertisement used for services
    - Electronic signature of the owner or authorized representative of owner or business
3. File your online TEAS application on the USPTO site at https://www.uspto.gov/trademarks-application-process/filing-online/initial-application-forms.
4. Monitor progress of your application diligently via the USPTO site at https://www.uspto.gov/trademarks-application-process/check-status-view-documents. The USPTO suggested that applicants check the status of their pending applications frequently, every three to four months. Expect a reply from the USPTO in approximately three months. An assigned examining attorney at the USPTO reviews the application. Modifications or minor application corrections are most typical.

    The examiner reviews the application to ensure it satisfies all federal legal requirements of the Lanham Act (15 U.S.C. §1051 et seq.) and the Trademark Rules of Practice (37 C.F.R. Part 2). Once a trademark application is approved for publication, you get a notice of publication from the USPTO. The weekly *Official Gazette* publishes your mark at https://www.uspto.gov/learning-and-resources/official-gazette/trademark-official-gazette-tmog. For thirty days, anyone may oppose your registration published in the *Gazette*. If there are no oppositions, you receive a certificate of registration. Common grounds for refusal of a federal trademark include likelihood of confusion with an established federal mark or merely a descriptive mark of the good or service, such as generic names, geographical references, or surnames.
5. Maintaining and taking care of one's mark is like taking care of one's own physical health and fitness. Unlike copyrights or patents, trademark ownership can be perpetual, so long as one maintains the USPTO fees, continues to use the mark in commerce, and follows the requirements of the Lanham Act. The renewal process is essential in maintaining one's right to use the trademark. The USPTO sends the owner of the trademark an email notice before the renewal is due. The first maintenance document is due between the fifth and sixth years after the registration date. Subsequent renewal maintenance filing is required between the ninth and

tenth years. Thereafter, the maintenance renewals occur every ten years from the registration date.

Throughout the life of a trademark, the owner of the mark is responsible for monitoring and enforcing their rights. In addition, the owner of a trademark could license its use for temporary or supplemental use by a third party, like sports teams do with authorized fan merchandise. In addition, the owner of a trademark could sell the trademark as part of a business sale or outright trademarked brand sale. The USPTO provides an electronic trademark assignment system (ETAS, https://etas.uspto.gov/) database for recording such assignment changes in the public records. Assignments are also helpful for name changes associated with a registered federal trademark.

FREEDOM OF EXPRESSION AND OTHER ISSUES AND CONTROVERSIES

In his article, "The Mark as Expression/The Mark as Property," Michael Spence says, "What I own when I own intellectual property, is not the subject matter of the intellectual property right, but the intellectual property right itself."[32] Spence articulates the difference between trademarks as commercial property versus expressive uses by others and potential challenges that ensue when others rely on such expressive uses. This section introduces aspects of trademarks related to fair use, free expression versus property ownership, use of trademark in commerce, the somewhat related identity rights, infringement defenses, fan culture, and social justice of controversial sports team logos.

According to the International Trademark Association, "A trademark owner can stop others from using its trademark in order to prevent the public from being confused about the source of the goods or services. In some circumstances, however, someone may use another party's trademark if the use is considered a 'fair use.'"[33] Such fair use or freedom of expression exceptions includes certain uses for instruction, research, publishing, and fan culture. Yet there are instances when owners of trademarks promote public controversy related to their own free speech, such as contentious sports team trademark logos. This section covers both sides of freedom of expression issues related to trademarks.

Free Expression Versus Property Aspects of Trademarks

Educators, librarians, and other nonprofit professionals are often unaware of their fair use boundaries related to the unlicensed expressive use of others' trademarks. In some instances, individuals rely on expressive use of others' trademarks for projects related to research, commentary, criticism, and other free-speech applications. When freedom of expression and trademarks meet, legal conflicts often emerge. Such threats of legal action are potential form of censorship. This section reviews what fair use defenses cover, including developments that exist to support educators, librarians, students, and other nonprofit professionals in reducing their risks of infringement for their expressive uses of trademarks.[34]

Trademark Trolls or Bullies

Trademark trolls are similar to patent trolls mentioned in Chapter 3. Trademark trolls or bullies often hide and wait to pounce on public creative cultural words and images tied to commercial branding. Even trademark bullying is associated with legitimate trademarks of high-profile companies. Cases are noted of trolls whose descriptive marks abuse their rights, as if their marks were more distinctive. Sometimes these types of marks may even be deceptive, which further detracts from possible registration with a government agency.[35] Intentional marketplace deception and confusion of products and services is both legally and ethically wrong. The focus here is on the legal creative and expressive uses by educators and other noncommercial users of trademarks and similar publicity-related intellectual properties more often associated with bullying by more familiar trademarks. Associated federal case laws, law review and trade press literature, and associated blogs related to the cultural fair use aspect of trademarks are referenced.

There is a tension-of-rights continuum between freedom of expression by consumers, educators, and critics, versus IP owners such as businesses, brands, or services. On one hand, freedom of expression or the First Amendment right to information is an inherently constitutional right in the United States, whereas on the other hand, information protected by IP has been shielded by monopolies that could stifle any new creative culture. Law and history scholar Susan Scafidi points out in her book, *Who Owns Culture?*, that if cultural products were "outside the scope of intellectual property protection," these works would "neither challenge the First Amendment nor limit the availability of their own expressive use."[36] Communications Studies Professor Kembrew McLeod, in his book *Freedom of Expression*, further discusses related situations where corporate culture has silenced artists due to fear of financial losses.

This act of stifling artists or imposing censorship presents a very pertinent point that social commentary, a vital First Amendment right, is often silenced by IP owners.[37] Parody artist Tom Forsythe learned this chapter well when he was sued by the toy manufacturer Mattel® for his photographic depiction of Barbie® dolls jammed in a kitchen appliance.[38] His photographic critique entitled *Food Chain Barbie* was a comment on the unrealistic beauty myth of a cultural icon. Forsythe was quoted stating, "Intellectual-property lawsuits limit the scope of artistic expression in such a way these days because everything's branded. . . . If you want to comment on society today, you're using somebody's brand if you're at all in touch with reality."[39] The artist merely expressed his opinion on a well-known cultural icon, but the toy producer saw this as an infringement of its copyrights and trademarks. After winning this case, Forsythe affirmed, "We may be free to express ourselves, but if that expression involves offending a rapacious corporation, they're equally free to sue; and unless we have the wherewithal to fight off high-powered attorneys, that's where our free speech ends."[40] Imagine if a similar situation occurred with a student art exhibit at a college or museum, and trademark infringements were imposed based on branding of a cultural icon. Fair use may be problematic for a college student or professor to defend.

Another topic for scholars to ponder deals with advocating for more academic freedom in terms of shared IPs within higher education, such as university-industry partnerships with business "incubators" where IP ownership and rights are questioned by researching faculty members. Academics are advocating for more academic freedom in terms of IP. Corynne McSherry, author of *Who Owns Academic Work?* and IP director of the *Electronic Frontier Foundation* (EFF), reminds us that symbolic information associated with trademarks of university-industry partnerships will become more common, especially in academic scientific works.[41] This is based upon the First Amendment eminence or eminent domain over a commercial asset viewpoint where there are many legitimate and legal fair uses of a trademark, especially in a noncommercial and educational setting. More about scholarly communication and IP is discussed in Chapter 7.

How does "use in commerce," covered earlier in this chapter, apply to fair use and freedom of speech scenarios for research, instruction, and publishing, especially noncommercial speech? Without "use in commerce" tied to the use of federal trademarked goods and services, there is no trademark infringement per the Lanham Act. The Act further excludes all noncommercial speech and applies to commercial uses only. This Lanham Act codified concept, Section 1125, exempting noncommercial speech from trademark infringement,[42] is further supported by the spirit of the First Amendment; otherwise, scholarly or consumer criticism, opinion, or parody (excluding defamation) would be ineffectual.

Identity Rights versus Trademarks

Right of publicity by famous personalities is a growing IP issue on the fringe of trademarks.[43] David L. Lange and H. Jefferson Powell comment on this rising trademark exclusivity versus appropriation where "the law professes to be concerned chiefly with confusion, but in reality often treats trade identity as though it too is property entitled to exclusivity."[44] This contemporary view of trademark protection has created confusion between trademark and rights of publicity or personality rights. The right of publicity has developed into private censorship of culture where, without permission, it could be an infringement to evoke a cultural image associated with a celebrity.[45]

Jonathan Faber, law professor and founder of Luminary Group LLL, a licensing agency specializing in personality branding, defines the right of publicity as "the right to control the commercial use of one's identity,"[46] or celebrity licensing. Faber believes that freedom of speech liberties related to celebrity licensing have not been suppressed, as the "judiciary is very good about safeguarding the First Amendment."[47]

On the other hand, Michael Madow, mass media law scholar, suggests that personality as property law in the United States is an uneasy case for publicity rights provides:

> famous persons considerable protection against the unauthorized use of their identities for commercial purposes. Unfair competition laws are an important source of protection, as are the invasion of privacy and defamation torts. However, in many

> states, an additional instrument of control is the so-called "right of publicity," which gives a celebrity a legal entitlement to the commercial value of her identity, and thereby enables her to determine the extent, manner, and timing of its commercial exploitation.[48]

Have rights of publicity gone too far? Madow and other scholars believe that freedom of expression should be confronted when censorship is alleged.

These recent developments have placed right of publicity in the shadows of trademark. Both areas provide rights-holders some measure of control over the meaning of their identities by permitting control of the use of associated symbols. In addition to identity, merchandising of the persona is another challenge for courts.[49] Faber also points out that trademark attributes to prevent unfair competition and its doctrine of misappropriation also promote similarities.[50]

These rights of publicity as celebrity licensing have developed the concept of celebrities as brands. For example, Gene Simmons of the 1970s rock group KISS has affirmed that "KISS is a brand, not a band." At business lectures, he asserts that individuals potentially are their own brand.[51] Other celebrities such as Paul McCartney follow this idea as they request trademark registration of their own identity name. However, applying for a trademark solely to guard others from using your trademark is not enough. A federally registered trademark must be supported by the "actual use in commerce." In some instances, estates of dead celebrities are able to obtain a trademark of the deceased's name because of his or her right of publicity.

A right of publicity guards the market value of one's persona or identity and allows an entity to keep others from unfairly appropriating this worth for their commercial gain. Protection includes:

> Section 43(a) of the Lanham Act, which holds that unauthorized use of an aspect of one's persona, or use of a persona feature confusingly similar to a feature of one's persona, on or in connection with any goods or services can constitute a false designation of origin, false or misleading description of fact, or false or misleading representation of fact;(2) State laws, extending protection to living and deceased persons; and (3) Common law, which differs state by state but generally holds that use of a person's identity for the "purposes of trade" without that person's consent constitutes unfair competition.[52]

Characters from copyrighted literary works that have entered into the public domain, such as Tarzan and Sherlock Holmes, may be protected further by trademark or right of publicity.[53] Although copyright associated with characters in books such as the original Sherlock Holmes series have entered into the public domain, authors should use caution when utilizing such characters in their own new works, including books, graphic novels, and films, among others. The Conan Doyle Estate of the Sherlock Holmes books has claimed common law trademark protection for Sherlock Holmes. Most of the original Sherlock Holmes books are in the public domain including illustrations such as the one shown in figure 5.14. Copyright on the few remaining titles were scheduled to expire on or before 2017. However,

Figure 5.14
One of Sherlock Holmes's Character Illustrations by Sidney Paget appearing in *The Strand Magazine*, now in the public domain.

the estate claims common-law trademark based upon its consistent licensing of its mark for recent motion pictures and television series.[54] If one looks ups Sherlock Holmes in the TESS trademark database of the USPTO, there are multiple federal trademarks registered on behalf of the estate. When neither copyright or trademark protection are viable options, right of publicity could be applied to protect fictional characters.

Photographs of the actual authors of recent public domain books or media celebrities might have right of publicity issues unless the subject died less than one hundred years ago.[55] Right of publicity prohibits unauthorized commercial use of a person's name, image, likeness, signature, and voice, particularly with commercial products, and as used in advertising goods or services. Noncommercial entertainment, informational, or editorial uses are not protected by right of publicity and could be applied to newer copyrighted works and associated subjects and their right of publicity. More on right of publicity related to cosplay and sports is discussed further below.

Infringement Defenses: Fair Use and Rights of Expression of Trademarks

For understanding which expressive uses by educators or nonprofit professionals are lawful or defendable as freedom of expression, a familiarity with most types of lawful infringement defenses with trademarks is needed. They are fair use and First Amendment rights for free expression, and each has many subsets.[56]

The first is fair use as a defense. A defendant asserting the classic fair use affirmative defense under the Lanham Act need only prove his or her use of the plaintiff's mark not as a mark, but rather as a fair use and good-faith description of the characteristics of a good or service.[57] This type of fair use often occurs when the user utilizes a competitor's weaker descriptive trademark that employs a common, everyday word or phrase. For example, company A brand, named *Makeup Express*, sells makeup and describes its cosmetic colors in marketing materials as a "beautiful rainbow of colors," while company B is named *Beautiful Rainbow Cosmetics*, which is also its trademark registered name. Company B sues company A for infringement of its registered trademark *Beautiful Rainbow*. Company A defends itself by claiming classic fair use whereby it is only using a common term as a good-faith description of the color characteristics of its goods. This case demonstrates why a common, descriptive mark is not as strong as distinctive marks covered earlier in this chapter.

Nominative fair use is the second type of fair use associated with trademarks. When the descriptive use of a trademarked term is virtually unavoidable, it becomes nominative fair use. For example, when a drug manufacturer compares its product brand X to competitor brand Z, it must use the competitor's name to demonstrate its point. Another example is when a computer repair shop advertises that it specializes in repair of a specific brand and displays that brand's logo, although the repair shop is not an authorized retailer. A test for nominative use basically states that one party may use or refer to the trademark of another if:

1. the product or service cannot be readily identified without using the trademark, remembering that a trademark is descriptive of a person, place, or attribute.
2. only as much of the mark is used as is necessary for its identification, such as the words but not the specific font or logo.
3. the user does nothing to suggest sponsorship or endorsement by the trademark holder—which applies even if the nominative use is commercial.[58]

The third example is fair use based on Copyright Law (Section 107) and the four factors test, as covered earlier. This is where the four-prong test is analyzed with regard to purpose, nature, amount, and market effect of the use of, in this case, a trademark rather than a copyrighted work.

The fourth example is noncommercial use, which could apply to educators, government, and nonprofit agencies. One of the best illustrations of noncommercial use was with the Strategic Defense Initiative by President Reagan in the 1980s. Reagan borrowed the name *Star Wars* from the trademarked name of the popular commercial movie owned by trademark owner, Lucasfilm Ltd. Lucasfilm Ltd. was denied an injunction against the use of the name as an expression for the Strategic Defense Initiative. The fair use doctrine in trademark law applied, as the owner of the trademark could not prevent its use to describe such a noncommercial government program.[59]

First Amendment rights of expression make up the other type of lawful infringement defense. These include parody and freedom of speech.

The first example is parody. In 2008 a trademark infringement suit was filed against the video game *Grand Theft Auto* by plaintiff *E. S. S. Entertainment 2000,* doing business as the *Play Pen*, which was a "gentlemen's club" in Los Angeles. This case was considered a First Amendment victory for the defendant, video game producer Rock Star Videos whose video game, *Grand Theft Auto*, had gamers navigating the "East Los Santos" virtual vicinity where they could visit a strip club called the "Pig Pen." The plaintiff said this was similar to their establishment, Play Pen. The court recognized that the game used attributes of the Play Pen to support its parody image of urban Los Angeles, but the court accepted the defendant's First Amendment argument. However, the plaintiff also claimed that the video game infringed its trademark associated with their real club. They presented evidence and testimony that questioned, with validity, the likelihood of confusion. Although parody prevailed, likelihood of confusion in future product placement in movies, video games, and other media should be carefully reviewed, especially in commercial scenarios.[60]

As shown above, parodies of trademarks are becoming more common than parody of copyrighted materials. The three types of parody associated with trademark are differentiated comparative advertising, confusion of services, and dilution of mark.

The first is differentiated comparative advertising. In theory, a business could legally use a competitor's mark or brand as necessary to fairly and accurately describe its products or services or to compare to those of its competitor. This is often used in commercial applications such as advertising for comparing an over-the-counter pharmaceutical product A to product B, whereby visual images of the brands are put side by side. However, another comparative advertising example was judged as an infringement despite its parody humor in *Deere & Co. v. MTD Products*. Both companies marketed riding lawn mowers. MTD Products distributed an advertisement where the John Deere trademarked deer symbol runs in fear from MTD's "Yard-Man" riding mower and a dog barking. Although clever, the court ruled it was not parody, as it was being employed to sell a product rather than to offer social commentary or entertainment. Further, the court held that the parody infringed Deere's right to prevent the dilution of its mark.[61] Many experts continue to debate this judgment. Many library customers, such as business start-ups or entrepreneur students, are likely to ask reference questions related to such commercial comparison scenarios. Librarians might utilize such comparisons of trademarked logos or names associated with subscription information databases from their collection in comparisons between competing brands. However, librarians, educators, or nonprofits might apply the following related scenarios.

The second type of parody deals with confusion of services. In 2005, the U.S. Supreme Court ruled that a fair use defense could be made in certain instances when the use resulted in consumer confusion.[62] This is more likely when a weak, nondistinctive, ordinary mark is copied, such as a descriptive created by McDaniel College, a private, nonprofit college in Maryland. McDaniel College placed a unique brand image, McLive!, on its website in 2012. If McDonald's restaurant lawyers approach McDaniel College with a cease and desist order, would

McDonald's fast food restaurant have a valid case here? Unless McDonald's goes into the business of higher education, these are noncompeting and different goods and services classifications.

Parody or satire are often exempt from trademark dilution, which is our third example with parody, as they are considered noncommercial. The First Amendment as well as the Trademark Dilution Revision Act of 2006 protects parodies that are noncommercial or not used to market goods or services commercially. However, when parody is used in commercial applications with federally registered marks, then such a parody must abide by federal dilution law.[63] Our example of the John Deere case above further demonstrates this point.

The second example of a right of expression is freedom of speech. Cybersquatting, also known as domain squatting, not to be confused with trademark trolls mentioned earlier in this chapter, is where an unaffiliated party registers, sells, or uses an internet domain name of another with the intent of profiting from the good will of another's trademark and often selling it to that associated party at a profit.[64] The Lanham Act provides civil remedies for such bad-faith actions.[65] For one such scenario, freedom of speech was the motive rather than an economic, commercial intention of cybersquatting. The case was *Lamparello v. Falwell 420 F.3d 309* (4th Cir., 2005). The dispute focused on the domain name fallwell.com. Christopher Lamparello produced a website to counter and criticize the antihomosexual statements of popular yet controversial Christian televangelist Reverend Jerry Falwell. Lamparello's website domain spelling varied with an additional letter "L" as fallwell.com. Falwell felt that confusion was created by the similarity between Lamparello's domain name and Falwell's name, domain name, and other trademarks. Falwell tried to legally stop Lamparello from using the trademark "fallwell" and transfer the misspelled domain name to Falwell. The original decisions decided in favor of Falwell, conceding Falwell's claims of federal trademark infringement, false designation of origin, unfair competition, and cybersquatting. On appeal in 2005, the court overturned the earlier decisions, determining that there was not a "likelihood of confusion" and that there was no trademark infringement based on "initial interest confusion." Lamparello's site was noncommercial, and the Court ruled there was no "bad faith intent to profit." Further, it was not considered cybersquatting.[66]

Another example of freedom of speech applied to the use of a trademark is illustrated by the following case. A customer sued Best Buy® for losing her laptop and displayed an original mash up on a grievance blog using the Best Buy logo. She struck out "best" and inserted the word "worst." The customer was disgruntled as she claimed identity theft had occurred due to the negligence of Best Buy. The lawsuit was ultimately dismissed in 2008.[67]

SPECIFIC SCENARIOS RELATED TO LIBRARIES OR NONPROFIT ORGANIZATIONS

Some libraries, such as the Jonesboro Public Library in Arkansas, posted a trademark FAQ page,[68] https://www.libraryinjonesboro.org/trademark-faqs, which not only defines trademarks but also codifies why it prohibits unlicensed trademarked items for sale at its event. The site also guides patrons and vendors on how to apply for licenses to sell such items at library events. Some libraries offer Comic-Con® events and have been approached by the official San Diego Comic Convention to request a license agreement to legally use their trademark.[69] Otherwise, one might genericize the comic theme to avoid potential trademark infringement. Yet the Wyoming Library Association exercised its trademark use by reappropriating the image of a woman's iconic silhouette often seen on semitrucks, but holding and reading a book. The image of the "library mudflap girl" campaign created some controversy, while increasing library card sign-ups.[70]

FAN CULTURE AND COSPLAY COSTUMES

What about fan culture that creates their own recreational derivatives of popular characters from comics and other popular media? Such derivative works range from fan fiction and fan art to costumes and cosplay. Could right of publicity and copyright concerns intersect for costumes or cosplay exhibited by attendees at comic conventions? What about freedom of expression and fair use?

Cosplay is a Japanese contracted expression of the words "costume" and "play." Most legal experts agree that fair use extends substantial protection to the cosplayer's customized derivative costume and prop. Right of publicity is another factor, which often favors a cosplayer at such public conventions.[71]

Is it an infringement for comic fan culture to create and publicly display such costumes? What about the rights of publicity for the comic convention attendees' images when others capture their photo images onsite? On a somewhat related fans' topic, there are similar rights of publicity issues with online fantasy sports as well as fan fiction. Keep in mind that both creator and consumer proprietary aspects are involved in these IP scenarios. Potential infringement lawsuits could challenge valid fair use and freedom of expression among such fan culture. Other similar fandoms include team-centric sporting events, film and music festivals, book fairs, and even neighborhood Halloween spectacles of homemade costumes based upon characters of popular media.

As noted throughout this book, both the creator and consumer aspects of IP have fundamental rights, such as those displayed at popular culture cons and festivals. Official producers of copyrighted and trademarked popular culture cannot mass-produce their creative works unless there is a mass audience to consume their works. Yet no mass audience could exist unless a creative work was produced and distributed. Fans need the producers, and producers need the fans.[72]

In addition, cosplay fans may even challenge their right of publicity for unauthorized images captured by others of themselves and their derivative works at Cons and Festivals.[73] There is a distinct difference between a vendor selling multiple unauthorized costumes at conventions and festivals and a single, homemade, derivative cosplay costume worn by comic or sci-fi enthusiasts. One only needs to return to our chapters on copyrights and fair use to apply facts and best practices in establishing policies and monitoring potential infringement at cons and festivals.

What about individually created Halloween costumes based upon popular superheroes for personal use? There are potential copyright, trademark, and patent infringements associated with mass-producing them or with individuals displaying them at public commercial venues, such as bars and restaurants. However, most traditional homemade costumes based on popular culture worn by trick-or-treat youngsters visiting neighbors door-to-door are most likely considered fair use. The same could apply for most trademarked character costumes worn at local community parades.[74]

Social Justice and Sports Team Logos

Proceeding with freedom of expression issues related to trademarks, there are touchy topics tied to free speech and sports' team logos. The three common challenges include:

1. Public opinion and good business public relations
2. Freedom of speech versus cultural sensitivity
3. Political, ethical, and moral status quo

With these three "code of behavior" challenges listed above in mind, reflect on the following story. Many years ago, a mascot was dressed in a stereotypical full headdress and pranced around a football field, mimicking an old-style Indian war dance. Some may believe this is entertaining. However, a growing number of IP scholars believe such exhibitions are not only offensive and derogatory, but they are also considered "unauthorized productions" carried out by persons from outside the mocked ethnic community.[75]

With that viewpoint, imagine if you were a proud Native American attending as an undergraduate or graduate student and a minority at a leading university. The university repeatedly exhibits an Indian-style costume-clad dancer at such football games in the San Francisco Bay Region, where numerous Native Americans reside. This is based upon a real situation reported by such a Native American minority student admitted to Stanford University in 1970. Stanford University was among the first to change its mascot due to such cultural sensitivities. Stanford, like many schools, had earlier adopted symbols of Native Americans in the 1920s. Stanford officially dropped its Indian symbol and name in 1972. A new team name, Cardinal, was adopted, and a tree mascot became its unofficial team icon. Stanford was a leader in recognizing and addressing cultural sensitivity with disparaging team names and mascots. Yet it was a question of free speech constitutionality for a professional football team involving the Supreme Court, many years later, that finally brought the disparaging trademark conversation to the mainstream.

In 2014, the NFL professional football team in Washington, D.C., was in the news over court appeals after the USPTO canceled their federal trademark registration for the name "Redskins." This dispute is the result of the team's name controversy by those who believe the name "Redskins" to be offensive and a disparaging racial slur.[76] Despite the initial cancellation of the federal trademark registration, the team was able to continue to use the name under state trademark registration as well as common-law use. It could continue using the TM symbol on its trademark displayed goods and services. Such a federal decision does not prohibit the use of the name "Redskins." The Redskins team has been in a legal battle to defend its federal registration since the early 1990s, when a Native American group filed a petition with the USPTO regarding the offensive nature of the mark. Since then, other Native American groups have continued to file similar complaints. Despite the ethics and morality of the dispute, most progressive opinions of the media and marketers believe the team is creating more bad publicity and diminishing its goodwill with such aggressive status quo persistence.[77] Additional discussion can be found in an article by John Woodward Cox of the *Washington Post*, found at https://www.washingtonpost.com/apps/g/page/local/timeline-the-furor-over-the-redskins-name/2035/.

Shortly thereafter, the USPTO and Pro-Football Inc. asked the Supreme Court to review the case to determine the constitutionality of banning a disparaging federally registered trademark. At the same time, an Asian-American music band challenged the Supreme Court with a similar case (*Matal v. Tam*[78]) involving their federal trademark registration for their band's name "The Slants." Despite an amicus brief filing by National Asian Pacific American Bar Association (NAPABA) supporting the constitutionality of the Lanham Act, the NAPABA stated, "Radical slurs should not be recognized as commercial speech through federally-protected trademarks. Freedom of speech does not require that the government allow racially derogatory terms to be trademarked so that a trademark owner can have exclusive rights to use and monetize such terms."[79]

In mid-2017, the Court ruled unanimously in favor of Tam, stating, "The disparagement clause violates the First Amendment's Free Speech Clause."[80] The court could not deny that such speech cited is offensive to "some portion of the population," yet free and open discussion must prevail in a democracy.[81] Because the Supreme Court ruled in favor of the Slants, the Native American petitioners dropped the Redskins case at that point.[82]

Nevertheless, the Redskins' questionable name debate is not over yet. Progressive views in favor of the Native American activists point out that the Tam victory dealt with a band's lead singer of Asian descent. He selected the moniker to redefine the negative-name perception and use it in a new, positive-connotation orientation. The owner of the professional Washington football team makes no claim to be of Native American heritage.[83] Despite the apparent trademark triumph by the Washington professional football team, the public perception and use of similar team names and mascots continue to decline among school and college teams.[84]

SAY SUPER BOWL® OR BIG GAME?

Trademarks and other IPs associated with the Super Bowl, Olympic Games, and NCAA's March Madness offer high-profile examples of exclusive sponsorships usually tied to licensing agreements. Ambush marketing is often the result of such exclusive sponsorships. Hence, other brand-named establishments attempt to associate their brands with such events without authorization or paying a sponsorship fee. Companies utilizing ambush marketing may not necessarily violate the Lanham (Trademark) Act in certain instances; nevertheless, such marketing could create confusion with consumers. Some companies utilize disclaimers to avoid liability.

The NFL is very strict about protecting its trademark of its branded name Super Bowl. However, as illustrated earlier in this chapter, there are instances of descriptive or nominative fair use that permit ordinary people to use the term in routine expressions for most everyday uses.

To show how bizarre some cease-and-desist claims have gone, keyword search the following terms from an online search engine: next big thing Samsung mobile 2013 super bowl commercial. The search engine should provide a link to the hilarious *Next Big Thing* commercial spoof with comedians Seth Rogen and Paul Rudd, directed by Jon Favreau.[85] It pokes fun at the overzealous trademark enforcement by the NFL. Rogen and Rudd are asked to brainstorm a new Samsung commercial for the Super Bowl. They are reminded not to speak the trademarked name of the event or teams.

Michael Atkins, trademark attorney blogger, reassures us that this scenario is merely a joke. "The game's called the Super Bowl, and if you want to refer to the Super Bowl, you don't have to call it the 'Big Game.' Using a trademark owner's trademark to refer to the owner's branded good is perfectly fair use. Not that I expect the NFL to agree with me."[86]

LICENSING AND RIGHT OF PUBLICITY MATTERS

Licensing commerce in entertainment and sports is big business. For example, the sports licensing industry is more than just official team jerseys or baseball cards. It is primarily a legal connection or agreement between the athletic leagues, sports teams, athletes/players, team fan subscribers, and/or sporting event sponsors.

Licensing professionals must be aware of IP to effectively navigate their way around licensing agreements with their clients. Businesses hire licensing agencies to facilitate their trademark branding business and media copyrights. Licensing agencies collect royalties and also monitor for unauthorized commercial uses or infringements of their client's IP. Group licensing agreements are common licensing mechanisms utilized by sports leagues to market their athletic players to potential licensees as an entire group. This concept reduces the need for individual negations with most players. Certain high-profile athletes may opt out or negotiate their own intellectual properties, including right of publicity covered below. Similar licensing practices apply in the entertainment industry with actors and musicians, as well as the highly branded fashion and apparel field. Apparel licensing is a major revenue generator in the sports licensing industry. Other licensing scenarios that intersect with sports include video games, player trading cards, and player and team collectibles.

Licensing negotiations involve licensing contracts similar to what libraries encounter with database subscriptions. Stipulations on usage of IP and right of publicity are included. Additional details include royalties and other payment responsibilities of the licensee.

Sports Image Rights of Publicity

Publicity rights are more often associated with the entertainment field. However, amateur and professional athletes are embracing their image rights by protections offered via trademark and their right of publicity. Athletes can register their well-known names, likenesses, signatures, slogans, or other insignia as trademarks to alert others of their claims.

In addition to trademarks, athletes can protect their image rights via the right of publicity. Right of publicity allows a well-known entity (an athlete in this case) the right to control the commercial licensing or misappropriation of their identity. Athletes and entertainers often avail themselves of both rights for their commercialization as well as protective measures against misappropriation. Taking such steps safeguards the value and integrity of a sports team and its athletes. Yet, fair use or freedom of speech might apply to unauthorized users of such designations in certain cases when utilizing trademarks or images of famous athletes.

DOMAIN NAMES, CYBERSQUATTING, FAKES, COUNTERFEITS, AND TRADEMARKS

The legal relationship between internet domain names and trademarks is still in flux as technology law develops. However, one should understand that a registration for an internet domain name does not necessarily grant trademark rights. Trademark owners could sue your customer if your customer's domain name confuses customers with regard to their mark or dilutes their mark.[87] The USPTO defines dilution as "the lessening of the capacity of a famous mark to uniquely distinguish its goods, either by tarnishing (weakening through unsavory associations) or blurring (an association arising from the similarity between a mark and a famous mark) its capacity to distinguish."[88]

Cybersquatting or domain squatting is defined as

> . . . registering, selling, or using a domain name with the intent of profiting from the goodwill of someone else's trademark. It . . . originated at a time when most businesses were not savvy about the commercial opportunities on the Internet. Some entrepreneurial souls registered the names of well-known companies as domain names, with the intent of selling the names back to the companies when they finally woke up. . . .

> Opportunities for cybersquatters are rapidly diminishing, because more businesses now know that nailing down domain names is a high priority.[89]

The Internet Corporation for Assigned Names and Numbers (ICANN) manages the international assignment of unique identifiers that keep the internet operating smoothly. These include four areas:

1. the management of assigning Internet Protocol parameters,
2. the authority administration of the internet domain name service (DNS) root zone management,
3. the assignment of internet numbering resources, and
4. other services related to top-level domains (TLDs).[90]

In Chapter 1, Grumpy Cat sued a licensed coffee maker for cybersquatting its trademark. ICANN addressed cybersquatting with its Uniform Domain-Name Dispute-Resolution Policy. This policy specifies that

> most types of trademark-based domain-name disputes must be resolved by agreement, court action, or arbitration before a registrar will cancel, suspend, or transfer a domain name. Disputes alleged to arise from abusive registrations of domain names (for example, cybersquatting) may be addressed by expedited administrative proceedings that the holder of trademark rights initiates by filing a complaint with an approved dispute-resolution service provider.[91]

Combating fake and counterfeit goods are a part of a business protecting its IP rights, or branding, which is vital to its profitability. Anticounterfeiting not only promotes innovation and growth of a business but also helps its customers identify its legitimate products and services. Yet recently, there has been increasing concern about the accelerated growth of counterfeiting and piracy and their effects on businesses, creators, and consumers or customers.

STOPfakes.gov is a service of the International Trade Administration and the U.S. Department of Commerce. The service was developed in reaction to the growing number of counterfeit goods and piracy of media. Such government services help businesses in the United States protect and enforce their global marketplace intellectual properties, which are at risk of being counterfeited and pirated. This is vital for both new business start-ups and established businesses as they expand their product lines or target markets.

According to a 2016 report by the Organisation for Economic Co-operation and Development (OECD), entitled *Trade in Counterfeit and Pirated Goods*, counterfeit and pirated goods are worth about half a trillion dollars, or approximately 2.5 percent of all global imports.[92]

The Office of the United States Trade Representative (USTR) affirms:

> Intellectual Property (IP) infringement, including trademark counterfeiting and copyright piracy, causes significant financial losses for right holders and legitimate

> businesses around the world. It undermines U.S. comparative advantages in innovation and creativity, to the detriment of American businesses and workers. In its most pernicious forms, IP infringement endangers the public. Some counterfeit products, including semiconductors, automobile parts, and medicines, pose significant risks to consumer health and safety.[93]

Often the challenge of counterfeiting and piracy is rooted in the brand name itself and not the actual good or service. A brand's powerful consumer appeal could be utilized by infringers to sell merchandise with little or no resemblance to any of the genuine goods manufactured by the authentic brand owner. Such appeal to the scammed customer has more to do with the brand than the item itself.[94] This is often the case for fashion and sports merchandise.

In addition to substandard counterfeit products scamming buyers, health and safety problems should be of concern to consumers. The use of potentially damaging materials in the manufacture of counterfeit products, as well as substandard functionality, can imperil the health and well-being of purchasers. For example, counterfeit and inferior quality child car seats endanger purchasers and their families.

CONCLUSION

This chapter has reviewed how IP library specialists assist entrepreneurs and small businesses needing support with the federal and state trademark resources. Topics covered included U.S. trademark law, searching trademarks, registration and maintenance of marks, freedom of expression issues, licensing and right of publicity matters, internet domain names, and protecting one's mark against fakes and counterfeit goods.

NOTES

1. Paul Goldstein, *Copyright's Highway: From Gutenberg to Celestial Jukebox* (Stanford, CA: Stanford University Press, 2003), 7.

2. Samira Kawash, "Hershey's Kisses: Got Lawyer?" *Candy Professor* blog, March 5, 2010, https://candyprofessor.com/2010/03/05/hersheys-kisses-facts-candy-professor-style/ (accessed December 3, 2018); P. K. Lo, "Free Kisses at Jacques Torres Today," *NBC New York*, July 17, 2009, https://www.nbcnewyork.com/the-scene/archives/Free-Kisses-at-Jacques-Torres-Today-.html (accessed December 3, 2018); Nicole Perlroth, "Sweet Talker: Jacques Torres' Showmanship Sets Him Apart in the Crowded Market for High-end Chocolate," *Forbes*, https://www.forbes.com/free_forbes/2009/0713/jacques-torres-chocolate-sweet-talker.html (accessed December 3, 2018); Sarah Feingold, "You Be the Judge: Chocolate Kisses," *Esty Journal* blog, June 12, 2009, https://blog.etsy.com/en/you-be-the-judge-chocolate-kisses/ (accessed December 3, 2018); Jeremy Olshan, "'Stolen' Kiss Riles Hershey: Cease and De-kiss!" *NY Post*, April 29, 2009, https://nypost.com/2009/04/24/stolen-kiss-riles-hershey/ (accessed December 3, 2018); and for actual viewing of Hershey's cease-and-desist letter and reply of Torres' attorney, see Daniel Mauer, "Hershey's v. Jacques Torres: The Lawyer-to-Lawyer Slapdown!" *New York Magazine's Grubstreet*,

April 22, 2009, http://www.grubstreet.com/2009/04/hersheys_vs_jacques_torres_the.html (accessed December 3, 2018).

3. http://www.uspto.gov/faq/trademarks.jsp#Search005 (accessed August 3, 2010).

4. http://www.ipwatchdog.com/trademark/trademarks-branding-business/ (accessed July 27, 2010).

5. Ewing Marion Kauffman Foundation, *Kaufmann Firm Survey Series*, http://www.kauffman.org/what-we-do/research/kauffman-firm-survey-series (accessed October 28, 2015).

6. Title 15 U.S. Code §1051 et seq., Trademark Act of 1946.

7. http://www.lib.utexas.edu/engin/trademark/timeline/tmindex.html (accessed March 20, 2011).

8. Title 15 U.S. Code § 1127.

9. Ibid.

10. United States Constitution, Article I, Section 8 empowers the United States Congress: To promote the Progress of Science and useful Arts, be securing for limited Times to Authors and Inventors the exclusive Right to their respective Writings and Discoveries.

11. Act of March 3, 1881, Chapter 138, 21 Statute 502.

12. United States Constitution, Article I, Section 8, Clause 3.

13. Trademark Manual of Examining Procedure (TMEP) 901.03 Commerce That May Be Lawfully Regulated By Congress, October 2017, https://tmep.uspto.gov/RDMS/TMEP/current#/current/TMEP-900d1e98.html (accessed October 8, 2018).

14. U.S. Constitution Article I, §8, Clause 8 (1787).

15. USPTO, About Trademark Infringement, https://www.uspto.gov/page/about-trademark-infringement (accessed November 6, 2018).

16. Title 15 U.S. Code §1051 et seq., Trademark Act of 1946.

17. U.S. Patent & Trademark Office, *Protecting Your Trademark: Enhancing Your Rights through Federal Registration*, Basic Facts About Trademarks brochure, 2015, p. 2.

18. Ibid.

19. Terry Fisher, "Overview of Trademark Law, Berkman Online Lecture and Discussion (BOLD) Series, Harvard University, https://cyber.harvard.edu/metaschool/fisher/domain/tm.htm (accessed May 18, 2017).

20. USPTO, 1202.02, Registration of Trade Dress, *Trademark Manual of Examining Procedure*, 2017, https://tmep.uspto.gov/RDMS/TMEP/current#/current/TMEP-1200d1e835.html (accessed December 29, 2017).

21. Two Pesos, Inc. v. Taco Cabana, Inc. 505 U.S. 763 (1992); Bryan K. Wheelock, "Trade Dress versus Design Patents: Understanding the Different Tests for Infringement," *Trademark Reporter* 105, no. 6 (November-December 2015): 1389–1408, http://www.inta.org/TMR/Pages/Vol105_No6_a3.aspx (accessed September 17, 2017); Julie Hopkins, "Understanding the Different Rights and Remedies Under US IP Law," *World Economics (Journal)* (Special Edition, 2015), http://www.tydingslaw.com/site/files/world_economics_journal_spring_2015.pdf (accessed December 15, 2018); Spear IP, "Fashion and IP, Part Two: Trade Dress," published September 21, 2015, https://spear-ip.com/fashion-and-ip-2-trade-dress/ (accessed December 15, 2018); and Julie Hopkins, "Differences Between Design Patents and Trade Dress," IPWatchdog.com, June 3, 2016, http://www.ipwatchdog.com/2016/06/03/differences-design-patents-trade-dress/id=69591/ (accessed December 15, 2018).

22. See Lanham Act, Pub. L. No. 79-489, § 43(a), 60 Statute 427, 441 (codified in 15 U.S.C. § 1125(a) (2013)).

23. Stephen Fishman, *Trademark: Legal Care for Your Business & Product Name* (Berkeley, CA: Nolo 2016), 23.

24. USPTO, *Trademark Manual of Examining Procedure*, 904.03(f) Specimens for Sound Marks, October 2018, https://tmep.uspto.gov/RDMS/TMEP/current#/current/TMEP-900d1e763.html (accessed November 6, 2018).

25. http://www.mondaq.com/unitedstates/x/373110/Trademark/Is+Taylor+Swift+Trying+To+Use+Trademark+Protection+To+Monopolize+Common+Phrases; and http://www.mondaq.com/unitedstates/x/375142/Trademark/Celebrity+Trademark+Watch+Shake+it+Off+Taylor+Swift+This+Sick+Beat (accessed October 23, 2015).

26. USPTO, Conducting a Trademark Search, https://www.uspto.gov/learning-and-resources/support-centers/patent-and-trademark-resource-centers-ptrc/resources (accessed October 15, 2018).

27. USPTO, Nice Agreement Eleventh Edition—Version 2019 (NCL 11-2019), https://www.uspto.gov/trademark/trademark-updates-and-announcements/nice-agreement-current-edition-version-general-remarks (accessed January 20, 2019).

28. Trademark Act Section 2(d), 15 U.S.C. Section 1052(d), TMEP §1207 et seq.

29. Jefferson C. Glassie et al., *Intellectual Property for Nonprofit Organizations and Associations* (Washington, D.C.: ASAE Association Management Press, 2012), 17–18; Timothy Lee Wherry, *Intellectual Property: Everything the Digital-Age Librarian Needs to Know* (Chicago: American Library Association, 2008), 79–81.

30. Stephen Fishman, *Trademark: Legal Care for Your Business & Product Name* (Berkeley, CA: Nolo, 2016), 33–34; U.S. Patent & Trademark Office, *Protecting Your Trademark: Enhancing Your Rights Through Federal Registration*, Basic Facts about Trademarks brochure, 2015, p. 9.

31. Ibid.

32. Michael Spence, "The Mark as Expression/The Mark as Property," *Current Legal Problems* 58, no. 1 (January 1, 2005), 491–515, https://doi.org/10.1093/clp/58.1.491 (accessed October 7, 2018).

33. International Trademark Association, "Fair Use of Trademarks," https://www.inta.org/TrademarkBasics/FactSheets/Pages/Fair-Use-of-TrademarksNL.aspx# (accessed October 8, 2018).

34. The section of this chapter entitled Freedom of Expression and Other Issues and Controversies is from an earlier journal article published by the author and the Patent & Trademark Resource Center Association: John Schlipp, "Fair Use and Freedom of Expression of Trademarks in Instruction, Research, and Publishing," *PTRCA Journal* 25 (2015), http://ptrca.org/newsletters/2015/schlipp (accessed December 15, 2018).

35. For more on Deceptive Matter—See 15 USC § 1052 (e) (1) & TMEP 1203.02(b).

36. Susan Scafidi, *Who Owns Culture?: Appropriation and Authenticity in American Law* (New Brunswick, NJ: Rutgers, 2005), 138.

37. Kembrew McLeod, *Freedom of Expression®: Overzealous Copyright Bozos and Other Enemies of Creativity* (New York: Doubleday, 2005).

38. *Mattel v. Walking Mountain Productions*, 353 F.3d 792 (2003).

39. Ibid., 144.

40. David Bollier, *Brand Name Bullies: The Quest to Own and Control Culture* (Hoboken, NJ: Wiley, 2005), 93.

41. Corynne McSherry, *Who Owns Academic Work?: Battling for Control of Intellectual Property* (Cambridge, MA: Harvard University Press, 2001), 2–3; 16.

42. Lanham Act, 15 U.S.C. § 1125, section on exclusions, including noncommercial use of a mark.

43. Schlipp, "Fair Use and Freedom of Expression of Trademarks."

44. David Lange and H. Jefferson Powell, *No Law: Intellectual Property in the Image of an Absolute First Amendment* (Stanford, CA: Stanford Law Books, 2009), 65.

45. Bollier, David, *Brand Name Bullies: The Quest to Own and Control Culture* (Hoboken, NJ: Wiley, 2005), 131–133.

46. Jonathan Faber, "Celebrity Licensing and the Right of Publicity: Navigating New Frontiers of Opportunity and Liability," *Licensing Journal*, September 2012.

47. Ibid.

48. Michael Madow, "Personality as Property: The Uneasy case for Publicity Rights," in *Intellectual Property and Information Wealth: Issues and Practices in the Digital Age*, Volume 3: Trademark and Unfair Competition, Peter K. Yu, ed. (Westport, CT: Praeger, 2007), 345.

49. Stacey L. Dogan and Mark A. Lemley, "What the Right of Publicity Can Learn from Trademark Law," *Stanford Law Review* 58, no. 4 (Feb., 2006): 1161–1220.

50. Jonathan Faber, "Indiana: A Celebrity-Friendly Jurisdiction," *RES GESTAE (Journal of the Indiana State Bar Association)* 43, no. 9 (March 2000): 24–30.

51. Jonathan Faber, "Celebrity Licensing and the Right of Publicity: Navigating New Frontiers of Opportunity and Liability," *Licensing Journal* 43, no. 8 (September 2012): 1–7.

52. Robert D. Litowitz, "Trademark Basics. The Rights of Publicity," *IP Strategist*, May/June 1995.

53. Kenneth E. Spahn, "Legal Protection of Fictional Characters," *University of Miami Entertainment & Sports Law Review* 9, no. 2 (1992), https://repository.law.miami.edu/umeslr/vol9/iss2/6/ (accessed October 7, 2019); Amanda Schreyer, "Overview of Legal Protection for Fictional Characters: Balancing Public and Private Interests," *Cybaris®*, 6, no. 1 (2015), https://open.mitchellhamline.edu/cybaris/vol6/iss1/3/ (accessed October 7, 2019).

54. Mike Masnick, "Sherlock Holmes and the Case of the Never Ending Copyright Dispute," TechDirt, May 26, 2015, https://www.techdirt.com/articles/20150524/17521431095/sherlock-holmes-case-never-ending-copyright-dispute.shtml (accessed May 27, 2015).

55. There is no single federal right of publicity law, so it varies from state to state. Indiana's publicity statute is the greatest, up to one hundred years, while as of 2012 over a dozen states have no right of publicity law. So it is safe to assume that anyone who died over one hundred years ago is not covered by any right of publicity. See following sites for additional information: *Right of Publicity*, "Brief History of the Right of Publicity," http://rightofpublicity.com/brief-history-of-rop (accessed October 7, 2018), adapted from "Indiana: A Celebrity Friendly Jurisdiction," by Jonathan Faber, published in *Res Gestae* 43, no. 9 (March 2000), and last updated July 31, 2015; International Trademark Association, "Board Resolutions US Federal Right of Publicity," March 3, 1998, http://www.inta.org/Advocacy/Pages/USFederalRightofPublicity.aspx (accessed October 7, 2018).

56. Schlipp, "Fair Use and Freedom of Expression of Trademarks."

57. 15 U.S.C. §1115(b)(4).

58. *New Kids on the Block v. News America Publishing, Inc.*, 971 F.2d 302 (9th Cir. 1992); *Playboy Enterprises, Inc. V. Welles*, 279 F.3d 796 (9th Cir. 2002).

59. 15 U.S.C. §1115(b)(4) regarding Fair Use for noncommercial use such as Lucasfilm Ltd. V. High Frontier, 227 USPQ 967 (D.D.C. 1985).

60. *E.S.S. Entertainment 2000, Inc. v. Rock Star Videos, Inc.*, 2008 WL 4791705 (9th Cir. 2008).

61. Deere & Co. v. MTD Products 41 F.3d 39 (2d Cir. 1994).

62. See Coca-Cola Co. v. Gemini Rising, Inc. 346 F. Supp. 1183, 1189 (E.D.N.Y. 1972); Hormel Foods Corp. v. Jim Henson Productions, Inc. 73 F. 3d 497 (2d Cir. 1996); and J. Thomas McCarthy, McCarthy on Trademark and Unfair Competition § 24: 104, 24:105 (4th ed. 2002).

63. See Pink Panther case regarding a gay group parody name association; Jordache Enterprises, Inc. v. Hogg Wyld, Ltd., 828 F.2d 1482 (10th Cir. 1987); L.L. Bean, Inc. v. Drake Publishers, Inc. 811 F.2d 26, 30-31 (1st Cir. 1987).

64. Nolo, "Cybersquatting: What It Is and What Can Be Done About It," https://www.nolo.com/legal-encyclopedia/cybersquatting-what-what-can-be-29778.html (accessed October 7, 2018).

65. U.S. Patent & Trademark Office, Report to Congress: The Anticybersquatting Consumer Protection Act of 1999, section 3006 concerning the abusive registration of domain names, http://www.uspto.gov/web/offices/dcom/olia/tmcybpiracy/repcongress.pdf (accessed March 1, 2015).

66. 420 F.3d 309 (4th Cir. 2005), Nos. 04-2122, 04-2011.

67. "Best Buy" vs. Consumer Protection Blog, Raelyn Campbell, http://bestbuybadbuyboycott.blogspot.com/ and PointofLaw.com Information and Opinion on the U.S. Litigation System, Carter Wood, April 30, 2008, http://www.pointoflaw.com/archives/2008/04/this-54-million-lawsuit-agains.php (accessed March 6, 2015).

68. Craighead County Jonesboro Public Library, "Trademark FAQ for Vendors," https://www.libraryinjonesboro.org/trademark-faqs (accessed October 8, 2018).

69. Erwin Magbanua, "A 'Comic-Con' by Any Other Name (Or, How Not to Commit Trademark Infringement with Your Library Comic Event," *Programming Librarian*, May 1, 2017, http://programminglibrarian.org/articles/comic-con-any-other-name-or-how-not-commit-trademark-infringement-your-library-comic-event (accessed October 8, 2018).

70. John Hubbard, "Top 20 Library Scandals in Recent History," *Librarian at the University of Wisconsin–Milwaukee* blog, May 10, 2017, https://medium.com/@hubbard/top-20-library-scandals-in-recent-history-bf237e1025b2 (accessed October 8, 2018).

71. Jon Garon, "Chapter 13: Fandom and Creativity: Fan Art, Fiction, and Cosplay," in *Pop Culture Business Handbook for Cons and Festivals: Business, Strategy, and Legal Reference Guide* (Fort Lauderdale, FL: Manegiare Publications, 2017), 175; and Amanda Bacoyanis, "Comic-Con Considerations: Coplay, the Right of Publicity, and Copyright Concerns," IP Watchdog, July 31, 2015, http://www.ipwatchdog.com/2015/07/31/comic-con-considerations-cosplay-the-right-of-publicity-and-copyright-concerns/id=60084/ (accessed July 31, 2015).

72. Garon, "Fandom and Creativity," 162–164.

73. Bacoyanis, "Comic-Con Considerations."

74. David Clark, "Is Your Halloween Costume an Infringement?" http://law-dlc.com/0/3923056/0/95912/ (accessed September 18, 2017); Tiff Graham, "Trademarked Costumes in Parades: Phenomenologically Speaking," October 6, 2017, https://networks.h-net.org/node/167585/blog/parade-talk/392141/trademarked-costumes-parades-phenomenologically-speaking (accessed October 8, 2017).

75. Kamil Idris, *Intellectual Property: A Power Tool for Economic Growth* (Genève, Switzerland: World Intellectual Property Organization, 2002), 258–259, ftp://ftp.wipo.int/pub/library/ebooks/wipopublications/wipo_pub_888e.pdf (accessed March 1, 2017).

76. NPR: *All Things Considered*, "Redskins' Cancelled Trademarks Spell A Symbolic Victory for Critics," June 18, 2014, http://www.npr.org/2014/06/18/323351064/redskins-cancelled-tradmarks-spell-a-symbolic-victory-for-critics (accessed June 18, 2014).

77. Michael Lewis and Manish Tripathi, "'Redskins' is Bad Business," *New York Times*, June 24, 2014, https://www.nytimes.com/2014/06/25/opinion/redskins-is-bad-business.html (accessed April 16, 2019); Clarence Page, "It's Time to Change the Name of the Washington Redskins," *Chicago Tribune*, May 4, 2014, http://articles.chicagotribune.com/2014-05-04/news/ct-redskins-clippers-nba-clarence-page-oped-20140504_1_washington-redskins-name-change-donald-sterling (accessed June 1, 2017).

78. Matal, Interim Director, United States Patent and Trademark Office v. Tam, 582 U.S. ____, (2017). Also, see Supreme Court Opinion at https://www.supremecourt.gov/opinions/16pdf/15-1293_1o13.pdf (accessed April 16, 2019).

79. "NAPABA Disagrees with Band in Trademark Case," *Asian American Press*, January 21, 2017, http://aapress.com/editorial/napaba-disagrees-with-band-in-trademark-case/ (accessed April 21, 2018).

80. U.S. Supreme Court, Slip Opinion 15-1293, Matal, Interim Director, United States Patent & Trademark Office, v. Tam, https://www.supremecourt.gov/opinions/16pdf/15-1293_1o13.pdf (accessed June 19, 2017).

81. John Richards, "It's 2018: The Impact of IP Decisions Form 2017—Matal v. Tam," *JD Supra*, April 12, 2018, https://www.jdsupra.com/legalnews/it-s-2018-the-impact-of-ip-decisions-91952/ (accessed April 12, 2018).

82. Ian Shapira and Ann E. Marimow, "Washington Redskins Win Trademark Fight over the Team's Name," *Washington Post*, June 29, 2017, https://www.washingtonpost.com/local/public-safety/2017/06/29/a26f52f0-5cf6-11e7-9fc6-c7ef4bc58d13_story.html?noredirect=on&utm_term=.1060ca6f07fe (accessed June 30, 2017).

83. Roger Groves, " Supreme Court's 'Slants' Ruling Isn't a Win Yet for the Washington Redskins," *Forbes*, June 20, 2017, https://www.forbes.com/sites/rogergroves/2017/06/20/supreme-court-ruling-is-not-the-savior-for-the-washington-redskins/#19d935c36915 (accessed April 21, 2017).

84. Erik Brady, "Appeals Court Vacates Decision that Cancelled Redskins Trademark Registrations," *USA Today*, January 18, 2018, https://www.usatoday.com/story/sports/nfl/2018/01/18/appeals-court-vacates-decisions-canceled-redskins-trademark-registrations/1046758001/ (accessed August 28, 2018).

85. Thomas Ricker, "Samsung's $15 Million Super Bowl Commercial Arrives Early," *Verge*, February 3, 2013, https://www.theverge.com/2013/2/3/3946972/samsung-super-bowl-commercial-with-paul-rudd-seth-rogan (accessed December 11, 2018).

86. Michael Atkins, "Commercial Pokes Fun at the NFL's Control of Its 'Super Bowl' Trademark," Seattle Trademark Lawyer, January 31, 2013, http://seattletrademarklawyer.com/blog/2013/1/31/commercial-pokes-fun-at-the-nfls-control-of-its-super-bowl-t.html (accessed December 11, 2018).

87. Stephen Fishman, *Trademark: Legal Care for Your Business & Product Name* (Berkeley, CA: Nolo, 2016), 59.

88. USPTO, Well-"Known Marks,"https://www.uspto.gov/trademark/laws-regulations/office-policy-and-international-affairs-well-known-marks (accessed November 4, 2018).

89. Nolo, "Cybersquatting: What It Is, and What Can Be Done about It," *Legal Topics*, https://www.nolo.com/legal-encyclopedia/cybersquatting-what-what-can-be-29778.html (accessed October 17, 2012).

90. ICANN, http://www.icann.org/ (accessed October 15, 2012).

91. ICANN website, Uniform Domain-Name Dispute-Resolution Policy, http://www.icann.org/en/help/dndr/udrp (accessed October 15, 2012).

92. OECD/EUIPO (2016), Trade in Counterfeit and Pirated Goods: Mapping the Economic Impact, OECD Publishing, Paris, http://www.oecd.org/gov/risk/trade-in-counterfeit-and-pirated-goods-9789264252653-en.htm (accessed April 12, 2018).

93. Office of the United States Trade Representative (USTR), 2017 Special 301 Report, https://ustr.gov/sites/default/files/301/2017%20Special%20301%20Report%20FINAL.PDF (accessed October 15, 2018).

94. Secretary General of the OECD (Organisation for Economic Co-operation and Development), *The Economic Impact of Counterfeiting and Piracy* (Paris, France: OECD, 2008), 48.

Chapter 6

LEGAL AND ETHICAL INFORMATION POLICIES

CHAPTER OBJECTIVES

1. To explore and examine legal and ethical information policies and their impact on libraries and information-based professions
2. To recognize how the context of information policies are established by various stakeholders such as government; business: information producers or distributors; and associations or organizations
3. To understand and apply intellectual freedom and its tie to freedom of expression as a fundamental right for library customers
4. To recognize varying legal and ethical aspects of privacy rights and data protection for employees in the workplace, customer data, and library archival and special collection personal information
5. To discuss how the Freedom of Information Act offers access to unpublished government information
6. To describe and compare plagiarism ethical issues versus author moral rights
7. To recognize and understand how internet copyright laws such as the Digital Millennium Copyright Act (DMCA) affect intellectual property and information rights

INTRODUCTION

This chapter is an overview of the legal and ethical applications related to information policies in the workplace environment of libraries and other information professions, including their customers. Libraries affect and are affected by information policies established at various levels—most often at national, state, and local levels.[1] This encompasses managing legal and ethical facets of information polices related to intellectual freedom, including free speech or expression, privacy and data protection, freedom of information or access to government information, and intellectual property (IP), including plagiarism and addressing the DMCA and other related IP laws. Such policies are often generated based upon different laws, regulations, standards, or codes by multiple stakeholders such as government, business and industry, information producers and disseminators, and associations or organizations that represent the common good of the public or professional norms.

The Declaration of Independence, the Bill of Rights, the Constitution, and other federal government documents are historical examples that address information policy issues such as those stated in the first paragraph, intellectual freedom, free speech/expression, access to government information, intellectual property rights, and dissemination of information.[2]

A policy is often defined as a law, regulation, rule, practice, or guideline. One should be aware that policies are not the same as procedures. Whereas policies are associated with laws and rules reflecting the credence of an organization, procedures outline how individuals should act policy out.[3]

Lee Ann Torrans, an attorney specializing in law and libraries, maintains that library policies should "represent the mission of the library and balance the rights of the library community as a whole with the individual's rights to access and use the library." Torrans adds that library "policies must be drafted to comply with laws that govern policies."[4] Within organizations such as libraries, the American Library Association (ALA) affirms that library policies:

> help define the values of the organization, and they help managers and staff translate those values into service priorities. Policies establish a standard for services that can be understood by users of the service and providers. Policies ensure equitable treatment for all and polices provide a framework for delivery of services. When policies have been adopted by a library's governing agents in a formal process and are consistent with local, state, and federal laws, they will be enforceable.[5]

The ALA offers additional details on how to develop library policies at its main site https://libguides.ala.org/librarypolicy and among its various affiliate sites for specific types of libraries. This chapter concentrates primarily on legal and ethical information policies that affect libraries and their customers.

Definitions of information policy include "a set of interrelated principles, laws, guidelines, rules and regulations, directives, procedures, judgments, interpretations, and practices"[6] that affect the creation, management, attainment, acquisition, organization, dissemination, evaluation, and/or use of information.[7] Information policies cover many aspects of information rights, including censorship, freedom of expression, privacy and data protection, freedom of information, and intellectual property.[8]

CONTEXT/STAKEHOLDERS: GOVERNMENTS, BUSINESSES, AND ASSOCIATIONS

Multiple stakeholders are involved in the context of establishing legal and ethical information policies. These include governments, businesses and organizations, and individuals, regionally, nationally, and, in some cases, internationally. Businesses include information producers and distributors of content in libraries. Associations and organizations usually represent the common good of the public or instill professional norms or standards. Often such stakeholders have economic or social goals in mind within a technological, legal, or human framework. Often, such goals are revealed when one identifies the needs of the stakeholders.[9]

A frame analysis study to better understand information policy needs by Rowlands et al.[10] reviewed the literature in the field to identify clusters of information policies of stakeholders with goal characteristics ranging from openness to control, as well as market regulation versus government control. Categorized objectives found among information policies include:

- Information protectionism such as privacy and data protection
- Information markets such as copyright laws to support information creators and consumers
- Broadcasting and telecommunications, balancing commercial and citizen interests including freedom of expression and universal service
- Public access to official information, such as government information, and the information society and provision of infrastructure for wider dissemination of information[11]

Library science scholars Case, Cornelius, and Rubin offer further elucidations about stakeholders related to information policies. Donald Case differentiates between social and economic interests of the stakeholders. He advocates that the economic interests promote investments in technology and the labor force to contribute to the financial wealth of society, including information products and services. The social interests address the needs of individual citizens and the cultural common good. Ian Cornelius expands on the overarching context of interests of the stakeholders to include the right of government, along with interests of business and the common good. Inclusion of government rights in a democracy often recognizes human rights, including information rights.[12]

Richard Rubin goes even further, offering more timely examples of social and economic aspects of the legal and political climate that affects information policy in libraries.[13] Today's political climate affects public policies and public perceptions, which shape information policies of the economic and social needs of the constituents of libraries. Examples include taxpayer calls for better accountability of public services, declining confidence of the community in public institutions, political ideology that favors private enterprises over public good, and libraries lacking effective advocacy and public relations of the libraries themselves. Social media policies covered below are a growing issue, too.

Stakeholders such as standards-setting organizations (covered in Chapter 3) develop policies known as standards. Such organizations often rely on patented technologies as benchmarks to develop their standards. Standards-setting organizations often publish policies or good-faith guidelines that attempt to establish standardized technology for the benefit of product and service compatibility, as well as consumer safety.

The facets of information rights associated with the information policies listed below often bolster significant social and economic benefit to the community. For example, intellectual property awareness supports social respect for the intellectual works of others while implanting a sense of entrepreneurship for rewarding creators of new intellectual works and business startups with intellectual properties. The following facets to managing information rights in libraries are expounded on next in this chapter:

Intellectual freedom (including free speech or expression)
Privacy and data protection;
Freedom of Information Act (FOIA)
IP legal and ethical aspects

INTELLECTUAL FREEDOM (INCLUDING FREE SPEECH OR EXPRESSION)

The first facet of information policy management in libraries, which is one with which librarians are most familiar, is intellectual freedom. The ALA defines intellectual freedom as:

> the right of every individual to both seek and receive information from all points of view without restriction. It provides for free access to all expressions of ideas through which any and all sides of a question, cause or movement may be explored.[14]

Although not directly related to intellectual property, intellectual freedom is fundamentally tied to freedom of expression, which, as this book explains, is fundamental to fair use of copyrighted and trademarked works. Intellectual freedom and the freedom to read advocates the freedom to hold, receive, and disseminate ideas.[15]

Freedoms of speech and expression are vital to an informed democracy. If such freedoms are stifled, censorship ensues, which could stop the creation, acquisition, organization, dissemination, evaluation, and/or use of certain types of information, as noted above. It is the primary function of an information policy in a democracy to promote the free flow of such information. Freedom of expression goes beyond free speech. Like intellectual freedom, it deals with actions to support one's expression or belief, not merely words.[16] The ALA reminds us that the First Amendment stands against such censorship tied to freedom of expression. It affirms that each of us has, "the right to read, view, listen to, and disseminate constitutionally protected ideas, even if a censor finds those ideas offensive."[17]

Intellectual freedom should not be confused with Freedom of Information Act (FOIA). It has to do with access to government information, not freedom of expression.

PRIVACY AND DATA PROTECTION

Privacy rights are not part of IP laws. Privacy rights, from a legal and ethical aspect, protect a person against unwanted public exposure and any consequential emotional harm. Libraries normally establish privacy information policies to protect the interests of their employees and customers. Online services frequently establish a privacy policy and post it online. Privacy policies describe how data is collected and how it will be utilized; often with a customer opt-out opportunity and offering patrons their data history.[18]

Privacy laws are more common at the state level and vary from state to state. State privacy laws reserve the privacy rights of individuals to be left alone.[19] Privacy rights are often associated with employee workplace scenarios, shared personal information held on internet service provider sites such as social media databases, cybersecurity settings, customer aspects of library patron data, and even historical research among personal information found in some special collections and archives.

Workplace privacy is a primary human resources subject for which librarians and personnel and members in other organizations and agencies should be aware. Some believe that employees should have strong privacy rights at work, while employers believe that they have a right to monitor employees to encourage productivity and suppress potential issues such as workplace bullying or sexual harassment. Yet, a worker's labor right to privacy is not always guaranteed under U.S. law.[20] The increased dependence on computers and email in the workplace offers employers additional productivity monitoring. Although employees may feel such technology-related eavesdropping is an invasion of their privacy, it is often legal for employers to do so. Only when privacy information policies are created by one's business or organization might that employee have some privacy rights related to the workplace environment.[21]

Online data and information privacy rights, cookies, web bugs, and spyware are ways commercial entities monitor consumer habits, especially on retailer websites. Some believe that these customer surveillance methods challenge the privacy rights of consumers. In the United States, it is lawful for online businesses to collect customer transaction information for marketing purposes without permission. Some websites inform their visitors and provide an opt-out model of permission marketing. Online commerce uses self-regulation to steer clear of privacy consumer protection legislation with such pacts as an industry created Online Privacy Alliance to promote self-regulation and developed privacy guidelines for its members.[22]

Data and information privacy laws prohibit the disclosure or misuse of data and information held by internet services on private individuals. The president of the United States introduced a new Consumer Privacy Bill of Rights in 2012.[23] The intent of these rights was to give individuals the ability to exercise control over what personal details companies collected and how the information was used. In 2018, after two days of congressional hearings with Facebook® founder Mark Zuckerberg,[24] the U.S. Congress introduced the Customer Online Notification for Stopping Edge-provider Network Transgressions (CONSENT) Act.[25] If passed into law, it would require the Federal Trade Commission (FTC) to establish privacy protections for customers of "online edge" providers like Facebook and Google.[26] A Federal Communication Commission (FCC) proposed rule defines an edge provider as an "individual or entity that provides any content, application, or service over the Internet, and any individual or entity that provides a device used for accessing any content, application, or service over the Internet."[27] The only law that addressed this topic somewhat is the Children's Online Privacy Protection Act (COPPA).[28] It addresses the online privacy of children under the age of thirteen. Similarly, individual medical records are now also protected by federal privacy law.[29] In the meantime, several information literacy instruction sessions in libraries now include this topic so that patrons may review their individual profiles to ensure that sensitive, personal information is protected, while still enjoying the benefits of online networking and research database sites.[30]

Beyond questionable privacy of customer data shared with legitimate online services such as Facebook or Google, cybercrimes still abound that jeopardize information security and privacy with communication technology for health care records, identity theft and credit card fraud, and other sensitive private information of individuals and businesses. Cybersecurity addresses such theft as it offers protection of computerized data,[31] while cybercrime refers to any criminal activity committed by means of the internet.[32] Technopedia defines cybercrime as "a crime in which a computer is the object of the crime (hacking, phishing, spamming) or is used as a tool to commit an offense (child pornography, hate crimes)."[33] Other computer crimes could also take place outside of the internet on private computers or networks.

Library Customer Data Collection and Privacy

Information security management and customer private data protection are key challenges for libraries. Confidentiality and security of patron information and its computer networks is a full-time job for librarians at their institutions. It is a challenge for libraries trying to balance between its information needs for collection development versus patron data privacy. For example, national security issues dealing with law enforcement inquires after the implementation of the USA PATRIOT Act[34] have been challenged in relation to First Amendment and intellectual freedom as well as privacy rights of library patrons. (See ALA site for additional details: http://www.ala.org/advocacy/advleg/federallegislation/theusa patriotact.)

As Judith Krug, freedom of speech proponent, related to privacy challenges for libraries in *Privacy in the 21st Century,* such issues are:

> brought forward by relentless change in technology, law, and social attitudes. Whether it is the question of adopting Radio Frequency Identification Devices (RFIDs) to track book inventory, devising policy to deal with law enforcement inquiries...or addressing a library user's concerns about the use of her personal information, each day finds librarians confronting new questions and new challenges concerning privacy and confidentiality.[35]

The ALA offers guidance on how to handle patron record privacy issues as privacy laws vary from state to state. The ALA Issues and Advocacy website proposes the following policy related to State Privacy Laws Regarding Library Records:

- To work with local legal counsel to ensure understanding of state confidentiality laws to be able to respond quickly to law enforcement requests
- To adopt a policy that specifically recognizes the confidentiality of information sought, received, consulted, or borrowed by a library user
- To refer to existing laws to control behavior that involves public safety or criminal behavior[36]

The ALA Issues and Advocacy site also encourages libraries to cooperate with law enforcement within the framework of their state law. This includes having a library policy in place with procedures for working with law enforcement when a legal order for customer records occurs.[37] Clear patron privacy policies should be crafted carefully recognizing all types of customer access and use of library facilities and resources.[38]

Social media guidelines are a growing privacy policy matter with libraries. Consideration of a library's own social media platform, as well as commercial social media accessed and utilized by patrons on library computers, should be considered in shaping such library policies. Library staff should be aware of these policies. If a library is unable to assure privacy, it should address this in its library customer privacy policy. For example, some states have records retention policies that could invade customer privacy. Seek support of legal counsel for additional guidance in such instances.[39]

To further guard privacy of library customers and maintain a secure computer network environment, investment in security of such challenges is necessary. Jo Bryson, author of *Managing Information Services: A Transformative Approach*, asserts that financial investment in security support alone is not effective without organizational culture support of all employees and any contractors in an organization. Bryson continues that the "objectives of information security management are to ensure confidentiality, integrity and availability of information and resources."[40] Information has varying levels of sensitivity and is secured through classification systems as to whom should have access to what.

Richard Spinello and Herman Tavani, editors of *Readings in CyberEthics*, also point out integrity, but add vulnerability concerns for cybersecurity of information on computers:

- The integrity of *data security* which resides in one or more computers
- The vulnerability of *system security* attacked by malicious programs on computers and system resources
- The vulnerability of *network/internet security* attacked on computer networks, including the internet[41]

Privacy Issues Related to Archives Content

Another aspect of privacy right goes beyond data collection of library information users. When library customers make use of resources from libraries, archives, or special collections, the privacy rights of authors must be considered. Especially when publishing sensitive information from diaries or personal files. As the Library of Congress points out on its American Memory website:

> Issues pertaining to privacy and publicity may arise when a researcher contemplates the use of letters, diary entries, photographs or reportage in visual, audio, and print formats found in library collections. Because two or more people are often involved in the work (e.g. photographer and subject, interviewer and interviewee) and because of the ease with which various media in digital format can be reused, photographs, audio files, and motion pictures represent materials in which issues of privacy and publicity emerge with some frequency.[42]

According to Sage Publication's related topics *Quick-Guide*, there are four types of privacy rights:

1. Public disclosure of private facts—revealing truthful private or embarrassing facts about a person without legitimate public concern or newsworthiness
2. False light—falsely portraying a person as something highly offensive that he or she is not
3. Intrusion upon seclusion—intrusion into private areas or affairs, including wrongful use of tape recorders and cameras
4. Misappropriation of name or likeness/right of publicity—unauthorized use of a person's name, photograph, likeness, voice, or endorsement to promote the sale of a commercial product or service[43]

The rights of privacy and data protection in information policies are significant for maintaining the security of libraries and their customers' private information, as well as workplace and research privacy issues. Having a better understanding of this subject should support making informed decisions related to privacy rights and data protection at one's library.

THE FREEDOM OF INFORMATION ACT (FOIA)

The Freedom of Information Act (FOIA) is a federal law that permits disclosure of information and documents controlled by the U.S. Government.[44] It offers access to unpublished information from the executive branch of the federal government. It does not include the legislative or judicial branches. The FOIA site states that its basic function is "to ensure informed citizens, vital to the functioning of a democratic society."[45]

Signed into law in 1966, the FOIA affords that "any person has a right, enforceable in court, to obtain access to federal agency records, except to the extent that such records (or portions of them) are protected from public disclosure by one of nine exemptions or by one of three special law enforcement record exclusions."[46] However, freedom of information only applies to information rights for access to the U.S. government documents.

FOIA was established for any individual, or group of people such as a business or organization, needing information. This right is especially useful for news journalists and library researchers. See https://www.foia.gov/index.html site for details. Also, the Reporters Committee for Freedom of the Press provides an easy-to-use

FOIA Letter Generator to make official requests of federal agencies that is available from https://www.rcfp.org/foia.

Federal government information is now available more freely online than ever before including the Government Printing Office (GPO) documents. Before submitting a FOIA request, one might consult with a government documents librarian at a Federal Depository Library Program (FDLP) library to see if the information needed is not already available among the wide-ranging collections of GPO documents or websites. However, as more of this information is contracted out to private sources or classified as national security exceptions, the threat to public access continues.[47] Librarians in all types of libraries espouse intellectual freedom to promote a civil society with equal access to information. The ALA offers support to libraries and the public with its two separate websites for Office for Intellectual Freedom and Government Information.

IP LEGAL AND ETHICAL ASPECTS

Management related to IP has become more prominent with the vast development of the online world of commerce, information, entertainment, and social networking interactions. Charles McClure, director of the Information Institute at Florida State University, considers that:

> Ownership of information, the ability to control who has access to that information and the conditions under which that information can be further disseminated, is perhaps one of the most contentious information policy issues. . . . Managing intellectual property rights in a global networked environment is extremely complex yet essential for the intellectual growth of society.[48]

As most IP laws are created and enforced at the national level, the internet is a challenge to control due to its international platform and different government levels of policies and regulations. Hence, copyright laws of disparate countries are encountered online. International individuals both consume and create copyrighted works in the digital world. These individuals want rights as creators as well as access to the widest spectrum of public information or creative works. Legal and ethical information policies help libraries and their customers sort out the copyright laws or ethical guidelines. Beyond the traditional ethics of originality and attribution, this section will focus on IP tied to the digital online environment and how to address it for libraries and their customers. Let's start with the most common ethical application for library customers, which is plagiarism.

Plagiarism

Sir Walter Scott is often quoted for saying, "Oh what a tangled web we weave, when first we practice to deceive!" This classic quote relates to plagiarism because persons who claim another's work as theirs are trying actually trying to deceive. Plagiarism not only deceives its readers, but it also withholds useful citations and attributions that readers might have used to seek additional information.

Plagiarism is not a legal issue in the United States but rather an ethical issue tied to IP. Plagiarism may violate academic principles and have dire consequences for a student's grade on a paper or even dismissal from one's university. It can develop into the grounds for dismissal for a writer on a news journal, but it is not an actual law. Yet in professional scenarios, a lawsuit could result after a breach of contract where plagiarism tarnishes originality requirements for contracted reports, books, or other intellectual works for hire.

Librarians may be asked to verify a plagiarism allegation by trying to locate the ownership of a passage in a document. However, before posing a plagiarism allegation, one should verify the authorship condition and understand what plagiarism is. Otherwise, privacy rights and even defamation could muddy the waters further. Defamation is when one party makes a false accusation about another party, which causes harm to the reputation or character of the accused party.

Understanding copyright law is helpful to differentiate between the legal and ethical aspects. Copyright is a law with a set of exclusive rights granted to the author of an original work. Plagiarism is an ethical issue, which could violate those rights by copying and distributing such a work without permission and claiming the copyrighted expression used is their own original work. Even when a work directly copied verbatim is from the public domain or open access, if not attributed to the rightful author, it is still plagiarism. This is why it is important for schools to establish information polices of academic integrity including originality as it relates to proactively preventing plagiarism.

A news headline from the *New York Times*, "Plagiarism Lines Blur for Students in Digital Age," says it all about this timely topic. It is contentious not only for teachers but also for App generation students who are redefining "the concept of authorship and the singularity of any text or image."[49] Many students cut and paste from the internet without attribution, truly believing there is no reason to credit others for such works, and then claim it as their own work.

The question of author originality even affects computer and data science students as plagiarism and copyright infringement of computer code is a growing challenge. Perhaps this is because programming content for computer code is a newer form of expression compared to traditionally authored books, music, and media.[50] A *New York Times* article recently stated:

> Computer science professors are now delivering stern warnings at the start of each course, and, like colleagues in other subjects, deploy software to flag plagiarism. They have unearthed numerous examples of suspected cheating.[51]

The same originality and copyright respect philosophy applied to traditional intellectual works applies to digital works such a computer code.

Kathryn Valentine, communication and writing instructor at New Mexico State University, maintains that plagiarism is a literacy practice whereby students learn about honesty through a social-situated enactment as well as how to cite sources.[52] Jon Alberti, a literature professor at Northern Kentucky University, ties this concept to citations in sharing information with others and creating knowledge based on learning from others.[53] However, Valentine states that it is more than learning from others. In today's climate, "the problem with teaching citation and plagiarism as rule following is that it is not enough for students to know the textual practices of citation. Rather, students need to know citation and plagiarism as literacy practices—as complicated ways of making meaning."[54] In other words, this means students getting back to honesty and doing the right thing by crediting the sources of others.

To further associate plagiarism and helping students avoid it as a literacy practice tied to social-situated enactment, Barbara Fister, academic instruction librarian at Gustavus Adolphus College, compares student research to the content of weblogs and social network sites. She includes an instructional point of view for web content that engages students to view knowledge as constructed by their peers. Fister believes that this promotes students to initiate "a genuine question and a genuine itch to see how they might answer it."[55] She continues by stating that this also helps students to shift "from aggregating sources to becoming a participant in creating knowledge."[56] A website can promote candid discussions with students in the classroom that model research integrity and reciprocity for referencing others' works. Alberti compares this same proactive concept to how students and other authors routinely share their favorite website attributions between friends on popular social networking services such as Facebook.[57]

Author attribution is also tied to author moral rights such as the 1990 Visual Artists Rights Act (VARA), as noted in Copyright Office Circular 40 entitled *Copyright Registration for Works of the Visual Arts*:

> For certain one-of-a-kind visual art and numbered limited editions of 200 or fewer copies, authors are accorded rights of attribution and integrity. The right of attribution ensures that artists are correctly identified with the works of art they create and that they are not identified with works created by others. The right of integrity allows artists to protect their works against modifications and destructions that are prejudicial to the artists' honor or reputation. These rights may not be transferred by the author, but they may be waived in a written instrument. Transfer of the physical copy of a work of visual art or of the copyright does not affect the moral rights accorded to the author.[58]

Moral rights of authors in the United States are most often associated with their limited right of attribution, right of integrity, and right to prevent the destruction of copies of certain works of art.[59] VARA covers only a small group of "works of visual art" including paintings, sculptures, drawings, prints, and still photographs produced for exhibition. Only single copies or signed and numbered limited editions of 200 or less are protected.[60]

Whenever an artist is approached to create a commissioned work, the copyright ownership should be clarified in a written agreement, as VARA does not apply to any "work made for hire" as covered in Section 101 of the Copyright Act, title 17 of the *U.S. Code*. "Works made for hire" prepared by an employee within the scope of their employment or works specially "commissioned" for use, include:

- a contribution to a collective work,
- a part of a motion picture or other audiovisual work,
- a translation,
- a supplementary work,
- a compilation,
- an instructional text,
- a test,
- an answer material for a test, or
- an atlas.[61]

INTERNET COPYRIGHT REGULATIONS

Because the internet is independent of any geographic location, it is a challenge to enforce copyright and other IP laws. An article, "Law and Borders—The Rise of Law in Cyberspace,"[62] published by David Johnson and David Post in *Sanford Law Review* in 1996, asserted that the internet exists as its own sovereign entity in light of its geography and identity quandary. Issues persist today on how to handle infringements of copyright and trademarks as well as cybercrime, privacy, and freedom of speech, in relation to its international environment without borders. Since Johnson and Post's article was published, their global self-governance concept of cyberspace has been challenged. They strongly discouraged a traditional territorial regulation of cyberspace, instead supporting that global computer-based communication have its own law and legal institutions. However, Johnson and Post admitted that "the activities that have traditionally been the subject of regulation must still be engaged in by real people who are, after all, at distinct physical locations."[63] It is no surprise that since 1996, internet regulations and governance via traditional territorial laws rule copyright and other IPs.

Another proponent of such online self-regulation is Lawrence Lessig, one of the founders of the Creative Commons. His book, entitled *Code and Other Laws of Cyberspace, Version 2.0* and an online edition *Codev2*, introduced what is known as the Pathetic Dot (also called the New Chicago School) theory.[64] Individuals are Lessig's "pathetic dot," influenced by four outside regulating modality factors, namely, law, the market (economic forces), societal norms (professional codes of conduct), and architecture (technology). All four of these factors also pertain to cyberspace. Lessig believes that regulation of the internet was an inevitable evolution based upon its advancing technology.[65] Cyberspace controls include the use of Code. Most may think of Code as codification of actual laws. However, Lessig is referring to Code as the software and hardware structure, literally the "architecture," of cyberspace. Lessig proposes that Code offers ways to suggest access to a system such as passwords and encryptions, among others.[66]

Lessig's theory takes into account that a delicate balance must be maintained between regulating cyberspace to protect IP, while also permitting freedom of speech and access to information. In other words, property rights and freedom of speech are both important elements of a democracy. How do we balance these in such a manner as to protect our IP from piracy and still provide freedom of speech? There is an interplay between all four factors, which requires that all parties are vigilant and active as regulation of cyberspace evolves.[67]

The four modalities of regulation can affect society or constrain the pathetic dot, as shown in figure 6.1. Code could be seen as a supplemental tool to enforce IP laws such as copyright.

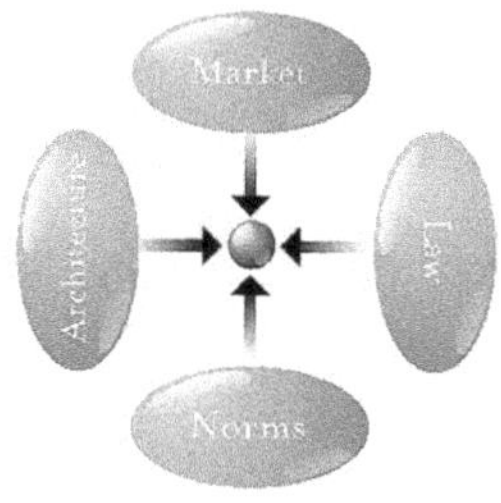

Figure 6.1
Four Primary Modalities of Code Affecting the Pathetic Dot. (Image source: www.socialtext.net)

DMCA

DMCA[68] is a law that effects information policy of libraries. It is the result of advances in information technology and the extensive growth of the internet as a communication medium. The Act regulates how digital copyrighted works are kept legal online. Besides the original Sections of the U.S. Copyright Act of 1976, Sections 1201 and 1202 of this complex law have most likely influenced more information policies for libraries related to IP than any other. It affects library information polices related to their online services, library employees, and library customers.

Enacted in 1998, the DMCA amends the Copyright Act. The Act "affords to copyright owners rights against those who circumvent copy protection technologies and insulates online service provides from liability for infringing acts of their subscribers subject to various limitations."[69] It prohibits circumvention of technological protection measures except for specified exemptions, such as classroom instruction covered in the TEACH Act in Chapters 7 and 9 related to academic and school libraries. In addition, there are limitations on copyright infringement liability for service providers. And specifically, significant for libraries, the Act revises rules and procedures for archival preservation. Some scientists, educators, and librarians have opposed certain aspects of the DMCA, as it was promoted by the entertainment and software content industries. The Act was related to treaties signed with the World Intellectual Property Organization (WIPO) in 1996.

The introduction of the DMCA initiated a controversial information rights debate between copyright owners and copyright consumers as the federal government had to balance between the exclusive copyright law rights of copyright owners and the free flow of information to copyright consumers online. The main provision of the DMCA found in Section 1201 of the Copyright Act states: "No person shall circumvent a technological measure that effectively controls access to" a copyrighted work.[70] Such violations could include hacking a password-protected site or breaking encryption on a DVD or online digital copy of a movie.

The ALA Advocacy, Legislation & Issues website summarizes key sections of the DMCA that affect libraries. These include Title I: New Prohibitions on Circumvention of Protection Technologies; Title II: Limitations on Online Service

Provider Liability; and Title IV: Digital Preservation. Highlights of ALA's summary of Title I of the DMCA[71] covering prohibitions on circumvention of protection technologies include:

- Prohibits the "circumvention" of any effective "technological protection measure" such as password or form of encryption used by a copyright holder to restrict access to its material.
- Prohibits the manufacture of any device, or the offering of any service, primarily designed to defeat an effective "technological protection measure."
- Expressly states that many valuable activities based on the "fair use" doctrine, including reverse engineering, security testing, privacy protection and encryption research, will not constitute illegal "anti-circumvention."
- Makes no change to the "fair use" doctrine or to other information user privileges and rights.

Notice the mention of fair use in the highlighted summary above. Some critics believe that the DMCA stifles fair use and, in some cases, access to information. For example, if one circumvents fair use portions of encrypted copyrighted works, in certain instances it is considered a violation of the DMCA. Only educators and similar parties have been granted restricted exemptions to lawfully circumvent the encrypted works such as online instruction in higher education. Under the terms of Section 1201(a)(1)(C) of the U.S. Copyright Act, the Librarian of Congress is delegated to publish new regulatory exemptions every three years, which is officially titled "Exemptions to Prohibition against Circumvention."[72] Such regulatory exemptions provide an opportunity for educators and librarians to make requests for the Librarian of Congress to develop new exemptions to support educational and information access needs of libraries their constituents.

The DMCA involves provisions dealing with online service providers (OSPs), those commercial providers including Google, YouTube, and noncommercial OSP; universities; and even public libraries. There are instances when people upload copyrighted content on the web without the permission of the copyright owner. Then the copyright owner sends a takedown notice to the OSP to remove the content. A good example of this is often seen on YouTube, when one returns to a link for a favorite site and it is no longer viewable, as it has been removed due to copyright restriction. This is officially known as a "notice-and-takedown" procedure codified by the DMCA, whereby copyright owners became responsible for locating infringing materials and notifying service providers. Then, in turn, OSPs are required to expeditiously remove infringing materials to avoid liability.[73]

So, whether OSPs are aware of the infringing activity by others on their site or not, they have a legal liability. Direct liability may result from the direct infringement by an OSP, whereas secondary liability, contributory infringement or vicarious liability, may result based on some actions of subscribers of an OSP. Kenneth Crews points out:

> A company or another party can be held liable for the actions of another person on at least two theories. *Contributory infringement* can occur when someone provides

> the equipment or other means for creating infringements and knows, or should have known, of the infringing actions. *Vicarious liability* can occur when someone has the right to supervise the activity and stands to benefit from it. Knowledge of the infringing activity is not necessary. Employers are often in exactly that situation, at least with respect to activity that are part of an employee's job.[74]

Based on the statement of Crews above, a school could be liable, depending on the level of oversight and knowledge. Congress included a safe harbor within the DMCA to address this challenge. Part of the DMCA included the Online Copyright Infringement Liability Limitations Act, eventually known as the "safe harbor" provision of DMCA. It was added as Section 512 to Title 17 of the U.S. Code (Copyright Act) and labeled "Title II: Limitations on Online Service Provider Liability." Title II exempts an OSP from copyright infringement liability if it follows four categories of conduct:

1. Transitory communications;
2. System caching;
3. Storage of information on systems or networks at direction of users; and
4. Information location tools.

According the ALA, the limitation for transitory communications "exempts any OSP or carrier of digital information (including libraries) from copyright liability because of the content of a transmission made by a user of the provider's or carrier's system (e.g., the user of a library computer system)."[75] The ALA summarizes categories two through four above as limitations that establish "a mechanism for a provider to avoid copyright infringement liability due to the storage of infringing information on an OSP's own computer system, or the use of 'information location tools' and hyperlinks, if the provider acts 'expeditiously to remove or disable access to' infringing materials identified in a formal notice by the copyright holder."[76]

The safe harbor conditions apply only when the limitations are followed and when the OSP registers an agent with the U.S. Copyright Office. The official agent registration site is known as the DMCA Designated Agent Directory. It is located at https://copyright.gov/onlinesp/. In addition, the University of Texas Libraries provide helpful DMCA compliance guidelines on their *Copyright Crash Course* site, which include DMCA agent selection and response tips at https://guides.lib.utexas.edu/copyright/libraryISP.

Once the OSP meets the Title II Limitations conditions and registers at the Copyright Office site, it could receive notices of claimed infringements on its site. If such notices are received, the agent is expected to remove the claimed infringed content immediately. For example, if a student at a university posts copyrighted music or movies on the school's website without permission, the copyright owner may discover this and object. When the university OSP agent gets the official objection, to reap or secure protection of the Safe Harbor, he or she must "expeditiously" remove or "take down" the claimed infringement. In other words, take down the item first and ask questions later. The claimed item infringed could be reposted later if proven to be fair use or subsequent permission is granted.

It is important to note that the safe harbor does not apply to the passive OSP itself, only to the third-party users of its online service. Libraries with online digital repositories or special collections must follow the letter of the copyright law. Hence, many librarians educate those third parties and their employees of the organization about copyright law and related rights. Some libraries even restrict third party access of any public content on their online services.

The ALA site covers Title IV in reference to Digital Preservation and this section's update to the preservation provision of Section 108 of the Copyright Act to:[77]

- expressly permit authorized institutions to make up to three, digital preservation copies of an eligible copyrighted work
- electronically "loan" those copies to other qualifying institutions
- permit preservation, including by digital means, when the existing format in which the work has been stored becomes obsolete

Section 108 of the Copyright Act has been vital to the copyright compliance effort of nonprofit libraries and archives. The DMCA focuses on the digital aspects of such copies and does have some limitation compared to analog copies. For example, digital copies for preservation and replacement may not be "made available to the public in that format outside the premises of the library or archives."[78] In this instance, one might consider conducting a fair use analysis upon Section 107 of the Copyright Act, as covered in chapter 2.

Lastly, another provision of the DMCA makes it a federal offense to remove or alter "copyright management information,"[79] such as a copyright notice or other identifying information such as a title of a work, an author name, a copyright owner, terms of use, web links, among others. However, if one wishes to review more details about the DMCA for one's own benefit, see the informative U.S. Copyright Office Summary document entitled, "The Digital Millennium Copyright Act of 1998," located at https://www.copyright.gov/legislation/dmca.pdf.

CONCLUSION

This chapter was an overview of the legal and ethical applications related to information policies in the workplace environment of libraries and other information professions. It demonstrated circumstances wherein libraries work with laws and regulations to prepare information policies that help libraries and their customers to use intellectual works legally and ethically. As expressed throughout this book, understanding IP laws and ethics supports consumers with access to a wide range of information resources and intellectual works while also respecting creators and owners with attribution and compensation for their creativity and investment. This chapter reviewed awareness and management of information polices by disparate stakeholders related to intellectual freedom, privacy and data protection, freedom of information, and IP. The remaining chapters apply information policies and procedures covered in this chapter as tied to specific IP and information rights by various library types such as academic, public, school, and special libraries.

NOTES

1. Charles R. McClure, "Information Policy: Libraries and Federal Information Policy," *Journal of Academic Librarianship* 22, no. 3 (1996): 214–218.

2. Harold C. Relyea, "Federal Government Information Policy and Public Policy Analysis: A Brief Overview," *Library & Information Science Research* 30, no. 1 (2008): 2–21.

3. Karthik Raman, "Protecting Intellectual Property Rights Through Information Policy," *Ubiquity* (June 2004), https://ubiquity.acm.org/article.cfm?id=1008537 (accessed November 15, 2018).

4. Lee Ann Torrans, *Law and Libraries: The Public Library* (Westport, CT: Libraries Unlimited, 2004), 237.

5. ALA, Library Policy Development: General, https://libguides.ala.org/librarypolicy (accessed November 9, 2018).

6. McClure, "Information Policy."

7. Ibid.; Richard E. Rubin, "Chapter 8: Information Policy: Stakeholders and Agendas," in *Foundations of Library and Information Science* (New York: Neal-Schuman Publishers, 2010), 309; Ian Cornelius, *Information Policies and Strategies* (London: Facet Publishing, 2010), 4.

8. Cornelius, *Information Policies and Strategies*, 9.

9. Donald O. Case, "Framework for Information Policies with Examples from the United States," *Library Philosophy and Practice* (October 2010): 1–10.

10. Ian Rowlands, Tamara Eisenschitz, and David Bawden, "Frame Analysis as a Tool for Understanding Information Policy," *Journal of Information Science* 28, no. 1 (2002): 31–38.

11. Ibid.

12. Case, "Framework for Information Policies"; Cornelius, *Information Policies and Strategies*.

13. Richard E. Rubin, *Foundations of Library and Information Science* (Chicago: Neal-Schuman, 2016), 410–411.

14. ALA, Intellectual Freedom and Censorship Q & A, https://www.ala.org/ala/oif/basics/intellectual.htm (accessed November 9, 2018).

15. Ibid.

16. Cornelius, *Information Policies and Strategies*, 88–90.

17. ALA, Intellectual Freedom and Censorship Q&A, http://www.ala.org/advocacy/intfreedom/censorship/faq (accessed November 9, 2018).

18. David L. Anderson, "Chapter 6: Security, Legal, and Ethical Issues for Entrepreneurial Technology," in *Entrepreneurship and Technology* (San Diego, CA: Cognella, 2012), 96.

19. Richard Stim and Stanford University Libraries, "Overview of Intellectual Property Laws," https://fairuse.stanford.edu/overview/introduction/intellectual-property-laws/ (accessed November 1, 2018).

20. "Workplace Privacy: Should Employees Have a Right to Privacy in the Workplace?" *Issues & Controversies*, Infobase Learning, March 21, 2008, http://icof.infobaselearning.com/recordurl.aspx (accessed November 10, 2018).

21. Privacy Rights Clearinghouse, "Workplace Privacy and Employee Monitoring," revised edition October 9, 2018, https://www.privacyrights.org/consumer-guides/workplace-privacy-and-employee-monitoring (accessed November 11, 2018).

22. Keith Laudon and Jane Price Laudon, "Chapter 4: Ethical and Social Issues in Information Systems," in *Management Information Systems: Managing the Digital Firm* (Upper Saddle River, NJ: Prentice Hall, 2007), 139–145.

23. President Barack Obama, *Consumer Data Privacy in a Networked World: A Framework for Protecting Privacy and Promoting Innovation in the Global Digital Economy*, http://www.whitehouse.gov/sites/default/files/privacy-final.pdf (accessed November 12, 2012).

24. Cecilia Kang and Kevin Roose, "Zuckerberg Faces Hostile Congress as Calls for Regulation Mount," *New York Times*, April 11, 2018, https://www.nytimes.com/2018/04/11/business/zuckerberg-facebook-congress.html (accessed November 15, 2018).

25. S.2639—CONSENT Act, April 10, 2018, https://www.congress.gov/bill/115th-congress/senate-bill/2639/text (accessed November 10, 2018).

26. Robin Kurzer, "Senators Introduce Privacy 'Bill of Rights' to Protect Consumer Data," Marketing Land, April 17, 2018, https://marketingland.com/senators-introduce-privacy-bill-of-rights-to-protect-consumer-data-238552 (accessed November 10, 2018)

27. Federal Communication Commission, "Protecting and Promoting the Open Internet NPRM," Notice of Proposed Rule Making, FCC 14-61, May 15, 2014, 67, https://www.fcc.gov/document/protecting-and-promoting-open-internet-nprm (accessed November 10, 2018).

28. 15 U.S. Code § 6501-6506—Children's Online Privacy Protection Act.

29. Amitai Etzioni, "Despite Facebook, Privacy is Far from Dead," *CNN.com*, August 16, 2012, http://www.cnn.com/2012/05/25/opinion/etzioni-facebook-privacy/index.html (accessed November 12, 2012).

30. Christopher Brown-Syed, "Roundup," *Library & Archival Security* 23 (2012): 55–58.

31. "Cybersecurity," *Issues & Controversies. Facts On File News Service*, August 23, 2010, http://www.2facts.com/article/i1500440 (accessed November 30, 2012).

32. Marjie Britz, "Chapter 1: Introduction," in *Computer Forensics and Cyber Crime* (Upper Saddle River, NJ: Pearson, 2009), 5.

33. Technopedia, "Cybercrime," https://www.techopedia.com/definition/2387/cybercrime (accessed January 24, 2019).

34. P.L. 107-56; Stat. 272 (2001), USA PATRIOT Act, or "Uniting and Strengthening America by Providing Appropriate Tools Required to Intercept and Obstruct Terrorism" Act, was introduced after September 11, 2001, and was signed into law on October 26, 2001.

35. Judith Krug, "Foreword," in *Privacy in the 21st Century*, Helen R. Adams et al., eds. (Westport, CT: Libraries Unlimited, 2005), ix–x.

36. ALA, Issues and Advocacy, "State Privacy Laws Regarding Library Records," http://www.ala.org/advocacy/privacy/statelaws (accessed November 11, 2018).

37. Ibid.

38. Torrans, *Law and Libraries*, Chapter 4, 34–35, 55.

39. American Library Association, "Social Media Guidelines for Public and Academic Libraries," approved by the Intellectual Freedom Committee in June 2018, http://www.ala.org/advocacy/intfreedom/socialmediaguidelines (accessed January 23, 2019).

40. Jo Bryson, "Chapter 27: Security," in *Managing Information Services: A Transformational Approach* (Hampshire, England: Ashgate, 2006), 271–281.

41. Richard Spinello and Herman Tavani, *Readings in CyberEthics* (Boston: Jones and Bartlett Publishers, 2004), 501.

42. Library of Congress, Privacy and Publicity Rights, http://memory.loc.gov/ammem/copothr.html (accessed November 12, 2012).

43. Sage, *Plagiarism, Defamation, and Privacy Rights Quick Guide*, www.sagepub.com/repository/binaries/bookAuthEdit/plagiarism_defamation_and_privacy_rights_quick_guide.pdf (accessed November 12, 2012).

44. Public Law 89-554, 80 Stat. 383; Amended 1996, 2002, 2007.

45. United States Department of Justice, FOIA.com, Home Page, https://www.foia.gov/index.html (accessed November 11, 2018).

46. http://www.foia.gov/about.html (accessed May 5, 2011).

47. Nancy Kranich, "Libraries: The Information Commons of Civil Society," in *Shaping the Network Society*, Douglas Schuler, ed. (Cambridge, MA: MIT Press, 2003), 11, http://dlc.dlib.indiana.edu/dlc/bitstream/handle/10535/4085/adingman_Libraries,_Civil_Society_and_the_public_sphere.pdf (accessed December 27, 2012).

48. McClure, "Information Policy."

49. Trip Gabriel, "Plagiarism Lines Blur for Students in Digital Age," *New York Times*, August 1, 2010, http://www.nytimes.com/2010/08/02/education/02cheat.html (accessed May 16, 2012).

50. Jonathan Bailey, "Plagiarism and Programming: How to Code without Plagiarizing," Turnitin.com, November 8, 2017, https://www.turnitin.com/blog/plagiarism-and-programming-how-to-code-without-plagiarizing-2 (accessed November 15, 2018).

51. Jess Bidgood and Jeremy B. Merrill, "As Computer Coding Classes Swell, So Does Cheating," *New York Times*, May 29, 2017, https://www.nytimes.com/2017/05/29/us/computer-science-cheating.html (accessed November 14, 2018).

52. Karen Valentine, "Plagiarism as Literacy Practice: Recognizing and Rethinking Ethical Binaries," *College Composition and Communication* 58, no. 1 (2006): 89–109.

53. John Alberti, "Chapter 2—Who Owns What? Ideas and Authority in the Information Age," in *Text Messaging: Reading and Writing About Popular Culture* (New York: Houghton Mifflin Harcourt, 2009).

54. Valentine, "Plagiarism as Literacy Practice," 105.

55. Michele Van Hoeck, "Barbara Fister: Playing for Keeps: Rethinking How Research Is Taught to Today's College Students," *Project Information Literacy, "Smart Talks,"* no. 12, July 26, 2012, http://projectinfolit.org/st/fister.asp (accessed August 6, 2012).

56. Ibid.

57. Alberti, *Text Messaging*.

58. U.S. Copyright Office, Circular 40: *Copyright Registration for Works of the Visual Arts*, http://www.copyright.gov/circs/circ40.pdf (accessed May 5, 2011).

59. *Copyright Act of 1976*, U.S. Code 17 §106A—Rights of Attribution and Integrity.

60. Cynthia Esworthy, *Guide to the Visual Artists Rights Act*, NEA Office of General Counsel, JD Washington & Lee Law School 1997, http://www.law.harvard.edu/faculty/martin/art_law/esworthy.htm (accessed November 12, 2012).

61. U.S. Copyright Office, *Circular 9: Works Made for Hire*, http://www.copyright.gov/circs/circ09.pdf (accessed November 12, 2012).

62. David Johnson and David Post, "Law and Borders—The Rise of Law in Cyberspace," *Stanford Law Review* 48, no. 5 (May 1996): 1367–1402.

63. Ibid., 1378.

64. Lawrence Lessig, *Code and Other Laws of Cyberspace: Version 2.0* (New York: Basic Books, 2006); and Codev2, http://codev2.cc/ (accessed November 12, 2018).

65. Lessig, *Code and Other Laws of Cyberspace*, 121–124.

66. Lawrence Lessig, "The Zones of Cyberspace," *Stanford Law Review* 48, no. 5 (May 1996): 1408.

67. Lawrence Lessig, "Code is Law: On Liberty in Cyberspace," *Harvard Magazine* (January-February 2000), https://harvardmagazine.com/2000/01/code-is-law-html (accessed January 24, 2019).

68. 112 Stat. 2860 (1998)—DMCA; also 17 U.S. Code § 1201 and 1202.

69. Peter S. Menell, Mark A. Lemley, and Robert P. Merges, *Intellectual Property in the New Technology Age: 2017, Volume II: Copyrights, Trademarks & State IP Protections*, Copyright Law (Berkeley, CA: Clause 8 Publishing, 2017), 496.

70. 17 U.S. Code § 1201—Circumvention of Copyright Protection Systems.

71. ALA, "Digital Millennium Copyright Act," Advocacy, Legislation & Issues, http://www.ala.org/advocacy/copyright/dmca (accessed November 9, 2018).

72. U.S. Copyright Act, 17 U.S. Code § 1201(a)(1)(C)-(D)—Circumvention of Copyright Protection System.

73. Jane C. Ginsburg, "Separating the Sony Sheep from the Grokster Goats: Reckoning the Future Business Plans of Copyright-Dependent Technology Entrepreneurs," *Arizona Law Review* 50, no. 2 (2008): 577, 596.

74. Kenneth Crews, *Copyright Law for Librarians and Educators*, 104.

75. ALA, "Digital Millennium Copyright Act."

76. Ibid.

77. Ibid.

78. U.S. Copyright Act, 17 U.S. Code §108 (b) and (c)—Limitations on Exclusive Rights.

79. U.S. Copyright Act, 17 U.S. Code § 1202—Integrity of Copyright Management Information.

Part II

SPECIFIC INFORMATION: INFORMATION ACCESS AND DELIVERY

Chapter 7

ACADEMIC LIBRARIES

CHAPTER OBJECTIVES

- To review copyright laws, the TEACH Act, and fair use as they relate to academic librarians for instruction, research, and scholarly communication
- To understand how licensing and contracts either promote or restrict use of copyrighted works for instruction, research, and scholarly communication
- To recognize the U.S. Copyright Act (Section 108) and the CONTU Rule of Five guideline for information delivery
- To understand and apply library policies for course reserves, information delivery, and scholarly communication services in academic libraries
- To inform faculty and students about all types of IP associated with their scholarly communications and innovations
- To assist faculty and students needing to learn how to search and to apply for patents or trademarks

This chapter reviews three areas of copyright: library course reserves and information for instruction environment, information delivery for research via interlibrary loan and document delivery, and scholarly communication for publishing and innovations. It concludes with the role of the academic librarian in helping faculty and students who may have ideas to patent or who may wish to trademark a product.

INTRODUCTION

Virtual library resources and online learning provide academic libraries with added teaching opportunities to contribute to instruction, research, and publishing in higher education. Because intellectual property (IP) library specialists deal well with IP matters such as copyright and fair use, they are better positioned to support instructor customers of the academic library with copyright and fair use related to instruction, research, and publishing. This beginning section is a guide for academic library specialists managing IP awareness, primarily copyright and fair use, to support information resources for instruction both face-to-face and virtually online. Supporting campus-wide instructional needs of faculty is primarily for library specialists responsible for library reserves, particularly electronic reserves. This means they should know about IP in relation to classroom instruction to assure compliance with the U.S. Copyright Law. Copyright for both traditional and online learning environments is reviewed, but the concentration is on copyright best practices for library reserves and classroom instruction related to online learning, materials placed in library reserves, instructor-posted audio and visual media in course management systems, and other displayed online classroom resources. Understanding the fair use doctrine, the TEACH Act, and database licensing agreements are vital for making certain a library's instructor customers are compliant.

The second section returns to topics from Chapter 2, reviewing copyright, fair use, and library special provisions related to information delivery to support research, including interlibrary loan and document delivery. Knowledge of Section 108 of the U.S. Copyright Law, CONTU Rule of 5, and licensing agreements are vital to ensuring copyright compliance of information delivered to all library customers.

The final section of this chapter focuses on the IP awareness aspects of scholarly communication to support institutional repositories and scholarly journals. Knowledge of copyright fair use, open access, contracts, and other IP topics are essential to support author rights and open access rights of research customers of institutional repositories and readers of scholarly journals. Patent and trademarks related to research and innovation are also covered.

Copyright is confusing and challenging. Its complexity leads some librarians and educators to err on the side that everything is fair use. Conversely, others are so scrupulous as to fear copying or reproducing anything.[1] Establishing copyright awareness programs and policies should help librarians to avoid fair use pitfalls and to know when to ask for permission when supporting the instruction, research, and publishing needs of their customers. For example, the case of a Georgia State University copyright lawsuit initiated in 2008 from publishers claiming that the school distributed unauthorized works through its electronic course reserve systems.[2] On May 11, 2012, Judge Orinda Evans of the U.S. District Court for the Northern District of Georgia ruled[3] that virtually all of the alleged infringements in this case were fair use. This was a victory principally for librarians, educators, and fair use, but appeared as a defeat for publishers. The plaintiff publishers were not pleased and appealed the decision in Fall 2012.[4] On October 17, 2014, the Eleventh Circuit Court of Appeals reversed and remanded[5] the District Court's decision in favor of the publishers. On March 31, 2016, the District Court Judge Evans reanalyzed the allegedly infringing works according to the direction of the Court of Appeals. The Court found[6] only four cases of infringement among 48 works and designated Georgia State the prevailing party. Again, the plaintiff publishers appealed the decision that was granted. On July 27, 2017, the Eleventh

Circuit Court of Appeals heard arguments. On October 19, 2018, the U.S. Court of Appeals for the Eleventh Circuit reversed the district court's fair use decision. The appeals court remanded the case to the district court for a revised verdict by Judge Evans.[7] Librarians and educators using electronic reserves in higher education should keep an eye on the resolution of this case to fine-tune their copyright permission policies.

Librarians and educators should understand copyright and take control of and exercise their fair use legal rights fully[8] so that they benefit from the legal exemptions. They must recognize options the law allows and make decisions about copyright that best advance their educational purposes. Not managing copyright fair use applications means losing valuable opportunities for attaining teaching and research goals.[9] U.S. Supreme Court Justice Sandra Day O'Connor expressed it best in reference to the *Feist* decision, which determined that factual information without creative expression could not be protected by copyright, stating that the primary purpose of copyright is to "build freely upon the ideas and information conveyed by a work. . . . It is the means by which copyright advances the progress of science and art."[10] O'Connor's legal opinion applies to instruction, research, and publishing to support educators, students, and colleagues in their IP awareness, including copyright and fair use. A good place to begin is understanding library course reserves.

LIBRARY COURSE RESERVES FOR INSTRUCTIONAL ENVIRONMENT

Library course reserves allow instructors to offer outside readings to students and supplement their lessons. Library reserves may be available in either traditional print or electronic formats, but electronic reserves have found greater favor among students of today's traditional classroom-based courses, as well as vital to the success of online learning students. It is obvious that traditional reserves, such as photocopied articles or entire books held at the students' host library, would not be easily accessible to students online. Since the introduction of electronic reserves, students now have 24/7 virtual access to reserve content. The Association of Research Libraries (ARL) describes electronic reserves as a collection of digital course materials made available over one or more computer networks.[11] With online technology, journal articles and many other library resources may be made available to all students remotely, with particular benefit to the online learning student. With the permission of the copyright holder, an entire book or an entire creative media resource such as music or film could be placed on electronic reserves. However, such electronic permission is not always so easy to obtain and can be costly. Otherwise, the fair use doctrine only permits small portions and limited time use tied to classroom instruction.[12] As online learning relies on electronic reserves to support its courses, the open nature of the Web potentially makes a school's reserves use presence more visible to the public and commercial publishers. Despite Georgia State University lawsuit, the open Web activity should encourage educators to become better aware of copyright laws, including fair use, to lawfully provide resources tied to online learning.[13] But who is responsible for getting copyright permission?

LIBRARY COPYRIGHT AND WORKFLOW ROLE

This important aspect of electronic reserves—who should hold responsibility for getting copyright permission—may seem the responsibility of the teaching faculty, but library specialists often handle such tasks. As librarians acquire and handle the vast majority of electronic subscription resources for their academic institution, it makes sense that the library staff is best to manage the workflow of copyright compliance. They are well suited to handle copyright compliance, as it generally fits their role better than the course instructors because it is more aligned to what librarians do in their daily work routine.[14] However, the library staff must also be mindful of the awareness level of technology and copyright related to the instruction and research needs of faculty and students. The faculty and student understanding of fair use helps librarians avoid earning a label as the "copyright police," as shown in figure 7.1 Instead, a role of coaching or tutoring library customers is more proactive and effective.[15]

Figure 7.1
"It's the new Copyright Compliance Center. We used to call it a library." (Courtesy of Bion Smalley. Used with permission. © Bion Smalley.)

Many colleges and universities use a special database or portion of a learning management system (LMS) to post their electronic reserves. To help manage the copyright compliancy for electronic reserves, library content electronic reserves portals such as those found in an online LMS make it possible for the librarians to post copyright compliant content into the online courses. For most LMS platforms, there is a designated place for electronic reserves that may be activated by the instructor and often shared with their campus librarian for copyright compliance or permission assistance.

The faculty and other instructors need to be made aware of much information concerning copyright and fair use, and this provides an opportunity for librarians to present copyright workshops and one-on-one copyright assistance to help faculty with their instructional and research needs. Working together with instructors and their LMS provides a collaborative model of course development between the teaching faculty and the library and promotes greater integration of library resources and instruction in traditional teaching and distance education. This collaboration demonstrates the "power of combining expertise, tools, and perspective to enhance teaching and learning."[16]

EDUCATION AND INSTRUCTION

Teaching faculty in academia may try to get permission to use information on their own; in this case, they need to be aware of the issues involved in seeking copyright permission. Or they may go directly to the library for assistance. In this case, once the library receives the faculty request, a fair use analysis or permission for copied works posted should be completed. As covered in Chapter 2, regarding fair use, the four factors are purpose, amount, nature, and effect on the market.[17] The Fair Use Checklist, prepared by Kenneth Crews and Dwayne Buttler,[18] has become the recognized standard for educators to determine if use of a document as a library reserve falls under the fair use umbrella.

Carrie Russell, director of the Program on Public Access to Information for the American Library Association's (ALA) Office for Information Technology Policy, suggests that understanding and using fair use habitually may reduce potential liability for educators using copyrighted works.[19] However, Kenneth Crews underscores the premise that educators should not become obsessed by exact numbers or percentages from some associations' or organizations' published guidelines. Fair use is not black and white. Lawmakers intentionally crafted fair use to be flexible for educators, but this was done in the era of print resources.[20]

Although recent technology has moved faster than the copyright laws, fair use generally applies specific mention of technology; it is technology neutral. The interpretation of fair use may vary and is decided in courts of law. For example, some academic librarians only utilize fair use for articles posted as traditional or electronic reserves for the first semester of a course, while permission is acquired for use in subsequent semesters for the same document by the same instructor.[21] Fair use does not stipulate this practice; this is a commonly accepted, conservative rule followed by most academic librarians based on the 1982 ALA *Model Policy* Section III-B, which will be discussed later in this chapter. This question of use in a subsequent semester is interpreted in varying ways. Some academic librarians have instructors who believe that as a new class arrives for a semester, it constitutes first-time fair use for those class students. Each institution should determine its own policy based on its interpretation of the law and the technology available. However, be prepared to justify a more liberal interpretation of fair use for a copyright policy if necessary. Georgia Harper reinforces the one-semester idea in her view that the publishers "clearly believe that fair use has time limits."[22]

Fair use conditions may differ depending on the types of customer use—for instance, library reserves, interlibrary loan, online learning course content posted by the instructor, or faculty and student research and writing. Most academic libraries are nonprofit and tend to have more liberal use of fair use for research and scholarship.

SUBSCRIPTION DATABASES

Many newspaper and journal articles in faculty members' and other course instructors' outside class readings may be available as full-text articles from a library's subscription databases. These database subscriptions have proven especially helpful for academic libraries for instruction and information delivery. When a library has an agreement through its electronic database licensing contract, the library could legally post a Uniform Resource Locator (URL) link instead of an actual electronic reserves image of an article because a URL link is an address and considered a fact. Facts are not protected by copyright.[23] Most databases provide persistent links to their URLs for uninterrupted posting of a document with no need to ask for permission or make an additional payment. Faculty members and instructors could also post URL links on their syllabus or their online course. If a dispute ever occurs over linking, it should be addressed by getting permission and having the linked site sign and provide a written agreement.[24] Also, free and open web pages usually may be linked to an electronic reserves site without requiring permission.

Educating faculty instructors on how to post persistent URL links is another coaching opportunity for librarians to collaborate. Often, persistent URLs are those links that are provided by the database source that remain constant and do not time out when posted as an electronic reserve or link within an online course shell. The library staff could post a webpage with directions on how faculty should link the persistent URLs within their LMS. Some faculty members may find their students prefer the outside readings posted within their LMS site rather than the library electronic reserves location. This also provides librarians an opportunity to assist with copyright permission for documents posted which are not be included in the library's databases. Additional fair use types of exemptions for distance learning are part of the TEACH Act passed in 2002.

THE "TEACH ACT" AND DISTANCE LEARNING EXEMPTIONS

The Technology, Education and Copyright Harmonization (TEACH) Act of 2002 Section 110(2)[25] expands existing face-to-face teaching exemptions of the copyright law allowing teachers at accredited, nonprofit educational institutions to use, in specific instances, copyright-protected resources including websites and other digital delivery methods in distance learning without obtaining permission from the copyright holder. These online learning instructional rights of the TEACH Act are closer to the exemptions employed in face-to-face classroom instruction in education under Section 110(1)[26] for audiovisual face-to-face teaching exceptions. Also known as face-to-face teaching display and performance, Section 110(1) limits exclusive rights of copyright owner in Section 106. It allows "performance or display . . . in the course of face-to-face teaching activities of a nonprofit educational institution, in a classroom or a similar place devoted to instruction." In other words, when showing an entire movie in the face-to-face classroom, it must be tied to the pedagogy of the lesson and not shown merely for entertainment purposes. It is important to note that this right only applies to works acquired under the First Sale Doctrine covered in Chapter 2. Licensed works may have qualifying terms that may that are similar or more limiting.[27]

Kenneth Crews[28] points out that the TEACH Act is relevant under Section 110(2) of the Copyright Act only to transmissions where instructors display or perform materials as they would in traditional face-to-face classrooms. If instructors are making copies and handouts to supplement their instruction, then fair use is likely the applicable statute.

Unlike the broader flexibilities of fair use Section 107 in the classroom, there may be limitations when utilizing the TEACH Act Section 110(2) for online instruction. The TEACH Act attempts to balance the rights of the copyright holders with the needs of educators and librarians and offers teaching exemptions allowing teachers at accredited, nonprofit educational institutions to use copyrighted resources in distance learning, including websites and other digital delivery methods, without permission from the copyright owner in specific instances. However, the TEACH Act requirements are assembled into three categories: institutional and policy requirements; technology requirements; and instructional requirements. Benefits of the TEACH Act only apply when all requirements are met. Below are the instructional requirements for which a library can offer resources.

INSTRUCTORS CAN:

Perform (show) a nondramatic literary or musical work or any other dramatic or audiovisual work in "reasonable and limited portions."

Display a work "in an amount comparable to that which is typically displayed in the course of a live classroom session."

Convert analog works into digital in the amount authorized by the list below if no digital version is available to the school.[29]

INSTRUCTORS CANNOT:

Perform or display a work marketed "primarily for performance or display as part of mediated instructional activities transmitted via digital networks."

Perform or display copies of works that are "not lawfully made and acquired" under the U.S. Copyright Act, if the college or university "knew or had reason to believe" that they were not lawfully made and acquired.[30]

INSTRUCTOR RESPONSIBILITIES FOR PERMITTED PERFORMANCE AND DISPLAY:

Performance or display must be "made by, at the direction of, or under the actual supervision of an instructor."

Materials are transmitted "as an integral part of the class session offered as a regular part of the systematic, mediated instructional activities" of the college or university.

Copyrighted materials are "directly related and of material assistance to the teaching content of the transmission."[31]

Before using the TEACH Act, the library should collaborate with instructors and their requirements listed above, as well as campus information technology experts and policy makers[32] regarding institutional and technology requirements listed below:

- The college or university must "institute policies regarding copyright."
- The college or university must "provide informational materials" regarding copyright which must "accurately describe, and promote compliance with, the laws of the United States relating to copyright."

- The college or university must provide "notice to students that materials used in connection with the course may be subject to copyright protection."
- The transmission of content must be limited to "students officially enrolled in the course for which the transmission is made."
- Technological controls are implemented to "reasonably prevent...retention of the work in accessible form by recipients . . . for longer than class session," as well as "unauthorized further dissemination of the work in accessible form by such recipients to others."[33]

As fair use is technology neutral,[34] it may supplement the TEACH Act. Although, if the amount of the resource posted is a mediated instructional activity and comparable to what the instructor would use in face-to-face classroom instruction, it satisfies that the performance and display is analogous to the type of performance or display that would take place in a live classroom setting.[35] In this instance, the TEACH Act or associated best practice guidelines could be applied for use within a password protected LMS or electronic reserves.[36] However, the online mediated instructional activity aspect, comparable to what the instructor would use in face-to-face classroom instruction, of posting documents under the TEACH Act should not substitute for course packs or supplementary readings used outside of the classroom instruction.

If an instructor posted a current newspaper article or recent journal article excerpt to demonstrate a point of his or her online lesson, this might qualify as an electronic reserve. Caution should be exercised when making this type of application an e-reserve, as it is very narrowly allowed under the TEACH Act. Under current copyright laws, librarians and educators should use fair use or copyright permission for virtually all electronic reserves. Again, the TEACH Act provides greater flexibility for instructors to display most copyrighted items for their online instruction which they would also display in the face-to-face classroom. The best way to make sure you are in compliance is to track electronic reserves.

TRACKING AND OBTAINING PERMISSIONS FOR ELECTRONIC RESERVES

Due to the physical difference between traditional and electronic reserves and some publishers' restrictive view of fair use, copyright compliance and fair use analyses require extra precautions for online learning. Password restriction to a website or access to an online LMS limited to those students enrolled in the course are the first step to supporting a fair use assertion.

As a rule, copyright fees are higher for the same resource requested for an e-reserve compared to a traditional paper reserve. This is because the permission cost factor established by the copyright holder is usually based on the number of students enrolled in the class using the electronic reserves, whereas the cost of a traditional reserve is based on how many physical copies, whether one or more, are held on reserve for students to share onsite at the library. Fair use analysis and copyright permission record keeping is the next step in this process.

Some electronic reserves platforms and other similar systems provide copyright management tracking. If these are not available, then either the library or the instructor should maintain records in a paper file or through an electronic database to track use of a document. The final aspect of tracking copyright management is obtaining permission from the publisher or the author, when required, to document disposition of the permission status.

A number of librarians have developed their own homegrown databases, which streamline the online faculty request process and also improve the workflow of electronic reserves and copyright compliance. This type of database could be built with at least three tables: reserve item, reserve instructor, and reserve copyright. Ideally, the database should be posted on the library's website. The database typically has two elements: a customer view with an online instructor request form and a staff view including document posting workflow and copyright compliance records. The staff view would have restricted access so that only library personnel may handle the workflow.

When getting permission to use electronic reserves, always ask for permission in writing. A permission request reference should include the resource title, author, page range, standard number (either ISBN or ISSN), and date. It is a practical measure to insist for the permission reply in a permanent written format, including the name of the authorizing party. Do not rely on verbal, telephone, or mobile text messages. An email, facsimile, or written letter with date and name of the permission-granting authorization should be saved in some type of copyright permission file.[37] To save time, the Copyright Clearance Center (CCC), is the first place to try to get permission.

If a document is being requested by the library for an instructor to be used for library reserve, and it is not registered with the CCC, then contact the publisher or author directly. For help with finding the author, the U.S. Copyright Office offers a free online database of copyright registration records since 1978 that may assist you at https://www.copyright.gov/.

Keyword searching for an author contact in a web search engine is another option. For electronic reserves, it is practical for librarians to maintain a file or database including all related information for each document posted such as source citation, instructor name and course, date posted, number of students, permission disposition and cost.

The pending Orphan Works Act discussed in detail in Chapter 2 may address a universal challenge in finding copyright owners after a realistic good-faith search. This type of copyrighted work could be considered an orphaned work. The pending act may limit the copyright owners in demanding only reasonable reimbursement at a later date, so long as the user of the work provides attribution. Further, there may be no infringement damages or attorney fees for the orphaned work used. For older, pre-1972 orphaned music recordings, see the Musical Works Modernization Act, covered in Chapter 2.

In addition to being unable to find a copyright owner, other challenges may include no reply from the permission request, a cost-prohibitive copyright fee, or the copyright owner refusing permission. When this occurs, returning to a fair use analysis may guide you or help you guide your colleague on what to do. Other options include replacing the work with an alternative work, using a smaller portion of the work, or conducting a risk-benefit analysis with legal counsel.[38] Most educators want to do the right thing. If copyright policies are posted and library awareness programs are presented, most educators will follow fair use guidelines or come to the library copyright specialist for help with the actual fair use doctrine. Otherwise, you could refer reluctant faculty to the copyright policies in the faculty handbook or on the library website.

FAIR USE GUIDELINES FOR ACADEMIC LIBRARIANS

Over time, some library and educator special interest groups, such as the ALA, have developed related guiding principles interpreting fair use for librarians to follow. It is important to remind anyone that these are someone else's guidelines and not the actual fair use doctrine as codified in the U.S. Copyright Law. Since fair use is technology neutral, these guiding principles may support a conservative threshold to conducting a fair use analysis for electronic reserves or online instructional displays. Merely applying the actual four fair use factors of the law may provide more flexibility. When in doubt whether or not your use is fair use, the following guidelines covered below could be helpful:

- 1976: Agreement on Guidelines for Classroom Copying in Not-for-Profit Educational Institutions with Respect to Books and Periodicals
- 1982: Model Policy Concerning College and University Photocopying for Classroom, Research and Library Reserve Use
- 2005: Using Electronic Reserves: Guidelines and Best Practices for Copyright Compliance, issued by the CCC

Some librarians create handouts of copying guidelines and how to use the actual fair use doctrine for their professors. Often librarians share such handouts during regularly scheduled copyright workshops for instructors. Copyright topics range from course reserves, fair use, the TEACH Act, obtaining permissions, scholarly publishing, and licensing.

CLASSROOM COPYING GUIDELINES

Classroom copying of copyrighted works used in face-to-face nonprofit academic settings are generally permitted in fair use portions if tied to the pedagogy of the instruction. However, the fair use percentage of copyrighted content one may copy is not specific. An analysis of a fair use checklist based upon the actual fair use doctrine, is strongly recommended. Using the Fair Use Checklist in Chapter 2, prepared by Kenneth Crews and Dwayne Buttler, to verify that one's use is indeed a fair use is highly advised.

As the quantitate question of copyrighted content use is not always clear according to the four fair use factors, a House Report guideline was created at the time of the introduction of the Copyright Act of 1976. Later in this chapter, examples of more contemporary qualitative guidelines to fair use are illustrated, such as those created by the American University's Center for Social Media.

The 1976 *Agreement on Guidelines for Classroom Copying in Not-for-Profit Educational Institutions with Respect to Books and Periodicals* covers the percentages of use published in House Report 94-1476.[39] Prompted by the encouragement of the U.S. Congress, the *Classroom Guidelines* were prepared by special interest author and publisher groups as part of the committee reports presented to the congressionally enacted 1976 copyright revisions. The *Classroom Guidelines* were endorsed by the House Report as "a reasonable interpretation of the minimum standards of fair use" without being an official part of the fair use statute, Section 107. Two special interest groups, The American Association of University Professors (AAUP) and the Association of American Law Schools (AALS) declined to participate or endorse the *Classroom Guidelines*, as they deemed them "too restrictive with respect to classroom situations at the university and graduate level."[40]

Depending on your interpretation of the fair use doctrine, you may find these and other guidelines too restrictive for face-to-face or online instruction. Some scholars such as Lindsey[41] believe that this guideline is "the most conservative and least contentious ground of fair use." Laura Gasaway, another expert scholar on this topic, adds that although the *Classroom Guidelines* point toward "minimum" rules, many educational institutions apply the *Classroom Guidelines* as if they are "maximum rules."[42] These limits include brevity, spontaneity, and cumulative effect.

AGREEMENT ON GUIDELINES FOR CLASSROOM COPYING (MULTIPLE COPIES)

The purpose of this quoted excerpt of *Multiple Copies for Classroom Use* is to state the minimum and not the maximum standards of educational fair use under Section 107. See pages 6-7 in Circular 21 from the Library of Congress entitled *Reproduction of Copyrighted Works by Educator and Librarians*, for complete details at https://www.copyright.gov/circs/.

BREVITY

(i) Poetry: (a) A complete poem if less than 250 words and if printed on not more than two pages or, (b) from a longer poem, an excerpt of not more than 250 words.

(ii) Prose: (a) Either a complete article, story or essay of less than 2,500 words, or (b) an excerpt from any prose work of not more than 1,000 words or 10% of the work, whichever is less, but in any event a minimum of 500 words.

(iii) Illustration: one chart, graph, diagram, drawing, cartoon or picture per book or per periodical issue.[43]

SPONTANEITY

(i) The copying is at the instance and inspiration of the individual teacher, and

(ii) The inspiration and decision to use the work and the moment of its use for maximum teaching effectiveness are so close in time that it would be unreasonable to expect a timely reply to a request for permission.[44]

CUMULATIVE EFFECT

(i) The copying of the material is for only one course in the school in which the copies are made.

(ii) Not more than one short poem, article, story, essay or two excerpts may be copied from the same author, nor more than three from the same collective work or periodical volume during one class term.

(iii) There shall not be more than nine instances of such multiple copying for one course during one class term.[45]

AUTHOR NOTE: This section on Multiple Copies for Classroom Use also stipulates that "each copy includes a notice of copyright."

Although the *Classroom Guidelines* have probably influenced more school library than academic library policies related to fair use, Kenneth Crews argues that these, "guidelines are a constraint on the law's flexibility," not to mention time-consuming to oversee. The fair use doctrine's four factors are based on the law, whereas the *Classroom Guidelines* are not. The four fair use factors from the U.S. Copyright Law may provide greater security than guidelines such as these. Lindsey and Crews suggest that although these guidelines are a good starting point in a fair use analysis, there are no legal grounds for the guidelines to control fair use policy in higher education. Crews further supports that fair use is open to technology changes and educators' needs, while these guidelines may be too restrictive.[46] However, the quantitative *Classroom Guidelines* or newer qualitative ones may be used as helpful, cautious measures to follow when a fair use analysis is uncertain especially when two of the four fair use factors lean for and two against fair use.

ALA Model Policy

The *Model Policy Concerning College and University Photocopying for Classroom, Research and Library Reserve Use* was originally published as an informational pamphlet by ALA in 1982.[47] Contrary to the earlier *Agreement on Guidelines for Classroom*, the ALA's *Model Policy* states that complete journal articles may be copied without counting words or authors.[48] While this is often used by librarians, it is not the law. It is covered here to show how an organization can create a guideline that is helpful for some needs, but academic librarians must realize this is not the law. It was a commonly accepted guideline that eventually influenced library course reserve policies.

The authors of the ALA policy included ALA Legal Counsel Mary Hutchings of the law firm Sidley & Austin, with recommendations and support from the ad hoc Copyright Subcommittee of ALA's Legislation Committee, Association of College and Research Libraries (ACRL) Copyright Committee, Association of Research Libraries (ARL), and other academic librarians, and attorneys. It was, "intended for the guidance and use of academic librarians, faculty, administrators, and legal counsel in response to implementation of the rights and responsibilities provisions of . . . the Copyright Law. . . ."[49] The ALA's *Model Policy* acquires much criticism for its statement in section III—Permissible Photocopying of Copyrighted Works: Classroom Use, where "the distribution of the same photocopied material does not occur every semester."[50] For library course reserves, some librarians found this too restrictive based on their fair use interpretation, while others have incorporated this into their library policy for workflow of handling reserves. This single-semester time limit factor has become the de facto policy for most academic libraries in the digital electronic reserve setting too. Yet the fair use doctrine in the copyright law includes nothing that supports a time limit in education for course reserves that could provide more flexibility for subsequent semester reuse. Newer fair use guidelines such as those listed further below from American University's Center for Social Media, offer more flexible interpretations of fair use to better balance such quantitative concerns.

Finally, several library copyright experts believe that these guidelines clearly imply that library reserves should not replace textbooks or legally acquired course packs. Reserves are designed to supplement textbooks.[51]

Kinko's Coursepack Case Affected Library Course Reserve Guidelines

The real fair use test for academia came from a lawsuit against the commercial photocopy chain, Kinko's, which implicitly questioned the authority of the *Classroom Guidelines* (1976) and the ALA's *Model Policy* (1982). It was the 1991 decision in *Basic Books, Inc. v. Kinko's Graphics Corp.*, 758 F. Supp. 1522, 1526 (S.D.N.Y. 1991).

> A New York Federal District Court ruled that Kinko's Graphics Corporation infringed copyrights when it photocopied materials (including chapters of books and articles from periodicals) for sale to students as course packs for their university classes. The copyrighted works infringed included hardback and paperback editions of in-print and out-of-print trade and professional works, as well as textbooks. The 12 copied excerpts in the case ranged from 14 to 110 pages and from 5% to 24% of the works. In addition to ruling against further photocopying by Kinko's without permission of the copyright owners, the Court awarded the plaintiffs damages, court costs, and attorney's fees resulting in $2 million. The Court's decision in the case did not prohibit the reproduction and sale of anthologies, but rather the reproduction and sale of anthologies made without obtaining proper copyright permission or meeting the criteria of either the *Classroom Guidelines* or the statutory "fair use" provisions in Section 107 of the Copyright Act.[52]

The Federal Court reported Kinko's as the party who profited and was found liable for not obtaining permission to copy. The publishers were awarded over $500,000 in damages from Kinko's. Professors of three schools, New School for Social Research, New York University, and Columbia University asked Kinko's to make the copies for ranges of 3 to 132 students charging students $11 to $24 per course pack.[53]

The Kinko's case not only affected the guidelines for coursepacks, it also added another layer of restricting guidelines established by most colleges and universities for library reserves. It also serves as a warning for electronic reserves. Crews observed that the court employed the statutory factors of fair use and easily found that three of the four factors, Purpose, Amount, and Effect, opposed fair use. The "Purpose" factor was considered commercial since Kinko's was involved. In this case, the "Amount" factor copied (5 to 25 percent) was considered substantial and its "Effect" factor on the market was seen as hindering the publisher's potential sale of books and photocopy permission royalties. Only the "Nature" factor favored fair use, as most of the copied materials were "factual works." The judge of this case refused to rule that all anthologies of photocopies, such as coursepacks, were unlawful. The decision was directed primarily against Kinko's for-profit motive within the framework of fair use. The *Classroom Guidelines* that were used by the defendant were deemed as not appropriate for Kinko's use as they were created only for nonprofit educational use.[54]

Copyright Clearance Center (CCC) Conservative Viewpoint

A more restrictive document was published in 2005 by the CCC and it was entitled, "Using Electronic Reserves: Guidelines and Best Practices for Copyright Compliance." Given the brokerage nature of the CCC as an intermediary between copyright holders and copyright users, it is not surprising that this document favors the publishers' perspective and should only be used as a conservative measure when establishing a library electronic reserves policy. Congress established the need for, and suggested the creation of, the CCC as a national rights clearinghouse to assist educators in obtaining permissions during the introduction of the Copyright Act of 1976. CCC saves librarians and educators much time in obtaining permission for the use of copyrighted works. "It is a voluntary, not-for-profit, industry-led licensing and infringement protection system for both electronic and paper-based works. CCC . . . completes approximately 2 million individual licensing transactions every year, collects over $100 million in royalties per year. . . ."[55] Although the CCC is a nonprofit organization, it primarily represents publishers first as a liaison to libraries as its copyright fees collected include a portion to cover their administrative expenses.

It is common knowledge that publisher studies have recognized a decline of traditional journal subscriptions for academic use.[56] One might question whether or not the lawsuit from publishers directed at Georgia State University was a result of such a decline? As the Yale University Library notes on its website, the CCC investigates alleged copyright infringement claims of the use of works by its customers.[57]

Copyright compliance requirement for campus bookstore or photocopy center making course packs vary greatly from library reserves. It is highly recommended to obtain permission and make copyright royalty payment when asked to do so, no matter the number of students or semesters a document is utilized. There are too many commercial aspects when a copy center is involved.

Audiovisual Fair Use Guidelines

When the initial *Guidelines for Classroom Copying* were introduced in 1976, part of that effort included *Guidelines for Educational Uses of Music*, H.R. Rep. No. 94-1476, at 70-71 (1976). In 1996, the *Fair Use Guidelines for Educational Multimedia*[58] were created. The newer *Guidelines* offer conservative benchmarks prepared by the Consortium of College & University Media Centers (CCUMC) for additional copyright compliancy in the classroom. These voluntary guidelines were the only part of the 1998 Conference on Fair Use (CONFU) report for which most of the major U.S. copyright owners participated and endorsed.[59] The three positive points for educational use of multimedia resources—the circumstances under which one does not need to seek permission to use copyrighted materials for two years—include the following:

1. The use is a multimedia project as described by the *Multimedia Guidelines*;
2. The rights owners are on record that fair use applies in an educational, digital environment; and,
3. The current Copyright Law's transmission restrictions of dramatic versus nondramatic sequential versus nonsequential performance versus display are minimized.[60]

The CCUMC *Guidelines* below offer examples of usable portion limitations of a single copyrighted work when presented in the classroom, especially for online instruction. As with the TEACH Act, these guidelines were not intended for electronic reserves. Use of portions larger than the illustrations below may be permitted, for which educators should refer to the four factors of the fair use doctrine to determine if it qualifies as fair use.

1. Motion media (e.g. film or video)—up to 10 percent or 3 minutes.
2. Text—up to 10 percent or 1,000 words.
3. Music/Lyrics/Music Video—up to 10 percent; 30 seconds maximum.
4. Photos/Illustrations—up to five from one artist.
5. Numerical Data Sets (e.g. databases)—up to 10 percent or 2,500 fields.[61]

The more creative the audiovisual resource, the more it must be tied to the pedagogy of the instruction to quality as fair use. For example, when a professor needs to display episodes of an imaginative story from television series to support teaching job interviewing skills, the videos offer engaging examples of different job interview scenarios for classroom discussion.[62] Due to the highly creative nature of such television and movie stories, only limited excerpts are lawful to display in a virtual classroom for related educational lecturing and class discussion. Yet, an instructor might be able to display an entire factual documentary film tied to his or her online lesson without any permission. To determine the lawful limit, educational instructors in the United States must refer to the U.S. Copyright Act's doctrine of fair use, 17 U.S.C. § 107; or audiovisual face-to-face teaching exemptions, 17 U.S.C. § 110(1) for face-to-face instruction' or the TEACH Act, 17 U.S.C. § § 110(2),

112(f), for online instruction which is equivalent to face-to-face. Again, when the TEACH Act does not fit one's unique audiovisual display needs online, refer to fair use, 17 U.S.C. § 107.

The 2010 regulatory exemptions of 17 U.S.C. § 1201(a)(1)(C)-(D) to the anti-circumvention provisions of the Digital Millennium Copyright Act, which make fair use and TEACH Act exceptions to U.S. Copyright Law more accommodating could also apply to your professor scenario. No longer must an instructor in higher education cue up a scene on a DVD or Blu-ray disc for the exact excerpt required to use film content as an educational tool. Instructors may now decrypt required DVD/Blu-ray content excerpts for pedagogical purposes tied to their instructional lessons and class discussions for either face-to-face or online instruction. For additional information, consult your institution's legal counsel for specific guidance related to your instructional use of copyrighted works. Some differences with use occur when the class is online.

Audiovisual resources posted online may require either limited portion use or network streaming access of an entire work. Password-restricted access to the e-reserve site for students enrolled in the course may also sway fair use in your favor. Password restriction or network streaming demonstrate the fair use "Purpose" factor supporting the limited students of a specific class. The technology of streaming supports copyright protection, as streamed resources are not saved to remote computers.[63] As with the TEACH Act, the CCUMC guidelines are for online instruction applications which would be equivalent to face-to-face.

Statement on the Digital Transmission of Electronic Reserves has been created by the Music Library Association (MLA), which considers that the use of musical works for class reserves falls within the character of fair use. The MLA promotes digital audio files copies of copyrighted recordings of musical works for outside class use in its *Statement*, under the following conditions:

- Access to such digital copies should be limited to individuals who have been authenticated as being enrolled in the specific course, or formal independent study, for which the copy was designated.
- Digital copies should be made only of works that are being taught in the course or independent study.
- Digital copies should, to the extent feasible, consist of no more than is necessary to satisfy the classroom pedagogical needs.
- The digital copy should be made from a lawfully-made original, owned by the library. The library should use lawfully-made material provided by the instructor only after it has made a good faith effort to purchase a commercially available copy, and only if the library retains the original for as long as the digital copy is retained.
- The library may store copies of library-owned materials for future re-use, but should remove access to the files at the completion of the course or independent study.[64]

Other support groups have created codes for best practices for fair use to support libraries and their constituents, such as the Center for Media & Social Impact (CMSI).

CODES OF BEST PRACTICES FOR FAIR USE

The Center for Media & Social Impact (CMSI) at American University collaborated with several groups of media creators and fair use experts, including attorneys, to develop Codes of Best Practices widely considered as fair use for various disciplines. Such codes offer specialized educational and nonprofit organizations guidelines introducing more qualitative aspects of fair use, such as transformative use. Informative Codes of Best Practice for fair use featured include Academic Libraries, Online Video, Documentary Filmmakers, Journalists, Media Literacy Education, and so forth. The Codes include principles describing how fair use applies to specified scenarios as well as limitations that should be followed to strengthen an argument in favor of fair use. See, for example, the Code for Academic and Research Libraries, Section One: Supporting Teaching and Learning with Access to Library Materials via Digital Technologies. The Code affirms that it is fair use for instructors to be able "to make appropriately tailored course-related content available to enrolled students via digital networks."[65] The Code further explains:

> Amounts of material used for online course support should be tailored to the educational purpose, though it will not infrequently be the case that access to the entire work (e.g., an illustrative song in a class on the history of popular music) will be necessary to fulfill the instructor's pedagogical purpose. It is also reasonable for works to be posted repeatedly from semester to semester to the extent that they are the most appropriate, relevant, and still timely materials for the course.[66]

See CMSI website for more details at https://cmsimpact.org/codes-of-best-practices/.

ELECTRONIC RESERVE LIBRARY POLICIES

Academic librarians should create electronic reserve library policies. Such posted policies on a library's website help faculty understand why they are asking for permission to use copyrighted works. Establishing an electronic reserves policy is vital for clarifying your library's requirement of faculty submitting content to supplement their face-to-face or online classroom instruction.

As this chapter has conveyed, there are no specific statutory exceptions that cover electronic reserves; therefore, fair use is applied. Academic librarians and publishers have different ideas on what polices should be followed. An attempt to address the varying views was an objective of the Conference on Fair Use (CONFU) proceedings in 1996. With no common agreement at CONFU, guidelines for electronic reserves were never produced. However, as mentioned earlier in the chapter, librarians are watching for the outcome of the Georgia State University electronic reserves case, as it may have some effect on related library policies in the future. The lack of such guidelines permits libraries to basically create their own policies and procedures.[67]

An academic library's reserves policy often has two sections. The primary part should cover the workflow submission instructions so that professors know how to submit content, often via an online template as covered earlier in this chapter, for the reserve's permission process. Then another section should provide copyright notice including Section 107 related to the fair use doctrine so that instructors are better informed about the legal aspect of course reserves. One may easily browse the web to view various electronic reserves policies. Many library policies follow fair use influenced by the library reserves guidelines from the ALA Model Policy.[68] Creating such policies also offers librarians an opportunity to provide some type of training for instructors about copyright, fair use, such as an online tutorial or regularly scheduled copyright workshops.

Copyright, fair use, and the TEACH Act are not as confusing as most would think for supporting face-to-face or online instruction for the institution of an academic library. Balance, compromise, and moderation are vital to copyright compliance in the classroom. For online instruction, remember to show instructors how to use fair use or TEACH Act checklists which are from the actual copyright law when possible, and always ask for permission whenever there is any doubt. The next section of this chapter will review information delivery for academic library customers including interlibrary loan, document delivery, and licensing.

INFORMATION DELIVERY FOR RESEARCH: ILL, DOCUMENT DELIVERY, AND LICENSING

A detailed overview of Section 108, the CONTU Rule of Five, and licensing related to ILL in Chapter 2 explains what an academic library needs to know to assistance its research customers in obtaining resources to fulfill their information delivery needs. Serials inflation crisis and budget challenges at academic libraries has forced librarians to rely on ILL, document delivery, consortia, and other library sharing alternatives to acquiring resources requested by students, faculty, and other researchers.

Interlibrary loan electronic delivery of resources directly to academic library patrons has transformed the role of libraries in delivering information to both traditional and distance learners. Some academic libraries provide document delivery for when an item is not available via interlibrary loan, or due to copyright restrictions. Only a few decades ago, most interlibrary loan requests took weeks to fulfill for customers. Today, an academic library may easily borrow a copyright compliant copy of an article from another library, or purchase an article from a publisher or document delivery website within hours. While acquiring a book or media item from another library or bookseller is often completed within a few business days. Academic libraries are no longer limited to what is available in their collection.

As reviewed in Chapter 2, Section 108 of the U.S. Copyright Law[69] offers limitations on a copyright holder's exclusive rights, such as reproduction by libraries and archives and allows librarians to make copies and to receive copies of articles, chapters, and other short works for purposes of private study and research. The National Commission on New Technological Uses of Copyrighted Works (CONTU) Rule of Five guidelines[70] supports a library to acquire limited photocopies or electronic copies of journal articles published within the last five years. CONTU is based upon the 1974 *Guidelines on Photocopying and Interlibrary Arrangements.* Under Section 108(a)2, for-profit academic institutions could use the CONTU Rule of Five, but they would need to be open to the public or provide virtual access by offering document finding services and interlibrary loan.[71] The CONTU guidelines do not include those article requests over five years old at the date of request. Section 107 related to fair use should cover those article requests.

As covered in Chapter 2, the borrowing library must specify whether its article request is copyright compliant with the CONTU guidelines on the request form (paper or electronic). The borrowing library is responsible in maintaining the copyright compliance records. The lending library is not responsible for maintaining copyright records.

Licensing agreements of the subscription databases must be followed for interlibrary loan and document delivery too. Depending on the negotiated contract with subscription databases, lending to other libraries may be permitted. Many libraries maintain a listing of databases that allow sharing as well as conditions and restrictions. This supports workflow of interlibrary loan and document delivery in following all their database licensing agreements. Consortia agreements also impact such licensing agreements as covered in the next section.

ILL CODES, CONSORTIA NETWORKS, AND RECIPROCAL AGREEMENTS

Organized policies support the interlibrary loan daily workflow as well as copyright compliance. As pointed out in Chapter 2, the *National Interlibrary Loan Code*[72] also available as the *Interlibrary Code for the United States*[73] promotes flexible interlibrary policies for state, regional, and local applications. These groups often create their own Code based on the *National Code.* State and regional policies are usually tied to consortia, network, or reciprocal agreements. Such library groups often collaborate to gain sharper pricing or favorable licensing terms.

Networks created at the local level usually provide express courier services and reciprocal agreements. *A Model Interlibrary Loan Code for Regional, State, Local or Other Special Groups of Libraries* was made available by the ALA in 1984 support such needs.[74] ILL Codes are also helpful for clarifying responsibilities, such as borrowing libraries liability for any damaged or lost items.

In 2006, the ACRL addressed ILL related to nonprint media resources with its *Guidelines for Media Resources in Academic Libraries Review Task Force.* The *Guidelines* affirmed that academic libraries may collect nonprint media resources that are as "vital and diverse" as any print collection in an academic library.[75] Nonprint media resources prominently support education and research. Such media resources make up a large portion of interlibrary loan requests. One need only look at the online explosion of audio and visual materials provided on blogs, social networking, and amateur film sites. Some academic libraries do not lend any nonprint media materials, while others may lend to their consortium or only to those libraries that lend media. Some videos and computer software requested may contain licensing restrictions for one user at a time, which is not conducive to interlibrary lending. Making copies of audiovisual resources is not considered an interlibrary loan function, unless the copying is considered to be a fair use. Generally, nonprint audiovisual resources are lent through interlibrary loan to traditional and online learner customers.

A growing concern for academic librarians in lending media resources deals with licensing. Some audio and visual resources are no longer sold but licensed to libraries, which potentially takes away certain statutory rights including the first sale doctrine. Some video producers of instructional films on DVD/Blu-ray discs from media services generally associated with educational classroom use have been involved in legal action toward educators. When purchasing audiovisual resources, watch for any licensing restrictions associated with the materials.[76] When uncertain of a disposition related to licensing, always consult with your institution's legal counsel.[77]

Subscription database licensing agreements of academic libraries restrict access of database content to faculty, staff, and students. For academic libraries, the authorized users should be defined as broadly as possible to include distance learners.[78] Distribution outside of the intended audience is usually prohibited, unless the library negotiates use for interlibrary loan lending. It cannot be emphasized how important contract negotiations are for libraries related to "right to use" conditions for interlibrary loan lending.

Resource requests of distance learning and traditional academic library customers may affect both collection development and ILL customer policies, such as access versus ownership. Not only does ILL fill in collection gaps, but such ILL request statistics are also an effective reference for what to collect in the future.[79] Hence, a borrowing policy for a library's ILL customers provides details on the service should be readily accessible for review. Interlibrary loan model policies among libraries depend on Section 108 of the Copyright Act and the CONTU Guidelines.[80] Many interlibrary patron-borrowing policies are posted on library websites that serve as model policies for comparison. In many cases, a separate policy regarding interlibrary loan and document delivery for distance learners may be posted in special section for distance learning students.

The setting for interlibrary loan and document delivery may continue to develop as both online and traditional courses use more electronic resources, or as librarians continue to evaluate their collection use and cancel low-use and high-cost journal subscriptions, they may implement an *access versus ownership* philosophy to further support these services. The next section of this chapter introduces scholarly communication and its support of publishing and innovation for students, faculty, and the community.

SCHOLARLY COMMUNICATION FOR PUBLISHING AND INNOVATIONS

Scholarly communication has evolved at academic libraries to promote open access and support its customers by removing barriers and making information as accessible as possible.[81] Open access, introduced in Chapters 1 and 2, empowers libraries to flourish and to meaningfully contribute to evolving changes and innovations necessary for customers' access to information. The Scholarly Publishing and Academic Resources Coalition (SPARC) defines open access as "the free, immediate, online availability of research articles coupled with the rights to use these articles fully in the digital environment. Open access ensures that anyone can access and use these results—to turn ideas into industries and breakthroughs into better lives."[82] Peter Suber, director of Harvard Library Office for Scholarly Communication, defines open-access literature as "digital, online, free of charge, and free of most copyright and licensing restrictions."[83] The open-access movement is inherently connected to the internet, as it has transformed scholarly communication and publishing.[84] As open-access journals offer free access, this addresses the serials crisis in libraries where commercial publisher raise subscription rates, while many academic library budget are reduced or remain flat.[85]

Scholarly communication mindfulness in libraries goes beyond open access, as it also includes IP awareness aspects of copyright, fair use, and other rights related to an academic library supporting its customers' instruction, research, and publishing. ACRL defines scholarly communication as

> the system through which research and other scholarly writings are created, evaluated for quality, disseminated to the scholarly community, and preserved for future use. The system includes both formal means of communication, such as publication in peer-reviewed journals, and informal channels, such as electronic mailing lists.[86]

Often librarians or specialists are appointed to coordinate and manage scholarly communications working with IP tied to information literacy; serials, electronic resources and reserves; interlibrary loan and document delivery; distance learning; digital preservation and institutional repositories; special collections and archives; open educational resources; or even patents and trademarks for students, faculty, or campus technology transfer offices.

SCHOLARLY COMMUNICATION LIBRARIANS (SCL): COMPETENCIES AND OUTREACH

SCLs wear many hats with related responsibilities that vary from library to library. While copyright, fair use, and open access are the common IP knowledge competencies for all SCLs, other tasks might include institutional repository management, academic publishing, data management, assessment and impact metrics, collaborating with archivists and special collections, and so forth.[87]

As with all types of IP specialists in libraries, outreach and instruction are vital to the success of any scholarly communication service. SCLs educate students and faculty about their rights and responsibilities as information creators and consumers. Target library customers include campus students, budding scholars, and academic researchers—and sometimes the greater community from professional peers to regional researchers and innovators. Campus faculty and graduate students are the primary customers needing assistance with publishing contracts, copyright, fair use, and open access.

Students often want help in obtaining a basic understanding of plagiarism and copyright associated with their school research, as well as personal use of others' creative works. Graduate students need to explore fair use, copyright permission, and registration while preparing their theses and dissertations for publication. For more about copyright and fair use for theses and dissertations, see Kenneth Crews' guide entitled "Copyright and Your Dissertation or Thesis: Ownership, Fair Use, and Your Rights and Responsibilities," at ProQuest (https://media2.proquest.com/documents/copyright_dissthesis_ownership.pdf).

Faculty and instructors on campus need support in gaining an understanding of copyright related to fair use for utilizing others' creative works in instruction and publishing applications, including institutional repository. They must learn when and how to obtain permission for using other others' works when fair use does not apply. They might need to get an agency registration of their own intellectual works, such as copyright, Creative Commons (CC), trademarks, or patents. Moreover, they might want to learn how to present plagiarism and copyright awareness lessons to their students.

Scientists, inventors, entrepreneurs, business professionals, musicians, authors, and artists from the campus or the community approach SCLs for assistance with protecting their creative and innovative works. SCL research consultations or presentations about all types of IP and related rights are likely for such outreach opportunities. For campus scientist and inventors, technology transfer related to campus research and innovation is an opportunity for some SCLs. In such cases, knowledge of patents, trademarks, trade secrets, open source, and licensing is supportive.

Some SCLs wear multiple IP hats, including managing a Patent and Trademark Resource Center (PTRC), as covered in Chapter 4. Patent and trademark searching instruction is the primary role of PTRCs. Outreach opportunities abound for both campus and community customers ranging from business entrepreneurs to engineering and science students, faculty, and community customers.

When a SCL is responsible for copyright awareness subject reference and outreach to its academic library customers, presenting information and best practices as opposed to legal advice is essential. Knowledge of copyright law and other IPs covered in earlier chapters of this book supports helping customers use such references. Academic librarians are responsible for such outreach endeavors without providing any suggestions or advice.

The following core copyright competencies based upon a list published by NASIG[88] are necessary for SCLs to understand and competently converse with their library customers:

- Knowledge of Relevant Copyright Laws
  - Exclusive rights and duration (Section 106), especially rights associated with reproduction and distribution, also covered in Chapter 2.
  - Exemptions such as fair use (Section 107), teaching (Section 110), and libraries (Section 108).
  - Determine if a work is in the public domain, also covered in Chapter 2.

- Judicial Environment Awareness
  - Current awareness of contemporary copyright cases such as Georgia State University reserves, as well as final case decisions covered throughout this book that have affected copyright in libraries and with customers.
- Author's Rights Overview
  - Including author copyright exclusive rights (Section 106), familiarity of publisher contracts and retaining any rights, and how to apply licensing such as CC for open-access publishing.
- Other Subject Awareness to Facilitate SCL Workflow and Outreach to Customers
  - Knowledge of orphan works, licensing, permission request process, and campus IP policies.

Once SCLs are educated about the IP aspects of scholarly communication and related subject disciplines, they are prepared to coach and educate students, faculty, and staff on campus, either face-to-face or online. Often the customers need IP awareness support for interacting with their campus institutional repository or publishing service, or another repository or publisher. Most institutional repositories are open access, while scholarly publishers could be traditional or open access. The subtle difference between IP policies of digital repositories versus open-access publishers are illustrated below.

IP AND INSTITUTIONAL REPOSITORIES

Institutional repositories host a wide variety of scholarly works of an academic institution such as faculty journal articles, and student theses and dissertations. As access to these resources are open and free, this helps address the serials crisis by distributing to journal articles to those without costly subscriptions. Some works may have been previously published, while others may have been unpublished. Sharing works which were previously unpublished extends new life to knowledge and offers "a means for faculty and students to make meaningful contributions to the global knowledge base of their disciplines."[89]

Obviously copyright law or other rights are associated with resources posted in an institutional repository. SCLs or specialists who manage institutional repositories should be aware of IP on behalf of the repository as well as its customers providing resources. Having policies in place to address copyright and other rights is vital to avoid any legal or ethical violations. SCLs also evaluate digital accessibility of the collections in institutional repositories.

Mandates for open access promote open content for institutional repositories. Research organizations, funders, or governments implement open-access mandates. Such mandates require researchers to openly publish their content in freely accessible intuitional repositories or open-access journals. The *National Institutes of Health (NIH)* Policy[90] (at https://publicaccess.nih.gov/policy.htm) requires that peer-reviewed research articles describing research funded by the NIH must be made publicly available for free through PubMed Central. Other mandates include the Bill & Melinda Gates Foundation Open Access Policy at https://www.gatesfoundation.org/How-We-Work/General-Information/Open-Access-Policy, as well as the Open, Public, Electronic and Necessary (OPEN) Government Data Act passed in 2019 that requires U.S. federal agencies to publish federally-funded research as open data.[91]

WORKS PREVIOUSLY PUBLISHED

SCLs regularly assist contributing authors of institutional repositories in verifying the copyright status of their previously published works with another publisher. With copyrighted works such as journal articles, authors must maintain control over at least two of their copyright exclusive rights, found in Section 106 of the U.S. Copyright Act, to permit the repository to reproduce the copy of and to distribute their copyrighted work submitted.[92] Traditionally, with published works, copyright has been transferred by authors to publishers, which means they need permission from the publisher before posting their work on an institutional repository. Yet lately, more authors insist on maintaining all or part of their copyright (such as reproduction and distribution), thus allowing to share with others such as with their organization's institutional repository.

SPARC offers an author addendum to address such needs at https://sparcopen.org/our-work/author-rights/brochure-html/. This is a legal tool for negotiating one's publisher agreement to maintain part or all of their rights of Section 106. The Author Addendum is a free resource developed by SPARC in partnership with Creative Commons and Science Commons. It is helpful to acquire and maintain books in your library collection that answer additional questions about publisher contracts for authors. Such resources often provide boilerplate contract examples with guidance on negotiating publisher contracts.

UNPUBLISHED WORKS IN SPECIAL COLLECTIONS AND ARCHIVES

On the other hand, assisting authors with their unpublished works presents other challenges such as plagiarism, copyright infringement, works made for hire, and privacy rights. Chapter 10 covers unpublished works in the section on museums, special collections, and archives. Student works include traditional course work to major projects such as theses and dissertations. Faculty works vary depending on whether work-related or scholarly publishing. For other types of faculty and student unpublished works, the university or college copyright or IP policy should be read carefully to ensure that works for hire and similar restrictions imposed by the campus policy are not violated.

CONTRACTS AND PUBLISHER AGREEMENTS

SCLs or managers of institutional repositories must also be familiar with contracts and publisher agreements. This facilitates the proper management of IP policies and requirements for their repository collection including its scholarly journals.

In addition, policies should be tied to the mission and goals of the academic library and its parent institution.

An author contract or agreement with the publisher must be reviewed on copyrighted works before they are added to the institutional repository. This confirms that the author maintained the right to grant the repository permission to reproduce and distribute their copyrighted work. To verify which exclusive rights in Section 106 of their copyright were maintained, simply review the two sections of their publication agreement customarily entitled "Copyright Ownership/Transfer of Copyright and Author/Contributor Rights." These sections reveal which exclusive rights were granted to the publisher.[93] One should also be mindful of works created as part of an author's job responsibilities such as, a commissioned effort, works made for hire, or as part of a grant. If this is the case, then another copyright holder might be involved in permission to reproduce or distribute such works in the repository.

Once an institutional repository has confirmed that the author has maintained enough of his or her exclusive rights in Section 106 to authorize reproduction and distribution of a published work contributed, then the author must review and sign a submission agreement of the repository. The central requirement of a submission agreement focuses on the IP rights of the author. In addition, the author must assure the repository that the submission is his or her original work, and the work does not infringe on an existing copyrighted works or other IP rights. This is especially important to assure when a work submitted is previously unpublished, as no publisher has scrutinized its originality. Usually repository agreements do not require any transfer or assignment of copyright over to the institutional repository. CC or other open-access licensing is often promoted if no traditional copyright was transferred or assigned to a commercial publisher.

Additionally, if photographs or images are a separate part of an author's prospective publication, permission (and payment for use) from another copyright party may be required to avoid infringement. Photographs are more challenging to deal with, as there are multiple layers of rights. Besides a photographer's copyright, right of publicity is another approval often recommended if identifiable images of other people are involved. Just because you purchased the photograph for your research does not mean that you own the copyright or have right of publicity to publish that photo on the university website or digital repository. Remember, photographers are authors too. A hired photographer, or a photo studio, is often the copyright owner. Likewise, photos captured and shared by students for faculty research may require their permission to use. Meanwhile, when photos utilized are from the public domain or CC, attribution may be required. Additional details about photographer copyrights are covered in Chapters 8, 9, and 10.

IP AND PUBLISHERS

As libraries and other units on college campuses are producing and publishing open-access scholarly journals, they must attempt to strike a balance between protecting the authors' rights versus the flexible open-access rights of its readers. Similarly, authors dealing with other publishers may have general questions for IP librarians and specialists about publisher agreements. Besides the SPARC author addendum cited above, the ACRL offers additional publisher agreement tips for authors entitled Copyright & IP: Author Rights at https://www.arl.org/focus-areas/copyright-ip/author-rights#.XAvnmFVKiUk. In addition, the Authors Alliance offer helpful guides to publication contracts at https://www.authorsalliance.org/resources/publication-contracts/.

Furthermore, the quality or even reputation of some open-access journals is critical, such as regarding issues with predatory publishers. Predatory publishers often lack quality assurance, peer reviewing, and editorial processing. Before submission to any open-access journal, an author might see if the title is included in an open-access journal directory, such as the Directory of Open Access Journals https://doaj.org/, or, if the journal is a member of the Open Access Scholarly Publishers Association, https://oaspa.org/.

For the editorial management team of an open-access scholarly journal, submission policies and requirements similar to what an institutional repository utilize are necessary. Permissions for an author's third-party copyrighted materials included in open-access articles is often the primary need of an agreement. Issues to consider when drafting guidelines for an open-access journal include who is responsibility for obtaining permissions, paying any fees, and documentation records of permissions; identifying rights holders; orphan works policies; and fair use. To assure ethical policies for an open-access scholarly journal, the Library Publishing Coalition published *An Ethical Framework for Library Publishing*,[94] version 1.0 in 2018 that offers recommendations for publishing and ethics. Topics include publishing practice, accessibility, diversity, privacy, and intellectual and academic freedom.

Fair use considerations are just as important as obtaining permissions. When contemplating how to incorporate a fair use policy for articles submitted, refer to best practices such as the *Code of Best Practices in Fair Use for Academic and Research Libraries* (found at https://publications.arl.org/code-fair-use/) from the Association of Research Libraries, and the Center for Social Media at American University School of Communication. This policy emphasizes the transformative aspects of fair use, which may apply to a fair use policy established for submission of articles to an open-access publication.[95]

The authors' rights versus the readers' rights to use an author's work to advance their research, writing, and instruction is a balancing act. Hence, CC or other types of open-access rights are helpful for guiding readers in building upon the works of other.

OTHER IP CONCERNS IN SCHOLARLY COMMUNICATIONS: PATENTS, OPEN SOURCES, AND TRADEMARKS

Finally, other IP rights such as patents, open sources, and trademarks are encompassed in research and innovation aspects of scholarly communications. The United Nations Educational, Scientific and Cultural Organization (UNESCO) considers patent literature as one of the many channels of scholarly communication.[96] Patents have been significantly tied to technology transfer of federally funded research at many universities since the Bayh-Dole Act was enacted in 1980.[97]

Technology transfer offices are now relatively common at academic institutions. Such offices manage IP owned by the organization and pursue commercialization opportunities for inventions that are the result of its research activities.[98] The Bayh-Dole Act "ultimately has motivated more and more universities to become actively involved in the transfer of technology from the lab to market."[99] Successful technology transfer from the campus workshop to marketplace include IP as part of the research process. Academic entrepreneurs often consider an IP strategy and licensing before initiating the actual research and product development. Effective academic entrepreneurs are not merely interested in designing novel inventions for the sake of inventing. They are more often interested in producing a commercially viable product while the novel invention facet is "simply a fundamental part of the patentable commercial viability of their future product."[100]

Chapters 3 and 4 of this book support librarians in teaching students, faculty, and community customers to recognize when they may need a patent for their innovation. Independent inventors from the community often look to librarians associated with IP to solve a specific problem with patent information, and campus students and faculty often need patent information for support in exploration and researching.[101] Chapter 3 covers patent fundamentals such as identifying parts of a patent, defining patentability and prior art, and recognizing the difference between provisional and non-provisional patent applications. Meanwhile, Chapter 4 offers insight on patent searching—for example, learning how to conduct a patentability search—including effective search strategies utilizing patent classifications and databases.

Different fields of science, engineering, or entrepreneurship require unique patent information to support discovery to potentially defend IP of innovations for students and researchers on campus. An introductory course or one-time class lecture should focus on awareness of all IP types including patents. An additional course might focus specifically on patents tied to a project or research paper. Patent literature as traditional research is another literacy aspect for course content.[102]

Divergent patent foci apply to different fields of engineering or science. For example, an engineering design course may emphasize patent drawings, whereas a chemistry course may encompass chemical compound identifiers or structures in patents.[103] Identifying such varying needs for patent information ensures focusing on the specific requirements of the target audience and strengthens the perceived quality of information presented.

INFORMATION LITERACY STANDARDS FOR SCIENCE AND ENGINEERING/TECHNOLOGY (PATENTS)[104]

The Association of College & Research Libraries (ACRL) offers Information Literacy Standards for Science and Engineering/Technology in 2006. Patent literature and research is included as part of the overall framework. The following lists include highlighted portions that apply to information literacy of patents for instruction associated with academic libraries:

STANDARD 1, PERFORMANCE INDICTOR 2, OUTCOME SECTION C

To identify the need for patent information.

STANDARD 1, PERFORMANCE INDICATOR 3, OUTCOME SECTION D

To understand patents and how they are produced, organized, and disseminated.

STANDARD 1, PERFORMANCE INDICATOR 4, OUTCOME SECTION D

To consider costs and benefits of the patent process including licensing.

STANDARD 2, PERFORMANCE INDICATOR 2, SECTION B

To acquire needed patent information effectively and efficiently with patent classifications.

STANDARD 3, PERFORMANCE INDICATOR 6, SECTION C

To evaluate patent information found by reviewing patent documents and determining if further searching should be considered.

STANDARD 5, PERFORMANCE INDICATOR 2, SECTION D

To keep up with innovation by utilizing current awareness tools and bibliometric analysis for competitive intelligence in the field.

PTRCs or other academic or special libraries collecting patents could aggregate patent documents for a distinctive scholarly communication need, such as regional legacy historical patent collections, color image plant patents, chemical patent compounds, or a specialized topical database of public domain patents, among others. Librarians focusing on IP could show customers how to utilize bibliometric analysis to track history of a technology or to reveal competitive intelligence. Chapter 10, on special libraries, demonstrates such patent analytic techniques.

The ACRL introduced the *Framework for Information Literacy for Higher Education* in 2016. Since then, various libraries representing specialized subject disciplines have applied its six frames into the information literacy instruction of different topics, including STEM subjects such as patents. Dave Zwicky, PTRC librarian at Purdue University, identified opportunities to incorporate patents into the STEM information literacy conversation based upon the six frames. This was reported in the *Journal of the Patent and Trademark Resource Center Association* in 2019. The most obvious frame which affords discussion is "Information Has Value," regarding the economic value of patents to inventors and society. The intricate steps to searching patents demonstrated in Chapter 4 could be tied to the frame "Searching as Strategic Exploration." Zwicky emphasizes that the role of patents in engineering design fits well with the frames "Research as Inquiry" and "Scholarship as Conversation." Further, the role of patents in general research and development supports the frame "Information Creation as a Process." Ultimately, as government documents, patents could be applied to discussion of the frame "Authority is Constructed and Contextual." The six frames tied to patents reinforce the role of library research consultations and instruction of intellectual property information literacy. Future PTRC publications and programs will most likely address further development of related IP information literacy.[105]

Campus researchers with potential patented inventions should be reminded that public disclosures, such as a presentation at a conference or publication in a scientific journal, occurring more than one year before a patent application is filed, could negate obtaining a granted patent.[106] One should at least submit a provisional patent application before public disclosure whenever possible. Conference papers or journal publications could also be included in a provisional application. Provisional patent applications are not the final application for a patent. They are a low-cost, one-year placeholder that could be referenced in a subsequent nonprovisional patent application. See Chapter 3 for more details about patents.

Open-access applications could relate to patents that are part of university research and innovation. Taking lessons from the software and health fields, the electric vehicle manufacturer Tesla created a limited, open-source patent pool to accelerate technology innovation in the field of electric vehicles.[107] Open IP scenarios may spur innovation, and some suggest they may diminish potential patent infringements such as patent trolls. Some believe that pools of open-source patents promote a sustainable future allowing competitors of new technologies to contribute to a larger shared portfolio in which they rely on essential inventions that are part of a larger part of a product like an electric vehicle. Professors in multiple disciplines may find it useful to know about such open-source patent pools, as these are beneficial to small and mid-sized companies in new technology fields lacking resources to battle patent infringement allegations.[108]

However, faculty and students on campus must use caution when using open-source software coding within potential applications for software patents. As covered earlier in Chapter 3, copyrights are used to protect software code, while patents are used to protect software function. Chapter 3 pointed out that some open-source licensing of computer software, GNU Public License (GPL) used by Linux, stipulates that using such open-source software within a patent means it "must be licensed for everyone's free use or not licensed at all."[109] Such an open-source license conflicts with most patent applications. One should always read the fine print of an open-source software license before interpolating such open-source IP into a new patent application.

Furthermore, trademarks are another IP that could apply to scholarly communications. Federal trademarks rights could apply in protecting the title name of an open-access journal. Products developed in technology transfer on campus may require trademarks.

Trademarks are common for branded names of mobile apps or computer software developed by students or faculty that are later commercialized. Non-law disciplines necessitating trademark branding awareness in their curriculum often include business management, marketing, entrepreneurship, sports business and event management, leisure and entertainment studies, engineering, computer science, and fashion design studies. See Chapter 5 for more about searching and registering trademarks.

CONCLUSION

Scholarly communication not only promotes open access in academic libraries but also has become a vital part of advancing academic instruction, research, and publishing tied to information access and delivery. The future of library reserves serving instruction, information delivery assisting research, and scholarly communication facilitating publishing will undoubtedly rely on the developing open-access movement. However, the traditional publisher model will continue to play a substantial role, too. Supporting student and faculty innovations with all types of intellectual property awareness, including patents and trademarks, will continue to expand as well to support STEM and entrepreneurship curricula.

This chapter prepares IP librarians or specialists to know, show, and tell their customers about IP topics, including copyright, fair use, open-access/source, patents, and trademarks as these relate to legal and ethical access of information for instruction, research, and publishing.

NOTES

1. David M. Marcovitz, "Copyright, Technology, and Your Rights," in *Advances in Educational Administration: Vol. 8. Technology and Education: Issues in Administration, Policy, and Applications in K12 Schools*, Sharon Y. Tettegah and Dr. Richard C. Hunter, eds., Advances in Education [Series], Volume 8, (London: Elsevier, 2006), 73–84.
2. Andrea L. Foster, "In Lawsuit, University Asserts That Downloading Copyrighted Texts Is Fair Use," *Chronicle of Higher Education* (June 27, 2008), http://chronicle.com/article/In-Lawsuit-University-Asse/942/ (accessed August 21, 2009).
3. *Cambridge Univ. Press v. Becker et al.*, 863 F. Supp. 2d 1190 (N.D. Ga, 2012), http://www.infodocket.com/2012/05/12/full-text-of-court-opinion-in-georgia-state-university-copyright-case/ (accessed November 30, 2012).
4. Steve Kolowich, "Publishers Double Down," *Inside Higher Ed*, September 11, 2012, http://www.insidehighered.com/news/2012/09/11/publishers-will-appeal-district-courts-decision-e-reserve-copyright-case (accessed November 30, 2012).
5. *Cambridge Univ. Press v. Patton*, 769 F.3d 1232 (11th Cir. 2014), defendant name change reflects different president at Georgia State University.
6. *Cambridge Univ. Press v. Becker*, Case 1:08-cv-01425-ODE Document 510 (N.D. Ga, 2016).
7. Krista Cox, "Eleventh Circuit Reverses and Remand Georgia State E-Reserves Case (Again)," *ARL Policy News*, October 22, 2018, http://policynotes.arl.org/?p=1738 (accessed December 6, 2018); Andrew Albanese, "GSU E-Reserves Case Goes On After Publishers Win Second Appeal," *Publishers Weekly*, October 22, 2018, https://www.publishersweekly.com/pw/by-topic/digital/copyright/article/78401-gsu-e-reserves-case-goes-on-after-publishers-win-second-appeal.html (accessed December 6, 2018); Kevin Smith, "GSU Copyright Case: Lather, Rinse, Repeat," *IO: In The Open*, October 20, 2018, https://intheopen.net/2018/10/the-gsu-copyright-case-lather-rinse-repeat/ (accessed December 6, 2018); Association of American Publishers: Newsroom, "Appeal Court Agrees with Publishers in Reversing Georgia State University Copyright Fair Use Decision," http://newsroom.publishers.org/appeals-court-agrees-with-publishers-in-reversing-georgia-state-university-copyright-fair-use-decision/ (accessed December 6, 2018).

8. Laura Gasaway, *Growing Pains: Adapting Copyright for Libraries, Education, and Society* (Littleton, CO: Rothman & Co., 1997), xii.

9. Kenneth D. Crews, *Copyright Law for Librarians and Educators: Creative Strategies and Practical Solutions* (Chicago: American Library Association, 2006), viii.

10. *Feist Publications, Inc. v. Rural Telephone Service Co.*, 499 U.S. 340, 349 (1991).

11. Cindy Kristof, *Electronic Reserves Operations in ARL Libraries: a SPEC kit* [Series] Flyer 245 (Chicago: Association of Research Libraries, May 1999).

12. The sections of this chapter on library course reserves and information for instructional environments is from an earlier chapter published by the author and the publisher of this book. John Schlipp, "Chapter Six: Electronic Reserves and Information Delivery," in *Distributed Learning and Virtual Librarianship*, Sharon Almquist, ed. (Santa Barbara, CA: Libraries Unlimited, 2011).

13. William W. Fisher and William McGeveran, *Digital Learning Challenge: Obstacles to Educational Uses of Copyrighted Material in the Digital Age: a foundational White Paper* (Cambridge, MA: Berkman Center for Internet & Society at Harvard Law School, August 2006), http://cyber.law.harvard.edu/media/files/copyrightandeducation.html (accessed August 8, 2009).

14. Rachel Bridgewater, "Shifting Responsibility for Electronic Reserves Copyright Permissions from the Academic Departments to the Library: From Confusion to Cooperation," *Journal of Interlibrary Loan, Document Delivery & Electronic Reserve* 18, no. 2 (2008): 141–152; David McCaslin, "Processing Electronic Reserves in a Large Academic Library System," *Journal of Interlibrary Loan, Document Delivery & Electronic Reserve* 18, no. 3 (2008): 335–346; Tomas A. Lipinski, *Copyright Law and the Distance Education Classroom* (Lanham, MD: Scarecrow Press, 2005), xi.

15. John Schlipp, "Coaching Teaching Faculty: Copyright Awareness Programs in Academic Libraries," *Kentucky Libraries* 72, no. 3 (2008): 18–22.

16. Kim Duckett and Dede Nelson, "Evolution of a Librarian: Instructional Designer Partnership in Higher Education," in *Academic Librarianship by Design*, Steven J. Bell and John D. Shank, eds. (Chicago: American Library Association, 2007), 74–77.

17. Kenneth Crews and Dwayne Buttler, "Fair Use Checklist," Columbia University Libraries, Information Services, Copyright Advisory Office, http://copyright.columbia.edu/fair-use-checklist (accessed April 26, 2009).

18. Crews, *Copyright Law for Librarians and Educators*, 124.

19. Carrie Russell, *Complete Copyright: An Everyday Guide for Librarians* (Chicago: American Library Association, 2004), 25–28.

20. Kenneth Crews, *Copyright, Fair Use, and the Challenge for Universities* (Chicago: University of Chicago Press, 1993), 22–25; Crews, *Copyright Law for Librarians and Educators*, 60–62.

21. Crews, *Copyright Law for Librarians and Educators*, 60–62; Andrew Richard Albanese, "Down with E-Reserves: Confusing, Contentious, and Vital, E-Reserves Fuel Higher Education—And an Ongoing Copyright Battle," *Library Journal* 132, no. 16 (2007): 36–38; and Janet Brennan Croft, "Electronic Reserves," *Journal of Interlibrary Loan, Document Delivery & Information Supply* 14, no. 3 (2004): 21–35.

22. Georgia Harper, *Fair Use of Copyrighted Materials* webpage, heading entitled, "Using the Four Factor Fair Use Test: A Note About Time Limits," affirms that publishers believe there is a time limit to Fair Use, http://www.utsystem.edu/OGC/intellectualProperty/copypol2.htm#note (accessed October 20, 2007); Georgia Harper, *Fair Use Guidelines for Electronic Reserve Systems* webpage, provides guidelines for library reserves based upon the

Conference on Fair Use (CONFU) in 1997. Section D entitled, "Storage and Reuse," states that permission from the copyright holder is required if the resource is reposted for the same class in future, http://www.utsystem.edu/OGC/intellectualProperty/rsrvguid.htm (accessed July 20, 2007).

23. *Feist* (1991) supports that facts themselves (such as a URL hyper link) are not copyrightable. For more, see Matt Jackson (April 1997) related article "Comment: Linking Copyright to Homepages," *Federal Communications Law Journal*, 49 Fed. Com. L. J. 731.

24. Stanford University Libraries, *Stanford Copyright & Fair Use: C. Connecting to Other Websites*, http://fairuse.stanford.edu/Copyright_and_Fair_Use_Overview/chapter6/6-c.html (accessed April 26, 2009).

25. *Technology, Education and Copyright Harmonization Act*, Public Law 107-273, *U.S. Statutes at Large* 116 (2002): 1910, codified at 17 U.S.C. §§ 110(2), 112(f).

26. 17 U.S. Code § 110(1)—Limitations on Exclusive Rights: Exemptions of Certain Performance and Displays.

27. Jeff Clark, "Chapter 5, Distributed Learning Copyright Issues," in *Distributed Leaning and Virtual Librarianship*, Sharon G. Almquist, ed. (Santa Barbara, CA: Libraries Unlimited, 2011), 200.

28. Kenneth D. Crews, "Chapter 12, Distance Education and the TEACH Act," in *Copyright Law for Librarians and Educators: Creative Strategies & Practical Solutions* (Chicago: American Library Association, 2012).

29. U.S. Copyright Act 17 U.S. Code § 110(2); TEACH Act.

30. U.S. Copyright Act 17 U.S. Code § 110(2); TEACH Act.

31. U.S. Copyright Act 17 U.S. Code § 110(2) (A)-(C); TEACH Act.

32. Crews, *Copyright Law for Librarians and Educators* (2012), 89.

33. U.S. Copyright Act 17 U.S. Code § 110(2).

34. Purdue University, *University Copyright Office: Fair Use Analysis*, http://www.lib.purdue.edu/uco/fair_use/ (accessed April 26, 2009).

35. *Technology, Education and Copyright Harmonization Act.*

36. Crews, *Copyright Law for Librarians and Educators,* 62.

37. Richard Stim, *Getting Permission: How to License & Clear Copyrighted Materials Online & Off* (Berkeley, CA: Nolo, 2004). Stim's book also provides ideas on how to write letters to contact author/publisher.

38. Crews, *Copyright Law for Librarians and Educators*, 111–112.

39. *Copyright Law Revision*, U.S. Congress. 94th Cong., 2d Sess. (1976). H. Doc. 1476: 68–70. "Agreement on Guidelines for Classroom Copying in Not-for-Profit Educational Institutions with Respect to Books and Periodicals, March 1976."

40. Marc Lindsey, *Copyright Law on Campus* (Pullman: Washington State University Press, 2003), 27.

41. Ibid.

42. Laura Gasaway, "Copyright Considerations for Electronic Reserves," in *Managing Electronic Reserves*, Jeff Rosedale, ed. (Chicago: American Library Association, 2002), 116–118.

43. Ibid., *Copyright Law Revision*, U.S. Congress. 94th Cong., 2d Sess. (1976). H. Doc. 1476: 68–70; Library of Congress, Circular 21, *Reproduction of Copyrighted Works by Educator and Librarians*, 6–7, https://www.copyright.gov/circs/circ21.pdf (accessed December 29, 2018).

44. Ibid.

45. Ibid.

46. Crews, *Copyright Law for Librarians and Educators*, 60–64; Lindsey, *Copyright Law on Campus*, 27.
47. American Library Association, *Model Policy Concerning College and University Photocopying for Classroom, Research and Library Reserve Use*, pamphlet, March 1982.
48. Ibid.; Crews, *Copyright, Fair Use, and the Challenges for Universities*, 51–52.
49. American Library Association, *Model Policy Concerning College and University Photocopying for Classroom, Research and Library Reserve Use, March 1982*, http://www.cni.org/docs/infopols/ALA.html (accessed April 26, 2009).
50. Gasaway, "Copyright Considerations for Electronic Reserves," 118–121.
51. Ibid.
52. Association of American Publishers, *Questions & Answers on Copyright for the Campus Community* (New York: Association of American Publishers, 2006), 25.
53. *Basic Books, Inc. v. Kinko's Graphics Corp.*, 758 F. Supp. 1522, 1526 (S.D.N.Y. 1991).
54. Crews, C*opyright, Fair Use, and the Challenge for Universities*, 53–55.
55. United States Patent and Trademark Office, *Technological Protection Systems for Digitized Copyrighted Works, Written Comments of Copyright Clearance Center, Inc.*, January 14, 2003, http://www.uspto.gov/web/offices/dcom/olia/teachcomments/copyrightcc.pdf (accessed August 9, 2009), Docket No. 2003-C-006.
56. Crews, C*opyright, Fair Use, and the Challenge for Universities*, 97.
57. Yale University Library, *Liblicence: Licensing Digital Information—Licensing Resources*, http://www.library.yale.edu/~llicense/liclinks.shtml (accessed May 4, 2009).
58. Consortium of College and University Media Centers, *Fair Use Guidelines for Educational Multimedia*, http://www.ccumc.org/assets/documents/MMFUGuidelines.pdf (accessed November 30, 2012).
59. Consortium of College & University Media Centers, *How the Fair Use Guidelines for Educational Multimedia Help Educators*, http://ccumc.org/node/209 (accessed August 21, 2009).
60. Fritz Dolak, Ball State University, Copyright & Intellectual Property Office, *Overview of the Fair Use Guidelines for Educational Multimedia*, http://www.bsu.edu/library/article/0,,14550--,00.html (accessed August 21, 2009).
61. Consortium of College & University Media Centers, *Fair Use Guidelines for Educational Multimedia*, http://www.ccumc.org/copyright-matters/fair-use-guideline (accessed August 21, 2009).
62. Janel Bloch, "Teaching Job Interviewing Skills with the Help of Television Shows," *Business Communication Quarterly* 74, no. 1 (March 2011): 7–21. See http://bcq.sagepub.com/content/74/1/7.abstract for details.
63. Sidney Eng and Flor A. Hernandez, "Managing Streaming Video: A New Role for Technical Services," *Library Collections, Acquisitions, & Technical Services* 30, no. 3–4 (2006): 214–223.
64. Music Library Association, "Statement on the Digital Transmission of Audio Reserves," *Copyright Guide for Music Librarians*, June 2010, http://copyright.musiclibraryassoc.org/Resources/DigitalReserves (accessed December 20, 2018).
65. Center for Media & Social Impact (CMSI) at American University, "Code for Academic and Research Libraries," http://cmsimpact.org/code/code-best-practices-fair-use-academic-research-libraries/ (accessed October 12, 2018).
66. Ibid.
67. Crews, *Copyright Law for Librarians and Educators*, 62–63.

68. Gasaway, "Copyright Considerations for Electronic Reserves," 121.

69. *Copyright Act of 1976*, U.S. Code 17 § 108—Limitations on Exclusive Rights: Reproduction by Libraries and Archives.

70. *1975 Senate Report on the New Copyright Law,* Senate Judiciary Committee, 94th Cong., 1st sess. (1975): S. Rep. No. 94-473, 70–71; for more on the CONTU Rule of Five, *Guidelines on Photocopying and Interlibrary Arrangements*, National Commission on New Technological Uses of Copyrighted Works (CONTU) Public Law 93-573 (1974), see http://www.copyright.gov/circs/circ21.pdf.

71. Carol Helgerson, "Copyright Issues in For-Profit Libraries: A Handbook for Non-Lawyers," in *Special Libraries Management Handbook: The Basics* (2004), http://www.libsci.sc.edu/bob/class/clis724/SpecialLibrariesHandbook (accessed August 11, 2009).

72. American Library Association, Interlibrary Loan Committee, *National Interlibrary Loan Code for the United States, 2003*, http://www.nmrls.org/ill/illcode.shtml (accessed April 18, 2009).

73. American Library Association, RUSA Reference Guidelines, *Interlibrary Loan Code for the United States, 2001*, http://www.ala.org/ala/mgrps/divs/rusa/archive/protools/referenceguide/interlibrary.cfm (accessed April 18, 2009).

74. American Library Association, Coalition for Networked Information, Information Policies, *Model Interlibrary Loan Code for Regional, State, Local, or Other Special Groups of Libraries, 1984*, http://www.cni.org/docs/infopols/ALA.html (accessed May 7, 2009).

75. *Guidelines for Media Resources in Academic Libraries Review Task Force, Association of College & Research Libraries, Guidelines for Media Resources in Academic Libraries, 2006*, http://www.ala.org/ala/mgrps/divs/acrl/standards/mediaresources.cfm (accessed April 26, 2009).

76. Carol Simpson, "Interlibrary Loan of Audiovisuals May Bring a Lawsuit," *Library Media Connection* 25, no. 5 (February 2008): 26–28.

77. Gretchen McCord Hoffmann, *Copyright in Cyberspace 2: Questions and Answers for Librarians* (New York: Neal-Schuman Publishers, Inc., 2005), 42.

78. Leslie Ellen Harris, *Licensing Digital Content: A Practical Guide for Librarians* (Chicago: American Library Association, 2009): 72–73.

79. Bruce R. Kingma, *Economics of Access versus Ownership: The Costs and Benefits of Access to Scholarly Articles via Interlibrary Loan and Journal Subscriptions* (New York: Haworth Press, 1996), 1–79. Copublished simultaneously in the *Journal of Interlibrary Loan, Document Delivery & Information Supply* 6, no. 3 (1996): 1–76.

80. Crews, C*opyright, Fair Use, and the Challenge for Universities*, 99–101.

81. Sigrid Kelsey, Director of Communication and Publications at Louisiana State University Libraries, Phi Kappa Phi *Forum* (Spring 2016): 26–29, http://www.phikappaphiforum-digital.org/phikappaphiforum/spring_2016?pg=28#pg28 (accessed May 1, 2018).

82. SPARC (the Scholarly Publishing and Academic Resources Coalition), Open Access, https://sparcopen.org/open-access/ (accessed December 7, 2018).

83. Peter Suber, Open Access Overview, 2015, https://legacy.earlham.edu/~peters/fos/overview.htm (accessed December 7, 2018).

84. Mikael Laakso et al., "Development of Open Access Journal Publishing from 1993 to 2009," *PLoS ONE* 6, no. 6 (June 13, 2011), https://journals.plos.org/plosone/article?id=10.1371/journal.pone.0020961 (accessed December 7, 2018).

85. ACRL, Scholarly Communication Toolkit: Economics of Publishing, 2016, https://acrl.libguides.com/scholcomm/toolkit/economics (accessed December 7, 2018).

86. ACRL (Association of College & Research Libraries), Principles and Strategies for the Reform of Scholarly Communication 1, June 24, 2003, http://www.ala.org/acrl/publications/whitepapers/principlesstrategies (accessed August 8, 2018).

87. NASIG (formerly the North American Serials Interest Group, Inc.), NASIG, Core Competencies for Scholarly Communication Librarians, August 11, 2017, http://www.nasig.org/site_page.cfm?pk_association_webpage_menu=310&pk_association_webpage=9435 (accessed August 8, 2018).

88. Ibid.

89. Isaac Gilman, *Library Scholarly Communication Programs: Legal and Ethical Considerations* (Oxford: Chandos Publishing, 2013), 15–16.

90. NIH Public Access Policy implements Division F Section 217 of PL 111-8 (Omnibus Appropriations Act, 2009).

91. "Heather Joseph, "Huge Win for Open Data in the United States," SPARC, January 14, 2019, https://sparcopen.org/news/2019/huge-win-open-data-united-states/ (accessed January 29, 2019).

92. Gilman, *Library Scholarly Communication Programs*, 23.

93. Beth Luey, "Chapter 5: Working with Your Publisher," in *Handbook for Academic Authors* (Cambridge: Cambridge University Press, 2010); William Germano, "Chapter 8: What a Contract Means," in *Getting It Published: A Guide for Scholars and Anyone Else Serious about Serious Books* (Chicago: University of Chicago Press, 2016); Gilman, *Library Scholarly Communication Programs*, 39.

94. Library Publishing Coalition, An Ethical Framework for Library Publishing, Version 1.0, July 2018, https://librarypublishing.org/resources/ethical-framework/ (accessed August 15, 2018).

95. Gilman, *Library Scholarly Communication Programs*, 207.

96. United Nations Educational, Scientific and Cultural Organization, *Scholarly Communication,* Module 1 (Paris: UNESCO, 2015), http://unesdoc.unesco.org/images/0023/002319/231938e.pdf (accessed August 10, 2018), page 10.

97. P.L. 96-517, Patent and Trademark Act Amendments of 1980.

98. Alexey Titov, "Commercializing Inventions Through an Office of Technology Transfer," in *Intellectual Property in Academia*, Nadya Reingand, ed. (Boca Raton, FL: CRC Press, 2012), 184.

99. University of Pittsburgh Innovation Institute, Bayh-Dole Act At a Glance, https://www.innovation.pitt.edu/resource/bayh-dole-act-at-a-glance/ (accessed December 8, 2018).

100. Ethel Machi and Peter Machi, "Chapter 7: University Patent Case Studies," in *Intellectual Property in Academia*, Nadya Reingand, ed. (Boca Raton, FL: CRC Press, 2012), 208–223.

101. David Zwicky, PTRCA listserv discussion about learning outcomes for patent presentations, October 26, 2018.

102. John Meier, "Chapter 6: Intellectual Property: Patents," in *Busy Librarian's Guide to Information Literacy in Science and Engineering*, Katherine O'Clair and Jeanne R. Davidson, eds. (Chicago: Association of College and Research Libraries, 2012).

103. Ibid.

104. Association of College & Research Libraries, "Information Literacy Standards for Science and Engineering/Technology," American Library Association, July 24, 2006, http://www.ala.org/acrl/standards/infolitscitech (accessed January 26, 2019).

105. Dave Zwicky, "Thoughts on Patents and Information Literacy," *Journal of the Patent and Trademark Resource Center Association* 29, no. 1 (2019): 1–16.

106. 35 U.S. Code § 102—Conditions for Patentability; Novelty.

107. Frank Tietze, "How a Free-For-All on Patents Could Help Build a Sustainable Future," *The Independent*, May 17, 2017, https://www.independent.co.uk/life-style/gadgets-and-tech/how-an-open-approach-to-patents-could-help-build-a-sustainable-future-a7738041.html (accessed August 15, 2018).

108. Sean D. Harding, "Meet the Patents: Fostering Innovation and Reducing Costs by Opening Patent Portfolios," *Journal of Business & Technology Law* 11, no. 2 (2016), https://digitalcommons.law.umaryland.edu/jbtl/vol11/iss2/5/ (accessed August 15, 2018).

109. Free Software Foundation, *GNU General Public License, Version 2*, Preamble, https://www.gnu.org/licenses/old-licenses/gpl-2.0.en.html (accessed March 11, 2017).

Chapter 8

PUBLIC LIBRARIES

CHAPTER OBJECTIVES

- To identify and understand the intellectual property (IP) associated with the workflow and customer information needs of public libraries
- To identify and understand the IPs associated with three-dimensional (3-D) printers
- To be aware of copyright and related rights associated with digitization of unique special collections of public libraries
- To be familiar with IP needs of public library customers
- To recognize the shared values between librarians and journalists associated with information access
- To identify unique aspects of IP and information rights relevant to blogging or news reporting, such as First Amendment rights and the Hot News Doctrine
- To understand and apply trademarks for protecting branding tag lines and logos tied to the public library's mission and vision

INTRODUCTION

IP in public libraries is not as apparent as in academic or school libraries. In addition to interlibrary loan, photocopier machine copyright notices, makerspaces, and Patent Trademark Resource Centers (PTRCs) located in some public libraries, IP is a growing part of information literacy for this environment. With information overload and ignorance of and need for help determining what is propaganda, versus factual types of information, many patrons of public libraries need assistance with navigating the vast sea of online information. Librarians at public libraries coach their colleagues and customers in the best ways to get the most value from information often providing information literacy and IP training via one-on-one reference assistance, workshops, interest groups, and one-on-one training. Much of this training is based on information shared from the American Library Association (ALA). The ALA's Advocacy and Public Policy site stress that "even in areas in which children are well served by fully developed information literacy curricula in their schools, adults may have little or no training in seeking and evaluating information on the Internet, and parents may seek training in guiding their children in Internet use."[1] Public library outreach programs address information literacy including evaluating quality of resources and respecting IP as information users. Other outreach efforts promote IP creators. Makerspaces and PTRC programs support creative and innovative customers from inventors to musicians.

As covered earlier in Chapter 1, information literacy concerning IP is a growing part of the knowledge shared for both coworkers and customers of public libraries. IP librarians or specialists at public libraries answer questions about copyrights, trademarks, and patents for artists, authors, business people, entrepreneurs, genealogists, inventors, journalists, musicians, students, and researchers of all ages. A report from the Aspen Institute promotes how public libraries drive innovation, inspire learning, and advance knowledge through people, place, and platform.[2] The library customers and partners are the people that use the physical and virtual place of their public libraries. While the platform includes the information content and services which a public library provides such as the needed reference resources and often, broadband internet access for answers to the most common types of IP topics. However, this platform also includes making the library a participatory enterprise as a central hub for learning and community connections related to IP awareness. Associated chapter topics ahead include makerspaces and three-dimensional (3-D) printers, digital collections of public libraries' unique local history and genealogy resources, IP resources for everyone from inventors to news journalists, and even IP for a public library's behind-the-scenes daily workflow or developing its own branding needs.

PUBLIC LIBRARIES FOSTER KNOWLEDGE, CREATIVITY, AND COMMUNITY CONNECTIONS

Benjamin Franklin founded the United States' first lending library in 1731, known as the Library Company of Philadelphia.[3] Franklin was an exceedingly curious and sociable person, which clearly promoted his success as an author, publisher, inventor, diplomat, and inventor, credited for bifocals, the Franklin stove, and using the lighting rod to discover electricity. Some recent historians consider him as the social network genius of the eighteenth century as he sent and received roughly 20,000 handwritten letters. Franklin used letters to share ideas and garner professional introductions as done today with LinkedIn. Perhaps it is no coincidence, that Franklin was the founder of a then new social platform of his era, the U.S. Postal Service.[4]

Franklin's curiosity and social networking attributes are evident as his group of fellow Philadelphia tradesmen and artisans determined they needed a lending library (see figure 8.1) to share information resources and establish community

Figure 8.1

Benjamin Franklin Opening First Subscription Library in Philadelphia. Illustration by Artist Charles E. Mills, published by Detroit Publishing Company, now in the public domain. (Courtesy of Library of Congress; https://www.loc.gov/item/2016817311/)

connections to nurture their business and political knowledge.[5] The origins of Franklin's lending Library Company of Philadelphia lives on today as public libraries continue to inspire knowledge, creativity, and community connections to benefit the public good. In fact, the Library Company promoted popular scientific exploration as Franklin used that library space to conduct his early experiments with electricity.[6] One might even say that the Library Company of Philadelphia introduced the first library makerspace in the eighteenth century.

Learning from Franklin's curiosity and sociability, today's public libraries are transforming their sites by offering customer spaces for technology tinkering. Makerspaces can go beyond arts and crafts centers or science project hubs. Makerspaces are more often organized centers in libraries that provide younger library customers an opportunity to create and innovate intellectual works utilizing library resources such as computers, 3-D printers, audiovisual tools, printing and publishing software, and the customary testing widget–type provisions. Public, academic, and even school libraries, perhaps on a lesser scale, have embraced large-scale centers frequently tied to community partners for financial and/or programming outreach support.

The maker culture also allows librarians to focus their science and technology information resources to supplement the makerspace. However, few makerspaces include IP as part of their agenda. PTRCs are well suited to support makerspaces with IP awareness, particularly patents. IP is intrinsically tied to the protection of the makers' unique creative and inventive works. IP awareness is also critical in developing customer policies and user training sessions to avoid potential infringements with copyrights, trademarks, and patents.

Miguel Figueroa, director of the Center for the Future of Libraries at ALA, affirms the maker movement as an integral part of libraries' "expanded mission to be places where people can not only consume knowledge, but create new knowledge."[7] Users of makerspace also report of networking opportunities with other makerspace users. A customer of a public library makerspace near the author of this book said that our makerspace was "an incubator for creativity, connections, and networking."[8]

Origins of contemporary marker movement in public libraries started with the Fayetteville Free Library in New York State.[9] The library calls its makerspace the Fabulous Laboratory, abbreviated as the FabLab.[10] The FabLab concept was introduced by MIT's Center for Bits & Atoms Fab Lab Program known as the FabFoundation.[11] Both institutions have inspired libraries nationwide with best practices on how to set up a makerspace and other logistics such as certification training sessions customers must attend before using the 3-D printer and other tools. Most makerspaces broadly follow a FabLab Charter[12] from the FabFoundation to:

- Serve as a community resource, offering open access for individuals in addition to scheduled access for programs.
- Respect IP choices of inventor, but make available works developed in lab for utilization and learning by others.
- Support commercial activities prototyped and incubated in the lab.
- Establish access to tools, capabilities, and processes to facilitate sharing within lab and project development.

IP OVERVIEW OF MAKERSPACES AND 3-D PRINTERS

Besides safety concerns and logistics of each makerspace location, 3-D printing and IP considerations present risk issues with copyrights, patents, trademarks, and even periphery issues such as free speech and privacy. Makerspaces often address such IP concerns associated with 3-D printers with waivers and agreements, equipment and personal safety assessments, staff and customer training, and signage similar to copyright notices for photocopiers. It is vital to get some policies and procedures in place before opening a makerspace.[13] Before a library creates such policies and procedures, understanding all IP matters involved with 3-D printers is very helpful. It is useful to refer to earlier chapters for their foundations of copyrights, patents, and trademarks before continuing this chapter.

Three-dimensional printing, also known as additive manufacturing or rapid prototyping, "enables physical objects to be constructed from a virtual 3-D model with the aid of computer-aided design (CAD) program."[14] At public libraries, 3-D printing empowers entrepreneurs, inventors, and business start-ups to prototype, to acquire needed IPs, and to advance their innovation to market. Public access to the printers and other tools of a library makerspace foster ambitious innovators and hobbyists to advance their creative ideas from discovery to reality. Access to such tools requires IP awareness for the makerspace host library as well as the makerspace customers.

To address IP awareness matters associated with library customers using a 3-D printer, the library administration and the makerspace support team must understand all aspect of IP related to their makerspace equipment and tools, such as 3-D printers. After the library staff has developed policies and procedures for its makerspace area, including IP aspects of 3-D printing, development of training sessions and posting signage are critical to prepare before opening the area.

ALA has published a template of a copyright warning notice created by Tomas Lipinski to post near 3-D printers that is similar to photocopiers notices that reference the Section 108 provision of the U.S. Copyright Act for libraries. Lipinski is a library copyright scholar and expert on such matters and his template includes reference to U.S. Patent Law and even torts related to product liability. For this copyright notice signage and other related policy concepts, see ALA's Office for Information Technology Policy series document by Charlie Wapner, "Progress in the Making: 3D Printing Policy Considerations through the Library Lens" (*Perspectives* no. 3, January 2015).[15] The Lipinski copyright warning notice template is located in the Appendix of this document. The ALA also offers a site entitled "3-D Printing in Libraries: Policies & Best Practices" at http://www.ala.org/advocacy/intfreedom/3d_printer_policy.

Wapner's *Perspectives* document concerning 3-D printing policies also emphasizes that public librarians must "understand where our rights and responsibilities begin and end as service providers and users"[16] in relations to 3P printing. Such rights include copyright, patent, and trademark considerations. Copyright is most prominent to 3-D printing as the CAD design file or software code could be copyrighted as pictorial, graphical, or literacy works. Software code is treated as a literary work for copyright registration with U.S. Copyright Office. CAD files could be copyrighted or open source code.[17] The bulk of infringement cases associated with 3-D printers are copyright disputes.[18] Most copyright litigation associated with 3-D printing usually deals with the anti-circumvention provision[19] of the Digital Millennium Copyright Act (DMCA) covered in Chapter 6. The DMCA possibly protects libraries[20] from liability for infringing acts of its makerspace customers circumventing CAD design files. However, makerspace customers are still liable for potential infringement. Hence, staff and customer training sessions reviewing CAD file copyright and displaying Lipinski's copyright notice signage are vital to protect both the library and its customers from infringement lawsuits.

Most of the original physical 3-D objects such as toy figures and jewelry created and printed by makerspace customers could be copyright protected as sculptural works. All copyright limits and exclusions like other copyrighted works could apply.

Replicating trademarks or trade dress designs of others could be an infringement too. As covered in Chapter 5, such trademarks infringement is pertinent to an unauthorized use of a distinctive brand or logo on the printed product.[21] While trade dress applies to inherently distinctive product visual designs that help determine product origin as discussed previously, the Coca-Cola bottle's distinctive contours and packaging is federally registered as a trade dress.[22] Action figures of proprietary pop culture characters could have both trademarks and copyrights associated.

Makerspace customers using 3-D printers should take care to avoid potential infringement of others as well as protecting one's own patentable inventions. Utility patents protect inventions and processes, while design patents protect ornamental designs for manufactured goods, but there are no fair use exceptions for patents.

The patent infringement scenarios that predominate with makerspace customers occur when a customer creates or copies a patented spare part of a machine, such as a vacuum cleaner that needs repair. Once again, posting Lipinski's copyright notice, which includes a reference to patents as well as dangerous product liability, could protect the library from any potential responsibility.

Inventors creating working models or prototypes for their original patent application gain the most value from use of 3-D printer at a makerspace. It saves inventors' time and money to prototype their products. Finally, their patent attorneys or agents will appreciate the 3-D printer prototype, as it helps them to understand the utility or design aspects of the invention as they construct claims for the patent application.

GENERAL COPYRIGHTS IN THE PUBLIC LIBRARY

Librarians are often steadfast advocates of following copyright law, respecting copyright creators, and promoting fair use for library customers. Copyright is the IP for which librarians are most familiar and able to assist library customers. Public librarians work at all times to ensure that their customer legally acquire the copyrighted, open access, or public domain resources to fulfill their information needs. In some instances, customers confer with librarians for assistance with locating online registration forms of the U.S. Copyright Office to register their copyrightable works.

As discussed in depth in Chapter 2, the legal foundation of all libraries in the United States lending books is built upon the First Sale Doctrine[23] Section 109(a) of the U.S. Copyright Act of 1976. Electronic resources such magazine and journals have become quite popular with patrons of public libraries as well as electronic books. These are all readable on common, multiple e-book readers and mobile devices. At a public library, a collection development or acquisition librarian is usually responsible for negotiating licensing contracts with electronic resources and e-book publishers. Copyright, fair use, and licensing contract terms are all significant for negotiating the best deals for customer access rights. Some publishers restrict access to single usage of an item and no fair use copying; while others allow multiple user access per item and fair use for personal and research needs. It is always helpful to read reference books about licensing, compare notes with other librarians for tips and suggestions, and even obtain legal counsel for help when negotiating such licensing contracts.

PUBLIC LIBRARY LOCAL COLLECTION

Historians and genealogists rely on local history and genealogy collections found at public libraries. Public libraries have often become the designated keeper or trustee of regional history for their communities. This author was introduced to such a special collection as a teenager in the 1970s, working part-time as a page/shelver in a suburban Carnegie library. A handsome wood-adorned back room featured shelved rows of long-play records that were very popular at the time. However, hidden in the corner of the phonograph records room, stood an old barrister bookcase locked with local history books, local family scrapbooks and letters, and many microfilm reels of local newspapers featuring the small town's golden past. The microfilmed newspaper collection was among the only items requested to view onsite by library patrons. Noticing the news headlines and advertisements of times about which he had heard of from his parents and grandparents, it was not long after that he too got the history bug to peruse fascinating facts and photos found about the little town. It is such collections and resources hidden away that many public libraries have unlocked by digitizing and publishing online to share with the world. A treasure trove of history and genealogy resources abound on websites of public libraries nationwide. However, before librarians digitize such collections, they must ensure that they have the right to copy and share the material online.

Besides specific regional history materials at public libraries, such common genealogical materials often include historical census documents, passengers' lists, city directories, military histories, maps, church and cemetery records, ethnic and cultural group historical records, and even photographs.

Photographs are probably the more challenging copyrighted materials to deal with for genealogy or library digitization projects. Matters to consider include fair use, public domain status, or where to get permission for both copyright and right of publicity.[24] Two different rights should be considered: the copyright owner of the photo, and the people captured in photos. A hired photographer or commercial studio are often the copyright holder of prepared photos, while whoever captured a personal snapshot is the copyright owner. If no rights of publicity forms are included with a photo, consider contacting the subject in the photo for permission as well as the photographer.

Audio or video recordings also have multiple layers of rights. For example, oral history interviews consist of separate copyright for the interviewee and the interviewer unless the interviewee signed a release form at the time of recording. Otherwise, fair use highlights could be considered. Music and other public performances have multiple layers of rights too. Review Chapter 2 for more about music copyright matters.

Donor agreements, in most cases, clear up any permission or rights issues as such agreements confirm that a library has rights to digitize. This would include how the donor holds copyright of such works. The library's customer policies also help so that there are no misunderstandings on what researchers can do with such resources.

Copyright matters related to genealogy resources are most challenging when family feuds occur about who owns copyright over genealogy compilations or when resources are prepared by another copyright cousin. Usually such misunderstandings are the result of lack of copyright awareness. Most genealogy resources published and placed in library collections offer compilations of dates and places of births, marriages, and deaths. The sources of these facts are often public domain. Facts cannot be copyrighted, and depending on the creativity, or lack thereof, compilation formatting of facts is often negligible and difficult to defend an alleged infringement.[25]

If the researcher of a published genealogy report inserted detailed narratives of history, personal information or repurposed the facts, and depending on how creative the arrangement or narrative is, such modified information might warrant copyright protection. Classifications or taxonomies of family records could be considered a creative endeavor since the final creation is based upon inclusion of facts chosen or excluded, as well as a method of organization created.[26]

No matter where the creativity line is drawn, courteous copyright cousins should always attribute fair use portions copied and ask for permission when not fair use. Therefore, librarians digitizing such resources may need to obtain permission, too. Recall the Supreme Court case covered in Chapter 2 entitled *Feist Publications, Inc. v. Rural Telephone Service Co.*, which addressed how facts are not copyrightable, but the compilation of facts might be protected if there is some creativity.

Digitization projects of public libraries often include a formal special collection department in the library. Sections 107 and 108 of U.S. Copyright Law afford such digitization projects to use fair use and other exemptions. For special collections, Chapter 10 reviews copyright matters, orphan works, donor agreements, finding rights holders, and getting permission. These workflow applications must be considered with multiples types of resources.

Fair use analysis of unpublished works applies to a large portion of content digitized in public libraries local history and genealogy collections. Unpublished works is also a topic that research customers, including authors and journalists, may encounter with legal issues when publishing such content from a library special collection. The fair use four factors—purpose, amount, nature, and effect—will apply. The nature of the copyrighted work factor, in relation to an unpublished work, often does not favor fair use. For example, in *Salinger v. Random House*, 484 U.S. 890:

> the Supreme Court in 1988 let stand a ruling that use of unpublished diaries and letters under the premise of research or news reporting may impair the future value of those writings. Such works are protected by a prepublication copyright. Further, there is a presumption that use of unpublished works is not fair use, the lower court concluded.[27]

The landmark case that set the precedence on how to apply the fair use "nature" factor to unpublished works dealt with the memoirs of former U.S. President

Gerald Ford. As introduced briefly in Chapter 2, Ford had signed a contract granting copyright ownership to the publisher Harper & Row, also giving them the right to license excerpts prior to the official release of the book. *Time* magazine paid for rights to publish 7,500 words of the text. Before *Time* published its authorized excerpt, another magazine, *The Nation*, acquired an unpublished manuscript of the memoir. *The Nation* published an article that only included approximately three hundred to four hundred words of direct quotes from the memoir. *Time* canceled its plans to publish its excerpt story, and Harper & Row sued *The Nation* for copyright infringement. Although the amount *The Nation* quoted from the memoir was brief, the qualitative aspect of the unpublished content was such that the short passage was the key content of the entire work about Ford's discussion of his pardon of Nixon. The Supreme Court found it to be the "heart of the work." When performing a traditional four-factor fair use test, including the amount factor, one must consider the "heart of the work" aspect into account. Even when only a very small portion of a factual work is copied, if it is the "heart of the work," one must make certain all other fair use factors favor the use. Since this work was unpublished, this further diminished the probability for defending it as fair use. In addition, the copyright holder's right of first publication, especially unpublished, tipped the fair use four-factor scale further toward copyright infringement. In the final decision from the U.S. Supreme Court, it was concluded that *The Nation's* publication of quoted excerpts from the unpublished manuscript was not fair use.[28]

Both Supreme Court cases mentioned above could apply to our library patrons. Copying content from unpublished works within special collections of public libraries more often requires permission of the copyright holder and/or author.

Besides regional history and genealogy, other types of authors, artists, musicians, and journalists may rely on public librarians for IP awareness and, in some instances, actual publishing, performance, or exhibition of their copyrighted works both at the library and out in the public. Fair use applications covered throughout this book may apply to such library customers.

Authors and musicians frequently need directions on registering copyright forms with the U.S. Copyright Office, while all of these creative customers may need directions on dealing with publishers and production services, such as original e-publishing of original content separate from library digital collections.

Blogs and informational websites are a growing part of the news media. Authors of such blogs and websites are the copyright owners of their content. To assure that one's blog or website content is protected, placing a © notice as well as registration with the U.S. Copyright Office is recommended. The party that establishes and maintains a blog is usually the copyright holder. Recognizing copyright ownership is essential when coauthors or guest contributors participate on the same blog site. Caution should be employed when copying quotes or paraphrasing from the blogs of others.[29] Challenges to fair use and the First Amendment occur with blogs and websites frequently. Librarian bloggers must be careful when publishing professional news articles and opinions.

LIBRARIANS AND JOURNALISTS MUTUAL VOCATION AND PASSION FOR SHARING INFORMATION

Like many of today's customers relying on public libraries for IP awareness, Benjamin Franklin authored, published, and printed news and viewpoints that influenced public opinion similar to what bloggers do today. Christopher Daly affirms this in his 2012 published history about journalism entitled *Covering America.* Daly states that through journalism, Franklin learned how to express himself to a broader audience, demonstrating a passion for civic engagement in the affairs of his city, his colony, and eventually, the entire world. Franklin gave journalism its "philosophical foundation" articulating the concept that "journalists serve the public by presenting controversial materials in their pages and should be thanked for going to the trouble, not sued, suppressed, or hanged."[30]

In 1731, Franklin published a historical document in his *Pennsylvania Gazette* entitled "Apology for Printers." According to Daly, Franklin asked his readers not to identify the views that appeared in a newspaper with the printer-editor. Instead, the newspaper should be the marketplace of ideas, where various opinions are up for debate. This was also known as an "open press" concept, whereby the printer-editor opens his pages to competitive points of view, providing a forum where truth and error can have "fair play." Franklin's "Apology" document faced political and legal implications under British rule. The Crown of Great Britain could censor the colonial press. Franklin's philosophy would eventually promote freedom of the press when the U.S. Constitution and the Bill of Rights were created over a half-century later. Today, journalists and librarians are carrying on the Franklin tradition with a mutual vocation and passion for sharing information by publishing books, news articles, and blogs. The day-to-day workflow may vary between librarians and journalists, but they each share many professional values, including fair use and freedom of speech.

In the early twenty-first century, the public appears to have credibility issues with the news media. A Knight Foundation and Gallup poll declares that only 33 percent of the public in the United States have a positive perception of the news media, and 66 percent claim most news media do not separate fact from opinion very well.[31] Yet another 2017 poll by the Pew Research Center clearly reveals that 78 percent say that public libraries help them locate trustworthy, reliable information, and 76 percent believe that libraries help them to learn new things.[32]

A recent trend reported by *American Libraries*[33] suggests that librarians and journalist can work together. Kate Torney, State Library Victoria CEO and former director of the Australian Broadcasting Corporation, recognizes that the two professions intersect as, "we are all in the information business. Journalists and librarians exist to share information and knowledge. Our goals are very similar."[34] Freedom of speech and freedom of the press are inherently in the democratic DNA work ethic of journalists. Librarians have always taken a firm stand supporting freedom of speech creating an alliance with the news media.[35] Some librarians write their own blogs or even grassroots, local newsletters. For example, the director of the Weare, New Hampshire, public library initiated a small newsletter after their local newspaper ceased operations. Their popular news resource offers calendar of events, library news, town politics and personalities. The library director claims that their grass roots publication instills a sense of community.[36] Librarian bloggers serve similar roles but must be cautious about potential libel scenarios

FIRST AMENDMENT RIGHTS AND HOT NEWS

Hot news may be defined as "breaking news" or a "news flash." Much confusion for journalists exists today to remain within the bounds of fair use to promote these freedoms, without infringing copyright or other legal implications and still report hot news. Recall the *Feist* Supreme Court case in Chapters 2 and 7 that dealt with facts versus published expression of content as it applies to copyright law.

Another landmark Supreme Court case that dealt with competitive Hot News and has renewed significance. The Hot News case falls more under competitive commerce law and misappropriation rather than copyright law of the similar aggregated intellectual content. See figure 8.2 for a visual continuum of the constitutional versus common law court cases in relation to freedom of speech discussed here.

Sherrie Callis, a law review author, relates the *Feist* case to the constitutional law that gives Congress the power to create copyright law to protect content format or originality. Callis suggests that there are natural tensions between protecting

Feist versus Hot News Doctrine court cases continuum

Overarching question of First Amendment (Free Speech and Free Press)

Copyright Law & Fair Use	Modern Hot News Doctrine	Original Hot News Misappropriation
(Federal Constitutional Law)	(State Common Law)	(Federal Common Law)
***Feist Publications, Inc. v. Rural Tel. Service Co.* (1991)** Fact versus Expression developed over time in federal court cases, such as *Feist*, which was based upon First Amendment and public access to facts. Also, legally affirmed that "sweat of the brow" did not matter with copyright law.	***NBA v. Motorola* (1997)** Common Law misappropriation limited to only five states and must pass "extra-element" test established in *NBA* case for preemption. Appealed and declared lawful for Motorola as alleged misappropriation were facts based on Federal Copyright Law and protected by First Amendment. *Barclays Capital Inc. v. Theflyonthewall.com, Inc.* (2011) was also appealed and overturned based on *Feist* and facts.	***International News Service v. Associated Press* (1918)** Supreme Court crafted a new variant of common law tort of misappropriation named the "hot news" doctrine. It protected "sweat of the brow," as it legally affirmed value of time in relation to the news. New technology prompted label of theft or piracy misappropriation under Federal Commerce Law. However, Federal Commerce approach was challenged and overturned in *Erie Railroad Co. v. Tompkins* (1938). It affirmed that the US Supreme Court should not add to federal common law those items clearly within the authority of state laws and state courts.

Figure 8.2
***Feist* versus Hot News Doctrine Court Cases Continuum by Author John Schlipp.**

the author's sweat of the brow and providing the public with access to copyrighted works. Copyright law reflects these tensions, as it distinguishes between fact versus expression. Callis points out that "facts have never been copyrightable, and therefore *Feist* should have come as no surprise. The First Amendment mandates copyright's idea/expression dichotomy, which ensures copyright law will not restrict freedom of speech by protecting ideas."[37] Further Callis states that "the Constitutional purpose of copyright is 'to encourage the widest possible production and dissemination of literary, musical and artistic works.'" Concurrently, the First Amendment supports that factual expression not be restricted by copyright.[38]

Yet Callis points out that a long-forgotten Supreme Court Hot News case associated with constitutional commerce law from 1918 has resurfaced whereby questionable copyright content of such aggregated works, such as databases, could be protected with "the use of contract and trade secret law."[39] Known as *International News Service v. Associated Press*, 248 U.S. 215 (1918), here is a case summary as posted on IP Watchdog:

> This was one of the first cases to address the issues raised by these technological advances, although the technology involved in the case was primitive by contemporary standards. The case involved two wire services, the Associated Press ("AP") and International News Service ("INS"), both transmitted news stories by wire to member newspapers. INS would lift factual stories from AP bulletins and send them by wire to INS papers. INS would also take factual stories from east coast AP papers and wire them to INS papers on the west coast that had yet to publish because of time differentials. The Supreme Court held that INS's conduct was a common-law misappropriation of AP's property.

Victoria Smith Ekstrand, a journalism scholar and professor, writes about this INS versus AP case in her book entitled *News Piracy and the Hot News Doctrine*.[40] She writes that in an early colonial news reporting era, the free exchange of newspapers promoted the technique of lifting news stories from other publications without attributing source credits. The belief that news and information belonged in the public domain persisted through the end of the nineteenth century. It became common knowledge that an informed democracy flourishes with free access to information. However, new technology presented challenges to this belief, as the telegraph offered instant news that provided competitive opportunities for reporters to scoop the news first. News soon became a commodity. Publishers defended their information products and rallied for a new "hot news" doctrine to protect them against the piracy of the latest, time-sensitive news scoops.[41]

The U.S. Supreme Court's 1918 ruling in the *International News Service v. Associated Press* case, establishing the hot news doctrine, requires some additional explanation. In essence, the U.S. Supreme Court made the ruling based upon federal common law tort cases involving property. Enlightenment thinkers like John Locke had long argued about the definition of what constituted property, and in the Supreme Court's 1918 decision, the justices were viewing the AP's collection of news about World War I as its quasi-property, gained at great expense to the organization and for which it was entitled some remuneration. Interestingly, Louis Brandeis was the sole justice dissenting in the decision, believing that it could impair basic constitutional rights. When the 1918 decision actually came before the U.S. Supreme Court, it made some of its most important First Amendment decisions the following year. Responding to the Espionage Act of 1917,[42] the 1919 cases of *Abrams v. United States* and *Schenk v. United States* resulted in decisions establishing the limits of First Amendment rights through the doctrine of "clear and present danger."[43] As Justice Oliver Wendell Holmes stated in these famous words: "The most stringent protection of free speech would not protect a man in falsely shouting fire in a theatre and causing a panic."[44]

The 1918 *International News Service v. Associated Press* case was essentially a decision based upon federal common law. Federal courts are only supposed to hear cases involving matters pertaining to citizens of different states, diversity jurisdiction, or cases involving federal law—federal-question jurisdiction. In the 1938 U.S. Supreme Court case *Erie Railroad Co. v. Tompkins*, the jurisdictional distinction between federal and state common law was questioned as an attorney attempted to apply federal common law for a case clearly within the authority of state laws and state courts.

Harry Tompkins had been seriously injured when walking along a track of the Erie Railroad in Pennsylvania. Tompkins's attorney sued in a federal district court in New York, home of the Erie Railroad, where the U.S. district court ruled on behalf of Tompkins and found the Erie Railroad guilty of negligence in the tradition of federal common law. The case was eventually appealed by the Erie Railroad to the U.S. Second Circuit Court, which argued that the lower court had ignored Pennsylvania common law dealing with negligence on the part of trespassers—in this case, Tompkins. Referred to the U.S. Supreme Court, the 1938 ruling of *Erie Railroad Co. v. Tompkins* led to a decision demarcating the boundaries between state and federal courts and limiting the practice of jurisdictional shopping. According to Justice Brandeis:

> Congress has no power to declare substantive rules of common law applicable in a state whether they be local in their nature or "general," be they commercial law or a part of the law of torts. And no clause in the Constitution purports to confer such a power upon the federal courts.[45]

In other words, the U.S. Supreme Court should not add to federal common law those items clearly within the purview of state laws and state courts.

In 1976, the U.S. Congress passed a revised Copyright Act. This new law, coupled with changing technologies in the decades to come, brought the "hot news doctrine" to the forefront again. A "hot news" case resurfaced in 1997, when the doctrine was argued by both parties of *National Basketball Association v. Motorola, Inc.*[46] The National Basketball Association (NBA) filed a hot news claim against Motorola for copying up-to-the-minute game scores and information from the NBA's copyrighted broadcasts to Motorola's "Sports Trax" pager customers. Initially, a U.S. District Court found the defendant, Motorola, liable for misappropriation;

but on appeal, a Second Circuit Court reversed the decision in favor of Motorola primarily because the scores and information of the alleged misappropriation were facts. In other words, the appeals court ruled on the basis of copyright law that facts, such as basketball scores, were not protected. The appeals court ruled against the "hot news" argument of the plaintiff, an argument that was based on common law and commerce law. The appeals court did not, however, deny that the common law and the commerce law were applicable. Rather, the plaintiff had not convinced the court with compelling evidence. Ekstand clarifies this, stating that the NBA case designed a new test for plaintiffs using the "hot news" argument, whereby the following points must be proven[47]:

(i) a plaintiff generates or gathers information at a cost;
(ii) the information is time-sensitive;
(iii) a defendant's use of the information constitutes free riding on the plaintiff's efforts;
(iv) the defendant is in direct competition with a product or service offered by the plaintiff; and
(v) the ability of other parties to free-ride on the efforts of the plaintiff or others would so reduce the incentive to produce the product or service that its existence or quality would be substantially threatened.[48]

Ekstand comments that "[t]he history of the hot news doctrine serves as an important reminder that common law, though imperfect and sometimes ill-defined, offers a measured approach to protections for the works delivered by new technologies, until the debate is fully argued."[49]

In earlier discussions in this chapter that facts and information are public domain, only the expression or the format of facts and information may be protected by copyright law. The *NBA v. Motorola* case strengthened this argument, yet, at the same time, provided for limited commerce rights to protect a competitive aspect of such information content.

"With the rise of the Internet and digital media, the largely dormant 'hot news' doctrine has become more relevant, as competitors can now copy content and repackage it as their own product with just a few keystrokes." This is *New York Times* reporter Peter Lattman's overview of "hot news" in light of U.S. Court of Appeals for the Second Circuit in Manhattan ruling in *Barclays Capital Inc. v. Theflyonthewall.com, Inc.*[50]

Patricia Aufderheide and Peter Jaszi published an article[51] about journalists and their lack of fair use awareness in 2012. This article addresses the hot news doctrine and its challenge to the First Amendment's freedom of expression speech clauses. The authors discuss the hot news doctrine, its challenges to the First Amendment, and how news organizations are on both sides of the copyright and fair use argument. On the one hand, some news services demand rights clearance and compensation for use of their content. Yet, on the other hand, they rely on fair use to copy direct quotes, facts, and information from the intellectual works of others. The article questions whether use of the "hot news" is constitutional under the First Amendment or the fair use doctrine of U.S. Copyright Law. The "hot news" doctrine is not a copyright law but rather a commerce law, and it is additionally tied to the common law of individual states.[52] As noted above, the NBA attempted to use the "hot news" doctrine to protect its competitive information content, Aufderheide and Jazi ask the following about similar uses, as they believe such applications are "fraught with problems":

> How could such a proposal be implemented while still observing the separation between facts (not copyrightable) and stories? How long is enough? What if embargoing information harms the public?[53]

An editorial in the journal, *Communication Lawyer*, entitled "Saving Journalism with Copyright Reform and the Doctrine of Hot News," considers that the "*Feist* case blocks any attempt by newspapers and journalists to claim that copyrights are being violated by Internet free riders."[54] The editorial does affirm, however, that "hot news has the potential to protect against types of content theft that copyright laws have struggled to cover—the theft of factual information rather than words or expression."[55] The idea of state common law to supplement the federal competitive commerce law behind the "hot news" doctrine is also presented as an alternative method of such content protection. However, the editorial cautions that, with the federalizing of the hot news doctrine, "care must be taken that such factors don't constrain the ability of the law to evolve . . . the doctrine must retain some flexibility if its purpose is to be fulfilled."[56]

In 2010, there was another attempt to override *Feist* using the "hot news" doctrine in *Barclays Capital v. Theflyonthewall.com*. In light of the recent *NBA* attempt to use the "hot news" misappropriation claim, Barclays, a financial brokerage information advisor, sued Theflyonthewall.com, a news aggregator, in the federal Southern District Court of New York. Barclays alleged that Fly's publication of investment recommendations of Barclays Capital and its brokers constituted an unlawful "hot news" misappropriation of Barclays's property. Barclays implied that Fly's unauthorized timely publication of Barclays's competitive recommendations was free-riding piracy as implied with the *NBA* case. When the five-factor *NBA* test was applied, the district court ruled in favor of Barclays, supporting the claim for "hot news" as valid.[57] The case was appealed by Fly, and the Second Circuit reversed the judgment of the district court, further narrowing the "hot news" doctrine, primarily based on *Feist*.[58]

As Applegate and Schermerhorn recap in an article, "as the U.S. Supreme Court clarified in *Feist*, U.S. copyright law does not protect facts or ideas, no matter how carefully or cleverly arranged, but only the particular expression of those ideas if sufficiently original."[59] Shyamkrishna Balganesh, professor at the University of Pennsylvania Law School, questions the future of "hot news" misappropriation based on the *Barclays* case, as it sends "an important signal to future litigants: that the hot news doctrine is today an unviable stand-alone claim in all but a very few situations."[60] Balganesh also promotes that the common law IP concepts such as this provide a "source of flexibility and pragmatism," with emerging new technologies where federal statutory law often lags behind the internet and other digital aspects. Caution is a virtue of the common law in these instances.[61]

The hot news scenario is a wakeup call for journalist to become more familiar with fair use. They should also be aware of hot news and how it applies to blogs and social media. Lack of such knowledge encourages self-censorship.[62] If it weren't for the now-common practice of news aggregators, the hot news doctrine would never have resurfaced. Those whose works are aggregated by others often cry piracy, while those aggregating such content claim fair use. The news aggregation process has made it essential that publishers and journalists have a better understanding of *Feist* related to facts and Fair Use, to avoid self-censorship as Aufderheide and Jaszi point out:

> Without either an understanding of the non-copyrightability of facts or a clear fair use rationale either for taking or for watching their material show up on others' website[s], journalists operated in a grey zone. They took without knowing whether it was legal or right, and exasperatedly watched others take without knowing which of such acts were legitimate. They confused business concerns with copyright violations, thus creating the possibility of reinforcing self-censorship in their own future work.[63]

LIBEL AND THE PRESS

While the well-known saying "Sticks and stones can break your bones, but words can never hurt you" sound fairly elementary, careless use of words can be hurtful to others, as well as libelous when published or broadcasted in the news or in documentaries. When a journalist's inaccurate words cause harm, there could be serious consequences. Just as IP infringement cases may be costly, libel lawsuits incur not only unplanned legal expenses for news media organizations but also loss of work time and organizational productivity.

Library customers may approach librarians to ask advice about libel and the press. Since information professionals cannot practice law or provide legal advice, they must refer customers to the many books, pamphlets, and articles that have been published to support such queries. One of these helpful resources, *The Starting Point: Young Journalists and the Law*, defines libel as "any published communication—words, photos, pictures or symbols—that is false and harms a person's reputation."[64] The Student Press Law Center publishes a website (https://splc.org/) with material to support student publications about libel and additional legal matters.

Another resource for all journalists that provides legal support is the Reporters Committee for Freedom of the Press, found at https://www.rcfp.org/. According to this organization's website, the Reporters Committee for Freedom of the Press offers "free legal advice, resources, support and advocacy to protect the First Amendment and Freedom of Information rights of journalists."[65]

You may also hear the term "slander" utilized for similar situations. Although not used exactly the same way, both words fall under the broader term of defamation. Any communication is potentially defamatory if it harms the reputation of another in the view of the allegedly defamed environment. *The Starting Point* publication differentiates that "libel is typically printed defamation; slander is usually spoken defamation."[66] When a defamatory comment is presented in the form of a written or permanent forum, such as statements published in a newspaper, it would be considered a libel. If the defamatory comment is spoken, such as what might transpire during a conversation, it is considered slander.

To prove that one has been libeled by a defendant, a plaintiff must establish the following four elements:

1. Publication
2. Identification
3. Harm (false allegation/injured reputation)
4. Fault (negligence)

If a plaintiff cannot prove each of these elements, such a libel claim often fails.[67]

When all four elements listed above are proven present in a libel case, the burden then shifts to the defendant. The alleged libel could be legally justified by the defendant under the following five conditions:

1. Consent (voluntary)
2. Truth
3. Privilege (fair and accurate accounts of official public proceedings)
4. Opinion defense (Constitution-based from 1974 Supreme Court decision)
5. Satire and cartoons (parody and spoof are protected more often than satire)[68]

The Student Newspaper Survival Guide, by Rachele Kanigel,[69] provides a chapter about legal issues including libel. The *Guide* includes a column entitled *Tips from a Pro*, by attorney James Wagstaffe, on how to remain legal when publishing:

1. Be a skeptic.
2. Get it right.
3. Get permission.
4. Write sensitive subjects sensitively.
5. Do not promise confidentiality lightly.
6. Watch for an unexpected plaintiff. (If you write about a teen drug addict, for example, you may inadvertently defame the teen's parents.)
7. Be wary of sources you yourself don't trust.
8. Obtain public record and documentary support.
9. Make sure that your headlines and teasers are factually accurate.
10. Treat demands for correction seriously.[70]

Aside from student newspaper writers, professional journalists and documentary producers likewise rely upon their information rights of freedoms of expression and of the press when others challenge them with defamation accusations. Philip Miller, author of *Media Law* points out that libel laws are a mixture of common law and state statutory law.[71] Yet when libel cases are tied to the First Amendment freedoms of speech and of the press, many rulings have come from the Supreme Court.[72] As with most topics covered in this book, common sense, informed factual knowledge, and moderation go a long way in keeping reported information legal.

LIBEL AND LIBRARY PROFESSIONALS' PUBLISHING

Librarians have published book reviews and annotated bibliographies on related resources for as long as professional library journals and resource guides have existed. With blogs becoming a common way for librarians and information professionals to share their expert opinions, one might use caution when analyzing a publication and writing "bad" reviews of their vocational viewpoint. In February 2013, the *Chronicle of Higher Education* printed an article entitled "Edwin Mellen Press Sues University Librarian for Libel."[73] Dale Askey, a librarian at McMaster University in Canada, published a criticism of Edwin Mellen Press in his personal *Bibliobrary* blog series, while he was employed at Kansas State University (KSU). In the original blog of September 22, 2010, Askey asserted that Edwin Mellen Press was a "dubious publisher," a "junk publisher," and a publisher of some books of "simply second-class scholarship," charging "egregiously high prices."[74] Edwin Mellen Press sued Askey, Kansas State University, and McMaster University for libel and asked for more than $4 million in damages. The charges against McMaster are that the university is "vicariously liable" for not requiring Askey to retract the blog, even though Askey was not yet working for McMaster when he wrote it. In March 2012, the blog was removed, although Askey declines to state why or when.[75] The press also claims that "the defendants are liable for statements made by others in the comments section of the blog post, including one scholar's claim that Edwin Mellen officials 'practically enslave their authors to a contract that NO ONE should ever sign.'"[76] The lawsuit was discontinued the next year.[77]

The Edwin Mellen Press case brings to the forefront a larger discussion of freedoms on both sides of the issue, both from the plaintiff's and the defendant's viewpoints, and many questions arise. For example, at what point does freedom of speech protect professionals who, on personal but professionally related blogs, engage in wholesale criticism of people or presses? How does defamation apply when a blogger's criticism is honest and factual based upon his or her expertise, such as this case? Is Askey an expert in the dozens of subject areas in which Edwin Mellen Press publishes? Has he read, or officially reviewed for peer-reviewed journals, any of their books? Has his statements caused the press economic hardship? Are there authors shunning the press, fearing that their books won't sell? Could this be considered censorship? Because Askey is paying for all of his own legal expenses,[78] what precedents might this case set for future blogs by library professionals? What should all of us learn from this developing case? To borrow from the declaration concepts of Voltaire and FDR: with great power comes great responsibility.[79]

BLOGGERS' FIRST AMENDMENT AND FAIR USE RIGHTS

Aufderheide and Jaszi affirm that "the practice of reporting timely news and information for public consumption—is driven by a mission widely articulated and shared among its practitioners. This collective vision finds its roots in the First Amendment, from which journalists draw their function as societal watchdog."[80] The transformative aspect of fair use helps to protect traditional journalists and online bloggers with their First Amendment rights of freedom of expression. "Under fair use, people can quote copyrighted work without permission or payment in some circumstances (broadly, when social benefit is larger than individual owners' loss)."[81] When bloggers use fair use in their writing, not only do they exercise their freedom of expression, society also benefits "when more culture is made."[82]

Blogs, also known as web logs, allow "individuals to become one-person online outlets of information covering subjects in detail. Blogs are online journals or diaries where individuals can post daily entries about the subjects of their choice."[83] However, as the lines continue to blur between newspaper journalists and online bloggers, the question is frequently asked whether bloggers should have the same freedom-of-the-press protection as the traditional press.

According to the Electronic Frontier Foundation (EFF) website, bloggers do have the same First Amendment protection as mainstream media.[84] The EFF site affirms that the Supreme Court said, "[I]n the context of defamation law, the rights of the institutional media are no greater and no less than those enjoyed by other individuals and organization engaged in the same activities."[85] Based upon a recent federal appeals court decision, Reuters News recently reported that "a blogger is entitled to the same free speech protection as a traditional journalist and cannot be liable for defamation unless she acted negligently."[86] The First Amendment Center website reminds us that just as the early Americans used political pamphlets and newspapers to counter political adversaries, today's bloggers are afforded the same First Amendment protection as sanctioned by our nation's founders, "paving the way for robust discussion of public issues, regardless of medium. That's something worth celebrating."[87] It's also worth fighting censorship.

Censorship is often challenged by traditional journalists and documentary producers. As noted in Chapter 6, the federal Freedom of Information Act further supports freedom of the press and also protects against some censorships by providing access to government information that might otherwise be suppressed. Similar to the Freedom of Information Act, the Supreme Court recognized that freedom of the press also applies to government prior restraint of classified government information that may be sensitive. In *New York Times Co. v. United States* (1971), the Pentagon Papers related to the Vietnam War were blocked by the Nixon administration. Subsequently, an appeal was expedited by the U.S. Supreme Court, clarifying that government may not issue prior restraints of publication except when there is an imminent threat to national security.[88] Supreme Court scholar Stanley Kutler[89] sums up the result this: "[T]he Supreme Court's decision legitimated the media's assaults against government secrecy and its self-assumed status as the people's paladin against official wrongdoing."[90]

Censorship and freedom-of-the-press issues are greater for bloggers when they do not get the same protections as traditional journalists. Public surveys reveal that "most Americans believe bloggers should not be allowed to publish sensitive personal information about individuals." Many recent news stories report the further challenges for the courts to rule whether a blogger is the same as a journalist. If they are not the same, bloggers would not be protected under shield laws for journalists.[91] Could this stifle the First Amendment rights of bloggers expressing their political belief? Does it suppress sharing a topic with your professional colleagues in one of your profession's online blogs? These questions should be considered for librarians who publish or assist bloggers as well as news media professions with their research needs.

TRADEMARKS LIBRARY BRANDING

Trademarks discussed in Chapter 5 are a vital part of a public librarians' role and particular those in PTRC libraries. IP awareness and information literacy are essential for entrepreneur and business customers. Conveying the meaning of a trademark, which is a word, phrase, symbol, or design that is a source identifier[92] and teaching how to perform a trademark search is not just for library customers, for many public librarians have grasped the power of trademarks to bolster their library's branding. Establishing and publicizing their trademarks help librarians make their libraries competitive among the increasing thousands[93] of brands that the average person is deluged by daily. Branding the library with a trademark takes some knowledge and skill.

Patrick Roughen contends that with public libraries,

> the most important part of branding is the expression of the mission and vision of the organization in a clear, comprehensible, and compact way to stakeholders. Even institutions that have no clear identity generate an image of themselves—a bundle of associations—in the minds of customers and so, arguably, branding happens, whether it is intended or not.[94]

A trademark might even exemplify the goodwill of a public library to advance its mission to garner tax levy or charitable support. Roughen differentiates that there are two types of branding in public libraries, a main brand of the entire library while there are minor but related sub-brands such as distinct library services, branches, department, or events.[95]

For help creating a brand, public libraries with limited budgets may need to rely on ready-made branding campaigns prepared for them from the ALA or ask for help from a volunteer from the Friends of the Library. They need to anticipate whether taxpayers would see such branding investment as a benefit for the community. However, when effectively crafted, a trademark can help a library to position itself in the public's minds. An article in *Public Libraries* asserts:

> One of the most successful, low-cost ways to convey the library's brand is to create a unified, consistent message through using a logo or tagline. Taglines or logos are useful as visual tools and help to develop and reinforce a stronger brand association. A logo is a symbol, graphic element, or trademark that is designed for easy and definite recognition of the brand. A logo influences its brand since people tend to think of that particular organization when they see the logo."[96]

Once a library develops an appealing or memorable tagline or logo as a potential trademark, it must make certain that it is unique and would not infringe on other registered marks for similar goods and services classified by the United States Patent and Trademark Office (USPTO). Ideally, legal counsel specializing in trademarks could guide libraries on such matters and also handle a library's trademark application process. As covered in Chapter 5, a trademark must be distinct enough that the USPTO does not consider it too descriptive. If a trademark application is declined by the USPTO, state registration or common law are other legitimate options.

Examples of illustrious federally registered trademarks associated with public libraries include the iconic library lions of the New York Public Library, named Patience and Fortitude, which have graced its library entrance since 1911.[97] More recently, the Charlotte Mecklenburg Library has developed several trademarks, most noteworthy is the branding of its ImaginOn® children's library branch, which infuses a playful, colorful atmosphere and extravagant, flowing celestial décor coordinating with its federally registered logo. The library website tagline states, "ImaginOn brings stories to life through extraordinary experiences that challenge, inspire and excite young minds."[98]

Furthermore, public libraries must be cautious about misappropriating commercial trademarks of others such as popular culture. Lee Ann Torrans asserts that "libraries cannot usurp trademark names to describe their reading programs, or borrow trademarked characters to enhance their appeal."[99] This includes painting original derivatives of popular book characters on the bulletin board or copying trademarked names wholesale. Parody or free speech exceptions related to trademarks covered in Chapter 5 might exempt a library from infringement in certain limited instances. However, be careful about famous characters of books and media that have entered the public domain, as trademarks of such characters may extend beyond the expired copyrighted works.[100]

INVENTORS, ENTREPRENEURS, AND BUSINESS STARTUPS

Businesspersons often use their local public library for business resources. However, unless they are aware of PTRC libraries, they may not associate trademarks or patents with libraries. Besides reference books on trademarks and patents, public libraries are able to support such customers through library reference assistance and workshops. Collaborative partnerships with likeminded community groups, namely, SBDC, SCORE, entrepreneurship programs at local colleges and universities, Chamber of Commerce, business start-up incubators and accelerators, and even local law firms could provide support.

Like trademarks, patent resources are freely available at public libraries that are designated PTRC libraries. U.S. patent documents have been freely available at larger metropolitan public libraries since 1871. Usually patent documents were part of a GPO document collection in these libraries. Over time, trademarks were included. At the time of this book publication, there are over eighty PTRCs, about half of the PTRCs are public libraries, and half are academic libraries.

Public libraries are well suited to assist inventors and entrepreneurs. Such customers often rely on public libraries for use of its makerspaces for prototyping their creations, and business information resources to support the marketing of their products or services. Public libraries offer an ideal platform for providing inventor youth programs, especially those with PTRCs. These PTRCs are usually able to collaborate with other libraries or schoolteachers for such IP awareness and information literacy directed to young inventors and creators.[101] For example, the PTRC at the St. Louis (MO) Public Library conducted a "Kids Inventing Day" to teach patent basics and marketing inventions, inspiring future entrepreneurs.[102] During these programs, an opportunity exists to educate youth about all types of IP. For teenagers, music and entrepreneurship could be included to add more about trademarks and copyrights, too.

CONCLUSION

This chapter has reviewed the common IP matters that apply to public libraries. Makerspaces are new platforms that assist public libraries in fulfilling their IP information literacy roles by advancing knowledge, inspiring learning, and driving innovation. All types of IPs apply in Makerspaces. Digitization projects are providing public library customers virtual access to each library's unique local history and genealogy resources. However, before digitizing such collections, copyright awareness is vital, as libraries must ensure that they have the right to copy and share these materials online. Additional users of library resources often need IP information literacy and particulars with copyrights, trademarks, and patents. Such customers include authors, inventors, musicians, and even journalists. Libraries and journalists share similar passions associated with information access, such as copyright, fair use, and freedom of the press. Finally, this chapter presented public library branding. Trademarks are essential for protecting branding tag lines and logos tied to public library's mission and vision. The next chapter on school libraries is primarily about their unique copyright issues associated with students and teachers, such as plagiarism, fair use, and other instruction exceptions to copyright law.

NOTES

1. ALA, "Information Literacy/Digital Citizenship: In Public Libraries," Libraries and the Internet Toolkit: Advocacy Legislation and Issues, http://www.ala.org/advocacy/intfreedom/iftoolkits/litoolkit/informationliteracy_digitalcitizenship (accessed December 19, 2018).

2. Amy K. Garmer, *Rising to the Challenge: Re-Envisioning Public Libraries* (Washington, D.C.: Aspen Institute, 2014), http://csreports.aspeninstitute.org/Dialogue-on-Public-Libraries/2014/report (accessed December 20, 2018).

3. Larry Nix, "Benjamin Franklin, Friend of Libraries," Library History Buff, http://www.libraryhistorybuff.org/benfranklin.htm (accessed November 24, 2012).

4. Alex Shashkevich, "Benjamin Franklin as the Social Network Genius of His Time? Yes, Says one Stanford scholar" (Stanford American historian Caroline Winterer), *Stanford News*, November 12, 2018, https://news.stanford.edu/press-releases/2018/11/12/benjamin-franklin-social-genius-18th-century/ (accessed December 20, 2018).

5. Edwin Wolf et al., *At the Instance of Benjamin Franklin: A Brief History of the Library Company of Philadelphia* (Philadelphia: Library Company of Philadelphia, 2015), https://librarycompany.org/about-lcp/, online version of book originally published in 1976 and later in 1995 by the Library Company of Philadelphia (accessed December 20, 2018).

6. Ibid., 11–13.

7. Deborah Fallows, "The Library Card," *Atlantic*, March 2016, https://www.theatlantic.com/magazine/archive/2016/03/the-library-card/426888/ (accessed September 19, 2018).

8. Carl Houston, artist and music producer customer of makerspace, quoted in "Level Up Workforce Development: Triiibe Member Creates Community, Positivity through Art at Makerspace," *Library Links* 27, no. 1 (Winter 2019): 7.

9. T J McCue, "First Public Library to Create a Makerspace," *Forbes*, November 15, 2011, https://www.forbes.com/sites/tjmccue/2011/11/15/first-public-library-to-create-a-maker-space/#25a6378f79cf (accessed December 19, 2018).

10. Fayetteville Free Library, FFL Fab Lab, http://www.fayettevillefreelibrary.org/make/fab-lab (accessed December 21, 2018).

11. FabFoundation, About Fab Foundation, http://www.fabfoundation.org/index.php/about-fab-foundation/index.html (accessed December 21, 2018).

12. FabFoundation, The Fab Charter, http://www.fabfoundation.org/index.php/the-fab-charter/index.html (accessed December 21, 2018); Theresa Willingham, *Library Makerspaces: The Complete Guide* (Lanham, MD: Rowman & Littlefield, 2018), 9.

13. Willingham, *Library Makerspaces*, 212–214.

14. Jessica R. M. Chan and Sandra Aya Enimil, "Copyright Considerations for Providing 3D Printing Services in the Library," *Bulletin of the Association for Information Science and Technology* 42, no. 1 (October/November 2015): 26.

15. Charlie Wapner, "Progress in the Making: 3D Printing Policy Considerations through the Library Lens," Office for Information Technology Policy, *Perspectives* no. 3 (January 2015): 19–20, http://www.ala.org/advocacy/sites/ala.org.advocacy/files/content/advleg/pp/pub/perspectives-3D_Library_Policy-ALA_OITP_Perspectives-2015Jan06.pdf (accessed December 20, 2018). Also, see ALA's 3-D Printing in Libraries site at http://www.ala.org/advocacy/intfreedom/3d_printer_policy.

16. Wapner, "Progress in the Making," 10.

17. Chan and Enimil, "Copyright Considerations for Providing 3D Printing Services in the Library," 27.

18. Stephanie M. Santoso and Stephen B. Wicker, "Future of Three-dimensional Printing: Intellectual Property or Intellectual Confinement?" *New Media & Society* 18, no. 1 (2016): 147.

19. 17 U.S. Code § 1201—Circumvention of Copyright Protection Systems.

20. Peter S. Menell, Mark A. Lemley, and Robert P. Merges, *Intellectual Property in the New Technology Age: 2017, Volume II: Copyrights, Trademarks & State IP Protections*, Copyright Law (Berkeley, CA: Clause 8 Publishing, 2017), 496.

21. Santoso and Wicker, "Future of Three-dimensional Printing," 138–155.

22. Wapner, "Progress in the Making," 12.

23. 17 U.S. Code § 109(a)—Limitations on Exclusive Rights: Effect of Transfer of Particular Copy or Phonorecord: First Sale Doctrine.

24. Sharon DeBartolo Carmack, *Carmack's Guide to Copyright & Contracts: A Primer for Genealogists, Writers & Researchers* (Baltimore: Genealogical Pub, 2005).

25. Lee Ann Torrans, *Law and Libraries: The Public Library* (Westport, CT: Libraries Unlimited, 2004), 65.

26. Ibid., 71.

27. Reporters Committee for Freedom of the Press, *First Amendment Handbook*, "10. Copyright: How to Avoid Copyright Infringement—Legal Action to Protect a Copyright," http://www.rcfp.org/first-amendment-handbook/how-avoid-copyright-infringement-legal-action-protect-copyright (accessed January 26, 2013).

28. *Harper & Row, Publishers, Inc. v. Nation Enterprises*, 471 U.S. 539 (1985).

29. Carrie Russell, "Copyright Concerns: The Copyright Implications of Blogs," *Public Libraries* (July/August 2005): 215.

30. Christopher Daly, *Covering America: A Narrative History of a Nation's Journalism* (Amherst and Boston: University of Massachusetts Press, 2012), 19–28.

31. Knight Foundation, "American Views: Trust, Media and Democracy," January 16, 2018, https://knightfoundation.org/reports/american-views-trust-media-and-democracy (accessed June 1, 2018).

32. Abigail Geiger, "Most Americans—Especially Millennials—Say Libraries Can Help Them Find Reliable, Trustworthy Information," Pew Research Center, August 30, 2017, http://www.pewresearch.org/fact-tank/2017/08/30/most-americans-especially-millennials-say-libraries-can-help-them-find-reliable-trustworthy-information/, (accessed June 1, 2018).

33. Marcus Banks, "Our Vocation Is Information: Exploring the Ways Librarianship and Journalism Can Work Together," *American Libraries* 49, no. 6 (June 2018): 40–43, https://americanlibrariesmagazine.org/2018/06/01/our-vocation-is-information-librarianship-journalism/ (accessed August 1, 2018).

34. Alison Peters, "What Libraries Can Learn From the Media, and Vice Versa," *Media Shift* (May 2, 2016), http://mediashift.org/2016/05/what-the-libraries-can-learn-from-the-media-and-vice-versa/ (accessed October 24, 2018).

35. International Federation of Library Associations and Institutions (IFLA), "Sustaining and Celebrating a Free Press through Libraries: World Press Freedom Day 2018," May 3, 2018, https://blogs.ifla.org/lpa/2018/05/03/sustaining-and-celebrating-a-free-press-through-libraries-world-press-freedom-day-2018/ (accessed October 24, 2018).

36. Banks, "Our Vocation Is Information," 41–42.

37. Sherrie Callis, "Copyright Protection in Factual Compilations: Feist Publications v. Rural Telephone Service Company 'Altruism Expressed in Copyright Law,'" *Golden Gate University Law Review* 22, no. 2; Notes & Comments, Article 13, 15 (September 2010): 541, 545.

38. Ibid.

39. Ibid., 546.

40. Victoria Smith Ekstrand, "Chapter One Introduction: The Scope of Piracy," *News Piracy and the Hot News Doctrine: Origins in Law and Implications for the Digital Age* (New York: LFB Scholarly Publishing, 2005), 1–13.

41. Ibid., 1–13.

42. The Espionage Act of 1917 prohibited not only spying but also a variety of other activities, including various forms of expression. Hence, this was an issue in U.S. Supreme Court First Amendment litigation. Source: Michal Belknap, "Espionage Acts," entry from *Oxford Companion to the Supreme Court of the United States*, edited by Kermit Hall (New York: Oxford Press, 2005), 301.

43. Kimberley Isbell, "The Rise of the News Aggregator: Legal Implications and Best Practices," *Berkman Center Research Publication No. 2010-10*, August 30, 2010, http://ssrn.com/abstract=1670339 or http://dx.doi.org/10.2139/ssrn.1670339 (accessed February 11, 2013); and Craig Ducat, "The 'Clear and Present Danger' Test," *Constitutional Interpretation* (Belmont, CA: Wadsworth/Thomson Learning, 2000), 831–833.

44. Oliver Wendell Holmes, *Schenck v. United States*, 249 U.S. 47, Opinion, http://www.law.cornell.edu/supct/html/historics/USSC_CR_0249_0047_ZO.html (accessed February 14, 2013).

45. Camille Calman and Robert Balin, "The Future of the Hot News Misappropriation Tort after Barclays Capital Inc. v. TheFlyontheWall.com," *DWT Media Law*, September 16, 2011, http://www.medialawmonitor.com/2011/09/the-future-of-the-hot-news-misappropriation-tort-after-barclays-capital-inc-v-theflyonthewall-com/ (accessed February 5, 2013); and Erie Railroad Co. v. Tompkins, 304 U.S. 64 (1938) Certiorari to the Circuit Court of Appeals for the Second Circuit, No. 367 Argued: January 31, 1938; decided: April 25, 1938, http://www.law.cornell.edu/supct/search/display.html?terms=constitutional%20or%20unconstitutional&url=/supct/html/historics/USSC_CR_0304_0064_ZS.html (accessed February 14, 2013).

46. National Basketball Association v. Motorola, Inc. 105 F.3d 845 (2nd Cir. 1997).

47. Smith Ekstrand, "Chapter One Introduction," 1–13.

48. National Basketball Association v. Motorola, Inc. 105 F.3d 845 (2nd Cir. 1997).

49. Smith Ekstrand, "Chapter One Introduction," 1–13.

50. Peter Lattman, "Big Banks Lose Ruling on Research," *New York Times*, June 20, 2011, http://dealbook.nytimes.com/2011/06/20/wall-street-banks-lose-ruling-on-research/?smid=pl-share (accesses January 15, 2013).

51. Patricia Aufderheide, Peter Jaszi et al., "Copyright, Free Speech, and the Public's Right to Know: How Journalists Think about Fair Use," July 30, 2012, http://ssrn.com/abstract=2119933 or http://dx.doi.org/10.2139/ssrn.2119933 (accessed January 8, 2013).

52. Ibid., 1–25.

53. Ibid., 6.

54. Bruce Sanford et al., "Viewpoint: Saving Journalism with Copyright Reform and the Doctrine of Hot News," *Communication Lawyer* 26, no. 4 (December 2009): 8–11.

55. Ibid.

56. Ibid.

57. Barclays Capital, Inc., v. Theflyonthewall.com, 700 F. Supp. 2d 310 (S.D.N.Y. 2010).

58. Barclays Capital, Inc., v. Theflyonthewall.com, 650 F.3d 876 (2d Cir. 2011).

59. David Applegate and Ryan Schermerhorn, "Hot News: The 'Hot-News' Doctrine Is Hot Again! Or Is It?

60. Shyamkrishna Balganesh, "The Uncertain Future of 'Hot News' Misappropriation after Barclays Capital v. Theflyonthewall.com," *Faculty Scholarship at Penn Law* 112 (June 11, 2012): 134–146.

61. Shyamkrishna Balganesh, "The Pragmatic Incrementalism of Common Law Intellectual Property," *Vanderbilt Law Review* 63, no. 6 (November 2012): 1543–1616.

62. Andrew Beaujon, "Study: Journalists' Lousy Understanding of Fair Use Leads to Self-Censorship," Poynter Institute, August 10, 2012, http://www.poynter.org/latest-news/mediawire/184600/study-journalists-lousy-understanding-of-fair-use-leads-to-self-censorship/ (accessed January 5, 2013).

63. Aufderheide et al., "Copyright, Free Speech, and the Public's Right to Know," 23.

64. Mark Goodman and Mike Hiestand, *The Starting Point: Young Journalists and the Law* (Arlington, VA: Student Press Law Center, Inc., 2006), 5.

65. Reporters Committee for Freedom of the Press, http://www.rcfp.org/ (accessed January 21, 2013).

66. Goodman and Hiestand, *The Starting Point*, 5.

67. Goodman and Hiestand, *The Starting Point*, 5–9; Rachele Kanigel, "Chapter 13—Legal Issues," *Student Newspaper Survival Guide* (Ames, IA: Blackwell, 2006), 122; Philip Miller, *Media Law* (Amsterdam: Elsevier, 2003), 170–172.

68. Goodman and Hiestand, *The Starting Point*, 10–13.

69. Kanigel, "Chapter 13—Legal Issues."

70. Ibid., 122.

71. Miller, *Media Law*, 170.

72. Ibid.

73. Jake New, "Edwin Mellen Press Sues University Librarian for Libel," *The Chronicle of Higher Education* (February 8, 2013), blog, http://chronicle.com/blogs/wiredcampus/edwin-mellen-press-sues-university-librarian-for-libel/42193 (accessed February 11, 2013).

74. Dale Askey, "Curious Case of Edwin Mellen Press," *The Bibliobrary*, retracted blog post archived at http://web.archive.org/web/20110630153231/http://htwkbk.wordpress.com/2010/09/22/the-curious-case-of-edwin-mellen-press/ (accessed February 11, 2013).

75. Colleen Flaherty, "An Academic Press Sues a Librarian, Raising Issues of Academic Freedom," *Inside Higher Ed*, February 8, 2013, http://www.insidehighered.com/news/2013/02/08/academic-press-sues-librarian-raising-issues-academic-freedom (accessed February 8, 2013).

76. New, *The Chronicle of Higher Education*, blog.

77. Casey Fabris, "Librarian Says Academic Press Has Settled Lingering Lawsuit against Him," *Chronicle of Higher Education*, February 5, 2015, https://www.chronicle.com/blogs/ticker/librarian-says-academic-press-has-settled-lingering-lawsuit-against-him/93413

78. Flaherty, "An Academic Press Sues a Librarian, Raising Issues of Academic Freedom."

79. Quote Investigator, "With Great Power Comes Great Responsibility, 23 July 2015, http://quoteinvestigator.com/2015/07/23/great-power/ (accessed November 12, 2015).

80. Aufderheide et al., "Copyright, Free Speech, and the Public's Right to Know," 2.

81. Ibid., 4.

82. Ibid.

83. David Hudson, "Freedom of the Press, Internet and First Amendment: Blogging, "First Amendment Center, http://www.firstamendmentcenter.org/blogging (accessed January 26, 2013).

84. Electronic Frontier Foundation, "Online Defamation Law," https://www.eff.org/issues/bloggers/legal/liability/defamation (accessed April 17, 2019).

85. Ibid.

86. Dan Levine, "Bloggers to Receive Same Freedom of Speech Protection as Journals, Court Rules," Reuters news posted on *Huffington Post* site, January 17, 2014, http://www.huffingtonpost.com/2014/01/17/blogger-journalist-protection-court-crystal-cox_n_4619271.html (accessed November 12, 2015).

87. Ken Paulson post, "Bloggers Enjoy First Amendment Protection against Libel Suits," First Amendment Center, January 24, 2014, http://www.firstamendmentcenter.org/bloggers-enjoy-first-amendment-protection-against-libel-suits (accessed November 12, 2015).

88. Lee Bollinger; revised by William Ross, "First Amendment," entry from *Oxford Companion to the Supreme Court of the United States*, edited by Kermit Hall (New York: Oxford Press, 2005), 345–346.

89. Stanley Kutler is author of the book *Abuse of Power: The Nixon Tapes* (New York: Free Press, 1997) and other works about American constitutional history.

90. Stanley Kutler, "New York Times Co. v. United States," entry from *Oxford Companion to the Supreme Court of the United States*, edited by Kermit Hall (New York: Oxford Press, 2005), 682.

91. Renai LeMay, "Blog Censorship Gains Support," *CNET*, April 13, 2005, http://news.cnet.com/2100-1028_3-5670096.html (accessed January 26, 2013); and Clifford Ward, "Media Shield Law Upheld for Some Bloggers: Cook County Judge's Ruling Says Independent Websites Can Protect Confidential Sources," *Chicago Tribune News*, August 15, 2012 (accessed July 30, 2014), http://articles.chicagotribune.com/2012-08-15/news/ct-met-shield-law-20120815_1_website-media-shield-law-bloggers (accessed April 17, 2019).

92. U.S. Patent & Trademark Office, *Basic Facts about Trademarks*, September 2018, p. 2, https://www.uspto.gov/sites/default/files/documents/BasicFacts.pdf (accessed December 19, 2018).

93. Caitlin Johnson, "Cutting through Advertising Clutter," *CBS News*, September 17, 2006, https://www.cbsnews.com/news/cutting-through-advertising-clutter/ (accessed December 19, 2018).

94. Patrick Roughen, "System Branding in Three Public Libraries: Live Oak Public Libraries, Charlotte Mecklenberg Library, and Richland Library," *Library Philosophy and Practice* 1442, October 10, 2016, http://digitalcommons.unl.edu/libphilprac/1442 (accessed December 19, 2018).

95. Ibid.

96. Arthur W. Hafner and Susan G. Akers, "Building the Libraries Brand: Using Taglines or Logos," *Public Libraries* (34, no, 1): 34–37, http://publiclibrariesonline.org/2013/04/building-the-librarys-brand-using-taglines-or-logos/ (accessed December 19, 2018).

97. New York Public Library, https://www.nypl.org/help/about-nypl/library-lions (accessed December 19, 2018).

98. Charlotte Mecklenburg Library, "ImaginOn: The Joe and Joan Martin Center," https://www.imaginon.org/ (accessed December 19, 2018).

99. Torrans, *Law and Libraries*, 216.

100. Ibid., 291.

101. Barbara J. Hampton, "Chapter 9, Kid-ventions with the US Patent Library," in *How to STEM: Science, Technology, Engineering, and March Education*, Vera Gubnitskala

and Carol Smallwood, eds. (Lanham, MD: Scarecrow Press, 2014); Carol Giles, "Patent Searching Presentations to Young Inventors," *Intellectual Property (IP) Journal of the PTDLA* (June/December 2001), http://ptrca.org/journal/2001giles (accessed September 14 2018); Harwell, "Legal Issues Relating to Patent Searching in Publicly Accessible Libraries," 399.

102. American Library Association, "One Small Business at a Time: Building Entrepreneurial Opportunities in America's Communities," *About America's Libraries*, November 2016.

Chapter 9

SCHOOL LIBRARIES

CHAPTER OBJECTIVES

- To identify and understand exceptions of copyright laws supporting learning in schools
- To understand classroom teaching exemptions within Section 110
- To recognize distinctions between various guidelines versus the fair use doctrine from the U.S. Copyright Act
- To understand how licensing promotes or restricts use of copyrighted works for information access, teaching, and learning in schools
- To recognize how the U.S. Copyright Act (Section 108) and the CONTU Rule of Five guideline support customer requests for interlibrary loan
- To recognize which types of IP support various student innovations and creative works from classroom to practical applications

INTRODUCTION

School librarians, sometimes called library media specialists or teacher librarians, serve in both public and private schools, supporting children starting in kindergarten through graduation from high school. The American Association of School Librarians (AASL) describes the role of school librarians as working with students and teachers:

> to facilitate access to information in a wide variety of formats, instruct students and teachers how to acquire, evaluate and use information. . . . As a collaborator, change agent, and leader, the school librarian develops, promotes, and implements a program that will help prepare students to be effective users of ideas and information, a lifelong skill.[1]

Respect for copyright and ethical use of information are an intricate part of a school librarian's responsibilities in empowering students and teachers and supporting these lifelong learning skills. Awareness of other intellectual properties (IPs), such as patents and trademarks, have recently entered the realm of schools with the cross-disciplinary inclusion of Science, Technology, Engineering and Mathematics (STEM) or Science, Technology, Engineering, Arts, and Mathematics (STEAM) project-based curricula. Such interaction between STEM and STEAM fields produces authentic learning experiences, which "broadly extend young people's understanding as they move from school to community as productive employees and citizens."[2] Trademark is perhaps the ugly duckling IP that has blossomed into the glitzier and more glamorous cousin to copyright and patents. A report from the World Intellectual Property Organization (WIPO) claims that trademark law is probably the easier IP for schoolchildren to understand in our increasingly brand-conscious culture.[3] See Chapter 5 for additional details on trademarks.

The AASL's *Empowering Learners: Guidelines for School Library Media Programs*[4] underscores the ethical facets of fostering students and teachers in the learning community, including copyright and other intellectual properties. The *Empowering Learners* resource affirms that "expertise in the ethical use of information . . . remains a cornerstone . . . of the. . .information specialists,"[5] and that they "must be versed in the theoretical grounding and practical application of . . . laws in order to teach the ethical use of information to the learning community. This involves new understandings of fair use and forms of licensing that allows users to modify original content."[6] Students and teachers depend on their school librarians to answer such legal and ethical aspects of using and creating information and innovations.

This chapter starts with copyright and fair use as it related to the ethical and legal use of information for teaching and learning. Sections 107, 108, and 110 of the U.S. Copyright Act offer certain exemptions that support information access, teaching, and learning in schools. Such exemptions are available for pedagogical purposes ranging from print and music resources to audiovisual and multimedia. Variations in exemptions for distance learning, computer software and internet usage are included. Finally, classroom to practical applications with students associated with patents, trademarks, and copyrights complete the chapter.

IP INFORMATION LITERACY K-12 SCHOOL SCENARIOS

During their time with students in basic education, one of the school librarians' major roles is to collaborate with their teachers so that students become information literate in any one of the many forms of literacy. As covered in Chapter 1, ethical and legal use of others' intellectual works related to information literacy have often dealt with respecting authors by citing their sources and recognizing when to ask for copyright permission if portions of copyright works used were beyond fair use. In this role, librarians teach the meaning of the © symbol that protects an author's creative work. From the earliest grades, this includes not only identifying an author in any use of an author's work, but also recognizing and crediting illustrators of the beautiful picture books enjoyed by younger students. This attitude demonstrates that a proactive information literacy curriculum, including IP awareness,[7] fosters the ethical and legal use of information as codified in the AASL Standards Framework for Learners.[8] Such IP information literacy and school library standards are reinforced as librarians teach and reteach the ethical need for students to give authors credit for their work with proper citations to help others locate the source of the quotation. Teaching and reminding students about originality and the meaning of plagiarism helps to demonstrate author attribution and proper paraphrasing or quoting. Discussions about research integrity and reciprocity for citing others' works allows librarians and teachers to tell students that such attribution is an indirect method of thanking the authors of their sources cited.[9] See inset box below for Creative Thinking, which is an example of online curriculum from the author of this book to help school librarians to teach IP information literacy in their schools.

The following situations are ideal opportunities when school librarians or media specialists could promote respecting IP and ethical and legal use of copyrighted works of others. These real-life, school applications will be addressed throughout this chapter.

When the photocopy machine often used by teachers is located in the library, it becomes problematic when the legal issues surrounding copyright are ignored, such as when a teacher duplicates copyrighted workbook pages for use in the classroom without permission, or the music teacher who only purchased twenty copies of sheet music, while making 20 additional unauthorized copies. Or the science teacher who has multiple chapters from his or her college text that would be perfect for the class to read on a topic that is not covered as well in their textbook.

It is further a challenge when you are asked to show a teacher's personal copy of a film, *Romeo and Juliet*, in the school auditorium for all the tenth graders studying the play in their class, and they have not secured permission to show this to an audience. It is even more difficult when a teacher boasts that the local Rotary Club has agreed to purchase a copy of that film so that the school won't have to continue to pay the charge to "rent" it. If the high school band has been invited to march in a nationally broadcasted parade, should you be assigned the task of video recording the broadcast of that parade for later presentation at a parent event, is this fair use or does it require permission?

Helping teachers with dramatic productions is another potential for copyright challenge. To perform a play for the students during school hours in the classroom or auditorium is one thing, but what if the same production is staged in the auditorium, with an admission fee for public attendance?

Classroom copies of assigned readings of novels are another potential problem. It is unlikely that a teacher would want to photocopy an entire book, but what about an entire class having access to an e-book?

Students work both as individuals and as groups to report research or other assignments. When can they use music and pictures to illustrate their reports?

Students often organize their own "garage" bands, where they hope to perform for a paying audience. What do you suggest to them to help them maintain ownership of their music? What do you tell them if they are going to publicly perform someone else's music at the school dance?

What do you suggest to the parent who has written a children's book and wants to get it published? How do you foster the great idea of a brainchild student who has come up with an invention that might be patentable? Then what if that same invention could be marketable with a clever branded name for a trademark? What about students' copyrights for classroom projects or individual real-world creative works?

All of these questions are answered in this chapter and offer teachable IP information literacy opportunities. Understanding copyright law and fair use are the first step toward promoting IP information literacy, as introduced in Chapter 1.

STUDENT-CENTERED APPROACH TO PLAGIARISM AND COPYRIGHT AWARENESS

Funded by a grant from the Cincinnati Bar Foundation, the W. Frank Steely Library at Northern Kentucky University (NKU) in Highland Heights, Kentucky, collaborated with campus students and community partners to produce Creative Thinking at https://inside.nku.edu/creativethinking.html. See figure 9.1 for cover art of companion DVD films for the Creative Thinking program.

Figure 9.1
Creative Thinking. (Courtesy of Northern Kentucky University)

> This educational plagiarism and copyright awareness curriculum is appropriate for upper elementary through high school students nationwide. The films, lessons, and activities offer a proactive approach to educating students on the importance of ethical use and respect for the intellectual works of authors and musicians. This awareness program was designed to be flexible for a variety of students and classroom disciplines.[10]

COPYRIGHT REVIEW

The first challenge for most school libraries dealing with copyright and fair use is to understand copyright and clear up any misconceptions. Generally, a school librarian is the only expert onsite with knowledge of copyright. Unlike academic or public libraries, discussions of copyright and fair use matters with local peers are uncommon. Customarily, school librarians attend a copyright workshop at a library association conference and then return to work, where they wear many different professional hats, and set aside learned copyright awareness skills. Others faithfully follow copyright and fair use guidelines, which are often too restrictive and, in some cases, incomplete or incorrect.[11]

While speaking at national and regional library conferences, the author of this book has observed that school librarians are often very cautious with copyright and fair use to avoid any potential lawsuits. In fact, such lawsuits have been almost nonexistent, as Carrie Russell, director for the Program on Public Access to Information for the American Library Association's (ALA) Office for Information Technology Policy, reports knowledge of only one copyright infringement lawsuit for a school in 1982, namely, *Encyclopaedia Britannica v. Crooks*.[12] This case acknowledged that schools could not record broadcasts for long-term retention.[13] Russell also affirms that nonprofit libraries and schools are protected from such liabilities. They have limits on penalties that copyright holders could expect to collect, per Section 504(c)(2)[14] of the Copyright Act, for nonprofit schools or libraries when the infringer acted within the scope of his or her job and believed his or her use was fair use. In addition, the Eleventh Amendment protects state entities from federal prosecution without their consent.[15]

Russell believes that many have erroneously confused cease and desist letters with lawsuits. Such cease and desist situations are only warnings, which are often cleared up by correcting the violation or making a reasonable payment for what an authorized use would have cost.[16] Caution is fine for avoiding cease and desist letters. Nevertheless, one might avoid overcompliance so as not to limit one's fair use rights. Ideally, librarians specializing in copyright try to help teachers and students utilize fair use to the broadest extend legally possible.[17] This is only possible when one understands and properly applies copyright law and fair use.

Copyright and Fair Use Serve Public Good

Article 1, Section 8 of the U.S. Constitution gave Congress the power "to promote the progress of science and useful arts, by securing for limited times to authors and inventors the exclusive right to their respective writings and discoveries."[18] Notice the phrase "to promote the progress of science and useful arts." Although authors retained exclusive rights, the primary idea about copyright in the Constitution supports the creation and distribution of new and original creative works to promote the advancement of learning and a well-informed community in our democracy. Fair use (Section 107) and other legal exemptions (Sections 108 and 110), mentioned throughout this book from the U.S. Copyright Act, allow teachers and students to use copyrighted materials for educational purposes under certain conditions without the need to ask permission. "Fair use is the safety valve in the law that allows citizens to exercise their first amendment rights when using copyrighted materials."[19] In the actual copyright law, the purposes of fair use that may be excused without permission include "criticism, comment, news reporting, teaching including multiple copies for classroom use, scholarship, or research."[20] These purposes apply moderately to virtually every scenario reflected in this chapter related to nonprofit educational applications. Yet fair use does not mean unlimited use. There are instances when larger portions utilized may require permission, or a smaller portion employed.

As reviewed in earlier chapters, one must be careful to not get too caught up in the measurement totals prescribed in fair use guidelines and best practices, especially when such restrictions do not fit your educational scenario. Understanding how to assess purpose, amount, nature, and effect of the four fair use factors in Section 107 from the actual copyright law is often a better gauge in determining how much constitutes fair use on a case-by-case basis. See Chapter 2 for how to apply Kenneth Crews' Fair Use Checklist, which is a four-factor test for specific case-by-case analysis.

School librarians should become fully familiar and comfortable with fair use. Read this book, other books, and journal articles from fair use experts to learn more. Browse academic library websites devoted to fair use, attend workshops at library conferences, and ask other academic or school librarians who utilize fair use frequently for educational applications for help if you are uncomfortable with your knowledge.

Public Domain, Open Access, Licensing, and Permissions

In addition to fair use, there are many public domain and open-access resources that do not require permission for making copies. These include classic literature books, classical music scores, and virtually all federal government documents. Most of these are in the public domain for the taking. Most open-access resources like Creative Commons (CC) are free to copy. Open-access resources often show a license or place a notice on any required conditions of use, such as attribution. Royalty payments for commercial use or other special requirements are seldom associated with open-access or open-source items.

In addition, most content from library subscription databases allow a teacher or student to make a copy for research purposes without permission. Yet when sharing articles from subscription databases, most licensed databases provide stable, persistent URLs for sharing with other teachers or students who have access to that subscription. Licensing also applies to click-through agreements found when uploading online apps, computer software, and online music services such as iTunes or Amazon. In many instances, one's fair use rights are relinquished upon agreeing to most licensing agreements.

Eventually, if an anticipated use of a copyrighted work, including licensed works, does not appear to be fair use, obtaining permission from the copyright owner is necessary. Always ask for permission in writing. A permission request reference should include as much bibliographic information as possible, including a description of how the work is going to be used for the course topic, number of students in the class, and time period of use, among others. It is a practical measure to insist that the permission reply be given in a permanent, tangible format, including the name of the authorizing party. To save time, the Copyright Clearance Center (CCC) offers a permissions service, too. Music licensing is available for different circumstances using copyrighted music, including performance rights licensing organizations such as ASCAP, BMI, and SESAC. Chapter 7 provides additional details on the permission process within the section on Electronic Reserves.

Understanding Copyright Law Section Numbers for K-12 Schools

Throughout this chapter and other chapters of this book, different sections of U.S. Copyright Act are prominently presented. The significant sections include 102, 106, 107, 108, and 110. Sections 107, 108, and 110 are especially vital for educators. More details on each of these sections are covered in Chapter 2. Nevertheless, and for easy reference, the section titles are repeated here with their essential roles for school libraries and the pedagogy of student learning:

Section 102—Scope of Protectable Works—This establishes what types of works are protected by copyright. "Original works of authorship" are vested as soon as they are created; they must be "fixed in any tangible medium of expression" to be copyrightable.[21]

Section 106—Rights of Copyright Owners—Copyright owners have exclusive rights to reproduce and distribute their work, prepare derivative works, and publicly display or perform their work.[22] However, Sections 107, 108, and 110 offer allowances for educators to use these works without permission in certain instances covered below.

Section 107—Fair Use Exceptions—These are exceptions to Section 106 rights of copyright owners.[23] This is the most important section of U.S. Copyright Law for all librarians. When it comes to classroom teaching, Section 107 provides fair use exceptions that are not considered an infringement of copyright for teaching, including "multiple copies for classroom use" in addition to scholarship and research.

Section 108—Library (and Archives) Copying Exceptions—This section is essential for what makes interlibrary borrowing and lending legal. It also provides libraries and archives further exceptions to Section 106 to support education and library customer research.[24] As covered in Chapter 7, Section 108 and the CONTU Rule of Five also provides lawful support for interlibrary loan paper copies of journal articles and book chapters in libraries.

Section 110—Teaching and Learning Exemptions—This section provides exemptions to Section 106 to support classroom instruction, both face-to-face and distance learning.[25] Chapter 7 provides additional details on Section 110 related to instruction.

PRINT RESOURCES

Despite the popularity and growth of electronic resources, the print format is still alive and well in school libraries. Likewise, print resources are the best place to start a discussion about copyright awareness for a school library and its customers. Photocopiers, scanners, and even mobile-device cameras make it too easy to generate unauthorized copies of copyrighted materials. However, fair use and other exemptions of the U.S. Copyright Act of 1976 permit copying in certain instances including educational and research applications covered in this chapter.

Photocopiers were commonplace at the time of the introduction of the revised U.S. Copyright Act of 1976. Many librarians were concerned about liability for copyright infringement when their customers made unauthorized copies on their library's photocopiers. Section 108(f)(1) protected libraries from copyright infringement "for the unsupervised use of reproducing equipment located on its premises: Provided, That such equipment displays a notice that the making of a copy may be subject to the copyright law."[26] This placed responsibility for any infringement on the user of the machine. Subsequently, the following notice is commonly display on photocopiers and other reproducing equipment:

> Notice: The copyright law of the United States (Title 17 U.S. Code) governs the making of photocopies or other reproductions of copyrighted materials. The person using this equipment is liable for any infringement.[27]

As the four factors of fair use are not quantitatively specific concerning an instructor's "multiple copies for classroom use" under Section 107 of the Copyright Act of 1976, a House Report guideline was created. Known as the *Agreement on Guidelines for Classroom Copying in Not-for-Profit Educational Institutions with Respect to Books and Periodicals*,[28] it addressed the percentages of use for "multiple copies for classroom use." As the *Guidelines* were introduced at the time of the revised Copyright Act of 1976, one must remember that these are guidelines and not the actual Section 107 fair use doctrine. However, the *Guidelines* were the result of an agreement between educators and publishers as a minimum benchmark when applying the four fair use factors. When you are comfortable using the actual fair use doctrine, you may go beyond a minimum benchmark such as the *Guidelines for Classroom Copying* without infringing.

> **AGREEMENT ON GUIDELINES FOR CLASSROOM COPYING (MULTIPLE COPIES)**
>
> The purpose of this quoted except of *Multiple Copies for Classroom Use* is to state the minimum and not the maximum standards of educational fair use under

Section 107. See pages 6–7 in Circular 21 from the Library of Congress entitled *Reproduction of Copyrighted Works by Educator and Librarians*, for complete details at https://www.copyright.gov/circs/.

BREVITY

(i) Poetry: (a) A complete poem if less than 250 words and if printed on not more than two pages or, (b) from a longer poem, an excerpt of not more than 250 words.

(ii) Prose: (a) Either a complete article, story or essay of less than 2,500 words, or (b) an excerpt from any prose work of not more than 1,000 words or 10% of the work, whichever is less, but in any event a minimum of 500 words.

(iii) Illustration: one chart, graph, diagram, drawing, cartoon or picture per book or per periodical issue.[29]

SPONTANEITY

(i) The copying is at the instance and inspiration of the individual teacher, and

(ii) The inspiration and decision to use the work and the moment of its use for maximum teaching effectiveness are so close in time that it would be unreasonable to expect a timely reply to a request for permission.[30]

CUMULATIVE EFFECT

(i) The copying of the material is for only one course in the school in which the copies are made.

(ii) Not more than one short poem, article, story, essay or two excerpts may be copied from the same author, nor more than three from the same collective work or periodical volume during one class term.

(iii) There shall not be more than nine instances of such multiple copying for one course during one class term.[31]

AUTHOR NOTE: This section on Multiple Copies for Classroom Use also stipulates that "each copy includes a notice of copyright."

For the typical unit of instruction, a teacher often uses supplemental resources to support their lessons. Two frequent examples of such applications might be when a teacher makes multiple copies of a copyrighted workbook pages or a newspaper article for use in the classroom without permission. Making copies from workbooks or textbooks, which are consumables for educational applications, is more often an infringement rather than fair use. The income of publishers for such educational resources depend on purchases by students. However, there are exceptions that both the *Guidelines for Classroom Copying* and the fair use doctrine support. If only a single chapter of a textbook were photocopied or shared as a library electronic reserve to supplement another legally acquired textbook students are reading, that could be fair use. If an instructor only copied one exercise and only one exercise from that same workbook to supplement another legally acquired workbook for instruction, that single copy could be fair use. Another exception is possible when waiting on newly purchased textbooks or workbooks that have not yet arrived in time for a class instruction. Copies could be made to fill in until the new textbooks or workbooks arrive.

One would need to perform a fair use analysis on a case-by-case basis to determine if similar uses were fair use. If not, then one should obtain permission from the publisher. It is important to note that when conducting a fair use analysis, you should always try to look at your analysis from the point of view of the publisher. Also, avoid copying if the amount copied appears to substitute for purchasing a book or journal subscription.

Chapter 2 reviewed how to perform a fair use analysis utilizing the Fair Use Checklist by Kenneth Crews. When one's fair use analysis is unclear and tied between fair and infringement, the following conceptual questions based upon a list prepared by Carrie Russell[32] should help make a confident fair use determination:

- Is the use transformative? Does the use incorporate, modify, or represent a portion of copyrighted content in a transformative way?
- Is the material copied from a book owned by the school or to a journal to which the library has a current subscription? If not, can the library purchase a copy?
- Is the material primarily factual in nature? Or is it more fictional? The more factual in nature, the more one could copy in some cases.
- Is it possible to post the material as a traditional library reserve, electronic reserve, or even provide a URL link to the students rather than make copies? (Fair use associated with library reserves and course packs are discussed in Chapter 7.)
- Can the teaching objective be met in another way? For example, paraphrase the copyrighted resource or locate a public domain or open access resource?

For more on utilizing the *Guidelines for Classroom Copying* and the fair use doctrine for classroom teaching purposes, the Library of Congress provides a document entitled Circular 21: Reproduction of Copyrighted Works by Educators and Librarians online at https://www.copyright.gov/circs/circ21.pdf.

MUSIC RESOURCES: PRINT AND RECORDED

Besides traditional print resources, music is conceivably a very challenging type of copyrighted work to comply with copyright and determine what is fair use in schools. Section 102(a) of the U.S. Copyright Act classifies music into two separate copyright types: sound recordings and musical works (sheet music). Returning to the exclusive rights of copyright owners in Section 106 of the U.S. Copyright Act, these rights are controlled either directly by the owner or indirectly by a (licensor) rights organization, authorized by the owner, to license the following rights listed below to a party (licensee) requiring permission to use copyrighted works:

- Mechanical Rights License for commercial recordings
- Performing Rights License for public performances
- Digital Rights License for online digital recordings
- Synchronization Rights License for television and movie music use
- Reprint Rights License for scores and sheet music.

Once again, these exclusive rights of Section 106 are subject to fair use and similar legal exemptions, especially for nonprofit education settings, K–12 schools. Such related exemptions covered throughout this book include Sections 107, 108, and 110. Also, when the *Guidelines for Classroom Copying* were introduced by the U.S. Congress in 1976, *Guidelines for Educational Uses of Music* were similarly comprised.

The music teacher scenario mentioned earlier needs forty copies of a sheet music score and only purchased twenty officially published copies. The sheet music is a copyrighted musical work. Making a single copy for research or an isolated emergency need is often exempt under Sections 107 or 108. However, making twenty photocopies is a likely infringement even in a nonprofit educational environment. If the sheet music is out of print, then obtaining permission for a reprint rights license from the publisher or rights holder of the score is highly advised. Otherwise, the school should purchase forty copies. If the published sheet music were in the public domain, then copying would not an issue.

When a teacher or student perform up to an entire music content of a score in a nonprofit educational face-to-face classroom setting, it is exempted from infringement under classroom exemptions of Section 110(1). However, music performed merely for entertainment purposes in the classroom setting including band classroom could be an infringement. Always tie educational or classroom music performances to pedagogy such as learning about music or even practicing music skills to prepare for concerts.

Students often organize their own "garage" bands where they are hoping to perform for a paying audience. This is a perfect opportunity for school librarians to either answer their questions directly or offer workshops for students about copyright and music. Collaborating with music teachers on such outreach is possible, too. During such encounters, helping the band to be aware of their ownership matters such as copyright registrations for protecting their works and registering separately with a single performance rights organization such as ASCAP, BMI, or SESAC is insightful. If they plan to publicly perform someone else's copyrighted music at the school dance, they might be exempted from the need for permission if the school dance meets the requirements of Section 110(4) listed below. However, if the band is compensated for its performance, Section 110(4) would not apply. When in doubt the band may need to obtain permission in advance from a performance rights organization. Then, if the band members decide to record and sell their music, mechanical and synchronization rights could be arranged by their publisher or their official representative to handle royalties. Many helpful books about the music business are available, which a high school librarian should consider adding to the library collection for its aspiring young musicians and junior achievement entrepreneurs.

School band directors may call on librarians with questions of when fair use or permission are required for sheet music played during the band's public halftime show performances at the school's own sporting events. These are considered public performances outside of the classroom. If the students are performing from music scores that are legally acquired, such as sheet music copies or reprint rights purchased from authorized publisher, then such use is most likely fair use or authorized by Section 110(4).[33] This copyright exception is discrete from fair use and probably more effective for such public performances.

What if the copies of the sheet music are used by the school band for performance in a nationally broadcasted parade? So long as the sheet music has been legally acquired, only performance and conceivably synchronization licensing rights are required. Performance licenses are the responsibility of the performance venue rather than the performers. If the school band performs copyrighted music at the parade or any other public venue outside of its school, it is the responsibility of the parade or television broadcaster to clear uses and obtain permission from a performing rights organization. Synchronization rights could also be needed for transmission aspects of performances.

What if you, the school librarian, have been assigned the task of video recording this national parade from an off-air broadcast of your school band for later presentation at a parent event? To whom can you lawfully show your recording? Section 110 only applies to an educational classroom setting, while Section 107 mainly applies to a home environmental setting for time shifting. Displaying a small segment of the parade broadcast that features the high school band could be defendable as fair use at a nonprofit parent association event. However, if such a nonprofit event needs more than a fair use portion to display in public, the librarian should contact the copyrighted party listed in the credits at the end of the recorded broadcast. It is helpful to convey to the copyright holder that the public display of the broadcast is noncommercial and related to an educational organization, such as a PTA meeting.

Section 110(4) is an exemption for school concert performances of nondramatic literary or musical works, if four specific requirements are met. First, the concert is restricted to an onsite, live audience. No broadcast transmissions are permitted unless licensed permission is obtained from a synchronization licensing rights organization. Second, the performance must be for nonprofit purposes, with no direct or indirect commercial purpose. Third, no fees or compensation can be paid to any associated parties. Fourth, there is no admission charge. However, an admission charge is permitted without permission for use of copyrighted works if the proceeds go to charity or education. Plus, be aware that Section 110(4) permits a copyright owner of a musical work to object to the exemption at least seven days in advance. Often, this occurs when there is a personal or political issue with the cause of a free public performance of their copyrighted work which the owner does not endorse.[34]

Public performance of copyrighted musicals or operas would require grand permission rights from the copyright owner or publisher, no matter what educational conditions exists. Like licensed databases and computer software, there are no fair use exemptions for recordings or even publicity media associated with such performances. Read the fine print of the grand permission rights for what is permitted to avoid any potential infringements. If the school wishes to produce and maintain a single archival video of the performance, it may need to pay an additional fee for a video recording license as part of the grand permission rights.[35] Distribution of copies of video or audio performance would also require additional permission, especially if students or their parents were being asked to purchase copies.

When the *Guidelines for Classroom Copying* were introduced in 1976, part of that effort included *Guidelines for Educational Uses of Music*, H.R. Rep. No. 94-1476, at 70–71. In 1996, the *Fair Use Guidelines for Educational Multimedia* were created. The newer *Guidelines* offer conservative benchmarks prepared by the Consortium of College & University Media Centers (CCUMC) for additional copyright compliancy in the classroom and are listed below.

AUDIOVISUAL RESOURCES

Audiovisual resources of school library collections support teaching and learning by aligning with curriculum needs, inquiry units, and student engagement.[36] Section 110 of the Copyright Act offers exemptions for use of audiovisual resources in both face-to-face and distance education. Besides documentary and factual films, entertainment movies are often included in an audiovisual collection. These can be used lawfully without permission when supporting the pedagogy of instruction.

What about our situation described earlier, the definitive *Romeo and Juliet* movie shown in the school auditorium for all the tenth graders studying the play in their class? It could be permitted under Section 110 if the auditorium is used as a "similar place devoted to instruction"[37] like in the classroom, and the audience is isolated only to the students enrolled in the course studying the story. Although the original book is in the public domain, a DVD copy of a movie version displayed is most likely copyrighted. If other students attend the auditorium public display of the film, or it is merely being shown for entertainment purposes, then permission from a movie rights service is needed. An allowance could exist for entertainment or outside classroom showing if the library acquired the copy of the movie with a public performance license. Further exemptions for an auditorium display isolated to the class studying the story could be defended with fair use (Section 107) if the teacher added value to the showing of the films with class discussion breaks.

Off-air broadcasts of programs such as the parade in which the high school band performs, if copied for classroom instruction, are considered legally acquired resources so long as the recordings are not maintained as a permanent part of the library collection. The 1982 *Encyclopaedia Britannica v. Crooks* case[38] acknowledged that schools could not record broadcasts for long-term retention. In addition, the *Guidelines for Off-Air Recording of Broadcast Programming for Educational Purposes* is a dated set of guidelines still used by many school libraries. It was drafted before the dawn of cable television, online media, or even the landmark 1984 Supreme Court decision of *Sony Corp. v. Universal City Studios, Inc.*, also known as the Betamax case, which permits time shifting of home-recorded broadcast as fair use. Time shifting means to record a broadcast for listening or viewing at a later time.

The *Guidelines for Off-Air Recording* apply to the recording, retention, and use with off-air antenna broadcasts for educational purposes. Recording and utilizing cable, satellite, and online transmissions for instruction require a fair use analysis or permission. However, if the cable, satellite, or online transmission is concurrent to the off-air broadcast, and especially if the quality is better than off-air, the alternative transmission source may be utilized.[39] Here are highpoints of the *Guidelines*:

- Nonprofit educational institutions can record television broadcasts for instructional purposes.
- Only off-air television broadcasted programs that are "free of charge" may be recorded.
- The television program may only be recorded once.
- Recordings cannot be made in anticipation of potential requests by teachers.
- The recording must be utilized for class purposes within ten days of the recording date. The recording can be viewed at a later time for "instructional reinforcement."
- The copy can only be retained for forty-five days.
- All recordings must include the copyright notice on the broadcasted program as recorded.

Remember that the *Guidelines for Off-Air Recording* are just that, guidelines. Not only are the *Guidelines* dated and challenging to apply to newer digital technology, but such strict application of the *Guidelines* could also confine one's lawful wider window of fair use opportunity for a pedagogically sound instructive endeavor. For extenuating circumstances, teachers may need to use the recording outside the ten-day window of the Guidelines. When best practices and guidelines restrict "criticism, comment, news reporting, teaching (including multiple copies for classroom use), scholarship, or research,"[40] then consider applying fair use instead. However, be careful not to abuse fair use. Recording or downloading programs to build a permanent media collection is not fair use, as it avoids the purchase of programs that may be readily available to purchase.[41]

Remember to check educational broadcaster sites such as PBS, Discovery, and even A&E for their latest classroom use guides. The help page at PBS and its Learning Media website offer additional details. For example, PBS posts that most of its programs offer "one year Educational Rights from the original broadcast date . . . you can record a PBS show and show that recording in the classroom for one year following the date the show originally aired."[42]

MULTIMEDIA RESOURCES

When Sara Kelly Johns was president of the AASL, she wrote, "Library media specialists empower students to be critical thinkers, enthusiastic readers, skillful researchers, and ethical users of information."[43] It is the "ethical users of information" factor that is part of the IP awareness equation reviewed here. School librarians should know how to guide students with ethical and legal applications of utilizing resources for multimedia projects tied to their school learning projects. Much content is easily found on the web and free for the taking. It is the school librarians' assignment to be the copyright coaches for both students and teachers in the K–12 setting. They serve as guides as students are preparing their responses to classroom assignments.

Students work both as individuals and as groups to report research or other assignments. When can they use music and pictures to illustrate their reports?

Many of the resources found in the library collection could be used in generous fair use portions. Some licensed library resources may offer unlimited use with proper author attribution. Clip art and audio recording collections are available that include unlimited educational use. Read the fine print of licenses before acquiring. Some licenses may even extend beyond the classroom to publicly display or broadcast.

Multimedia works are perhaps the most challenging for school librarians and researchers to determine fair use and when permission is needed. Returning to Section 107 for the classroom setting, the "purpose" (nonprofit/educational) factor tilts in favor of fair use. However, students and teachers should be reminded that when images are displayed publicly outside of the classroom or educational onsite school events, the fair use window narrows, and permission may be required.

Images found online, including photographs, graphics, and videos, are often missing copyright notices. Many persons believe that the absence of copyright notice means that it is public domain, when in fact that is merely public dissemination. Neither copyright notice nor registration is required since the Copyright Act of 1976. Unless an open-access or public domain notice is attached, it is safe to assume that virtually all images found online are copyrighted resources. Observe how some sites display copyrighted images without permission and post disclaimers that it is your responsibility to secure rights for use of an image shown. When uncertain of the copyright status, consider it copyrighted. For educational purposes, refer in Chapter 2 to the Fair Use Checklist by Kenneth Crews, based on the actual copyright law.

Use of sound recordings for multimedia projects presents another challenge to determine when it is fair use or when permission is needed. Two best practice guides listed below offer some assistance. As noted in Chapter 10, with regard to museums, there are some instances when the copyright owner of some vintage music is unknown, and it has become an orphan work. The Music Modernization Act of 2018 brings some pre-1972 recordings into the public domain sooner, too.[44] See the latest Cornell University *Library Copyright Term and the Public Domain* chart (https://copyright.cornell.edu/publicdomain) to determine when certain vintage music enters the public domain.

Besides the Fair Use Checklist, there are two dissimilar guidelines most librarians refer to for benchmarks when performing a fair use analysis regarding copyright content used in multimedia teacher instruction and student learning projects. Keep in mind, when applying such guidelines, that if one's use exceeds the recommended limits, it could still be fair use.

The first guideline is the *Fair Use Guidelines for Educational Multimedia.* This guideline was prepared by the Consortium of College & University Media Centers (CCUMC) in 1996. The quantity limit recommendations below are conservative examples of usable portions of a single copyrighted work when presented in classroom multimedia presentations. Use of portions larger than the illustrations below may be permitted, for which educators should refer to the four factors of the fair use doctrine to determine if it qualifies as fair use.

1. Motion media (such as film or video)—up to 10 percent or three minutes
2. Text—up to 10 percent or 1,000 words
3. Music/lyrics/music video—up to 10 percent; thirty seconds maximum
4. Photos/illustrations—up to five from one artist
5. Numerical data sets (e.g., databases)—up to 10 percent or 2,500 fields[45]

The second guideline is a set of best practices steeped in a more progressive application of transformative fair use. As mentioned in Chapter 2, transformative fair use of copyrighted materials adds value, repurposes, or produces new meaning. The term "mash-up" has also been applied to such applications. This concept advances the purpose of copyright by fostering the creation of new expression built on access to established works, which ultimately benefits society. Transformative uses add substantial fair use opportunities to multimedia projects of students.

Such transformative fair use principles were crafted for classroom media use in the *Code of Best Practices in Fair Use for Media Literacy Education* in 2008. The *Code* encourages both teachers and students to use the principles described to develop an understanding of fair use and then apply analysis and reasoning to determine fair use within one's own pedagogical needs of their educational media projects. This includes using copyrighted works of others in creating their own new material, especially if their work incorporates, modifies, and re-presents a portion of existing media content in a transformative way. It affirms that in certain instances, "[e]ducators' and students' fair use rights extend to the portions of copyrighted works that they need to accomplish their educational goals—and sometimes even to small or short works in their entirety."[46] The complete *Code* is available to read at https://cmsimpact.org/code/code-best-practices-fair-use-media-literacy-education/.

DISTANCE LEARNING

Distance learning, also known as distributed learning or distance education, is not only for higher education. Online distance learning is now common in K–12. It is also known as K–12 online learning, cyber school, and virtual school. Some K–12 programs are taught entirely online, whereas others utilize a hybrid, blended approach. The National Education Association (NEA) defines distance education as "a form of education in which courses are delivered via the Internet (or other forms of digital technologies that may evolve from the Internet that exists today) without face-to-face interaction between student and instructor."[47] Clearly, copyright compliancy concerns are a high priority in distance education. The Technology, Education and Copyright Harmonization (TEACH) Act of 2002[48] (Section 110(2)) and fair use (Section 107) support strategies utilized by librarians in assisting online teachers with supplementary readings in library electronic reserves, information about the TEACH Act and fair use, licensing requirements of subscription database content posted online, and so on.

The TEACH Act amended part of the limitations on exclusive rights in Section 110 of the U.S. Copyright Act to permit digital transmission of copyright protected content for nonprofit, educational purposes. The new law Section 110(2) affirms that distance education should receive comparable copyright exemptions as Section 110(1)[49] audiovisual face-to-face teaching exceptions. Because rights holders of copyrighted works were wary about the ease of digital duplication and potential violations, the TEACH Act is complicated in contrast to the more flexible fair use doctrine in Section 107. The information in this chapter applies only to nonprofit and outside classroom support role scenarios for K–12 rather than full-time online high school. When use of the TEACH Act is full-time or for-profit, such as online charter schools, you need to determine an IP policy with your legal counsel. For-profit educators cannot use the TEACH Act exemptions. Fair use or other copyright exemptions could apply in certain instances.[50]

The TEACH Act could apply to online transmissions where the instructor is displaying or performing copyrighted materials as they would in traditional face-to-face classrooms. If the instructor is making copies and handouts to supplement their instruction, then fair use (Section 107) is likely the applicable statute. In addition, all posted content must be tied to the pedagogy of the instruction. In other words, it should not be presented as entertainment, reward, or enrichment.[51] In addition, it is wise to have content posted online include a copyright warning statement. Most online learning platforms post a copyright notice on their home page or gateway.

Unlike Section 110(1) in the face-to-face classroom (or Section 107), there may be limitations when utilizing the TEACH Act Section 110(2) for online instruction. The TEACH Act requirements are assembled into three categories: institutional and policy requirements, technology requirements, and instructional requirements. Benefits of the TEACH Act only apply when all requirements are met. Below are the instructional requirements[52] for which a library can offer copyrighted resources.

INSTRUCTORS CAN:

Perform (show) a non-dramatic literary or musical work or any other dramatic or audiovisual work in "reasonable and limited portions."

Display a work "in an amount comparable to that which is typically displayed in the course of a live classroom session."

Convert analog works into digital in the amount authorized by the list below if no digital version is available to the school.

INSTRUCTORS CANNOT:

Perform or display a work marketed "primarily for performance or display as part of mediated instructional activities transmitted via digital networks."

Perform or display copies of works that are "not lawfully made and acquired" under the U.S. Copyright Act, if the school "knew or had reason to believe" that they were not lawfully made and acquired.

INSTRUCTOR RESPONSIBILITIES FOR PERMITTED PERFORMANCE AND DISPLAY:

Performance or display must be "made by, at the direction of, or under the actual supervision of an instructor."

Materials are transmitted "as an integral part of the class session offered as a regular part of the systematic, mediated instructional activities" of a government body or an accredited nonprofit educational institution.

Copyrighted materials are "directly related and of material assistance to the teaching content of the transmission."

Policy makers such as a board of education must verify the nonprofit educational status. The board must adopt a copyright policy. Other institutional and policy requirements include making certain that the faculty, staff, and students are trained in copyright awareness and that distance learning content is limited only to students enrolled.[53]

The information technology staff is responsible for technology requirements. They must assure that technological controls are implemented to "reasonably prevent . . . retention of the work in accessible form by recipients . . . for longer than class session" as well as "unauthorized further dissemination of the work in accessible form by such recipients to others." Information technology staff must protect digital rights management or "technological measures used by copyright owners to prevent such retention or unauthorized further dissemination."[54]

Once again, posting complete articles or textbook chapters that are intended as homework or supplemental library readings is not covered under the TEACH Act, unless permission is acquired or a persistent link to the school library's subscription database is utilized. However, fair use from Section 107 could cover certain supplemental resource distributions, such as library electronic reserves.[55] In addition, the TEACH Act addressed Section 112(f) where it does not cover conversion of audiovisual resources from analog to digital formats, except when the converted resource is used only for authorized transmissions under the TEACH Act and when no digital version of the resource is available or is inaccessible because of protection measures.[56]

Discussions over what is allowed and not allowed under the TEACH Act continue—for example, whether posting an entire film is permitted. The TEACH Act indicates that only "reasonable and limited portions"[57] can be shown. Fair use might permit posting an entire film online in certain instances. There is a difference in what fair use could cover between an entertainment film versus a factual documentary. However, portions of an entertainment film could support the pedagogy to illustrate a point tied to a lesson. When an online instructional application does not fit within the conditions of the TEACH Act, many schools rely on fair use or another exception in the copyright law, or they merely secure permission from the copyright holder. However, higher education offers many TEACH Act best practices and guidelines which K–12 should review, such as the Copyright Crash Course at University of Texas Libraries at https://guides.lib.utexas.edu/copyright/teachact. The Crash Course site offers a TEACH Act Checklist.

Recently, questions have been raised regarding who owns the online content developed for distance learning by teachers and potential liability issues of school districts. Many school districts are revisiting the TEACH Act and other aspects of copyright law to determine such matters. CC and open access may become more prevalent, too, as Open Educational Resources (OER) are addressing more IP facets of online instructional content.[58] School librarians should watch for articles and news related to distance learning to keep up with any significant changes to support their instructors.

COMPUTER SOFTWARE AND INTERNET USAGE

Unauthorized copies and other misappropriations of computer software reflect similar concerns with other licensed library resources. Users of computers should always follow copyright laws and licensing agreements, as with other library resources. Otherwise, copyright infringement consequences are just as rigid as with traditional library resources. Some school librarians collaborate with their computer information technology staff to create an accessible database site of license agreements for teachers to review to know and identify the different sharing restrictions or other limitations. Computer software licensing is usually tied to individual computer use. Before purchasing computer software for the library, read the fine print. Explore to see what user options are available. Otherwise, a multiple-use license or multiple purchases would be a wise investment. Open-source software is often free to share, but look for any potential restrictions such as CC stipulations for commercial use.

As with other library resources, fair use and some exemptions to copyright infringement of computer software exist. Unless prevented by licensing contracts, there are some Section 107 fair use rights for certain unauthorized reproduction, distribution, adaptation, and public performance and display to support the basic fair use rights such as criticism, comment, news reporting, teaching, scholarship, and research.[59]

Section 109(b) provides an exemption from software licensing agreements that restrict lending software to others. It permits nonprofit libraries and educational institutions to lend software to other nonprofit libraries and educational institutions,[60] whereas Section 117 provides an exemption for archival backup copies and modifications essential for using computer software.[61]

Internet usage also presents potential infringement issues when such unlawful activities occur. Teachers and students may not be aware that certain copying and sharing of resources from the web are just as problematic as licensing issues associated with computer software or library subscription databases. Outside of the TEACH Act to guide online instruction, there are no formal guidelines and few copyright laws tied to educators and their students use of the internet. The Digital Millennium Copyright Act (DMCA) covered in Chapter 6 applies somewhat. Otherwise, fair use from Section 107 is supportive. Some school librarians create and post computer and internet usage policies on their website for easy reference.

Printing pages from the internet follows similar guidelines and copyright laws associated with the *Guidelines for Classroom Copying* and fair use covered earlier in this chapter. However, other matters to consider include emails and chats, websites, social networking, podcasting, and blogs. Use caution when reposting or sharing images, music, and videos. Consider all content found copyrighted, unless otherwise noted from the site of a resource utilized.

The DMCA offers some defense to infringement for schools as it regulates digital copyrighted works online. The DMCA amended the Copyright Act in 1998. The Act "affords to copyright owners rights against those who circumvent copy protection technologies and insulates online service provides from liability for infringing acts of their subscribers subject to various limitations."[62] The DMCA prohibits circumvention of technological protection measures except for specified exemptions, such as the TEACH Act Section 110(2). In addition, there are limitations on copyright infringement liability for service providers. However, such limitations extend only to the school or district, not the individuals committing an infringement.

PATENTS, TRADEMARKS, AND COPYRIGHTS: CLASSROOM TO PRACTICAL APPLICATIONS

We now return to some questions from the beginning of the chapter. How do you foster the great idea of a brainchild student who has come up with an invention displayed at the school science fair, which might be patentable? Then what if that same invention could be marketable with a clever banded name for a trademark? What if a student has coauthored a children's book with a parent and wants to get it published? Often, neither the student nor the parent knows much about copyright from the creator point of view. How do you help other students with their copyright needs for publishing original poetry, short stories, artwork, blog or podcast series, or even new music from the neighborhood garage band? This section of the chapter covers these scenarios as they apply to IP library specialists.

Patents for School Students

News stories abound in the media of whiz kids and teens and their invented gadgets and gizmos. Inventions range from science and technology to health innovations and even assistive devices for around the house. You or another clever teacher in your school could also develop a better gadget requiring information about patents and trademarks. You might even have a student whose parent has an idea for a product and wonders how to get a patent or other IP.

Support from regional Patent and Trademark and Resource Center (PTRC) libraries are covered in depth in Chapters 4 and 5. They are available to help to prepare students and teachers with an understanding of patents and other IPs aligned with various information literacy principles. Information literacy tied to younger inventors includes identifying, discovering, and synthesizing needed information, a part of IP information literacy, as well as using other types of related information effectively, ethically, and legally.[63]

Often PTRC librarians reach out to support K–12 school librarians and teachers. PTRC librarians participate in regional science fairs, makerspace programs, and support K–12 science and technology classroom curricula. A successful example of such a program series was the *InventorFest*, which drew nearly 750 people during one weekend in 2006. Educational activities were included for children, teens, and adults related to intellectual property and inventing.[64]

Although patent searching exercises are more practical for high school students, patent awareness presentations and classroom exercises are ideal for upper elementary and middle school students. Some PTRC librarians have created websites or class lessons to support curriculum activities where students produce their own inventions or creative works, such as the Creative Thinking program at https://inside.nku.edu/creativethinking.html. PTRC librarians might even visit the school to assist the librarian or science teacher with lessons. Students are taught about the different types of IPs and how they apply to their inventions and creative works. The United States Patent and Trade Office (USPTO) and the U.S. Copyright Office websites are employed for real-world applications to the students' inventions and creative works. For one such PTRC program, students documented their inventions beforehand and shared them with the PTRC librarian. Then, similar patents were located in advance and attached to a Great Idea certificate presented to each student at the patent program. Such programs could be adapted to support science, art, and history classes. In addition, many PTRCs created regional historic inventor/patent databases that could support local history projects.

PTRC patent and other IP awareness lessons support all K–12 students participating in regional or national science and makerspace fairs. Many established science and makerspace fairs nationally are available for students. The Smithsonian's Lemelson Center for the Study of Invention and Innovation (https://invention.si.edu/tags/kid-inventors) and the USPTO Kids (https://www.uspto.gov/kids/index.html) are examples of quality websites offering venue date announcements for young inventors, online activities, and inventing process guidelines.

However, if your school plans to create and host its own event, community buy-in, class-related projects, community publicity and sponsorship and building science or maker activities into the curriculum are helpful for its success.[65] Curriculum ties could include student-project entry-forms with rubrics aligned with educational standards encompassing creativity and innovation; critical thinking; communication and collaboration; and evidence and IP.[66] Makerspaces are covered in detail in Chapter 8.

To help students and even their parent inventors understand the process of applying for a patent, outreach presentations could be offered at science fairs or makerspace events, or even separately. PTRC IP librarians, technology transfer, or entrepreneur program directors of regional universities, patent attorneys, or directors of business incubators or accelerators could offer informative inventor/entrepreneur topical presentations.

As this book suggests in Chapters 3 and 4, the patent application process is very challenging. PTRC librarians can attest to the time involved and the effort of making sure an invention is unique will absorb an incredible amount of time. At the beginning of the process, these would-be entrepreneurs need to understand that for expanding beyond the search process, the services of a patent lawyer will often be required.

As school librarians expand their outreach with science fair or makerspace programs and involve volunteer members of the community to help these students with their ideas, it becomes even more likely that students will create something that could be marketed. Understanding the long road to getting a patent can begin in your school library. Trademarks and copyrights are tied to such outreach, too.

Professional Development and IP

Most school librarians are surprised when it is suggested that they get a patent lawyer or trademark lawyer to speak to teachers or parents. They will consider it a waste of time because so few students may need the information. However, if you have planned a session tied to STEM or STEAM with your regional PTRC librarian from an academic or public library and invited interested parents and other members of the community, it should encourage a large enough audience to warrant a guest speaker. The presenter could cover the basics of applying for a patent or trademark, the search process to begin to avoid any infringement issues and verify whether the patent or trademark are indeed unique, and then the need to consult an expert through the actual application process.

Professional development for copyright awareness is often necessary for teachers and even parents who have gifted children who wish to become authors, musicians, and artists. Consider that fact that students write creative poetry, multimedia, and essays for class assignments. Other students might capture photographs or write news stories for the school newspaper. Who owns the copyright for such student works? Hopefully a school copyright policy exists to address any copyright matters.

For teenagers, an IP program might be the answer for such copyright matters. It must provide engaging material tied to what teens do, including writing poetry, short stories or complete books, comic or graphic novels, composing music, and even inventing. A teen program is a hybrid blend of the younger inventor programs and information from more adult programs for entrepreneurs and businesses.[67]

CONCLUSION

School librarians should remain up-to-date with basic copyright laws and fair use for teaching, establish networks, and building relationships with regional IP librarians. School librarians should also be part of any school-wide committees to contribute expertise on numerous library matters, including IP rights. Collaborating with teachers, school administrators, and the community are all vital for long term planning at one's school library, which positively affects the information literacy skills needed for student achievement and becoming active in the global information society.[68]

This chapter supports librarians in school libraries in facilitating copyright and fair use, as it relates to the ethical and legal use of information for teaching and learning. Exemptions of Sections 107, 108, and 110 of the U.S. Copyright Act have been reviewed, indicating how each supports information access, teaching, and learning in schools. Such exemptions are available for pedagogical purposes, ranging from print and music resources to audiovisual and multimedia. Variations in exemptions for distance learning, computer software, and internet usage were also addressed. Classroom to practical applications for students associated with patents, trademarks, and copyrights wrapped up the content presented.

NOTES

1. American Association of School Librarians, "What Does a School Librarian Do?" http://www.ala.org/aasl/about/ed/recruit/learn (accessed December 11, 2018).
2. Cherie P. Pandora and Kathy Fredrick," *Full STEAM Ahead: Science, Technology, Engineering, Art, and Mathematics in Library Programs and Collections* (Santa Barbara, CA: Library Unlimited, 2017), xviii.
3. Jeremy Philips, "Teaching Trademark Law," in *Teaching of Intellectual Property: Principles and Methods*, Yo Takagi, Larry Allman, and Mpazi A. Sinjela, eds. (Cambridge: Cambridge University Press, 2008), 75.
4. American Association of School Librarians, *Empowering Learners: Guidelines for School Library Media Programs* (Chicago: American Association of School Librarians, 2009), 17.
5. American Association of School Librarians, *Empowering Learners.*
6. Ibid.
7. Nicholas Joint. "Teaching Intellectual Property Rights as part of the Information Literacy Syllabus," *Library Review* 55, no. 6 (2006): 330–336.
8. American Association of School Libraries, AASL Standards Framework for Learners, National School Library Standards, 2018, https://standards.aasl.org/framework/ (accessed December 11, 2018).
9. John Alberti, "Chapter 2—Who Owns What? Ideas and Authority in the Information Age," in *Text Messaging: Reading and Writing about Popular Culture* (New York: Houghton Mifflin Harcourt, 2009); Michele Eodice, "Man Bites Dog: The Public, Press, and Plagiarism," in *Pluralizing Plagiarism: Identities, Context, and Pedagogies*, R. M. Hoard and A. E. Robillard, eds. (Portsmouth, NH: Boynton/Cool Publishers, 2008); David P. Noskin, "A Proactive Approach to Plagiarism," *English Leadership Quarterly* 28, no. 1 (August 2005): 14–16.
10. John Schlipp, "Creative Thinking: A Student-Centered Approach to Plagiarism and Copyright," *Kentucky Libraries* 74, no. 3 (2010): 28–32.
11. Carrie Russell, *Complete Copyright for K–12 Librarians and Educators* (Chicago: American Library Association, 2012), 1.
12. Ibid., 8, cites the following as the only copyright infringement case for a school—Encyclopaedia Britannica Educational Corp. v. Crooks, 542 F. Supp. 1156 (W.D.N.Y. 1982).
13. Kenneth Crews, *Copyright, Fair Use, and the Challenge for Universities* (Chicago: University of Chicago Press, 1993), 45.
14. U.S. Copyright Act, 17 U.S. Code §504(c)(2) - Remedies for infringement: Damages and profits.
15. Kenneth Crews, "Chapter 14: Responsibilities, Liabilities, and Doing the Right Thing," in *Copyright Law for Librarians and Educators: Creative Strategies and Practical Solutions* (Chicago: American Library Association, 2012), 101–107, cites 17 U.S.C. § 504(c)

(2), and U.S. Constitution, Eleventh Amendment; Russell, "Complete Copyright," 4, cites Copyright Act of 1976, 17 U.S.C. § 504(c)(2), regarding remission of statutory damages and limit on the remedies which rights holders could expect to collect if they sued schools or libraries; also cites U.S. Constitution, Eleventh Amendment protecting state entities from federal prosecution without consent.

16. Russell, "Complete Copyright," 3.

17. Ibid., 8.

18. U.S. Constitution, article I, §8, clause 8 (1787).

19. Tammy Ravas, "Everyday Fair Use in Libraries," *District Dispatch*, blog, American Library Association, February 25, 2016, https://www.districtdispatch.org/2016/02/16420/ (accessed December 11, 2018).

20. U.S. Copyright Act, 17 U.S. Code §107—Limitations on Exclusive Rights: Fair Use.

21. U.S. Copyright Act, 17 U.S. Code §102(a)—Subject Matter of Copyright: In General.

22. U.S. Copyright Act, 17 U.S. Code §106—Exclusive Rights in Copyrighted Works.

23. U.S. Copyright Act, 17 U.S. Code §107—Limitations on Exclusive Rights: Fair Use.

24. U.S. Copyright Act, 17 U.S. Code §108—Limitations on Exclusive Rights: Reproduction by Libraries and Archives.

25. U.S. Copyright Act, 17 U.S.C. §110—Limitations on Exclusive Rights: Exemption of Certain Performances and Displays.

26. U.S. Copyright Act, 17 U.S. Code §108(f)(1)—Limitations on Exclusive Rights: Reproduction by Libraries and Archives.

27. Reference and User Services Association (Division of the American Library Association), "Language Suggested for the Notices Required by the Copyright Revision Act of 1976," http://www.ala.org/rusa/resources/guidelines/languagesuggested (accessed December 14, 2018).

28. *Copyright Law Revision*, U.S. Congress. 94th Cong., 2d Sess. (1976). H. Doc. 1476: 68–70, "Agreement on Guidelines for Classroom Copying in Not-for-Profit Educational Institutions with Respect to Books and Periodicals, March 1976."

29. Ibid.; Library of Congress, Circular 21, *Reproduction of Copyrighted Works by Educator and Librarians*, 6–7, https://www.copyright.gov/circs/circ21.pdf (accessed December 29, 2018).

30. Ibid.

31. Ibid.

32. Russell, "Complete Copyright," 87–88.

33. U.S. Copyright Act, 17 U.S. Code §110(4)—Limitations on Exclusive Rights: Exemption of Certain Performances and Displays.

34. David J. Moser, *Moser on Music Copyright* (Boston: ArtistPro and Thomson Course Technology, 2006), 97.

35. Phillip L. Harris, "Can Our Play/Musical Show Be Recorded?" *School Video News*, 2018, http://schoolvideonews.com/Copyright/Can-our-Play-Musical-Show-Be-Recorded (accessed December 14, 2018).

36. American Association of School Librarians, *Empowering Learners*, 38–39.

37. U.S. Copyright Act, 17 U.S. Code §110(1)—Limitations on Exclusive Rights: Exemption of Certain Performances and Displays.

38. Russell, "Complete Copyright," 8, cites the following as the only copyright infringement case for a school—Encyclopaedia Britannica Educational Corp. v. Crooks, 542 F. Supp. 1156 (W.D.N.Y. 1982).

39. Carol Simpson, *Copyright for Schools: A Practical Guide* (Santa Barbara, CA: Linworth, 2010), 84.

40. U.S. Copyright Act, 17 U.S. Code §107—Limitations on Exclusive Rights: Fair Use.

41. Russell, "Complete Copyright," 74.

42. PBS, "I Am a Teacher and I Want to Hold a Screening of a PBS Show for My Students. Can I Do That?" May 7, 2018," PBS Help, https://help.pbs.org/support/solutions/articles/5000673774-i-am-a-teacher-and-i-want-to-hold-a-screening-of-a-pbs-show-for-my-students-can-i-do-that- (accessed December 14, 2018).

43. Eric Weil, "Meet Your New School Media Library Specialist," *Scholastic Administrator*, http://www.scholastic.com/browse/article.jsp?id=3748779 (accessed December 16, 2018).

44. Mitch Stoltz, "New Music Modernization Act Has a Major Fix: Older Recordings Will Belong to the Public, Orphan Recordings Will Be Heard Again," Electronic Frontier Foundation, September 19, 2018, https://www.eff.org/deeplinks/2018/09/new-music-modernization-act-has-major-fix-older-recordings-will-belong-public (accessed November 30, 2018).

45. Consortium of College & University Media Centers, *Fair Use Guidelines for Educational Multimedia*, http://www.ccumc.org/copyright-matters/fair-use-guideline (accessed August 21, 2009).

46. Center for Media and Social Impact, *Code of Best Practices in Fair Use for Media Literacy Education*, http://cmsimpact.org/code/code-best-practices-fair-use-media-literacy-education/ (accessed December 16, 2018).

47. National Education Association, Distance Education, 2002, http://www.nea.org/home/34765.htm (accessed January 27, 2019).

48. *Technology, Education and Copyright Harmonization Act*, Public Law 107-273, *U.S. Statutes at Large* 116 (2002): 1910, codified at 17 U.S. Code §§ 110(2), 112(f).

49. 17 U.S. Code § 110(1)—Limitations on Exclusive Rights: Exemptions of Certain Performance and Displays.

50. Carrie Russell, "Tough Act to Follow: Although the TEACH Act Aims to Clarify the Use of Digital Technology, the New Copyright Law Is Difficult to Decipher," *School Library Journal* 49, no. 11 (November 2003): 52.

51. Simpson, *Copyright for Schools*, 129.

52. U.S. Copyright Act 17 U.S. Code § 110(2)—Limitations on Exclusive Rights: TEACH Act.

53. Simpson, *Copyright for Schools*, 127.

54. U.S. Copyright Act 17 U.S. Code § 110(2)—Limitations on Exclusive Rights: TEACH Act.

55. John Schlipp, "Fair Use & TEACH Act," Intellectual Property Awareness Center, https://inside.nku.edu/ipac/worksofothers/teachact.html (accessed January 27, 2019).

56. Simpson, *Copyright for Schools*, 129; and U.S. Copyright Act 17 U.S. Code § 112(f)—Limitations on Exclusive Rights: Ephemeral Recordings.

57. U.S. Copyright Act 17 U.S. Code § 110(2)—Limitations on Exclusive Rights: TEACH Act.

58. Greg Krabacher and Bryan Evans, Bricker & Eckler LLP, "Copyright Law & Teacher-Created Digital Content: Important Policy Considerations," Ohio School Boards Association, 2014 OSBA Capital Conference and Trade Show, November 9–12, 2014, http://conference.ohioschoolboards.org/2014/wp-content/uploads/sites/3/2014/11/330PM1111C210Karbacher.pdf (accessed January 27, 2019).

59. U.S. Copyright Act, 17 U.S. Code §107—Limitations on Exclusive Rights: Fair Use.

60. David Ensign, "Resource Sharing and Copyright among Library Consortia Members," in *Growing Pains: Adapting Copyright for Libraries, Education, and Society*, Laura Gasaway, ed. (Littleton, CO: Rothman & Co., 1997), 151–171; Russell, "Complete Copyright," 157, regarding U.S. Copyright Act, 17 U.S.C. §109(b).

61. U.S. Copyright Act, 17 U.S. Code §117. Limitations on Exclusive Rights: Computer Programs.

62. Peter S. Menell, Mark A. Lemley, and Robert P. Merges, *Intellectual Property in the New Technology Age: 2017, Volume II: Copyrights, Trademarks & State IP Protections, Copyright Law* (Berkeley, CA: Clause 8 Publishing, 2017), 496.

63. ALA/ACRL/STS Task Force on Information Literacy for Science and Technology, "Information Literacy Standards for Science and Engineering/Technology," Standard 4, 1, d, Association of College and Research Libraries, http://www.ala.org/acrl/standards/infolitscitech (accessed December 18, 2018).

64. John Schlipp, "Best Practices and InventorFest: Community Partners and Patent and Trademark Depository Libraries (PTDLs)," *Intellectual Property Journal of the PTDLA,* November 2007, http://ptrca.org/journal/2007schlipp (accessed January 27, 2019).

65. Collen Graves, "Starting a School Maker Space from Scratch," Edutopia, July 16, 2015, https://www.edutopia.org/blog/starting-school-makerspace-from-scratch-colleen-graves (accessed December 18, 2018).

66. John Schlipp, iMAGiNExpo Project-Based Learning imagine_factory assignment and submission checklist for students, https://inside.nku.edu/creativethinking/teachersguide/imaginexpo.html (accessed December 18, 2018).

67. John Schlipp and Linda Kocis, "Using Popular Fiction to Spark Student Creativity and to Teach Intellectual Property Information Literacy (IPIL)," *Kentucky Libraries* 77, no. 1 (Winter 2013): 26–32.

68. American Association of School Librarians, *Empowering Learners*, 47–48.

Chapter 10

SPECIAL LIBRARIES

CHAPTER OBJECTIVES

- Review common copyright exemptions and special provisions shared among special libraries
- Recognize and identify fair use continuum associated with special libraries
- Analyze and apply impact of pertinent copyright court cases
- Examine and distinguish specific U.S. Copyright Law exceptions beyond fair use that support unique types of special libraries
- Explore and apply specific copyright concerns in special libraries
- Identify when to draft or revise onsite polices regarding clearances to avoid infringements and/or ownership issues
- Discuss and differentiate related permission organizations for various types of special libraries and tie to associated intellectual property (IP) workflow responsibilities
- Distinguish patents and trademarks in special libraries

SPECIAL LIBRARIES AND COMMON IP CHALLENGES

Librarians and information professionals at special libraries provide focused subject information assistance, often for parent organizations that are not libraries. For example, hospital librarians assist doctors and nurses with specific research needs for medical treatments, while corporate librarians locate and collect defined information to support their businesses' decisions of product development or competitive intelligence.[1]

Despite the specialized nature and advanced knowledge of information research involved, some librarians and customers of special libraries are often oblivious to any copyright concerns and carelessly share copyrighted information with others without confirming copyright compliance. This chapter also covers other IPs, such as patents and trademarks associated with special libraries and their parent institutions. Common IP challenges begin with copyright infringement.

Specific copyright infringement lawsuits targeted to special libraries cited in this chapter reinforce the need for librarians and information professionals to know their fair use limitations, to recognize when to ask for permission of copyrighted works used, and to grasp IP laws related to their library and its employees and customers.

Recognizing and identifying the fair use continuum between nonprofit and for-profit special libraries is helpful when trying to determine whether one is copyright compliant or infringing. Fair use (Section 107) varies greatly in special libraries, as opposed to academic, public, and school libraries reviewed in other chapters. Using fair use of other creators' intellectual works varies by library types within the category "special": for-profit company information centers, law, medical, museum, church/faith-based/theological, and government, among others. Academic, public, and school libraries have a greater window of opportunity for fair use. Government agency libraries also have more liberal fair use flexibility similar to academic, public, and school libraries.[2]

Fair use (Section 107) in a for-profit setting, such as the *American Geophysical Union v. Texaco* case, is much narrower than in similar nonprofit scenarios. According to fair use scholar Laura Gasaway "While fair use exists in the corporate . . . world, it is more restricting and less likely to be found than is fair use in the non-profit environment."[3] In addition to fair use, there are library exemptions (Section 108), which Gasaway asserts that "many corporate libraries find . . . so limited that it is easier to pay royalties . . . in order to avoid the restriction."[4] Yet, some fair use scholars such as Kyle Courtney claim that such "commercial uses were far from dispositive in deciding fair use."[5] In other words, the commercial versus noncommercial aspect of a statutory exception analysis, such as fair use, depend on how much of Section 108 is followed or how transformative the use is under Section 107. In certain instances, it could be fair use when such use by a private, for-profit library is transformative and falls within the bounds of the three fair use factors unassociated with the fourth factor; effect on the market. Each kind of special library may have unique aspects of Sections 107 and 108 that may augment their transformative fair use to support the research needs of their customers. This further supports the need to conduct a fair use analysis on a case-by-case basis.

Before reviewing the commonalities of copyright and other IP matters in special libraries, definitions related to special libraries and the professionals who work with IP in these environments are needed.

Special libraries are located in focused environments mentioned above such as corporations, hospitals, museums, professional associations, government and military, law firms, theological colleges, and so on.[6] According to the Special Library Association (SLA), there were approximately 4,000 SLA members associated with special libraries in 2018.[7] The SLA site endorses its Professional Ethics Guidelines, within its Competencies for Information Professionals[8] section. Its Competencies foster the information ethics principles of its members working in special libraries in relations to IP, privacy, and proper use of information by "recognizing ethical issues relative to information handling, including but not limited to privacy and confidentiality, information security, intellectual property and copyright, and intellectual freedom." The site encourages information literacy to educate and maintain professional knowledge and competencies for such matters as IP and information right rights.

As defined above, special libraries vary greatly as they support disparate types of customers with diverse yet focused information topics. The virtual aspects of many special libraries with digital technology has revolutionized the way such libraries offer access to information. Special library customers are typically able to access their needed information via online subscription databases, document delivery and interlibrary loan, and other digital delivery methods. As it is so easy for customers of special libraries to access and share library content, potential copyright infringement occurs when shared erroneously. For example, most licensing agreements of databases require that users share links of articles rather than PDF copies. Even when one shares a free-access article found on the web, providing a URL link to another party is preferable to sending a PDF or cut-and-pasted HTML text. Such copyright violations place the special library and its parent organization at risk of legal and financial jeopardy, as well as possible ethical concerns, such as plagiarism.[9]

U.S. COPYRIGHT LAW SECTION 107 AND FAIR USE IN SPECIAL LIBRARIES

Knowledge of Sections 107 and 108 of U.S. Copyright Law assists librarians of special libraries to avoid risking potential copyright infringement. Such knowledge supports librarians in educating their customer when fair use or other copyright exemptions are legal for research and information access scenarios, especially for-profit or those special libraries that are not academic, public, or school libraries.

Section 107, fair use, is broader and more flexible, whereas Section 108, limitations for libraries and archives, is narrower and more specific as to what special libraries are able to do without permission of the copyright owner. While fair use is often denounced as vague and difficult to apply, several fair use scholars such as David Hansen cite that, "a growing body of research has emerged showing that while fair use is flexible, it is not entirely unpredictable."[10] Hansen describes the limitations for libraries and archives as

> a narrow set of preservation and lending activities in which libraries and archives frequently engage. Through the application of several rules, stipulations, and exceptions to those stipulations, section 108 carves out a complex but workable framework for library reproduction and distribution of copyrighted works in a variety of common archival and lending situations.[11]

In Chapter 7, fair use was tied to educational classroom copies and the Kinko's copy center case to avoid risks associated with library course reserves. Because fair use is often perceived as narrower in for-profit versus nonprofit libraries, there are two copyright cases to review to better understand when Sections 107 and 108 could apply to special libraries versus when permissions or subscriptions are needed. The first is *American Geophysical Union v. Texaco Inc.*[12]

Section 107 applies to limitations on the exclusive rights of the copyright owner, known as fair use. Fair use in special libraries such as corporate information centers could vary compared to other libraries. Texaco scientists routinely made copies of entire articles from scientific journals for later use in commercial research, without permission. Yet this case focused only on one scientist and his eight articles photocopied from the *Journal of Catalysis.*

In applying the fair use "Purpose" factor, these articles were kept in the scientist's file for just-in-case use. It was not transformative, where new value or utility is added. Instead, the courts considered this systematic copying. If the scientist had made a copy of the table of contents for just-in-case later use, and then requested the articles as he needed later during his actual research, copyright infringement may not have been found.

Purpose—Commercial; not transformative, just-in-case use, systematic copying; **did not favor fair use.**

The courts found that only the single "Nature" factor favored fair use in this commercial application.

Nature—Factual/research content; **favored fair use.**

When it came to the "Amount" factor, the courts determined that eight articles from a single issue of a journal was excessive and not fair use.

Amount—Entire articles; eight articles out of same issue; **did not favor fair use.**

Finally, the courts determined that the "Effect" on the market factor was violated, as the company negatively impacted the *Journal of Catalysis* by avoiding the purchase of additional subscriptions.

Effect—Market was impacted; Copyright Clearance Center was available for practical permission and payment method; **did not favor fair use.**

The Texaco case affirmed "large scale routing of journals to researchers in a for-profit company and the copying of articles by researchers who file them away to create their own mini-libraries, without using them in a transformative way, is not fair use."[13] The lesson learned here is that systematic just-in-case copying is most likely not fair use in a for-profit scenario unless there is some type of transformative use.

Section 108 offers traditional and special libraries multiple exemptions to avoid risking potential copyright infringement in certain instances. Section 108(g)(2) prohibits systematic reproduction or distribution of aggregate quantities of copies that would substitute for subscription to, or purchase of, a work, similar to what happened with Texaco. For-profit librarians should be especially aware of this application as noted above. However, isolated, spontaneous photocopying without systematic action to substitute for subscription or purchase may be covered by

Section 108. The copying must be research-based, with no commercial gain from the copied document's distribution. This research exception is also permitted in a for-profit environment.

Another example of non-transformative and unfair use of a subscription-based resource in a corporate environment occurred in *Lowry's Reports, Inc. v. Legg Mason, Inc.*[14] A jury found Legg Mason liable for $20 million[15] to Lowry for breach of contract and willful copyright infringement for internal copying of content from the copyrighted newsletter *Lowry's New York Stock Exchange Market Trend Analysis*, for which Legg Mason signed a subscription agreement. The defendant subscribed to only one copy of the newsletter. Copies were duplicated and shared via internal photocopy, intranet, and email distribution on a daily and weekly basis without permission or further payment.[16]

The defendant argued that copying within its research department was fair use. The court declared that the "Purpose" factor weighed heavily against the defendant and exploited the use of the newsletters for the commercial benefit of the defendant with a single subscription. The "Nature" factor also weighed against the defendant's use of factual information with added creative content. Because the newsletters were copied in their entirety for commercial gain of the defendant without compensation for unauthorized users, the "Amount" factor of fair use weighed against the defendant. Lastly, the "Effect" on the market factor harmed the primary subscription income of Lowry's. In other words, the unauthorized copying of the newsletters was an intentional exploitation to avoid additional subscription costs. The court concluded that the reproductions of the newsletters were not fair use.[17]

If the defendant's reproductions in this financial newsletter case were transformative and followed at least three of the fair use factors, the legitimate use outcome might have been different. This is a virtuous IP lesson for all special libraries, both for-profit and nonprofit, to know to avoid potential infringements.

U.S. COPYRIGHT LAW SECTION 108 AND SPECIAL PROVISIONS FOR REPRODUCTION

As covered in previous chapters, the relationship between the rights granted to copyright owners in Section 106 and exceptions granted to users in Section 107 of U.S. Copyright Law (U.S.C. Title 17) are deliberately flexible to promote the balance between creator and user rights of copyrighted works. However, limitations on the exclusive rights granted to users in the special provisions for reproduction by libraries and archives (Section 108) allow libraries to make lawful copies for customers without permission only under very specific conditions, such as interlibrary loan, as discussed in Chapter 2. Such conditions are very specific and are especially important for special libraries, such as subsection (g) related to prohibiting systematic copying related to the reproduction scenarios of special libraries shown above.

The legislative history of Section 108 from the 94th Congress House Report, at the time of its introduction in 1976, clarifies that special provisions apply to both for-profit and nonprofit libraries and archives:

> Isolated, spontaneous making of single photocopies by a library in a for-profit organization, without any systematic effort to substitute for photocopying for subscriptions or purchases, would be covered by section 108, even though the copies are furnished to the employees of the organization for use in their work. Similarly, for-profit libraries could participate in interlibrary arrangements for exchanges of photocopies, as long as the production or distribution was not "systematic." These activities, by themselves, would ordinarily not be considered "for direct or indirect commercial advantages," since the "advantage" referred to in this clause must attach to the immediate commercial motivation behind the reproduction or distribution, rather than to the ultimate profit-making motivation behind the enterprise in which the library is located. On the other hand, section 108 would not excuse reproduction or distribution if there were a commercial motive behind the actual making or distributing of the copies, if multiple copies were made or distributed, or if the photocopying activities were "systematic" in the sense that their aim was to substitute for subscriptions or purchases.[18]

The essentials of Section 108 consist of four key parts:

1. Eligibility requirements—Section 108(a)
2. Archival uses and preservation—Section 108(b) and (c)
3. Copies for private study, including lending and user-requests—Section 108(d) and (e); this is crucial for special libraries to avoid infringements like the Texaco and Legg Mason cases.
4. Additional limitations and enhancements including interlibrary loan, photocopy machines, and types of works that may be copied—Section 108, subsections (f), (g), (h) and (i).

Eligibility requirements: Section 108(a) applies only to a library or archive that makes a single copy of a work as long as that library is (1) open to the public, or at least researchers in the field, (2) copies are made without direct or indirect commercial advantage, and (3) copies include a copyright notice.[19] For special libraries to qualify, they must admit outside researchers in the field of their collection, even selectively.[20] For interlibrary loan aspects of the Section 108 requirements, if the library participates in reciprocal borrowing and lending, it may meet the qualification of being open to the public or to researchers in a specialized field.[21]

Archival uses and preservation: Section 108(b) and (c) allows eligible libraries to make up to three copies of a work for preservation and replacement purposes. For preservation of unpublished works, section 108(b) allows for the reproduction and distribution of three copies if it is "solely for purposes of preservation and security or for deposit for research use in another library or archives," and only if the copy is currently in the collections of the reproducing library or archives.[22]

Section 108(c) covers published works, allowing libraries to make three replacement copies of published works that are damaged, deteriorating, lost or stolen, or in obsolete formats. A format is considered "obsolete" if the machine or device necessary for the format "is no longer manufactured or is no longer reasonably available in the commercial marketplace." Section 108(c) also specifies that copies can only be prepared if, "after a reasonable effort," the library or archive determines that an unused replacement copy cannot be acquired at a fair price.[23] Both sections 108(b) and (c) specify that reproductions in digital formats may not be made available to the public outside the premises of the library or archives.[24]

The Digital Millennium Copyright Act[25] amended these rights related to preservation in digital formats for both published and unpublished works as specified above. However, works that are reproduced in digital format may not be "made available to the public outside of the premises of the library or archives."[26]

Copies for private study, including lending and user-requests: Sections 108(d) and (e) allow libraries and archives to make copies for library customers to study and keep. In addition, when a for-profit library meets the requirements of subsection (a), this one-copy rule could apply to such special libraries without the need for permission of the copyright owner. Section 108(d) permits the copying of an article or small excerpts of a copyrighted work.[27] It has three main stipulations:

1. The copy becomes the property of the library customer;[28]
2. The library has no notice that the copy is for any use other than private study, scholarship, or research;[29] and
3. The library displays a copyright notice for library customer.[30]

Section 108(e) permits reproduction and distribution of an entire work or substantial part, rather than just an excerpt or article, at the request of a library customer.[31] The 108(d) conditions likewise apply here, but section 108(e) also requires that libraries or archives "first determine, on the basis of a reasonable investigation," that a copy cannot be obtained at a "fair price."[32]

Additional limitations and enhancements are covered in subsections (f), (g), (h), and (i): including more details on interlibrary loan, photocopy machines, and types of works that may be copied. See Chapter 7 on academic libraries for greater details on interlibrary loan and document delivery including the CONTU Rule of Five, which could be vital with for-profit special libraries. The U.S. Copyright Office has prepared a discussion document reviewing Section 108 in the context of the digital environment and special copyright exceptions for libraries and archives. The discussion publication is entitled "Section 108 of Title 17."[33] See endnote for website URL to view document.

PERMISSIONS, POLICIES, AND PURCHASING AGREEMENTS

Besides common copyright matters shared among special libraries from Sections 107 and 108 of U.S. Copyright Law, permissions, policies, and purchasing licensed information resources associated with copyright matters are integral to all types of special libraries. This is especially for when they must determine whether such scenarios are fair use or when permission is required.

Many special librarians use commercial document delivery services where copyright royalties are paid up front, whereas other librarians establish accounts with the Copyright Clearance Center (CCC) to obtain permission and make payments on their behalf. Yet other special libraries have experts that understand Sections 107 and 108 and ask for permission and make payments directly to copyright content owners.

It is important to make certain such document delivery services include copyright royalties in your payment; otherwise, you may be responsible to obtain permission and pay for copyright. A single document purchase is for one employee's use only, not for further employee distribution. Either request multiple copies from a document delivery service or ask for permission to make additional copies in-house. Some document delivery services provide electronic copies of reprints for multiple users of the same document, with copyright royalties prepaid.

Copyright policies reflecting interlibrary loan and licensing concerns for use of subscription information databases, such as sharing copyrighted content, are often established and posted to employees of a parent institution of a special library. Such policies are especially helpful for customers of for-profit libraries to avoid costly infringement scenarios, as covered above.

It is wise for libraries to create a database site of license agreements for librarians and employees to review. Subscription commercial databases may have different copy-sharing restrictions or sanctions. For example, computer software licenses are often limited to one user. Before purchasing for library or department use, read the fine print. Some software only allows one-user-at-a-time or only a single user period. Investigate if a cloud-based, one-user-at-a-time capability is available. Otherwise, a multiple-use license or multiple purchases are a wise choice.

CORPORATE FOR-PROFIT LIBRARIES

The retrieval of information in a global knowledge economy is beneficial to the competitiveness and bottom line of a for-profit company. Therefore, one would think that corporate libraries and information centers would be highly valued. Yet closures, staff reductions, and reorganizations abound in many corporate libraries. While this "rightsizing" and reorganization of corporate libraries occurs, the need for librarians to promote IP awareness remains more vital than ever before. As shown with the two high-profile companies above, for-profit special libraries of larger institutions are potential targets for copyright infringement lawsuits. Information literacy and training workshops related to responsible information sharing, copyright, fair use, licensing, and other IPs are essential. Librarians and information specialists are ideal for this role. Constance Ard considers that "training is an ongoing necessity in the knowledge culture" for corporate libraries and information centers.[34] Librarians and specialists in corporate libraries offering such IP awareness is perhaps the one of the best means for them to demonstrate value to their company.

Corporate library professionals may potentially deal more often with IP restrictions than other special library professionals due to their information management roles within a for-profit organization. In some instances, they may wear multiple hats as solo librarians for an entire company. The unique IPs and information rights associated with corporate library professionals may include copyrights, trademarks, patents, trade secrets, nondisclosure agreements, inventor/scientist lab notebooks, copyright clearance for document delivery, licensing agreements for journal databases and computer software, web content posting and sharing policies, copyright works made for hire, patent assignments for inventions, and company IP policies.

IP MANAGEMENT AND AUDIT

One of the major challenges in for-profit corporate libraries is the ongoing debate about how many fair use (Section 107) and special provision (Section 108) exceptions are available compared to nonprofit libraries. Certain applications that may be fair use in nonprofit libraries may require permission in for-profit libraries. Copyright compliance is not so simple as demonstrated in the *Texaco* and *Legg Mason* case scenarios above. Conversely, the parent institution of a for-profit corporate library usually holds valuable IP of its own, including trademarks and patents for the company's products or services. Besides legal use of others' copyrights, the corporate library personnel must often understand IP laws from a creator/owner perspective to safeguard and manage the IP of their company. An audit of a company's IP is helpful so that one knows what the company owns as well as the value of the IP.

Ian Cockburn of DLA Piper global law firm defines an IP audit as "a systematic review of the IP assets owned, used or acquired by a business."[35] For example, auditing the company-owned copyrighted works found in its library may include the following:

- Product user manuals and guides
- In-house created computer software and databases
- Product-related website and other electronic resources created in-house
- Sales literature and promotional media
- Product designs such as sculptural copyrights
- Architecture blueprints and building designs

Some companies perform an IP audit beyond the copyrighted works listed above, such as patents, trade secrets, and trademarks. A comprehensive IP audit provides a record to identify nontangible assets and opportunities to derive new revenue. An IP audit could reveal underutilized IP assets, identify threats to a company's bottom line, and formulate strategies to maintain or improve the market position of a company.[36] For more about auditing IP, go to the World Intellectual Property Organization (WIPO) website at https://www.wipo.int/, keyword search: IP audit, for many free useful guides.

All of this IP management accentuates the significance of copyright and other IP awareness within corporate libraries. As noted earlier, instances of fair use could apply with for-profit libraries and information centers when the library is open to the public, or is open to researchers in a specialized field, or participates in reciprocal interlibrary loan agreements.

COPYRIGHT FUNDAMENTALS IN A FOR-PROFIT SETTING

The growing world of digital information on the web has supplied a wealth of information. With this abundance of information comes responsibility for legal and ethical use in the corporate culture. Copyright fundamentals in a for-profit environment are reviewed below and include:

- CCC for internal and external permissions
- Downloading and sharing free web resources
- Document delivered papers and e-articles
- Onsite database research content and storage
- Database licensing and article handling
- Computer software licensing agreements and legal sharing among multiple users
- Copyrighting the corporate library organization's software and databases
- Establishing an onsite library copyright policy
- Establishing an electronic communications policy

Copyright Clearance Center's Copyright License

As copyright compliance is an onerous challenge in a for-profit setting, the CCC offers a blanket agreement for legal copying of a library's paper and electronic format copyrighted resources. Subscribing to this type of blanket copyright permission service helps researchers to legally make such copies. It is important to note that just because a corporate library owns a copy of a copyrighted work does not mean that anyone can make copies of such resources without permission, unless it is fair use. CCC may also be used on an as-needed basis for such copyright fees.

At times, the CCC or a stand-alone document delivery service may not be able to provide permission for some works. In such cases, a for-profit corporate library or information center should always request permission from a publisher or author when required or needed by a member of the organization.

Multiple Copyright Compliance Levels

In a corporate environment, there is often a need for multiple copyright clearance levels. For-profit library copyright compliance policies usually only recognize internal use of copied documents and external use of large-volume document reprints when there could be a unique need for external distribution of single journal article copies for individual outside customers or fulfillment of government regulatory requirements. When this is the case, separate permission by the copyright owner may differ from typical internal use or large-scale reprints. To assure company associates that their requested documents are compliant with such unique external requests, a special copyright notice might state something about external use permission for "this copy only" as copyright cleared. CCC and some commercial document delivery services offer copyright compliance for disparate internal and external applications.

Sharing Web Documents

If a work is public domain or clearly labeled free to copy, such as open access or Creative Commons (CC), you are free to copy and share it others. Because a URL link is considered a fact, you would generally be allowed to share links without permission. Blogs should be treated as copyrighted works. When your use is indeed a fair use of any copyrighted work, this does *not* mean unlimited use. Especially in a for-profit environment, it is wise to obtain permission before sharing copies of copyrighted works to avoid unlawful systematic copies, as noted in the *Texaco* and *Legg Mason* cases above.

Document Delivery in For-Profit, Corporate Environments

Make certain outside document delivery services include copyright royalties in your payment; otherwise, you are responsible to obtain permission and pay for copyright. As noted above, single-document purchase is usually for one employee's use only and not for further employee distribution. Either request multiple copies from a document delivery service or ask for permission to make additional copies in-house. As noted above, CCC and document delivery services often provide ePrints for multiple users of the same document.

Onsite Resources and Commercial Database Content for Internal Use Only

Is a for-profit library posting articles on its company intranet from subscribed journals? If so, it is important to read the fine print in the journal subscription agreements. Are employees sharing electronic articles from subscribed databases? If so, the library or the parent organization should negotiate to use persistent/constant links for internal sharing with other company employees. Are company employees photocopying outside source reports, articles, and book chapters? Unless the company has a CCC blanket payment program or only small fair use excerpts are copied, then permission should be requested and correspondence documented in writing.

Sending a friend or colleague an electronic news article is fine so long as it is only the URL link. Personal or occasional sharing may be fair use. However, recurrent-use distribution of the same resource is *not* fair use.

Journal article licensing may be negotiated in all types of library environments. Some article databases may have licenses that prevent copying for others. Try to negotiate for research-use copies, including:

- Intranet access
- Unlimited/limited number of internal users

- Persistent/constant links
- Table of content alerts
- Posting PDF documents on intranet database
- E-archives, abstracts versus full-text; html or PDF format, etc.

As mentioned earlier, some libraries have created an in-house database of license agreements for librarians and employees to review. Each commercial database may have different copying requirements.

Computer software licensing has similar requirements as mentioned earlier in this chapter. Read the contract fine print before purchasing or renewing such subscriptions. Open-access software is often free to share, but look for any potential restrictions, such as CC stipulations for commercial use.

Copyrighting Software of the Library's Parent Organization

Utility patent protects the underlying function of computer software. Copyright can protect against unauthorized copying of software script/code and even database formats. The copyright term of protection is seventy-plus years versus twenty years with a utility patent. Open-access computer software is often registered with CC.

Establishing a Copyright and Related Policies

A copyright policy provides guidelines for users of copyrighted works. It helps to determine whether permission is necessary. It also helps to prevent unauthorized use of copyrighted works. Even when libraries have a CCC licensed plan or pay-per-use account, a copyright policy is useful, as some copyrighted works are not covered. The organization's legal counsel should help establish guidelines.

Establishing a copyright policy helps educate administrators regarding policy and consequences, particularly when they are represented during policy development. This supports ongoing copyright awareness for all employees on the items in the bulleted list above. The policy may delegate who will deal with repeat violators and how a company takes action or accepts consequences.

A copyright policy generally includes defining copyright and clarifying fair use, works for hire, preinvention assignment agreements, and electronic communications. The first, fair use, should be reflected in relation to balancing fair use and the rights of copyright owners as well as fair use of the company's own copyrighted works. Details on interlibrary loan, document delivery, and licensing agreements are helpful. Indicating who is in charge of copyright compliance and how to handle infringements are vital too.[37]

A works-made-for-hire policy could be part of a copyright policy. This is especially important for contracted works of those who are not long-term employees of a business. This is discussed further in the section below on church, faith-based, and theological libraries. See a related guide from the U.S. Copyright Office (https://www.copyright.gov/circs/circ09.pdf) for more about works made for hire and U.S. Copyright Law.

Another work-related IP policy could be associated with preinvention assignment agreements. Assignment agreement licenses are fairly common in business. These licensing contracts are intended for engineers and scientists but may be required for all employees throughout an organization, regardless of their capacity to invent. These agreements are also known as an employment agreement contract, signed upon initial hiring of an employee. In academia, commercialization agreements are often utilized by technology transfer offices. Assignment agreements may legally secure all IP rights of an employee's creative and innovative work within and outside the range of his or her employment.

Electronics communications policies are often an ethical and company-related policy document. A written policy should be posted for all to see. It includes legal liability aspects related to all electronic communications, web, intranet, and email, among others. Another important topic includes appropriate versus inappropriate uses, such as personal use that affects work productivity. It prohibits illegal or unethical activities. In some cases, employer monitoring rights are implemented, if warranted. Policy violation consequences are clearly stated.

PATENT LANDSCAPE SEARCHING AND COMPETITIVE INTELLIGENCE

Patent landscape searching supports the legal and business research purposes of a company. Besides auditing the patents of the company and the obvious identification of technological competitors, such patent landscape searches help corporate library customers to conduct a patent literature review of prior art, as covered in Chapter 4. The patents retrieved allow the researcher to analyze patent trends and to forecast technological developments that support strategic research and product development. In addition, a patent landscape analysis could help to identify and avoid potential infringements. Applying a patent landscape outlook often identifies promising patents for market viability and identifying technological vacuums and hotspots.[38]

Patent landscaping and business trends are easy to collect via free online patent-searching databases, including those covered in Chapter 4. A patent landscape search often realizes competitive intelligence and market opportunities, identifies potential customers, and determines niche markets of a specific patented product or technology. As covered in depth in Chapter 4, one is able to search patent databases by inventor or company, patent number, or invention keyword. A searcher is able to identify relevant patent classification groups and analyze patent trends by company or other unique bibliographic fields of the patents. With these databases, one is able to look at patent references backward (cited works on original patent application) and forward (citing works of a patent in future patents) to compare technology's level of development. It is important to note that the number of forward citations of patent increases over time.[39] The PubWEST database (available at most patent and trademark resource centers, or PTRCs) and the Espacenet online database offer spreadsheet conversion tools to display one's findings via visualization tools such as bar charts, graphs, and cluster graphics. PubWEST and Espacenet provide assignee/applicant field searching to isolate patents by company name too.

When one pursues a patent landscape analysis, one must ask five questions. These five questions also provide the five steps to the patent landscape searching process demonstrated below:

1. In what areas does a company patent?
2. Who are its competitors?
3. How strong is a patent?
4. What is the patenting trend in a specified field?
5. Can we predict a likely scenario for the future?

A hypothetical patent landscape search is demonstrated below with new and improved snowboard bindings classified as the truncated CPC code A63C10/, entitled Snowboard Bindings. Figure 10.1 displays the snowboard binding patent document example of our patent landscape search.

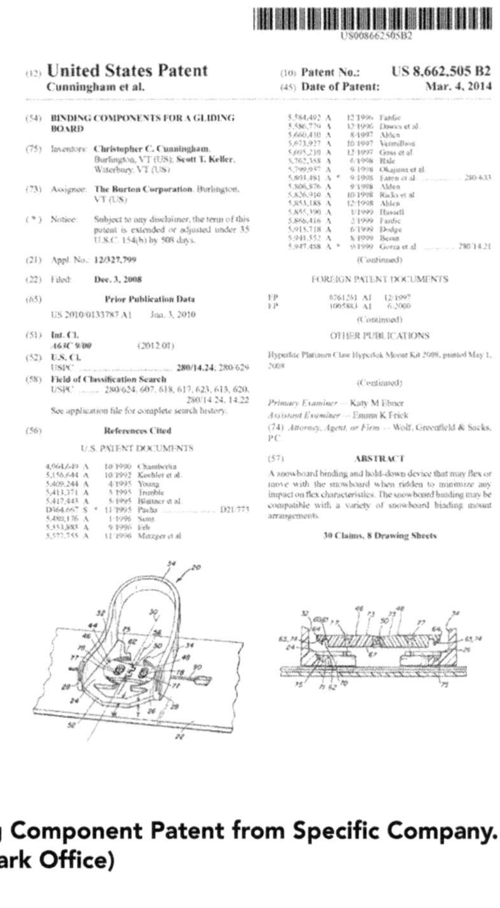

US008662505B2

(12) **United States Patent**
Cunningham et al.

(10) **Patent No.: US 8,662,505 B2**
(45) **Date of Patent: Mar. 4, 2014**

(54) **BINDING COMPONENTS FOR A GLIDING BOARD**

(75) Inventors: **Christopher C. Cunningham**, Burlington, VT (US); **Scott T. Keller**, Waterbury, VT (US)

(73) Assignee: **The Burton Corporation**, Burlington, VT (US)

(*) Notice: Subject to any disclaimer, the term of this patent is extended or adjusted under 35 U.S.C. 154(b) by 508 days.

(21) Appl. No.: **12/327,799**

(22) Filed: **Dec. 3, 2008**

(65) **Prior Publication Data**

US 2010/0133787 A1 Jun. 3, 2010

(51) **Int. Cl.**
A63C 9/00 (2012.01)

(52) **U.S. Cl.**
USPC **280/14.24**; 280/629

(58) **Field of Classification Search**
USPC 280/624, 607, 618, 617, 623, 613, 620, 280/14.24, 14.22
See application file for complete search history.

(56) **References Cited**

U.S. PATENT DOCUMENTS

4,964,649 A		10/1990	Chamberlin	
5,156,644 A		10/1992	Koehler et al.	
5,409,244 A		4/1995	Young	
5,413,371 A		5/1995	Trimble	
5,417,443 A		5/1995	Blattner et al.	
D364,667 S	*	11/1995	Pacha	D21/773
5,480,176 A		1/1996	Sims	
5,553,883 A		9/1996	Erb	
5,577,755 A		11/1996	Metzger et al.	
5,584,492 A		12/1996	Fardie	
5,586,779 A		12/1996	Dawes et al.	
5,660,410 A		8/1997	Alden	
5,673,927 A		10/1997	Vermillion	
5,695,210 A		12/1997	Goss et al.	
5,762,358 A		6/1998	Hale	
5,799,957 A		9/1998	Okajima et al.	
5,803,481 A	*	9/1998	Eaton et al.	280/633
5,806,876 A		9/1998	Alden	
5,826,910 A		10/1998	Ricks et al.	
5,853,188 A		12/1998	Alden	
5,855,390 A		1/1999	Hassell	
5,868,416 A		2/1999	Fardie	
5,915,718 A		6/1999	Dodge	
5,941,552 A		8/1999	Beran	
5,947,488 A	*	9/1999	Gorza et al.	280/14.21

(Continued)

FOREIGN PATENT DOCUMENTS

EP	0761251 A1	12/1997
EP	1005883 A1	6/2000

(Continued)

OTHER PUBLICATIONS

Hyperlite Platinum Claw Hyperlok Mount Kit 2008, printed May 1, 2008

(Continued)

Primary Examiner — Katy M Ebner
Assistant Examiner — Emma K Frick
(74) *Attorney, Agent, or Firm* — Wolf, Greenfield & Sacks, P.C.

(57) **ABSTRACT**

A snowboard binding and hold-down device that may flex or move with the snowboard when ridden to minimize any impact on flex characteristics. The snowboard binding may be compatible with a variety of snowboard binding mount arrangements.

30 Claims, 8 Drawing Sheets

Figure 10.1

Snowboard Binding Component Patent from Specific Company. (Courtesy U.S. Patent and Trademark Office)

To determine the classification of a technology, one should conduct a preliminary patent search, as demonstrated in Chapter 4 with the *Seven Step Strategy*. Then by utilizing a classification gateway of any free or commercial patent searching database, one should be able to locate classifications to complete a patent landscape search. Five questions about this process are answered below. The first question refers to patents from a specific company; the second is for multiple companies.

1. *In what areas does a specific company patent?*

   Start from the PubWEST or the Espacenet database to avoid manual aggregation of content. Search assignee fields for all years to get patents from a single company.

   Go into the first patent listed and look for primary CPC class number. For design patents, use the former U.S. Patent Classification class and subclass codes. See Chapter 4, Patent Searching, for details on classification systems. Navigate through the results list; note, first, the primary class numbers on each patent. Aggregate the patents by primary class number to determine which one(s) predominate(s).

   After you have located the patent listing from a single company from PubWEST or Espacenet, you should be able to create a grid display to import the essential fields to an Excel spreadsheet via a CSV function. Once the content is in an Excel spreadsheet, you should be able to consolidate the CPC classes by count to compare how many patents are listed by class for your company. Next, select one of the visualization tools from Excel to display the numbers by count such as a pie chart, as shown in figure 10.2 below.

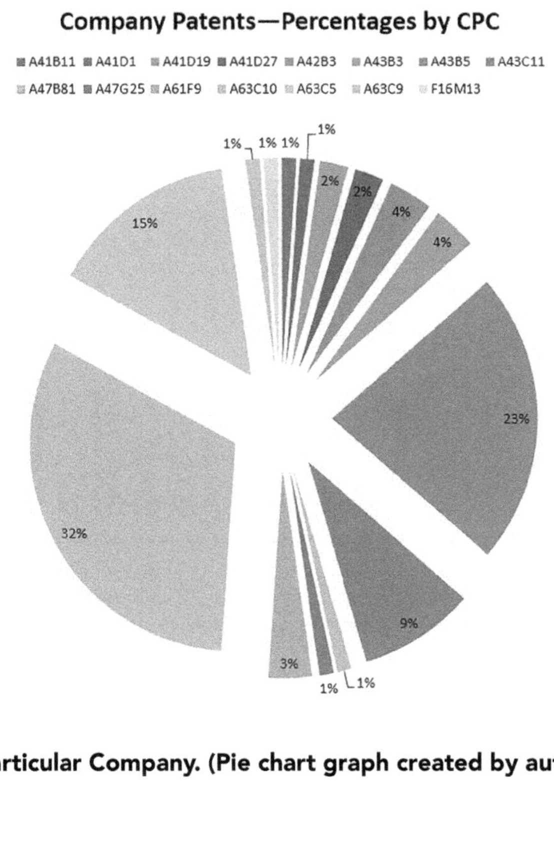

Figure 10.2
Patents from a Particular Company. (Pie chart graph created by author John Schlipp)

2. *Who are its multiple company competitors?*

   To view the competitive patents of a company, search the current classification field, using the classes found. CPC classes may need to be truncated. For example, if the closely related CPC classes are A63C 10/04, A63C 10/22, and so on, truncate the CPC class as A63C 10$. Go into the first patent and note assignee name. Navigate to move through the results list; note assignee for each patent. Aggregate the patents by assignee for a tally count to see which firms have patented most heavily in this area. After the content is transferred to a spreadsheet as directed in step one, and select one of the visualization tools such as a bar graph to display the number of patents listed for each competitor. See figure 10.3 below.

3. *How strong is a patent?*

   To determine the strength of a patent, enter the patent number in one of the databases suggested above. Examine the patent document for the following strengths:

   - Is the assignee company well-known?
   - Is there less than a two-year period between application and granted patent date?
   - Are there ample prior art citations?
   - Does prior art include nonpatent literature?

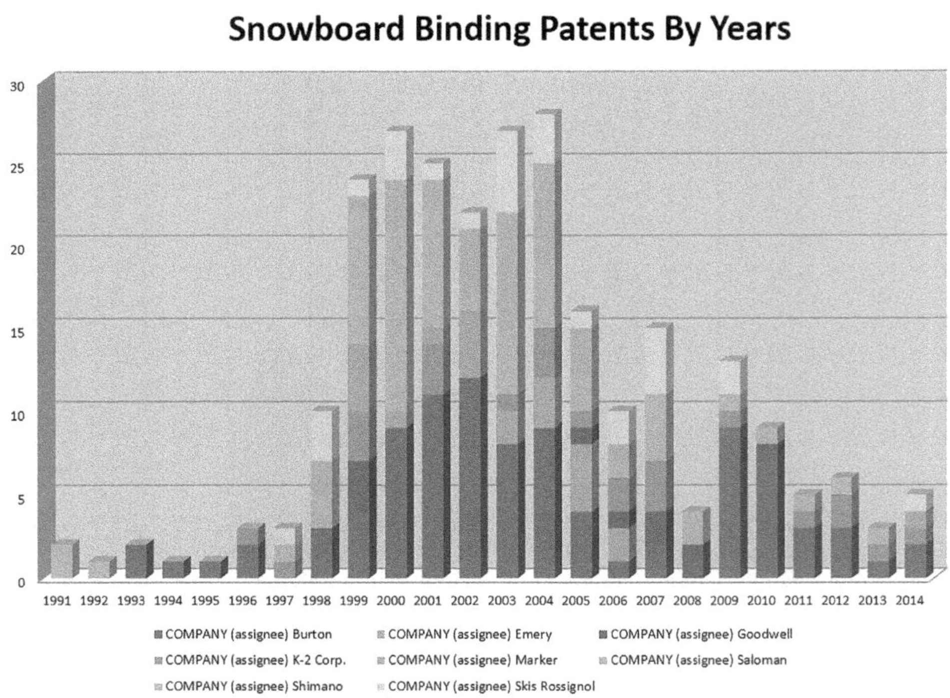

Figure 10.3

Comparison of Same Class Patents by Competitors and by Years. (Bar graph chart created by author John Schlipp)

- Is there more than one inventor?
- Are foreign patents cited?
- If a patent is cited "reference by" many later patents, this validates its strength/value.

4. *What is the patenting trend in a specified field?*

   Search the current classification field for the area of investigation. Examine results by frequency and year. Also, analyze the movement in the number of patents over time. These statistics can be collected when researching assignee and company areas as researched in Question 2.

5. *Can you predict a likely scenario for the future?*
   - Review trends from patent searches completed above.
   - Search patent databases for applications by current classification number to see patents pending in the same area.
   - Subscribe to free patent application alert services such as the one the USPTO partners with LexisNexis, available at https://www.uspatentappalerts.com.

Other related resources that patent landscape searchers should review to complete their analysis include:

- Company annual reports and sales figures
- Business periodicals and newspaper articles (trade journals)
- Mergers/partnerships/licensing agreements
- Budget devoted to research and development
- Government/university research connections
- Track record in developing new products
- Current litigation news and alerts
- Subscription business databases of the organization's library

The USPTO also offers a Patent Assignment Search database. Patent assignment records provide history of ownership transfers. Looking up company names in this database determines the most current assignee data on record. Often assignee names listed on patents are not the current owner found in the Assignment database. Such information could provide clues to future trends of companies listed.

Numerous articles are published on patent landscape searching techniques for business researchers. This concept, shown above, was originally shared with PTRC librarians by colleague Donna Hopkins in her article "Using Patents to Plot Business Trends,"[40] published in *DttP (Documents to the People).*

OPEN ACCESS AND OPEN SOURCE

Lastly, open access and open source are growing areas that not only supplement a collection of subscription databases and onsite resources but also offer freely accessible scholarly and scientific research and resources with no fees. Open-access journal repositories and indexed databases include the following:

- Directory of Open Access Journals (DOAL) https://doaj.org/
- MEDLINE and PubMed https://www.nlm.nih.gov/bsd/pmresources.html
- Science.gov https://www.science.gov/
- National Technical Information Service (NTIS) https://www.ntis.gov/
- GoogleScholar https://scholar.google.com/

Open-access books are easy to locate via the Directory of Open Access Books (DOAB) found at https://doabooks.org/. Not only do such open-access resources support scholarly and scientific research needs of corporate libraries, but business-related titles are also more common now. However, one should be mindful of any open-access notices, such as those from CC, to see if there are any restrictions for further distribution beyond authorized individual research. Also, open-source resources are available to support corporate libraries. These are often free and include customizable computer software programs, some specifically designed for library applications.

As with all library environments, a corporate organization's information professionals should not become the copyright police. Following license agreements and promoting copyright awareness should be the library's number-one copyright information literacy role. Increasingly, IPs, including patents and trademarks, are now recognized as more valuable assets of for-profit companies than in the past. Some companies have dedicated IP departments with a dedicated patent librarian to administer their growing proprietary rights. Special librarians and information professionals, with the additional background they may gain from this book, may be well poised to offer added-value to the administration of IP and information rights.

FOR-PROFIT OR NONPROFIT LAW LIBRARIES

Nonprofit law libraries include those in academic institutions serving faculty, students, and government agencies for employees; private law firm libraries are for-profit. The Law Library of Congress, established in 1832, primarily serves Congress.[41] In some instances, academic law libraries of publicly funded colleges or law libraries that support government agencies may provide research assistance to attorneys and walk-in public patrons. Private law firm librarians assist lawyers and paralegals in their practice.[42] Recognizing the fair use continuum noted earlier in this chapter between for-profit and nonprofit is helpful when applying exemptions of the U.S. Copyright Law. This is why one should recognize whether a law library is for-profit or nonprofit when conducting a fair use analysis.

Specialized IP Research and Resources in Law

In law libraries, librarians normally direct their customers to the associated IP resources and assist them in how to use the research tools. For example, many nonprofit law libraries open to the community encounter walk-in customers from the public. Unless the librarian is a licensed attorney specializing in IP, he or she should be mindful not to give legal advice. For further legal information, librarians could offer referrals to free and low-cost legal services.[43] Such customer encounters of all types offer librarians teaching opportunities with reference guides to instruct how to perform routine research of IP resources in the collection. Law librarians often create and publish specialized legal research guides to support the curriculum of their law school.

Many academic law schools utilize open access for their law journals published on their open archival digital repositories. Such free and open distribution of academic law journals offers wider circulation for lesser-known titles. Many of these publications represent specialized law practice areas, including IP.[44] For example, Cornell Law School offers the *Journal of Open Access to Law*, while Stanford Law School produces the *Stanford Technology Law Review*, which includes IP related to science, technology, and industry. The development of open-access books and open educational resources for law instruction is offered at sites such as CALI (Center for Computer-Assisted Legal Instruction, at https://www.cali.org/).

Private law firms offer structured specialized research guides and collections. For librarians there, IP could include federal statutes as well as state frameworks. Such IP law research guides could include books and subject headings, current awareness resources, legal practice aids, treatises and loose-leaf services, statutes and legislative histories, case law and administrative law research, and journal and law review finding tips.[45]

Both free and subscription patent and trademark databases support law libraries that specialize in patents or trademarks. For private law firms and some universities, commercial databases offer advanced searching features such as saving search sets, customizable search result lists with filtering, immediate foreign language translations, graphical patent family analysis, visualization tools, identification of highest assignees, peak classifications, systematic classifications tailored to chemical structures, reactions, biological sequences, and more.[46]

Subscription Resource Licensing in both Nonprofit and For-Profit

Besides the instructional and current awareness support of the IP collection in a law library, other unique copyright and licensing concerns include licensing restrictions and customer access of electronic content such as subscription databases. For example, with law firms, immediate access to resources is often vital to their professional responsibilities such as information for court cases. Mobile technologies place a virtual law library at the fingertips of its customers. Licensing of the databases and document delivery services is vital to supporting such timely needs of lawyers.

Because law libraries resources are legal in nature, IP should be a concern close to their core ideals. Such inherent IP awareness should promote the cautious outlook in copyright compliance and avoiding infringement. Once again, Sections 107 and 108 of the U.S. Copyright Act are just as vital for private law firm libraries to observe as corporate libraries. Going back to *American Geophysical Union v. Texaco* and *Lowry's Reports, Inc. v. Legg Mason, Inc.*, law librarians have an opportunity to work with the management of their firms to establish copyright policies about the subscription databases and their document delivery services. Once a policy is established, it should be publicized with educational efforts to explain "the firm's positions on whether and to what extent fair use applies to the reproduction and distribution of copyrighted works within the firm."[47] Case examples such as *Geophysical Union v. Texaco*, and *Lowry's Reports v. Legg Mason* could illustrate preventative measures as well as reminders of the damage costs associated with both cases.

When law libraries negotiate with subscription databases and electronic resources, familiarity of Sections 107 and 108 of the U.S. Copyright Law are helpful to maintain such terms related to copyright and IP. Understanding the customer needs of the law library assure that negotiated terms are not only a favorable value for the library but also satisfactory for the authorized users of the contract. Law librarians must be attentive to user restrictions in a licensing agreement. Often contracts include "a confusing array of legal restrictions imposed on patron access and usage."[48] A negotiating strategies paper, published by Mattson and Schneider in the American Association of Law Libraries (AALL) magazine *Spectrum*, reminds us that, "the end user—typically a lawyer or law student—is not necessarily the entity facing a legal risk if he or she violates the terms of the license."[49]

The AALL publishes *AALL Principles & Practices for Licensing Electronic Resources*,[50] an essential guide with strategies, checklists, and appendixes with additional resources to foster an effective negotiation for licensing contracts of electronic resources. Principles and practices covered include licensing preparedness, licensing components, authorized use and authorized users, copyright and IP, archiving, usage tracking and user privacy, termination/renewal, dispute resolution, and warranties/quality of service. The *Principles and Practices* publication includes much material regarding inclusion of fair use provisions of Section 107 and interlibrary loan provisions of Section 108 in contract content. The section on authorized users' practice includes a principle vital for lawyers with their court and customer interactions: "Licensors should agree that occasional and irregular use of limited portions of the licensed materials for inclusion in organization documents, communications to members of the organization or clients, or incorporating into government agency or court filings is permitted."[51]

MEDICAL AND HEALTH SCIENCE FOR-PROFIT OR NONPROFIT LIBRARIES

Medical and health sciences libraries may be found in both for-profit and nonprofit settings. Some are academic libraries at colleges and universities. For-profit health science libraries often include corporate libraries at pharmaceutical and health product companies, such as Eli Lilly or Merck. As such libraries are highly specialized, in some instances library professional staff may have PhDs in health, biology, or chemistry. Often those advanced-degree colleagues have some level of library background or an associate's or bachelor's degree in library science to complement their advanced degrees. Document delivery and copyright compliance as well as research and technical services may offer a vital role in which those with only the library degrees could fit well.

Medical and health sciences libraries are fundamental to both patient-related and research-based environments, including educating nursing professionals. When accessing information for scientists, physicians, or nurses of these organizations, timely delivery of information and copyright compliance is critical. The Medical Library Association (MLA) affirms "knowledge of copyright is essential for health sciences librarians, faculty, and those who use the library and its resources."[52]

Licensing of electronic resource subscriptions is also vital to ensure copyright compliance. Often the manager of the document delivery area of a health science library is responsible for copyright and licensing matters. Licensing considerations such as the following apply to authorized use and users:

1. Concurrent use—How many organization customers have access to the same resource at the same time? Some databases limit the number of concurrent users depending upon the subscription agreement.
2. Sharing—Fair use and interlibrary lending transaction: if your organization plans to lend to other libraries, review the ILL lending authorization agreed upon within the licensing contract.
3. Delivery and access—Do you have proxy server remote access off-campus for network access or not?
4. Consortial licensing—Besides larger hospital networks or universities with branch campuses, does your licensing agreement permit ILL sharing with library consortia?
5. Other legal issues—These include indemnification issues with third parties and lawsuits based upon information delivered to physicians or scientists.[53]

Copyright awareness begins with introducing the basics of copyright, such as creators and consumers of copyrighted work, explaining Section 106 of U.S. Copyright Law about the rights of copyright owners and then Section 107 about fair use rights of consumers. Specifics about Section 108 related to ILL, avoiding systematic copying, and sharing full documents from subscription databases and the web, as noted earlier in this chapter, should also be covered. Such awareness one-on-one or in formalized instructional settings supports the advocacy charge[54] of the Medical Library Association as well as its Standard 8 for hospital libraries, which articulates that all knowledge-based information functions are "performed in compliance with applicable federal, state, and local laws and regulations."[55]

Open-Access Research

The open-access movement of health sciences and medical information resources made significant progress with the National Institutes of Health (NIH) Public Access Policy[56] implemented in 2008. The NIH is the largest funder of medical research worldwide and primary financial supporter of nonclassified U.S. federal government research. The policy requires that peer-reviewed research articles describing research funded by the NIH must be made publicly available for free through PubMed Central within twelve months of publication. PubMed Central is a digital repository for such publications. Copyright is reserved by the authors with use of one of the CC licenses. Since the implementation of the policy, additional open-access resources are available freely via online open access directories and some subscription database services. Open-access resources support the growing number of online educational programs for health and nursing professionals.

The TEACH Act, covered in earlier chapters, is often utilized for posting copyrighted content online for such educational programs. To qualify to use the TEACH Act, the institution and its instructors should be accredited with a certification organization, such as the American Nurses Credentialing Center (ANCC, located at https://www.nursingworld.org/ancc/).

MUSEUMS, SPECIAL COLLECTIONS, AND ARCHIVES FOR-PROFIT OR NONPROFIT LIBRARIES

IP rights are significant in the daily function and utility of museums, galleries, special collections and archives. Typically, museums or galleries have special collections or archives, whereas special collections or archives exist on their own outside of museums or galleries in other institutions. While Section 108 of the U.S. Copyright Law specifically limits its copyright exemptions to libraries and archives, nowhere does it mention museums. However, Section 108 could apply to libraries and archives within museums if they are open to the public or to specialized researchers. What makes museums and galleries similar to libraries and archives here are the unique and analogous IP topics to museums. Examples include open-access digital repositories, orphan works, restrictions of unpublished public domain works and privacy, copyright and preservation, copyright conveyance for donations and gifts, moral rights of artists and authors, fair use of copyrights and trademarks, among others.

The American Association of Museums connects IP to collection building and preservation, researching and interpreting collection content, organizing exhibits, and providing educational programs and services. Museums also use works created by others while simultaneously creating their own original works for exhibits, selling products, and licensing their brand for others to use. The Association believes that:

> As educational institutions, museums are also entitled to fair use of the copyrighted works of others. A working knowledge of the basic principles of intellectual property is essential if museums are to respect and maintain the legal relationships that define and govern these various roles. . . . While museums are concerned about protecting ownership rights, they are at the same time concerned about protecting and preserving fair use and use of works in the public domain.[57]

Museums, special collections, and archives personnel dealing with copyright matters include archivists, curators, registrars, special collection librarians, records managers, and others. Copyright concerns could include accurately informing customers about copyright ownership and reproduction rights in papers, records, and images in a collection; creating user-friendly yet copyright compliant polices for using a collection; negotiating copyright ownership conveyance when acquiring items from donors; advising an institution's personnel of its publishing policies; and protecting the institution's own rights as authors and photographer.[58]

COPYRIGHT CONVEYANCE OF ORIGINAL CREATIVE WORKS TO MUSEUMS

"Ownership of a copyright . . . is distinctive from ownership of any material object in which the work is embodied."[59] —U.S. Copyright Law, Section 202

Artists could maintain their copyright when they donate their works of art, or the donor of the work may not hold the copyright. The assignment of copyright often rests with the artist; it is not automatically assigned to the museum as part of a Deed of Gift. If copyright of the gift is an issue and not included in the Deed of Gift, then a separate "nonexclusive use" agreement must be obtained from the copyright holder.[60] Possessing the container does not grant copyright ownership. For further details, see a free online international guide entitled, *WIPO Guide on Managing Intellectual Property for Museums*, at https://www.wipo.int/copyright/en/museums_ip/.

The term "Deed of Gift" is one of the most common obstacles as it involves a contract. Similar to licensing, a contract can override any fair use or special library provisions to support research customers in certain situations. As noted in the inset box about conveyance, copyright scholar Peter Hirtle and colleagues affirm that

> laws relevant to the physical embodiment of the collection item can also be important, most notably personal property law and contract. For example, it is common for material held by an institution to have been acquired according to a deed of gift, loan agreement, or other transfer document. Such documentation may include restrictions on how the repository may use the material."[61]

Hirtle also points out that failure to comply with a Deed of Gift could result in a breach of contract and that

> restrictions specified in contract take precedence over any rights specified in copyright. This is particularly true for the Section 108 libraries and archives exemptions; Section 108(f)(4) states explicitly that nothing in the section overrides any "contractual obligations assumed at any time by the library or archives when it obtained a copy . . . of a work in its collections."

Section 108 Special Provisions to Support Needs of Research Customers

Once again, Section 108[62] of the U.S. Copyright Law specifically lists copyright exceptions that favor archives. Archivists may make copies for preservation, replacement, or security and may make or permit others to make single copies of printed materials or manuscripts for research. However, musical, pictorial, graphic, or sculptural works or motion pictures are not covered and must refer to fair use (Section 107), or one must ask for permission from the copyright holder.

Archives may also reproduce up to three copies of an unpublished work for its own use, to distribute to another repository for preservation and security, or to deposit in another repository for research use. Archives may produce up to three copies of a published work to replace a damaged, deteriorating, lost, or stolen item, or if the item format becomes obsolete and if, after a reasonable effort, no unused replacement is obtainable at a fair price. Digitally reproduced copies under these circumstances may not be distributed to the public outside of the archives.

As covered in Chapter 7 regarding interlibrary loan, Section 108 permits archives to copy and distribute, for private study, scholarship, or research, fair use portions of articles from a periodical or small parts of any copyrighted work. A copyright notice must be included, as is the case with ILL copies. (See the U.S. Copyright Office website at https://www.copyright.gov/title17/92chap1.html#108 for other related archival topics in Section 108.)

Unpublished Works and Orphan Works

As covered in Chapter 2, it is fairly simple to determine if an item is in the public domain or requires permission. However, unpublished works in the special collections of museums and archives introduce IP challenges unlike those associated with other libraries. Jean Dryden, of the International Council of Archives, Paris, France, stresses that "the unpublished nature of the majority of archival holdings has several consequences. Rights holders are unlikely to be interested in monetizing their IP; in fact, many are unaware that they are copyright owners. Archival holdings also contain a high proportion of orphan works, that is, works for which the copyright owners cannot be identified or located. In general, this is because copyright owners of these materials have no vested interest in being readily traceable to grant permission for use or to derive income from their creations."[63] The latest legislative appraisals regarding orphan works is covered below.

For unpublished copyrighted works created since 1978 under the U.S. Copyright Act of 1976, this is not an issue. However, unpublished works created before 1978 (under the 1909 Copyright Act) were not associated with federal copyright law. Such unpublished works were protected under state copyright laws, also known as common-law copyright. An author had extensive protection if the work remained unpublished. This creates a challenge for archives to determine when unpublished works such as creative art works or manuscript letters fall into public domain. See Cornell Library's "Copyright Terms and the Public Domain" chart in Chapter 2 or https://copyright.cornell.edu/publicdomain for details. These copyright laws apply to copying and distributing larger parts of unpublished works. They usually do not apply to smaller fair use portions for noncommercial research.

Unpublished and public domain works held in special collections may introduce other moral challenges. Often customers dealing with certain special collections do not understand why they must obtain permission for publishing rights related to some public domain works. Often donor agreements or rare, fragile resources are attributed for such policies. So, does a library have the legal right to enforce such restrictions on reuse of public domain resources? Lawfully, no, it does not. Physical ownership of a public domain work does not give the owner the right to direct how such works may be used. However, possession and ownership of a physical document could control access, especially for rare or fragile works.[64]

Libel, privacy, and right of publicity, covered in earlier chapters, should be considered with unpublished and public domain works. Objects such as diaries, letters, photos, music, and artwork could be troublesome for posting on public websites or permitting large-portion copies by research customers. Once again, "documenting the status of the copyright of any material donated to a historical institution is one of the reasons for obtaining a donor agreement."[65]

Orphan works flourish within special collections and archives more than most other types of libraries. Orphan works in this situation occur when the copyright ownership and the copyright status are unknown, and an archival researcher needs to use the work in a way that requires copyright permission. Archivists are reluctant to offer access to orphan works. As mentioned above, a fair use (Section 107) analysis may be an archivist's only lawful response with these kinds of customer copy requests. Orphan works in the case of special collections and archives might warrant a copyright and publishing rights policy for your collection.

When Congress commissioned the Copyright Office study group in 2006, it recommended enacting legislation to limit the legal actions against legitimate users of orphan works. They suggested that users' "good faith" and "reasonable effort" to locate a copyright owner should be enough to protect them from later potential copyright infringement liability.[66] See Chapter 2 for additional information on orphan works.

Since 2018, the Music Modernization Act provides a means for using orphan work sound recordings freely. The user must direct the questioned orphan work to the U.S. Copyright Office for notice, so that its copyright owner has ninety days to object to its use. If no rights holder appears, or if the user demonstrates the use is for noncommercial fair use, the recording is free to use.[67] Additional updates may always be found at https://copyright.gov/orphan/.

To Ask Permission or Risk Fair Use, That Is Always the Question

When resources are clearly known to be copyrighted works, one might ask if it is for research or commercial use. If it is research, personal notes, copies, or quotes for scholarly work, then a fair use analysis is suggested. If the analysis reveals an unfair use, or if it is for commercial use, then ask for permission. Moral rights of artists are yet another aspect of permission to be considered.

But what do you do when your fair use analysis of a public-view digitization website project reveals a tie with two factors favoring fair use and the other two factors disfavoring fair use? Then a strong fair use defense might include the factual and/or transformative nature of the materials being digitized. Hirtle suggests that an organization might identify possible risks associated with such a project prior to its start and plan how to alleviate some of those risks. Hirtle promotes a risk management analysis, including the following relevant factors:

- Nature of the materials being digitized
- Accessibility of digital content
- Likely remedies in the event of legal proceedings
- Availability of sovereign immunity
- Arguable existence of an implied license
- Likelihood of a complaint being made
- Potential impact of project on an institution's reputation or relationship with current and future donors
- Institution's level of comfort with risk
- Availability of legal advice
- Perceived social utility of proceeding with the project[68]

When performing risk assessments, photographs usually have more layers of rights and permission than textual documents. In addition to the copyright of the photographer, there may be the fine art of an artist or an identifiable individual within a photograph that requires a release permission form to use. Fair use may not cover these extra permission layers.

Other Types of IP Concerns

Right of publicity issues likely occur with photographs for exhibits or when copied for research customers. As Jeremy Rowe of Arizona State University has discussed on his Vintage Photography webpage, entitled *Copyrights and other Rights in Photographic Images*:

> Another issue currently in flux is the right of publicity, and the use of the likeness of recognizable personalities such as Charlie Chaplin, W. C. Fields, James Dean, as well as unauthorized pictures of private individuals. Strong lobbying, particularly by the entertainment industry and estates of prominent people, has led to increasing control of the use of photographs by individuals and their estates. Again, even though you own an original copy of a photograph, the right of publicity may limit your ability to use the image without obtaining permission from the subject.[69]

What about photographs of a museum or gallery's works of art on display? A federal district court decision, *Bridgeman Art Library v. Corel Corp.* ruled that exact photographic copies of public domain images were not protected by copyright due to lack of originality, which is a key element for copyright eligibility.[70] The *Bridgeman* case has raised great concern among museums and archives as this may promote piracy of, and erode their revenue from licensing, photographs of objects and works in their holdings.[71]

Museums and galleries often struggle with artists' moral rights and the moral integrity of their works onsite. One of a few moral rights recognized within U.S. Copyright Law is found in Section 106A and is known as the Visual Rights Act (VARA).[72] The Act recognizes an author's moral rights, including right of attribution, right of integrity, and right to prevent the destruction of copies of certain works of art. VARA applies to limited types of artworks: paintings, drawings, prints, sculptures, and still photographs. Before VARA was enacted, moral rights of artists were protected by defamation and misappropriation laws.

Use of sound recordings for an exhibit or website poses another challenge to determine when it is fair use or when permission is needed. What is more problematic is that many exhibit designers at museums may not realize that sound recordings before 1972 were not protected by federal copyright law until the Music Modernization Act (MMA)[73] was passed in 2018. Only the underlying musical scores or lyrics were covered by federal copyright law, as covered throughout this book. The pre-1972 recordings were protected by a patchwork of state statutory and common laws, most through the year 2067.[74]

The MMA confers federal copyright protection to pre-1972 recordings, as this preempts related state copyright laws. It also brings most sound recordings into the public domain sooner than the state copyright laws. Federal protection for pre-1972 recordings will expire after ninety-five years, subject to certain additional periods after the date of their first publication, depending on the date range. Recordings made before 1923 will exit from all copyright protection on December 31, 2021. Recordings made from 1923 to 1946 will enter the public domain following an additional five years after the general ninety-five-year term. Recordings from 1947 to 1956 will expire fifteen years after the general ninety-five-year term. Recordings made between 1957 and 1972 will not expire until February 15, 2067, as before with most state laws.[75]

Trademarks are another IP to consider when performing a risk assessment for exhibits, digitization, or research needs of customers of museums and archives. Trademark owners may sue for infringement against any party that uses a trademark in a manner likely to cause confusion in the marketplace or that tarnishes the reputation of the product or service. Just as there are fair use exemptions to the exclusive rights of copyright owners, similar fair use of trademarks exists, as covered extensively in Chapter 5.

For example, if a Coca-Cola trademark were visible in a photograph that a customer wishes to include in a scholarly work, as long as the display of the trademark is not for any commercial gain, does not tarnish the reputation of the product, and does not imply any sponsorship or endorsement by the trademark owner, an infringement suit is less likely. Trademark infringement normally deals with potential consumer confusion by a competing product. Therefore, a noncommercial use of the Coca-Cola mark in the background of a historic photo would likely be fair use. However, for a high-profile exhibit or online website, one must use caution and conceivably add a disclaimer of the noncommercial use and educational application of the display tied to historical or cultural references. Use of the trademark in news reporting and commentary would likely also be fair use.[76]

CHURCH, FAITH-BASED, AND THEOLOGICAL NONPROFIT LIBRARIES

Many might believe that the religious or nonprofit status of such a library and its parent organization would enjoy abundant fair use. As noted in Chapter 2, Mark Twain said it best: "Only one thing is impossible for God: to find any sense in any copyright law on the planet." Due to the nature of religious and spiritual organizations, few legal topics trouble these organizations more persistently than copyright.

The primary copyright violation is often related to duplicating and distributing sheet music or lyrics without first obtaining permission for worship bulletins or via overhead projection devices.[77] However, video recording or display of movies or television broadcasts in a public sacred space is likewise a violation in certain instances. For example, the National Football League (NFL) sent a cease-and-desist order to an Indianapolis church planning a Super Bowl® party displaying the broadcast that included a minor cover charge. Not only did the NFL claim copyright infringement for the public viewing of the televised sporting event, it also challenged the church's use of the trademark term "Super Bowl" associated with an announcement of the church party. Ultimately, the NFL toned down its complaint to avoid poor public relations.[78]

Religious and theological libraries share the same types of resources. Although seminary students are the primary customers of theological libraries, both types of libraries may contain copyrighted liturgical, print, video, audio and musical resources. Unless a professional librarian works or volunteers in a church or other religious library, the person in charge of such a library or music collection is often unfamiliar with copyright and fair use. Then there are issues with computer software licensing usage, copyright rights of original authored sermons or lectures of spiritual leaders, and staff musicians' original music.

Attorney Richard Hammar has published multiple editions on the subject of copyright and churches. In his 2010 edition, entitled *Essential Guide to Copyright Law for Churches*, he points out the following examples as common church practices that are directly affected by copyright law:

> Copying of choral music or church school literature, insertion of hymn or chorus lyrics in church bulletins, compilation of "church booklets," use of video projectors in worship services and in teaching, making of audio and video recordings of church services, copying computer programs, websites, the broadcast of religious services over radio or television, streaming sermons over the Internet, the use of copyrighted translations of the Bible, performance of copyrighted music in the course of religious services, and showing DVDs during youth worship services and events.[79]

Hammar's list of copyright cautions are imperative for a religious organization to be aware of to stay legal. Copyright involves applying special policies and an understanding of the fair use doctrine, which is not always clearly understood by church members, pastors, and musicians. This may lead to misinformation and lack of compliance for copyright law, which in turn could result in a court case.

While many religious leaders may not like the copyright law and its limited fair use, they need to understand that aversion or ignorance of copyright law does not justify copyright violation. Such aversion is also admitting to intentional infringement that only makes matters worse. Damages are much greater when an infringement is willful.

Fair Use in Nonprofit Religious Scenarios

For customers of church, faith-based, and theological libraries, the first "Purpose" factor of a fair use analysis is often for a nonprofit purpose, which sways in favor of the user. Otherwise, the remaining three factors must be analyzed with caution. The second "Nature" of work factor is usually highly creative, such as music or videos, which is less likely to be considered fair, unless the next third "Amount" factor is met or the "Nature" factor meets the religious services exemption of U.S. Copyright Law Section 110(3). The third "Amount" factor depends on how much is used; the more one uses, the less likely it is fair. However, a smaller amount could be fair. Finally, the "Effect" on the market factor is most obviously not fair if one is avoiding a sale of a work. Always review the factors from the viewpoint of the copyright owner. How would the owner perceive your fair use argument?

Copyright attorney Hammar suggests the following scrutiny when applying the fair use factors for church and faith-based groups to determine if a use is indeed fair:

- What is the purpose and character of the use? Duplicating a work solely to avoid paying for it isn't fair use.
- What is the nature of the copyrighted work? There is a broader privilege to copy and quote from resources like dictionaries and encyclopedias than from a song or magazine article.
- How much of the copyrighted work is being used? The higher the percentage copied, the less likely it constitutes fair use. One thing is clear: verbatim or nearly verbatim reproductions of an entire copyrighted work are rarely considered fair use.
- The key question is: Does my use diminish the return the copyright owner can expect? This is a main consideration of the courts when determining copyright judgments.[80]

Getting Permission for Reproduction of Music and Video Works

One of the major permission services that churches turn to for authorization is Christian Copyright Licensing Inc. (CCLI, found at https://us.ccli.com/). Although not the only permission service available, it acts as a clearinghouse for several publishers and composers. Churches may purchase a blanket license, which authorizes them to make copies of music from the CCLI repertory of over 200,000 musical works. If one looks closely at most church service bulletins or programs where lyrics of songs are reprinted in full, a CCLI permission notice is often posted after a song title. The CCLI website[81] promotes its practical licensing solutions for music used for congregational singing, which allows a church to legally:

- Print songs, hymns, and lyrics in bulletins, programs, liturgies, and song sheets for use in congregational singing.
- Create customized songbooks or hymnals for use in congregational singing.
- Create overhead transparencies, slides, or use any other format whereby song lyrics are visually projected (such as computer graphics and projection) for use in congregational singing.
- Arrange, print, and copy one's original arrangements (vocal and instrumental) of songs used for congregational singing, where no published version is available.
- Record workshop services (audio or visual), provided that only live music is recorded. Accompaniment tracks cannot be reproduced. The website specifies what churches may charge for digital media sold under the licensing agreement.

CCLI licenses do not authorize copying music for church choir performances but only duplication rights for music sung by the congregation. CCLI also provides licenses for churches to publicly show copyrighted motion pictures and other programs from any legally obtained source intended for personal, private, home use only—such as DVDs—in its facility.[82] The Motion Picture Licensing Corporation (MPLC, https://www.mplc.org/) is an additional movie rights organization that licenses churches or schools to show videos in public. Another option for congregational music clearances is One License at https://www.onelicense.net/.

J•License of Transcontinental Music found at https://jlicense.com/ is a music licensing service for the Jewish community. It offers similar services as CCLI. J•License is nondenominational and also licenses for international customers.

Religious Services Exemption—Section 110(3)

A religious services exemption, Section 110(3) of the Copyright Act,[83] states that "the following are not infringements of copyright . . . performance of a nondramatic musical work . . . of a religious nature, or display of a work, in the course of services at a place of worship or other religious assembly." Here, both the choir and the congregation may sing any religious or spiritual copyrighted music without the need to obtain permission to do so during a church service. However, performance licenses or permission must be obtained for any musical performances outside of a specific "worship service," including concerts and special musical programs.[84] Christian Copyright Solutions (CCS, found at https://www.christiancopyrightsolutions.com/) collaborates with music performance rights organizations such as ASCAP and BMI for one-stop performance licensing needs outside of the religious services exemption.

Displaying Copyrighted Music for Religious Services

Section 109 of the Copyright Act[85] has special significance to church and faith-based communities related to the use of copyrighted transparencies and slides during worship services. Section 109(c) limits the exclusive right of the copyright holder by allowing a lawful owner of a copyrighted work to place the original copy on public display without the permission of the copyright owner. Hence, it is copyright compliant to display legally acquired computer slide programs containing music lyrics for use during a religious service. Even a legally acquired original copy of a music book may be displayed via an opaque projector during a service. However, if the song lyrics are copied, scanned, or manually retyped and displayed with a computer slide program or an opaque projector, copyright permission must be obtained.

Obviously, if the music copied for display is public domain, no permission is required. Look for copyright notice and year and then check Cornell's latest "Copyright Terms and the Public Domain in the United States" chart (found at https://copyright.cornell.edu/publicdomain) to determine status. Be watchful for new arrangements of traditional music or lyrics that often are under copyright protection. For authorized duplication of copyrighted works, the church or synagogue should acquire a blanket annual license from CCLI or J*License, or it should contact each publisher of any works copied. For any permission methods, the licensing fee is customarily based upon variable such as congregation size and the nature and scope of duplication.[86]

Worship Leaders, Musicians, and Works Made for Hire

For pastors' or rabbis' sermons and staff musicians' musical compositions, paid for by the religious organization, everyone should be aware of how works made for hire may influence the ownership party for such copyrighted works. Theological libraries are academic in nature and often promote the copyright of sermons and lectures as the IP of the creator of the content. However, for most churches, when sermons are prepared on church time and published, the church owns the copyright unless it specifically assigns rights to the pastor. The same applies to the original music and lyrics composed by musicians on church time.[87] Although authors are normally considered the copyright owners of their creative works, Section 201(b) entitled "Ownership of Copyright" within the Copyright Act states:

> In the case of a work made for hire, the employer or other person for whom the work was prepared is considered the author for purposes of this title, and, unless the parties have expressly agreed otherwise in a written instrument signed by them, owns all of the rights comprised in the copyright.[88]

A work made for hire is defined as "a work prepared by an employee within the scope of his or her employment," according to Section 101 of U.S. Copyright Law. If an intellectual work is created by an employee within the labor of his or her employment, it is usually considered a work made for hire. If it is created within the labor of an independent contracted assignment, a written agreement should specify who owns copyright upfront. It is highly advisable to consult with legal counsel to draft an official policy to address ownership of works created by clergy and other staff members such as musicians. Once again, the U.S. Copyright Office provides an informative circular entitled "Works Made for Hire," found at https://www.copyright.gov/circs/circ09.pdf.

CONCLUSION

This chapter has reviewed common and unique copyright exemptions and provisions shared among special libraries from Sections 107 and 108 of the U.S. Copyright Law, the fair use continuum between nonprofit and for-profit libraries, and public versus private customer bases. Specific U.S. Copyright Law exceptions beyond fair use that support unique types of special libraries and their customers, such as Sections 108, 109, and 110, were examined. Specific information for special librarians was detailed concerning permission organizations, computer software and database licensing, interlibrary loan, document delivery, photocopying or displaying content, posting content on organization intranet, orphan works, sharing content one-on-one, open access and creating digital archives, preservation, copyright conveyance, and works made for hire. Patents and trademarks may apply to fewer special libraries but are applicable to corporate and law libraries.

NOTES

1. Olivia Crosby, "Librarians: Information Experts in the Information Age," *Occupational Outlook Quarterly* (Winter 2000–2001): 3, https://www.bls.gov/careeroutlook/2000/Winter/art01.pdf (accessed November 25, 2018).
2. *Williams & Wilkins Co. v. United States*, 16 B.C.L. Rev. 141 (1974). The U.S. Supreme Courts permitted the National Institutes of Health to photocopy many journal articles for researchers and other libraries. Since then, there have been no other major cases regarding government agency reliance on fair use.
3. Laura N. Gasaway, "Copyright Law and the Practice of Law in the Digital Age," in Intellectual Property Course Handbook Series, No. G-856, *Law Library 2006: Skills, Strategies, and Solutions* (New York: Practising Law Institute, 2006), 136.
4. Ibid., 134.
5. Kyle K. Courtney, "Chapter 3: Copyright in the Digital Age," in *Law Librarianship in the Digital Age*, Ellyssa Kroski, ed. (Lanham, MD: Scarecrow Press, 2014), 38–39.
6. ALA, Education & Careers, Explore a Career in Libraries, Types of Libraries, http://www.ala.org/educationcareers/careers/librarycareerssite/typesoflibraries (accessed November 23, 2018); Pamela H. McKellar, *Accidental Librarian* (Medford, NJ: Information Today, 2008), 40–41: Cornell University Library, LibGuide: *Books & Bytes: Librarians as Information Managers: Types of Libraries*, October 12, 2018, https://guides.library.cornell.edu/c.php?g=30898&p=198569 (accessed November 23, 2018).
7. E-mail correspondence with author of this book regarding number of members by Stephanie Bossing, SLA, November 19, 2018.
8. SLA, Competencies for Information Professionals, https://www.sla.org/about-sla/competencies/ (accessed November 19, 2018).
9. Sabrina I. Pacifici, "Risky Business of Information Sharing: Why You Need to Care about Copyright," *Law and Technology Resources for Legal Professionals*, February 2011, https://www.llrx.com/2011/02/the-risky-business-of-information-sharing-why-you-need-to-care-about-copyright/ (accessed November 20, 2018).

10. David R. Hansen, "Copyright Reform Principles for Libraries, Archives, and Other Memory Institutions," *Berkeley Technology Law Journal* 29, no 3 (2015), https://scholarship.law.berkeley.edu/btlj/vol29/iss3/5/ (accessed November 19, 2018).
11. Ibid.
12. American Geophysical Union v. Texaco, Inc., 60 F.3d 913 (2d Cir. 1994, 1995).
13. Merilyn Burke and Susan J. Heron, "Copyright Issues and 'For Profit' Libraries: Problems and Solutions," *Journal of Interlibrary Loan, Document Delivery & Information Supply* 14, no. 4 (2004) 5–21.
14. Lowry's Reports, Inc. v. Legg Mason, Inc., 271 F.Supp.2d 737 (D. Md. 2003).
15. Martin Samson, "Lowry's Reports, Inc. v. Legg Mason Inc., et al.," *Internet Library of Law and Court Decisions,* http://www.internetlibrary.com/cases/lib_case520.cfm (accessed November 19, 2018).
16. Lowry's Reports, Inc. v. Legg Mason, Inc., Complaint, 2001 WL 34898871 (No. 01CV3898, December 18, 2001).
17. Tomas A. Lipinski, *Complete Copyright Liability Handbook for Librarians and Educators* (New York: Neal-Schuman Publishers, 2006), 48; 118–119; Tomas A. Lipinski, "Towards a Functional Understanding of Fair Use in U.S. Copyright Law," *Annual Review of Information Science and Technology* 45, no. 1 (2011): 589–590.
18. H.Rep. 94-1476, at page 75 (1976), https://www.copyright.gov/history/law/clrev_94-1476.pdf (accessed November 25, 2018). [House Report, 94th Congress, 2nd session, 9/13/1976]
19. U.S. Copyright Act, 17 U.S. Code § 108 (a)—Limitations on Exclusive Rights: Reproduction by Libraries and Archives.
20. Kenneth Crews, *Copyright Law for Librarians and Educators* (Chicago: American Library Association, 2012), 94.
21. Burke and Heron, "Copyright Issues and 'For Profit' Libraries," 13.
22. U.S. Copyright Act, 17 U.S. Code § 108 (b)—Limitations on Exclusive Rights: Reproduction by Libraries and Archives.
23. U.S. Copyright Act, 17 U.S. Code § 108 (c)—Limitations on Exclusive Rights: Reproduction by Libraries and Archives.
24. U.S. Copyright Act, 17 U.S. Code § 108 (b) and (c)—Limitations on Exclusive Rights: Reproduction by Libraries and Archives.
25. Digital Millennium Copyright Act, § 404(2), Pub. L. No. 105–304, 112 Stat. 2829 (1998).
26. U.S. Copyright Act, 17 U.S. Code § 108 (b)(2)—Limitations on Exclusive Rights: Reproduction by Libraries and Archives.
27. U.S. Copyright Act, 17 U.S. Code § 108 (d)—Limitations on Exclusive Rights: Reproduction by Libraries and Archives.
28. U.S. Copyright Act, 17 U.S. Code § 108 (d)(1)—Limitations on Exclusive Rights: Reproduction by Libraries and Archives.
29. Ibid.
30. Ibid.
31. U.S. Copyright Act, 17 U.S.C. § 108 (e)—Limitations on Exclusive Rights: Reproduction by Libraries and Archives.
32. Ibid.
33. Library of Congress, "Section 108 of Title 17," Discussion Document of the Register of Copyrights, September 2017, https://www.copyright.gov/policy/section108/discussion-document.pdf (accessed December 15, 2018).
34. Constance Ard, *Next-Generation Corporate Libraries and Information Services* (London: Ark Group, 2009), 3.

35. Ian Cockburn, "IP Audit—A "How to" Guide," *Small and Medium-Sized Enterprises*, World Intellectual Property Organization, https://www.wipo.int/sme/en/documents/ip_audit_fulltext.html (accessed December 15, 2018).

36. Ibid.

37. Pacifici, "Risky Business of Information Sharing"; and Laura Gasaway, "Copyright Corner: Drafting an Organizational Copyright Policy," *Information Outlook* 8, no. 9 (September 2004): 36.

38. A. Abbas et al., "Literature Review on the State-of-the-Art in Patent Analytics," *World Patent Information* 37 (2014): 3–13.

39. John Schlipp, Northern Kentucky University, IPAC (Intellectual Property Awareness Center): Patent Citations, https://inside.nku.edu/ipac/ipbasics/patentcitations.html (accessed November 29, 2018).

40. Donna Hopkins, "Using Patents to Plot Business Trends," *DttP (Documents to the People)* 30, no. 3/4 (Fall/Winter 2002): 10–13.

41. Law Library of Congress, About the Law Library, http://www.loc.gov/law/about/ (accessed November 25, 2018).

42. Jennifer Wertkin, "Law Librarianship 2.0," in *Law Librarianship in the Digital Age*, Elyssa Kroski, ed. (Lanham, MD: Scarecrow Press, 2013), 4–8.

43. Ibid.

44. James G. Milles, "Redefining Open Access for the Legal Information Market," *Law Library Journal* 98, no. 4 (2006): 619–637; and Cheryl Kelly Fischer and Vicki Steiner, "Chapter 4: Open Access to Legal Scholarship," in *Legal Librarianship in the Digital Age*, Ellyssa Kroski, ed. (Lanham, NJ: Scarecrow Press, 2014).

45. Mary Whisner, "On Specialized Legal Research," *Law Library Journal* 108, no. 3 (2016): 483–488.

46. Vikram Singh, Kajal Chakraborty, and Lavina Vincent, "Patent Database: Their Importance in Prior Art Documentation and Patent Search," *Journal of Intellectual Property Rights* 21 (January 2016): 42–56, https://core.ac.uk/download/pdf/44684007.pdf (accessed November 30, 2018).

47. Gasaway, "Copyright Corner," 14.

48. Sallie Smith, Susanna Leers, and Patricia Roncevich, "Database Ownership: Myth or Reality?" *Law Library Journal* 103, no. 2 (2011): 233–247.

49. Ingrid Mattson and Linda-Jean Schneider, "Negotiating and Complying with Electronic Database Licensing Agreements," *AALL Spectrum* (February 2013): 9–12.

50. American Association of Law Libraries, "AALL Principles & Practices for Licensing Electronic Resources," https://www.aallnet.org/advocacy/vendor-relations/criv-tools/principles-practices-for-licensing-electronic-resources/ (accessed November 25, 2018).

51. Ibid.

52. Medical Library Association, "Copyright Law and the Health Sciences Librarian," revised edition, 2007, 3.

53. Holly Phillips, "Chapter 4: Collection Development in Health Science Libraries," in *Health Sciences Librarianship*, M. Sandra Wood, ed. (Lanham, MD: Rowman & Littlefield, 2014), 98–101.

54. Medical Library Association, Advocacy: Intellectual Property and Copyright, https://www.mlanet.org/page/intellectual-property-and-copyright (accessed November 30, 2018).

55. Medical Library Association, "Special Report: Standards for Hospital Libraries 2007, Hospital Libraries Section Standards Committee," *Journal of the Medical Library Association* 96, no. 2 (April 2008): 162–169.

56. NIH Public Access Policy website, NIH Public Access Policy implements Division F Section 217 of PL 111-8 (Omnibus Appropriations Act, 2009), https://publicaccess.nih.gov/policy.htm (accessed November 30, 2018).

57. Michael Shapiro et al., *Museum Guide to Copyright and Trademark* (Washington, D.C.: American Association of Museums, 1999), 6–7.

58. Menzi Behrnd-Klodt, *Navigating Legal Issues in Archives* (Chicago: Society of American Archivists, 2008), 203.

59. U.S. Copyright Act, 17 U.S. Code § 202—Ownership of Copyright as Distinct from Ownership of Material Object.

60. For further details about copyright conveyances in museums, see Sharon Smith Theobald and Laurette E. McCarthy, eds., *To Give and to Receive: A Handbook on Gifts and Donations for Museums and Donors* (Washington, D.C.: American Association of Museums Press, 2011); and Rebecca A. Buck and Jean Allman Gilmore, eds., *MRM5: Museum Registration Methods 5th Edition* (Washington, D.C.: American Association of Museums, 2010).

61. Peter Hirtle, Emily Hudson, and Andrew T. Kenyon, *Copyright and Cultural Institutions: Guidelines for Digitization for U.S. Libraries, Archives, and Museums* (Ithaca, NY: Cornell University Library, 2009), 185–186.

62. U.S. Copyright Act, 17 U.S. Code § 108—Limitations on Exclusive Rights: Reproduction by Libraries and Archives.

63. Jean Dryden, "Copyright Exceptions: An Archivist's Perspective," *WIPO Magazine* no. 4 (August 2017): 16–19, https://www.wipo.int/wipo_magazine/en/2017/04/article_0003.html (accessed November 30, 2018).

64. Rick Anderson, "Asserting Rights We Don't Have: Libraries and 'Permission to Publish,'" *Library Journal* (August 21, 2014), http://lj.libraryjournal.com/2014/08/opinion/peer-to-peer-review/asserting-rights-we-dont-have-libraries-and-permission-to-publish-peer-to-peer-review/#_ (accessed October 21, 2014).

65. Lois Hamill, *Archives tor the Lay Person* (Lanham, NJ: AltaMira Press, 2013), 93.

66. "A Report of the Register of Copyrights: Report on Orphan Works," January 2006; also see http://www.copyright.gov/docs/regstat030806.html (accessed April 4, 2011).

67. Mitch Stoltz, "New Music Modernization Act Has a Major Fix: Older Recordings Will Belong to the Public, Orphan Recordings Will Be Heard Again," Electronic Frontier Foundation, September 19, 2018, https://www.eff.org/deeplinks/2018/09/new-music-modernization-act-has-major-fix-older-recordings-will-belong-public (accessed November 30, 2018).

68. Hirtle et al., *Copyright and Cultural Institutions*, 193–194.

69. Jeremy Rowe, "Copyrights and Other Rights in Photographic Images," http://vintagephoto.com/reference/copyrightarticle1.htm (accessed April 23, 2011).

70. Bridgeman Art Library v. Corel Corp., 25 F. Supp. 2d 421 (S.D.N.Y. 1998).

71. Susan Bielstein, *Permissions, a Survival Guide: Blunt Talk about Art as Intellectual Property* (Chicago: University of Chicago Press, 2006), 42–46.

72. U.S. Copyright Act, 17 U.S. Code § 106A(a)—Exclusive Rights in Copyrighted Works.

73. Kevin J. Hickey, "Music Modernization Act: Extending Copyright Protection to Pre-1972 Sound Recordings," *Congressional Research Service—Legal Sidebar*, October 15, 2018, https://fas.org/sgp/crs/misc/LSB10181.pdf (accessed December 1, 2018); and U.S. Copyright Office, Music Modernization Act, https://www.copyright.gov/music-modernization/ (accessed December 1, 2018).

74. U.S. Copyright Office, "Study on the Desirability of and Means for Bringing Sound Recordings Fixed before February 15, 1972, Under Federal Jurisdiction," http://www.copyright.gov/docs/sound/ (accessed April 24, 2011).

75. Hickey, "Music Modernization Act"; and U.S. Copyright Office, Music Modernization Act.

76. Hirtle et al., *Copyright and Cultural Institutions*, 177.

77. John R. Throop, "Right Those Copyright Wrongs," in *Copyright Law: What Every Church Must Know*, Jeff Hanna, ed. (Carol Stream, IL: Christianity Today International, 2008), 7.

78. Ted Olsen, "NFL Cracks Down on Church Super Bowl Events," *Christianity Today International*, February 2, 2007, https://www.christianitytoday.com/ct/2007/februaryweb-only/105-51.0.html#superchurch (accessed November 30, 2018); and Mike Masnick, "NFL Wants to Remind You That Having People Over to Watch the Super Bowl on a Big Screen Is Copyright Infringement," TechDirt, February 2, 2017, https://www.techdirt.com/articles/20070201/140812.shtml (accessed November 30, 2018).

79. Richard Hammar, *Essential Guide to Copyright Law for Churches* (Carol Stream, IL: Christianity Today International, 2010), ix.

80. Richard Hammar, "Making Peace with Copyright Law," in *Copyright Law: What Every Church Must Know*, Jeff Hanna, ed. (Carol Stream, IL: Christianity Today International, 2008), 16.

81. Christian Copyright Licensing, "What You Can Do," http://www.ccli.com//WhatWeOffer/WhatYouCanDo.aspx (accessed April 22, 2011).

82. Church Video License, License Terms: Annual License, https://us.cvli.com/about/terms/ (accessed November 30, 2018).

83. U.S. Copyright Act, 17 U.S. Code § 110 (3)—Limitations on Exclusive Rights: Exception of Certain Performances and Displays.

84. http://mpa.org/copyright_resource_center/church_musician (accessed November 17, 2010).

85. U.S. Copyright Act, 17 U.S. Code § 109(c)—Limitations on Exclusive Rights: Effect of Transfer of Particular Copy or Phonorecord.

86. Hammar, "Making Peace," 15.

87. Throop, "Right Those Copyright Wrongs," 8.

88. U.S. Copyright Act, 17 U.S. Code § 201(b)—Ownership of Copyright (Works Made for Hire).

INDEX

Page numbers followed by *f* indicate figures.

About the Author

JOHN SCHLIPP is an intellectual property librarian and professor of library science at the W. Frank Steely Library at Northern Kentucky University. He manages the Intellectual Property Awareness Center (IPAC), which is a designated Patent and Trademark Resource Center representing the U.S. Patent and Trademark Office. Schlipp won the 2011 Kentucky Library Association's Outstanding Feature Article award for "Creative Thinking: A Student-Centered Approach to Plagiarism and Copyright" that appeared in the *Kentucky Libraries* journal. His contributions include scholarly articles, book reviews, and an online intellectual property awareness program for teens called Creative Thinking. He is an associate editor of the *Encyclopedia of Northern Kentucky*.

CPSIA information can be obtained
at www.ICGtesting.com
Printed in the USA
LVHW012035190422
716645LV00012B/372

9 781440 870705